ns Engineering **642**

Editorial Board Members

Ozgur Akan, *Middle East Technical University, Ankara, Türkiye*
Paolo Bellavista, *University of Bologna, Bologna, Italy*
Jiannong Cao, *Hong Kong Polytechnic University, Hong Kong, Hong Kong*
Geoffrey Coulson, *Lancaster University, Lancaster, UK*
Falko Dressler, *University of Erlangen, Erlangen, Germany*
Domenico Ferrari, *Università Cattolica Piacenza, Piacenza, Italy*
Mario Gerla, *UCLA, Los Angeles, USA*
Hisashi Kobayashi, *Princeton University, Princeton, USA*
Sergio Palazzo, *University of Catania, Catania, Italy*
Sartaj Sahni, *University of Florida, Gainesville, USA*
Xuemin Shen, *University of Waterloo, Waterloo, Canada*
Mircea Stan, *University of Virginia, Charlottesville, USA*
Xiaohua Jia, *City University of Hong Kong, Kowloon, Hong Kong*
Albert Y. Zomaya, *University of Sydney, Sydney, Australia*

The LNICST series publishes ICST's conferences, symposia and workshops.
LNICST reports state-of-the-art results in areas related to the scope of the Institute.
The type of material published includes

- Proceedings (published in time for the respective event)
- Other edited monographs (such as project reports or invited volumes)

LNICST topics span the following areas:

- General Computer Science
- E-Economy
- E-Medicine
- Knowledge Management
- Multimedia
- Operations, Management and Policy
- Social Informatics
- Systems

Haiquan Zhao · Maria Pia Fanti
Editors

Internet of Things, Artificial Intelligence and Mechanical Automation

5th EAI International Conference, IoTAIMA 2024
Hangzhou, China, July 19–21, 2024
Proceedings, Part II

Editors
Haiquan Zhao
Southwest Jiaotong University
Chengdu, China

Maria Pia Fanti
Polytechnic University of Bari
Bari, Italy

ISSN 1867-8211   ISSN 1867-822X (electronic)
Lecture Notes of the Institute for Computer Sciences, Social Informatics
and Telecommunications Engineering
ISBN 978-3-032-00220-4   ISBN 978-3-032-00221-1 (eBook)
https://doi.org/10.1007/978-3-032-00221-1

© ICST Institute for Computer Sciences, Social Informatics and Telecommunications Engineering 2026

This work is subject to copyright. All rights are solely and exclusively licensed by the Publisher, whether the whole or part of the material is concerned, specifically the rights of translation, reprinting, reuse of illustrations, recitation, broadcasting, reproduction on microfilms or in any other physical way, and transmission or information storage and retrieval, electronic adaptation, computer software, or by similar or dissimilar methodology now known or hereafter developed.
The use of general descriptive names, registered names, trademarks, service marks, etc. in this publication does not imply, even in the absence of a specific statement, that such names are exempt from the relevant protective laws and regulations and therefore free for general use.
The publisher, the authors and the editors are safe to assume that the advice and information in this book are believed to be true and accurate at the date of publication. Neither the publisher nor the authors or the editors give a warranty, expressed or implied, with respect to the material contained herein or for any errors or omissions that may have been made. The publisher remains neutral with regard to jurisdictional claims in published maps and institutional affiliations.

This Springer imprint is published by the registered company Springer Nature Switzerland AG
The registered company address is: Gewerbestrasse 11, 6330 Cham, Switzerland

If disposing of this product, please recycle the paper.

Preface

As one of the major international conferences in the fields of Internet of Things (IoT), artificial intelligence (AI) and mechanical automation, and held in Hangzhou, China from July 19th to 21st, the 2024 5th International Conference on Internet of Things, Artificial Intelligence and Mechanical Automation (IoTAIMA 2024) was created to provide an important platform for researchers around the world to exchange the latest research results, share innovative ideas and discuss future directions in relevant domains.

With the rapid development of technology, the IoT, AI and mechanical automation have become an important force driving social progress and industrial upgrading. IoTAIMA 2024 gathered about 100 participations both as speakers and participants, including scientists, researchers, industrial experts, students and other practitioners from all over the world to discuss the latest advances and applications of IoT, AI and mechanical automation. It not only promoted the research and developmental activities in related fields and scientific information interchange among the participants, but established connections for participants to find global partners for potential collaboration in the future.

The keynote speech session was one of the highlights of the conference. Several renowned scholars and industry leaders, such as Guangjie Han (Hohai University, China) and Yonghui Li (University of Sydney, Australia), brought us wonderful speeches with their profound academic attainments and rich practical experience. Guangjie Han shared his latest research results and insights on the cutting-edge areas of industrial IoT, smart ocean, artificial intelligence and mobile computing. Yonghui Li, on the other hand, focused on the latest technologies in the field of wireless communications, especially innovative applications in IoT, machine-to-machine communications and millimeter-wave communications, which provided valuable academic inspiration for the attendees. These speeches not only demonstrated the latest developments of science and technology, but also provided important references for future research directions, triggering lively discussions and a good number of informal talks among all the participants.

In addition, oral presentation is an important platform for participants to demonstrate the in-depth research exploration in their respective fields and exchange academic ideas, and also provides participants with valuable communication opportunities and inspires new research. Moreover, some participants also presented their research results and experimental data visually through beautifully designed posters. This not only facilitated the participants to quickly understand the research progress in other fields, but also provided a more direct and convenient communication opportunity between researchers.

We received 126 submissions in total, and after months of preparation and hard work, the Proceedings of IoTAIMA 2024 covering 55 excellent contributions, having been checked through a double-blind review process with each submission receiving three reviews on average, is smoothly published. This paper volume includes 38 full papers and 17 short papers.

We extend our sincere gratitude to the organizers, speakers, authors and all the participants of IoTAIMA 2024, for their fruitful work and contribution to the success of the conference. We are also thankful to the reviewers for providing constructive criticisms, stimulating comments and suggestions on the submissions. May this event be a spark that ignites many more new inventions in the fields of and related to Internet of Things, artificial intelligence and mechanical automation!

The Committee of IoTAIMA 2024

Organization

Conference General Chairs

Guangjie Han	Hohai University, China
Xiangjie Kong	Zhejiang University of Technology, China
Guan Gui	Nanjing University of Posts and Telecommunications, China

Conference Co-chair

Yonghui Li University of Sydney, Australia

Program Chairs

Marco Claudio Campi	University of Brescia, Italy
Maria Pia Fanti	Polytechnic University of Bari, Italy
Kaikai Chi	Zhejiang University of Technology, China

Local Chair

Xinwei Yao Zhejiang University of Technology, China

Publication Chairs

Zike Zhang	Zhejiang University, China
Sukhpal Singh Gill	Queen Mary University of London, UK
Haiquan Zhao	Southwest Jiaotong University, China

Organizing Committee

Kechen Zheng	Zhejiang University of Technology, China
Dongyan Guo	Zhejiang University of Technology, China
Jiaxin Du	Zhejiang University of Technology, China

Program Committee

Liang Hu	Tongji University, China
Praveen Kumar Donta	Vienna University of Technology, Austria
Jinping Liu	Hunan Normal University, China
Juan Luo	Hunan University, China
Junzhao Du	Xidian University, China
Zhikui Chen	Dalian University of Technology, China
Yihong Chen	China West Normal University, China
Yanguo Jing	Leeds Trinity University, UK
Chunlei Wang	Shanghai University, China
Huiyu Zhou	University of Leicester, UK
Yang Li	Changchun University of Science and Technology, China
Rachid El Alami	Sidi Mohamed Ben Abdellah University, Morocco
Bing Wang	Shanghai University, China
Nima Jafari Navimipour	Kadir Has University, Turkey
Shiwei Ma	Shanghai University, China
Guo-Jun Qi	University of Central Florida, USA
Aziz Fellah	Northwest Missouri State University, USA
Raj Mani Shukla	Anglia Ruskin University, UK
Chee Keong Tan	Monash University Malaysia, Malaysia
Jin Zhang	Shanghai University, China
Haider Abbas	National University of Sciences and Technology, Pakistan
Baoyan Duan	Xidian University, China
Zhengming Gao	Jingchu University of Technology, China
Li Guo	Hunan University, China
Kaoru Ota	Muroran Institute of Technology, Japan
Igor Bisio	University of Genoa, Italy
Qixin Cao	Shanghai Jiao Tong University, China
Jun Cai	Concordia University, Canada
Arun Balodi	Visvesvaraya Technological University, India
Arumugam Nallanathan	Queen Mary University of London, UK
Minoru Sasaki	Gifu University, Japan
Willy Susilo	University of Wollongong, Australia
Jelena Misic	Ryerson University, Canada
Abderrezak Rachedi	Paris-East Créteil University, France
Xu Zhang	University of Exeter, UK

Contents – Part II

Intelligent Sensing and Fault Detection Technology

Enhancing Fault Detection in Electric Vehicle Lithium Batteries Using Unlabeled Data 3
   Shaoxuan Xia, Zhengxing Dai, Yusheng Liu, Mingzi Bao, Rongjian Cheng, Ben Wang, Xiabing Huang, Xin Li, and Yiqiang Liu

Bearing Faults Diagnosis Based on EEMD and Probability Density Analysis 10
   Xiangyang Liu, Zhifeng Li, Shuanglong He, and Zhangliang Xu

Deep Learning-Based Hand Keypoints Detection for Industrial Manipulation Gestures 18
   Shengdang He, Yuanyuan Zou, and Cheng Peng

Development of Static Calibration Device for Eddy Current Sensors 29
   Ling Zhang, Xiang Xu, Yang Liu, Mao Zheng, Qingping Wang, Jinjiang Han, Jun Wang, Bin Lei, and Chengbo Yang

Prediction of Landing Spare Parts Consumption Based on Multiple Linear Regression 43
   Feng Guo, Hongwei Zhu, Shusong Yu, Hailu Liu, and Bin Tan

Navigation Fuel Consumption Prediction Based on Improved LSTM Network 51
   Xiaohu Lu, Nan Ye, Kang Bai, Jie Shi, and Qijin Tan

Research on a Radar Image Alignment Method 58
   Yanbing Hu and Lingyu Wang

One-Shot Talking Head Generation with Audio-Aware Identity Compensation 70
   Ruihong Yuan and Zhiguang Wang

Lightweight End-To-End Enabled Joint Source-Channel Coding for Wireless AUV Image Transmission 81
   Guang Liu, Zhenguo Zhang, Minghui Wang, Bo Chen, Zesheng Liu, and Xiaojie Zhang

Method for Predicting Impact Point of Trajectory Correction Projectile
Based on IDBO-XGBoost 94
  Dong Sun, Bo Zhang, and Feiyu Wang

Research on Insulator Fault Detection Based on Improved YOLOv5 101
  Lu Liao and Fenghua Jin

Design of Attitude Calculation Algorithm Based on Kalman and Mahony
Complementary Filtering 107
  Feiyu Wang, Bo Zhang, and Dong Sun

Robot Modeling and Automation Control

Research and Design of Terminal Logistics and Distribution Robots 115
  Hongji Chen, Yansheng Zhang, Yonghuan Yan, Qianhua Luo,
  and Kaishun Su

Research and Implementation of Anti-Pinch Function for Car Windows
Based on Microcontroller 127
  Zhiguo Zheng, Zhujun Jiang, Xiaowei Zhao, and Jie Chen

Design of Non-standard Injection Mold with Hot Runner for Outdoor
Measuring Cup of Electric Vehicle 139
  Lijun Huang and Aldrin D. Calderon

Multi-objective Electric Vehicle Route Optimization for Low-Carbon
Cold Chain Logistics Under Time-Dependent Networks 150
  Pingping Zhao, Meiyan Li, and Yanhua Yuan

Swin-MPGM: A Swin-Transformer Based Method for Content Separation
in Challenging Environments 162
  Yufeng Ding and Yan Feng

Flow Field Analysis and Structure Optimization of Silica Sol Shell Drying
Chamber 174
  Zhiqiang Hu, Fang Wang, Hongfang Qi, and Tao Chen

Design of Personalized and Lightweight Rehabilitation Fixators Based
on nTopology 188
  Yaohua Feng, Xuerong Yang, Siyuan Cheng, Zhengyang Chen,
  Bojian Fang, and Zhixi Chen

Study on the Profiling of the Header and the Method for Measuring Cotton
Stalk Height 198
   Kai Wu, Jianming Jian, Xiuying Tang, Ziyang Tian, Kaihuan Ju,
   and Junming Yin

Pump Equipment Fault Diagnosis Based on an Improved DenseNet Model 210
   Chao He, Jiarula Yasenjiang, Debo Wang, and Yang Xiao

Research on the Residual Controllable Robot Grinding Technology
of 500 kV High-Voltage Cable Insulation Layer 223
   Hai Zhu, Kailin Duan, Bo Yan, Mi She, Bo Wang, and Jingli Jia

A Peg-in-Hole Assembly Method Based on Hybrid Visual Information 235
   Jian Zhang and Yongpeng Tian

Robotic Grasping Object Recognition Method Based on 3D Point Cloud
in Multi-object Stacking Scenes 246
   Bingyuan Zhu, Minglun Dong, Yongpeng Tian, and Jian Zhang

Time-Optimal Trajectory Planning of a Robotic Arm Based on an Improved
Adaptive Inertia Weight Particle Swarm Algorithm 256
   Sirui Liu, Hua Zhang, Gang Zhao, and Kai He

An Automatic Generation Method for Business Process Specification
Based on Large Language Models 268
   Kai Wang, Shan Li, Lizong Zhang, Yongjian Zhang, Baobing Xia,
   Lei Zhang, and Yihong Qian

Design of a Smart Wearable Power Supply Scheme for Abrasive Water Jet
Equipment in Troubleshooting Condition 275
   Xianding Xue, Shiyou Xu, and Shenglin Wu

Design of an Automatic Take Tooth Threading Robotic Arm Based
on Solidworks 286
   Shiyou Xu, Xianding Xue, Yunfeng Wu, and Ruyi Wang

Author Index 297

Contents – Part I

Internet of Things Model Construction and Strategy Analysis

A Structural Design Optimization Framework Based on the Integration of SolidWorks, Patran, Nastran and Isight 3
    Wenwei Li, Ru Chen, Zhenyu Zhong, and Jianan Liang

Innovating Fire Monitoring System of High-Rise Building Around Internet of Things Technology 15
    Shuang Sha and Zhijia Tian

An Authentication Method Based on Improved Butterfly Optimization Algorithm and XGBoost 21
    Heng Ding

Strategies for Improved Data Transmission in LoRa IoT Systems: Evaluating Adaptive Data Rate and Shannon-Based Approaches 33
    Jingtong Wang and Jiachen Qu

Robustness Analysis and Improvement of Networked Control Systems Based on Time-Delay Compensation 44
    Juan Song

Classification of Early Stages of Retinopathy of Prematurity Based on Convolutional Neural Networks of Weighted Ensemble Strategy 52
    Honghao Lu, Madhavi Devaraj, and Pengfei Yang

Research on the Data Storage Model for a Blockchain-Based Agricultural Product Traceability System 59
    Jing Li, Jian Xie, Xuefei Du, Zhuoping Wu, Youhang Jiang, Zongyou Cai, and Lipeng Yan

A Method for On-site Unmarked Identification of Product Assembly States 69
    Weibo Li, Hui Li, and Jie Zhang

A Research on Perception Control and Simulation Modeling of an Industrial Internet Platform 75
    Xinghui Zhang, Huafeng Xiong, Liang Chen, and Li Li

A Memristive Neural Network for Learning and Generalization Based on Albert Associative Memory 86
  Mi Zhang, Hui Chang, Xintong Yue, Xinzhe Zhang, and Baoxing Han

TIM-GCN Speech Emotion Recognition Network Based on Generative Adversarial Network 92
  Liyan Zhang, Jiaxin Du, Jiayan Li, and Shuang Chen

Machine Learning Based Network Attack Warning and Predictive Precision Protection 103
  Aihua Liu, Hong Hao, and Jinlei Tao

A Bayesian Update-Based Strategy for Fusing Extended Traversability Maps 109
  Yonghang Zheng, Yan Peng, and Dong Qu

Acoustic Parameter Model of Consonants in Dunhuang Dialect 119
  Yanhua Duan, Yonghong Li, and Xianghe Meng

Innovative Heuristic-Based Periodic Iterative RRT* Trajectory Planning Algorithm 131
  Yonggang Zhang, Jun Li, Chaosheng Huang, Xinyu Zhang, and Yuan Li

Design and Construction of the Typical Application System of the Agricultural Internet of Things 143
  Yongge Yao and Jiazhen Liu

Risk Assessment System for Digital Workshop 151
  Hua Yang, Yi Hu, and Jinjiang Liu

Research on Multi-AGV Hierarchical Intelligent Scheduling Method Based on Bidirectional A* 162
  Min Lv, Jun-ao Tang, Yu-peng Zhou, and Xun Xu

Controllable Emotional Speech Synthesis Based on the Ranking of Relative Emotional Attributes 176
  Yolwas Nurmemet and Qichao Liu

Design of an Event Tracing Mechanism Based on a Domestic Hypervisor 184
  Yueyang Wu and Xiaoli Chai

Intelligent Sensing and Fault Detection Technology

Smart Meter Data Management and Visualization for Intelligent Energy Development 199
   Xu Di, Wei Fei, Liu Xue, and Li Lin

An Improved Zernike Moment Subpixel Edge Detection Algorithm Based on Adaptive Threshold 211
   Yuanyuan Zou, Shilong Xu, and Boxuan Chen

Railway Foreign Body Intrusion Algorithm Based on Improved YOLOv7-Tiny MS YOLOv7-Tiny 223
   Hong Yuan Liu and Xia Hong Niu

Self-supervised Graph Autoencoder with Node Feature Convolution for Community Detection 235
   Haoran Tan, Hongkai Xie, Xiaofeng Wang, Jianhao Chen, Qianyi Qian, and Haoran Tang

YOLO-GNN: An Improved GNN Based YOLOv4 Algorithm for Street Pedestrian Detection 243
   Furong Peng and Yuyu Chen

Application of the RT-LSTM Model with Multi-dimensional Feature Extraction in PM2.5 Concentration Prediction 254
   Lili Wang, Zexia Li, Tongyang Liu, and Fuqiang Ye

Research on Identification of Apple Leaf Diseases Based on an Improved YOLOv5s Model 266
   Kaiyan Lin, Chuanyu Li, Fei Mei, Junhui Wu, Jie Chen, and Huiping Si

Author Index 277

Intelligent Sensing and Fault Detection Technology

Enhancing Fault Detection in Electric Vehicle Lithium Batteries Using Unlabeled Data

Shaoxuan Xia[1,2,3], Zhengxing Dai[3], Yusheng Liu[2], Mingzi Bao[3], Rongjian Cheng[3], Ben Wang[3], Xiabing Huang[3], Xin Li[4], and Yiqiang Liu[3(✉)]

[1] Postdoctoral Research StationZhejiang Geely Holding Group Co., Ltd., Hangzhou 310052, Zhejiang, China
[2] State Key Lab. of CAD and CG, Zhejiang University, Hangzhou 310058, Zhejiang, China
[3] Ningbo Geely Royal Engine Components Co., Ltd., Ningbo 315336, Zhejiang, China
liuyiqiang@geely.com
[4] Beijing Institute of Astronautical Systems Engineering, Beijing 100076, China

Abstract. Fault detection in electric vehicle lithium batteries is a crucial task to ensure the safety and reliability of electric vehicles. However, the scarcity of labeled data is a major challenge in achieving high-accuracy fault detection. This paper proposes a novel training method to address the issue of limited labeled data. The method begins with unsupervised pre-training of a feature extractor using a large amount of unlabeled data, followed by training a base classifier on a small set of labeled data. Then, through progressive training with self-generated labels, the base classifier predicts the unlabeled data to generate high-confidence labels, iteratively enhancing model performance. We validated the effectiveness of this method on the task of fault detection in electric vehicle lithium batteries. Experimental results demonstrate that the proposed method significantly outperforms traditional methods in handling the problem of labeled data scarcity.

Keywords: Electric Vehicle · Lithium Battery · Fault Detection · Semi-Supervised Learning · Self-Generated Labels

1 Introduction

Electric vehicles (EVs) are gaining popularity due to their environmental and energy efficiency benefits. However, lithium batteries, as the core component, significantly impact EV reliability and user experience [1]. Faults in lithium batteries can lead to severe safety incidents, making accurate and timely fault detection crucial [2]. Most current fault detection methods require large amounts of labeled data, which is costly and often scarce due to varying conditions [3]. Traditional supervised learning struggles with this scarcity.

Fault detection in EV lithium batteries is a research hotspot, focusing on model-based and data-driven methods. Model-based methods use physical models for monitoring but face practical limitations due to battery complexity [4, 5]. Data-driven methods leverage historical data with machine learning and deep learning algorithms, including random forests, and neural networks [6]. Deep learning, particularly convolutional neural networks (CNNs) and recurrent neural networks (RNNs), has excelled in fault detection [7].

With scarce labeled data, semi-supervised learning and self-generated labels become effective solutions. Semi-supervised learning combines a small amount of labeled data with a large amount of unlabeled data, using methods like self-training, co-training, and generative adversarial networks (GANs) [8]. Self-generated labels are created through initial models and iteratively improve performance [9].

This paper proposes a novel method to enhance fault detection in EV lithium batteries using unlabeled data. It involves unsupervised pre-training of a feature extractor, training a base classifier on a small labeled set, and iterative progressive training with self-generated labels to improve performance. This research aims to provide an effective fault detection solution for EV lithium batteries and offer insights for related fields.

2 Methodology

2.1 Framework

We use two types of data: labeled and unlabeled. Labeled data (D_l), with known labels indicating battery state (normal or faulty), are manually labeled by experts or recorded by reliable sensors, making them costly but reliable. Unlabeled data (D_u), lacking labels, are automatically collected in large volumes through monitoring systems, containing rich information about the battery's state. Combining labeled and unlabeled data allows us to leverage the reliability of labeled data and the abundance of unlabeled data, enhancing the model's overall performance.

The proposed method's framework is shown in Fig. 1 and consists of three steps: feature extractor pre-training, base classifier training, and progressive training with self-generated labels. These steps maximize the use of unlabeled and limited labeled data to enhance fault detection model performance and robustness.

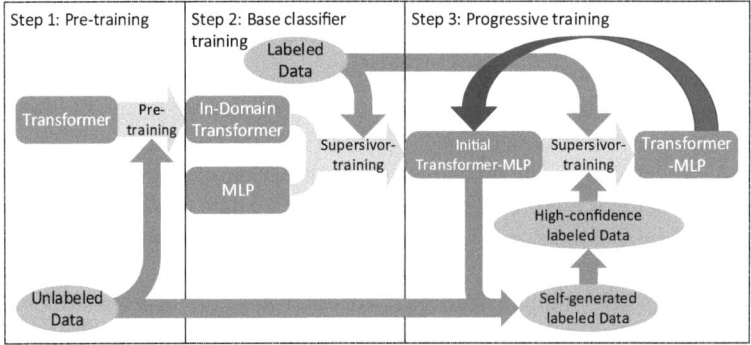

Fig. 1. Overall framework.

First, we pre-train the feature extractor on a large amount of unlabeled data, using a transformer for its effectiveness with time-series data. Next, we combine the pre-trained feature extractor with a new multilayer perceptron (MLP) classifier and train this model using labeled data. Finally, we use the initial classification model to predict unlabeled data, generate high-confidence labels, and iteratively improve the model through progressive training.

2.2 Feature Extractor Pre-training

We perform unsupervised pre-training on the transformer feature extractor using a large amount of unlabeled data to capture underlying patterns through self-supervised learning. The data is fed into the transformer model, which, using its self-attention mechanism, captures global information and key features in the time-series data.

For pre-training, an MLP is appended to the Transformer, with the task of predicting indicator values at the last time step of each sample. This helps the Transformer learn effective feature representations, using the mean squared error (MSE) as the loss function. The pre-training results in a Transformer feature extractor with strong representation capabilities, supporting subsequent classification tasks.

2.3 Base Classifier Training

We combine the pre-trained transformer with a MLP classifier and perform supervised learning using a small amount of labeled data to form the initial classification model. The MLP consists of several fully connected layers, with the output layer matching the number of classes.

During training, features from each time-series sample are fed into the combined model, which uses the transformer for feature extraction and the MLP for classification. The objective is to minimize classification error using the cross-entropy loss function. Training continues until validation performance converges, resulting in the initial classification model M_0.

This phase effectively uses labeled data, enabling initial fault detection capabilities and setting the stage for progressive training with self-generated labels.

2.4 Progressive Training with Self-generated Labels

We use the initial classification model M_0 to predict unlabeled data D_u, generate high-confidence labels, and iteratively improve model performance. This approach leverages the abundance of unlabeled data to enhance the model's robustness and accuracy. To ensure the quality of self-generated labels, we introduced a confidence threshold in each iterative step to select high-confidence label samples.

First, the initial model predicts the unlabeled data, generating labels $\hat{y}_u$ and confidence scores $\hat{c}_u$. High-confidence samples, determined by a set threshold τ, form a new training set. This set, combined with the labeled data, trains a new model. The new model is evaluated on a validation set. If its performance improves or remains stable, the threshold is lowered for the next iteration. If performance deteriorates, the previous model is restored, and the threshold is increased. This process repeats until validation performance stabilizes, resulting in the final model.

We designed a dynamic confidence threshold adjustment strategy to ensure high-quality self-generated labels:

1) Initial Confidence Threshold: Set a high initial threshold τ_0 to ensure quality.
2) Dynamic Adjustment Strategy: Adjust the threshold based on validation performance. Lower the threshold if performance improves or remains stable; increase it if performance deteriorates.
3) Threshold Adjustment Formula: Adjust using an adaptive strategy based on performance change. In each iteration, we dynamically adjust the confidence threshold using the following formula: $\tau_{t+1} = \tau_t - \alpha \times \Delta p$, where α is an adjustment coefficient and Δp is the change in model performance.
4) Stopping Condition: The iterative process stops when the validation performance stabilizes. Specifically, if there is no significant change in performance over several consecutive iterations, the model is considered to have reached its optimal state, and the iteration is stopped.

This strategy maximizes the use of unlabeled data without sacrificing performance stability. The quality of self-generated labels directly affects final performance, particularly in EV lithium battery fault detection.

3 Experiments and Results

In this chapter, we introduce and evaluate the proposed algorithm named Transformer Progressive Self-generated Labeling (TPSL). Through detailed experimental setup and result analysis, we validate the effectiveness and advantages of the TPSL algorithm in fault detection of electric vehicle lithium batteries.

3.1 Dataset Description

The dataset from Tsinghua University's EV data platform includes over 690,000 charging segments from 347 EVs, split into 70% training, 10% validation, and 20% testing sets. Only 1% of the training data is labeled, with the rest treated as unlabeled. Each sample represents a charging segment with time-series data on current, voltage, and temperature. Fault labels, derived from driver reports and validated by engineers, focus on issues like lithium plating and unexpected voltage changes. Anomalous data during or before faults are excluded. The model predicts potential battery issues days in advance by analyzing historical data [10]. No further preprocessing is required due to the dataset's good structure.

The dataset covers various battery fault types and states. However, due to diverse real-world scenarios, some fault types and states may still be uncovered. Future work will focus on collecting more comprehensive datasets and testing the model under different fault types and battery states to enhance its applicability.

3.2 Experimental Results

We evaluated the TPSL algorithm's performance using comparative and ablation experiments to demonstrate its effectiveness in lithium battery fault detection for electric vehicles.

We compared the TPSL algorithm with long short-term memory (LSTM), gated recurrent unit (GRU), CNN, and a fully labeled transformer. The results, shown in Table 1, indicate that TPSL outperforms LSTM, GRU, and CNN across all metrics and achieves an F1-score of 95.0%, comparable to the fully labeled transformer. This demonstrates TPSL's ability to utilize unlabeled data effectively and enhance model performance through progressive training.

Table 1. Performance comparison of different models

	Performance			
	Accuracy	Precision	Recall	F1-score
LSTM	85.2%	84.7%	83.5%	84.1%
GRU	86.1%	85.9%	84.3%	85.1%
CNN	88.5%	87.3%	87.1%	87.2%
Transformer (Full Labeled)	94.5%	94.0%	95.5%	94.7%
TPSL (Proposed)	95.8%	94.2%	95.8%	95.0%

To assess each component's contribution, we conducted ablation experiments: TPSL without pre-training, TPSL without iterative training, and TPSL without both. The results in Table 2 confirm the importance of pre-training and iterative training, as removing these components reduces performance. The fully labeled Transformer performs well, but TPSL further improves performance by incorporating unlabeled data.

Table 2. Ablation study results for TPSL

	Performance			
	Accuracy	Precision	Recall	F1-score
TPSL (without Pre-training)	89.0%	88.5%	87.9%	88.2%
TPSL (without Iterative Training)	89.7%	89.0%	88.3%	88.6%
TPSL (without Both)	72.3%	70.5%	71.0%	70.7%
TPSL (Proposed)	95.8%	94.2%	95.8%	95.0%

In the experiments, TPSL performed exceptionally well in specific scenarios. Pre-training significantly improves feature extraction, while iterative training enhances the use of unlabeled data. In the experiment, we observed that the accuracy of the TPSL model improves with the number of iterations, as shown in Fig. 2. This demonstrates the significant role of the iterative training module in enhancing the model's performance. Future work will analyze these mechanisms to better understand and optimize TPSL.

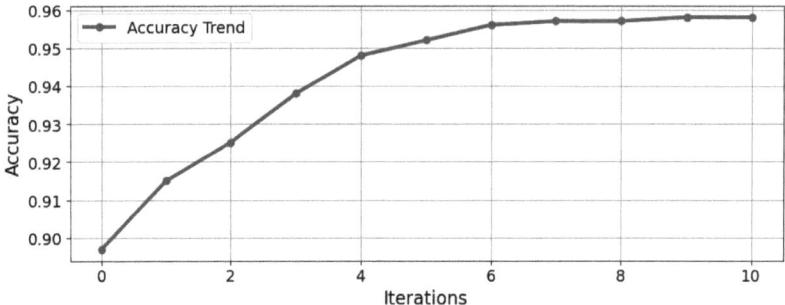

Fig. 2. Accuracy Improvement over Iterations.

Comparative and ablation experiments validate TPSL's effectiveness in fault detection. TPSL enhances performance with scarce labeled data and improves generalization through progressive training with unlabeled data.

4 Conclusion

The TPSL algorithm effectively uses unlabeled data for EV lithium battery fault detection through unsupervised pre-training and progressive self-generated labeling, boosting performance with scarce labeled data. Experimental results show TPSL outperforms traditional methods in precision, recall, and F1-score, and is comparable to fully labeled Transformer models. However, TPSL has high computational costs, especially during iterative training. The quality of self-generated labels is crucial, as poor initial labels can lead to incorrect fault detection.

Future work should optimize TPSL's computational efficiency with more efficient models or distributed computing and enhance self-generated label quality through complex strategies or ensemble methods. Validating TPSL in real-world scenarios will ensure its robustness and reliability under different conditions. Although the proposed model structure performed well in experiments, future work will explore more efficient structures, such as deeper neural networks or hybrid models, and adopt distributed computing techniques.

Experimental results show excellent performance of TPSL in fault detection of EV lithium batteries, but its generalization under different working conditions needs further verification. Future work will test the algorithm's robustness and reliability in a broader range of real-world scenarios.

Acknowledgments. This work was supported by Yangtze River Delta Science and Technology Innovation Community Joint Key Task under Grant No. 2023CSJGG1500 and the National Key Technology Support Program under Grant No. 2023YFB3307201.

References

1. Xu, J.J., et al.: High-energy lithium-ion batteries: recent progress and a promising future in applications. Energy Environ. Mater. (2023). https://doi.org/10.1002/eem2.12450
2. Wang, N., et al.: Thermal fault diagnosis method of lithium battery based on LSTM and battery physical model. In: 41st Chinese Control Conference (CCC). Hefei, Peoples R China (2022)
3. Tran, M.K., et al.: A review of lithium-ion battery thermal runaway modeling and diagnosis approaches. Processes **10**(6), 1192 (2022). https://doi.org/10.3390/pr10061192
4. Lin, C.P., Xu, J., Mei, X.S.: Improving state-of-health estimation for lithium-ion batteries via unlabeled charging data. Energy Storage Mater. **54**, 85–97 (2023)
5. Yao, L., et al.: An intelligent fault diagnosis method for lithium battery systems based on grid search support vector machine. Energy **214**, 118866 (2021). https://doi.org/10.1016/j.energy.2020.118866
6. Yang, X.L., et al.: A survey on deep semi-supervised learning. IEEE Trans. Knowl. Data Eng. **35**(9), 8934–8954 (2023)
7. Khan, N., et al.: Batteries state of health estimation via efficient neural networks with multiple channel charging profiles. IEEE Access **9**, 7797–7813 (2021)
8. Pan, T.Y., et al.: Generative adversarial network in mechanical fault diagnosis under small sample: a systematic review on applications and future perspectives. ISA Trans. **128**, 1–10 (2022)
9. Yang, L.H., et al.: ST plus plus: make self-training work better for semi-supervised semantic segmentation. In: IEEE/CVF Conference on Computer Vision and Pattern Recognition (CVPR). New Orleans, LA (2022)
10. Zhang, J.Z., et al.: Realistic fault detection of li-ion battery via dynamical deep learning. Nat. Commun. (2023). https://doi.org/10.1038/s41467-023-41226-5

Bearing Faults Diagnosis Based on EEMD and Probability Density Analysis

Xiangyang Liu, Zhifeng Li, Shuanglong He(✉), and Zhangliang Xu

School of Electronic Information Engineering, China West Normal University,
Nanchong 637009, Sichuan, People's Republic of China
18216065158@163.com

Abstract. In order to achieve high-precision detection of bearings under different working conditions, this paper proposes a bearing fault diagnosis method based on ensemble empirical mode decomposition (EEMD) and probability density analysis. The time-domain and frequency-domain characteristics of different bearing fault signals are analyzed. The kurtosis factor is selected to characterize bearing condition. The original vibration signal is decomposed into multiple intrinsic mode functions (IMF) by the EEMD algorithm, and each IMF component contains local feature information of the original signal at different time scales. The time-domain fault characteristics are extracted by calculating the kurtosis factor of each IMF component and doing probability density analysis. The frequency-domain fault characteristics are extracted by performing Fourier Transform and Hilbert transform on IMF. This paper uses the Case Western Reserve University (CWRU) bearing dataset for simulation analysis, as well as field test data for validation. The experimental results show that the diagnostic method proposed in this paper achieves 99.2% accuracy for field test data collected by the acceleration sensor.

Keywords: bearing fault diagnosis · kurtosis factor · EEMD · probability density

1 Introduction

Bearings are extremely vital components in rotating machinery systems [1], and bearing fault diagnosis has an important impact on the reliability and safety for modern industrial systems [2]. Therefore, the early fault analysis and feature extraction of rolling bearings is a hot research topic in recent years [3]. How to obtain the characteristics of bearing faults has become the focus of bearing fault diagnosis.

Time domain and frequency domain analysis is a simple and effective method which is used to diagnose the early bearing fault. A typical time-frequency signal decomposition method called empirical mode decomposition (EMD) was developed by N.E. Huang for analyzing non-linear and non-smooth signals [4]. The bearing signals are decomposed into multiple intrinsic mode function (IMF) through EMD. However, EMD still suffers from modal conflation, which affects feature extraction, model training, and pattern recognition. Ensemble empirical mode decomposition (EEMD) is a later improved method proposed by N.E. Huang to solve the modal aliasing phenomenon by adding white noise to the original signal [5]. The spectrum obtained by EEMD can accurately reflect the bearing failure characteristics.

Deep learning is also one of the popular methods for bearing fault detection. The key to bearing fault diagnosis based on deep learning lies in the extraction of fault features and the accuracy of classification [7]. Nowadays, there are many diagnostic methods that can reflect the relationships between bearing faults and features, such as decision trees [8], support vector machine(SVM) [9], K-Nearest Neighbors(KNN) [10], and artificial neural networks [11]. As a result, these diagnostic methods can automatically extract the REB fault features and possess a high diagnostic accuracy [6]. However, the bearing fault diagnosis method based on deep learning relies on historical data and requires strictly training of the model, and is not easy to diagnose bearing faults under different working conditions.

This paper proposes a bearing fault diagnosis method based on EEMD and probability density analysis. The problem of EMD decomposition modal confusion is solved and the accuracy of feature extraction is improved. At the same time combining with probability density from a numerical point of view to analyze the bearing failure, the method can be practical for a variety of bearing operating conditions detection. The bearing fault diagnosis method proposed in this paper does not rely on historical data and fixed models, which is an important guideline for variable working condition bearing fault detection in actual engineering.

2 Methodology

2.1 Probability Density Analysis

Probability density function is used to describe the probability distribution obeyed by a continuous random variable. Our work selects inner race bearings with different failure sizes to investigate the relationship between the probability density distribution of kurtosis factor and the depth of bearing failure. The vibration signal of normal bearings is the process of each state ephemeris, and its probability density distribution conforms to the normal distribution. The degree of deviation of the bearing signal from the normal distribution is detected by calculating the mean and standard deviation of the normal probability plot. Therefore, the bearing failure depth can be determined.

2.2 EEMD

EMD is a signal decomposition based on its own time-scale characteristics, which can handle any non-linear, non-stationary signal with high signal-to-noise ratio [6]. EMD does not require any pre-set basis functions, therefore it has adaptability [12]. EMD is achieved by taking the maximum and minimum points of the original signal separately, obtaining the maximum and minimum envelope lines. The IMF is the mean envelope subtracted from the original signal. This method mainly decomposes the complex engineering signal into a finite number of IMF components, and each IMF component contains the local feature information of the original signal at different time scales. The essence of EEMD is a multiple EMD with superimposed Gaussian white noise, which takes advantage of the statistical property that Gaussian white noise has a uniform frequency distribution [14]. By adding different white noise of equal amplitude each time to change the polar characteristics of the signal, the IMF components obtained after multiple EMD are averaged overall to cancel the added white noise, thus effectively suppressing the EMD modal aliasing. The EEMD flow chart is shown in Fig. 1.

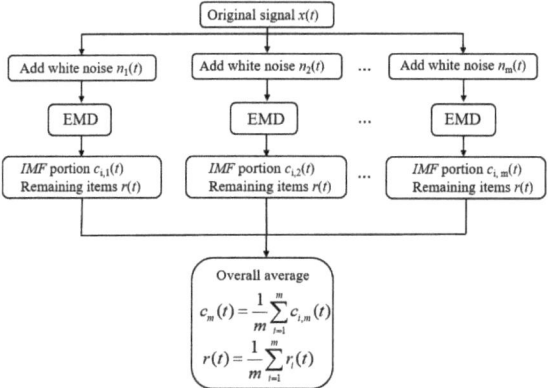

Fig. 1. EEMD flow chart

From Fig. 1, it can be seen that EEMD has added multiple sets of different white noise sequences. The signal with added white noise are seen as a whole to be decomposed. Compared with EMD, EEMD increased the computational complexity and improved the decomposition effect of signal end effects [13].

In this part, three kinds of time-domain signals of bearing inner race fault, outer race fault and rolling element fault are selected. EEMD will be used to decompose the time-domain signal into multiple IMF components, and the Fourier transform will transform each IMF into a frequency spectrum. The spectrum characteristics can reflect the bearing fault location. Theoretically, the formula for calculating the characteristic frequency of different fault locations is shown in formula (1), (2) and (3) respectively.

$$f_{inner} = \frac{z}{2}(1 + \frac{d}{D} \cos \alpha) f_i \qquad (1)$$

$$f_{outer} = \frac{z}{2}(1 - \frac{d}{D} \cos \alpha) f_i \qquad (2)$$

$$f_{roller} = \frac{D}{2d}(1 - (\frac{d}{D})^2 \cos^2 \alpha) f_i \qquad (3)$$

where f_{inner}, f_{outer} and f_{roller} represent the characteristic frequencies of the inner ring, outer ring and rolling element respectively. z represents the number of bearing balls, D indicates bearing pitch diameter, d indicates rolling element diameter, α indicates contact angle, f_i represents the rotation frequency, determined by the speed.

The inner race fault bearing with failure depth of Grade 1 is selected to decompose into multiple IMF components, and the Fourier transform will transform each IMF into a frequency spectrum. The spectrum characteristics can reflect the bearing fault location. Each IMF component is divided into 10 segments of the same length, and the length of each segment is 1024. The kurtosis factor of these IMF components is calculated and counted.

2.3 Field Experimental Data Verification

In this part, the proposed method is further verified by the field test data. The bearing failure test conditions selected in the field test data are shown in Table 1. The type of sensor we use is YND-187T02 with IEPE low noise and strong anti-interference capability. The bearing drive end accelerometer is used to analysis. The sampling frequency is 25600 Hz. The specific parameters of the bearings are shown in Table 2. The gearbox inner race fault bearing with damage grade 1 is selected to verify the diagnosis method proposed.

Table 1. CRRS gearbox running test bench experimental conditions

Experimental Conditions	The specific parameter value
Sample rate	25600 Hz
Approx motor speed	200 rpm
Data acquisition end	Drive end accelerometer
Damage level	Grade 1, 2, 3
Bearing type	Gearbox bearings R215

Table 2. Type 26 circular roller bearing dimensional parameters

Parameters	Size
Outer race diameter/r_1	240 mm
Inner race diameter/r_2	130 mm
Bearing pitch diameter/D	185 mm
Rolling element diameter/d	32 mm
Number of rolling element/Z	14
Contact angle/α	0–45o

3 Result and Discussion

3.1 Experimental Result and Discussion

The results of the bearing inner race fault with fault depth Grade 1 of EEMD is shown in Fig. 2. Figure(a) is the IMF components after EEMD. Figure(b) is the spectrum of the IMF components corresponding to (a).

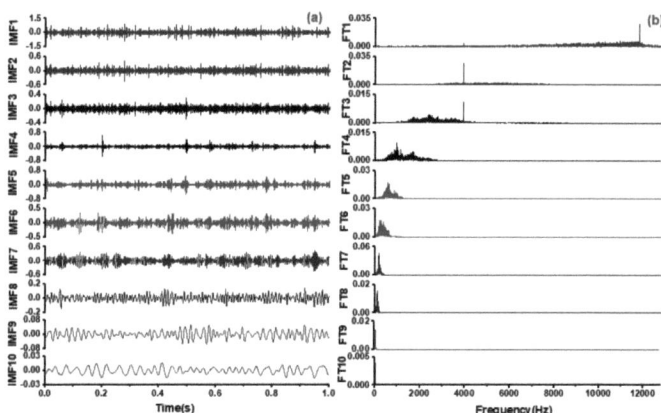

Fig. 2. Field experimental data analysis. Flow chart of EEMD of (a) time-domain waveform of IMF components, (b) spectrogram of IMF components.

The original bearing fault signal is decomposed into multiple IMF components with fault characteristics. The current bearing fault characteristic frequency can be obtained from the frequency spectrum of IMF components. The spectrum of IMF component is selected to analysis. As shown in the following Fig. 3.

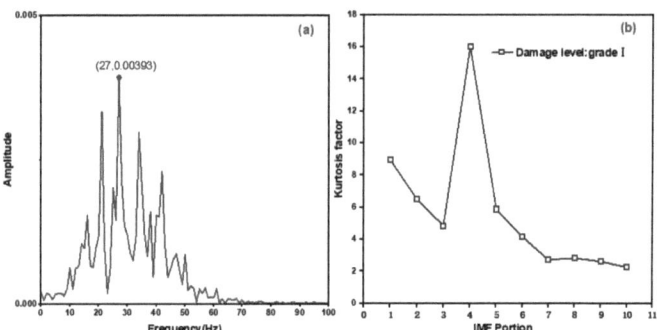

Fig. 3. Field experimental data analysis. (a)envelope spectrum with fault characteristics of the IMF component. (b) kurtosis factor of the IMF components.

The actual fault characteristic frequency is 27 Hz. According to Table 2, the theoretical failure characteristic frequency of the gearbox bearing is calculated as follows:

Inner race characteristic frequency:

$$f_{inner}(\min) = \frac{14}{2}(1 + \frac{32}{185}\cos 0°)\frac{200}{60} = 26.19 \quad (4)$$

$$f_{inner}(\max) = \frac{14}{2}(1 + \frac{32}{185}\cos 45°)\frac{200}{60} = 27.37 \quad (5)$$

Rolling element characteristic frequency:

$$f_{roller}(\min) = \frac{3 \times 185}{2 \times 32}(1 - (\frac{32}{185})^2 \cos 0°)\frac{200}{60} = 28.04 \quad (6)$$

$$f_{roller}(\max) = \frac{3 \times 185}{2 \times 32}(1 - (\frac{32}{185})^2 \cos 45°)\frac{200}{60} = 28.47 \quad (7)$$

After comparing the theoretical characteristic frequency of the gearbox bearing, 27 Hz is just within the inner race characteristic frequency range. Therefore, the fault location is detected as inner race fault and the fault location accuracy rate of 99.2%.

The Fig. 3 (b) is the trend plot of the kurtosis factor calculated from the IMF component. The characteristic value of the normal bearing kurtosis factor is 3. From the Fig. 3 (b), it can be seen that kurtosis factor deviates from 3, and the bearing malfunctions.

The probability density analysis results are shown in the following Fig. 4. In a normal probability plot, the mean mu determines the location of the probability density function, and the probability density plot reaches a maximum at the mean mu and is symmetrical about the variable X = mu. The normal bearing kurtosis factor probability density graph should be symmetric about the mean mu – 3. It can be seen that the mean $mu = 4.21406$, the standard deviation sigma = 3.22329 for the gearbox bearing failure criteria, that slightly deviates from the standard normal distribution of mu = 3, sigma = 1. It means that the bearing has failed, but its deviation is not large. Therefore, it can be diagnosed that the gearbox bearing is in the first level of damage at this time.

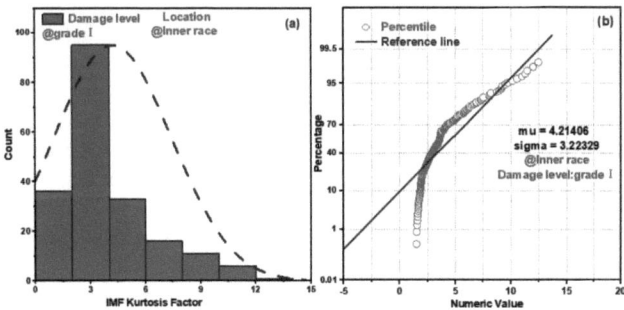

Fig. 4. Frequency distribution histograms of (a) kurtosis factor. Probability density diagrams of (b) kurtosis factor.

4 Conclusion

This paper proposed a bearing fault diagnosis method based on probability density analysis and EEMD. The mean and standard deviation were calculated from the probability density of the kurtosis factor. This paper combined the field experimental data to verify the diagnosis method proposed in this paper, and the accuracy rate reached 99.2% in determining the location of the bearing fault, and the depth of the fault was diagnosed as first-grade damage. In a nutshell, the diagnosis method propose in this paper can accurately detect the bearing fault location and fault depth, and the diagnosis method is practical and applicable not only to detect a variety of bearing fault types, but also to detect a variety of bearing operating conditions.

Acknowledgements. We acknowledge support from the Natural Science Foundation of Sichuan Province (No. 2022NSFSC1996) to Z. L. Xu. Authors would like to thank the support of Nanchong Key Laboratory of Electromagnetic Technology and Engineering.

References

1. Liu, R.N., Yang, B., Zio, E., Chen, X.F.: Artificial intelligence for fault diagnosis of rotating machinery: a review. Mech. Syst. Signal Process. **108**, 33–47 (2018)
2. Wang, X.L., Jiang, B., Wu, S.M., Lu, N.Y., Ding, S.X.: Multivariate relevance vector regression-based degradation modeling and remaining useful life prediction. IEEE Trans. Industr. Electron. **69**(9), 9514–9523 (2021)
3. Li, H., Liu, T., Wu, X., Chen, Q.: An optimized VMD method and its applications in bearing fault diagnosis. Measurement **166**, 108185 (2020)
4. Gupta, P., Pradhan, M.K.: Fault detection analysis in rolling element bearing: a review. Mater. Today Proc. **4**(2), 2085–2094 (2017)
5. Cui, H.J., Guan, Y., Chen, H.Y.: Rolling element fault diagnosis based on VMD and sensitivity MCKD. IEEE Access **9**, 120297–120308 (2021)
6. Zou, P., Hou, B., Lei, J., Zhang, Z.J.: Bearing fault diagnosis method based on EEMD and LSTM. Int. J. Comput. Commun. Control (February) **15**(1), 1010 (2020)
7. Chen, X.H., Yang, R., Xue, Y.H., Huang, M.J., Ferrero, R., Wang, Z.D.: Deep transfer learning for bearing fault diagnosis: a systematic review since 2016. IEEE Trans. Instrum. Meas. **72**, 3508221 (2023)
8. Amarnath, M., Sugumaran, V., Kumar, H.: Exploiting sound signals for fault diagnosis of bearings using decision tree. Measurement **46**(3), 1250–1256 (2013)
9. Konar, P., Chattopadhyay, P.: Bearing fault detection of induction motor using wavelet and support vector machines. Appl. Soft Comput. **11**(6), 4203–4211 (2011)
10. Tian, J., Morillo, C., Azarian, M.H., Pecht, M.: Motor bearing fault detection using spectral kurtosis-based feature extraction coupled with K-nearest neighbor distance analysis. IEEE Trans. Industr. Electron. **63**(3), 1793–1803 (2015)
11. Yu, Y., Cheng, J.S., Yu, D.J.: A roller bearing fault diagnosis method based on EMD energy entropy and ANN. J. Sound Vib. **294**(1–2), 269–277 (2006)
12. Lei, Y., He, Z., Zi, Y.: Application of the EEMD method to rotor fault diagnosis of rotating machinery. Mech. Syst. Signal Process. **23**(4), 1327–1338 (2009)

13. Ding, C., Zhou, Y.Y., Ding, Q.C., Wang, Z.Y.: Loss prediction of ultrahigh voltage transmission lines based on EEMD–LSTM–SVR algorithm. Front. Energy Res. (2022). https://doi.org/10.3389/fenrg.2022.811745
14. Lv, T., Tao, A.F., Zhang, Z., Qin, S.F., Wang, G.: Significant wave height prediction based on the local-EMD-WaveNet model. Ocean Eng. **287**, 115900 (2023). https://doi.org/10.1016/j.oceaneng.2023.115900

Deep Learning-Based Hand Keypoints Detection for Industrial Manipulation Gestures

Shengdang He[1,2], Yuanyuan Zou[1,2(✉)], and Cheng Peng[1]

[1] School of Mechanical Engineering, Shenyang Jianzhu University,
No.25, Hunnan Middle Road, Shenyang 110168, China
yyzou@sjzu.edu.cn
[2] National-Local Joint Engineering Laboratory of NC Machining Equipment and Technology of High-Grade Stone, Shenyang 110168, China

Abstract. Keypoints detection of Industrial manipulation gestures is a crucial need in a human-machine collaboration system. A high number of hand gesture keypoint detection problems are being presently solved. However, the accuracy as well as the reliability of hand gesture keypoints detection approaches still face challenges when they need to deal with more detailed hand manipulation behaviors such as gestures in the industrial manipulation. To solve the issue, a deep learning-based keypoint detection method for industrial manipulation gestures is proposed in this paper. Moreover, an industrial manipulation gesture dataset is established and a visualization software is designed for displaying the detection results. In addition, hand gesture keypoints detection experiments on the InterHand 2.6 M public dataset and the proposed industrial manipulation gesture dataset are conducted respectively. The experimental results show that the method can detect the keypoint position with high accuracy and can effectively detect the keypoints of industrial manipulation gestures.

Keywords: Industrial Manipulation Gesture · Keypoint Position Detection · Deep Learning · Human-computer Interaction

1 Introduction

Gestures are one of the most common types of body language used in communication and interaction. While the rest of the body exhibits a more general state in everyday communication, gestures can contain specific linguistic content. Gestures are widely used in human-computer interaction systems due to their speed and expressiveness in interaction [1]. However, the accuracy as well as the reliability of gesture recognition algorithms still face challenges when gesture recognition techniques need to deal with more detailed hand manipulation behaviors. Moreover, in human-computer interaction, in addition to the need to recognize gesture categories, application scenarios such as human-computer co-manipulation and robot imitation learning also require the acquisition of information about the location of the keypoints of gestures [2].

In gesture keypoint position detection algorithms, deep learning models are usually used to predict the keypoints position after being trained, which can be classified into three types of methods, namely, depth image-based method, RGB image-based method, and multimodal visual information-based method. In depth image-based gesture recognition methods [3], the depth image is sensitive to ambient light and the diversity of industrial environments, which leads to a decrease in the accuracy of gesture keypoints detection. Multimodal visual information-based method [4] needs to consider data synchronisation and calibration of various visual sensors. Certainly, the system complexity is high. In contrast, the RGB image-based method [5, 6] is suitable for large-scale application scenarios and has better real-time performance due to the RGB images are easy to obtain, have low processing costs, and are highly popular. Therefore, this paper finally chooses the RGB image-based gesture recognition method for hand keypoints detection.

Accurate acquisition of keypoints of gestures not only facilitates a highly accurate interaction experience, but also serves as the basis for robot imitation learning to achieve complex action recognition and imitation. However, in practical and industrial applications, the mutual occlusion of hands, the occlusion of objects on the hands, and the similarity between left and right hands in appearance lead to the problem of false detection and omission of keypoint location in hand keypoints detection. To address the above problems, this paper proposes a deep learning based keypoint location detection method for industrial manipulation gestures.

2 Related Works

In gesture keypoint position detection algorithms, deep learning models are usually used to predict the keypoints position after being trained, which can be classified into three types of methods, namely, depth image-based method, RGB image-based method, and multimodal visual information-based method.

In depth image-based methods, Tompson et al. [3] proposed a method to achieve a probabilistic heat map for each joint by using a linear hybrid masked hand model. Moreover, Zhou et al. [7] additionally considered the function of each finger and the importance of each finger. They proposed a network called Hand Branch Ensemble (HBE). Based on above methods, Du et al. [8] decomposed the hand pose estimation into palm pose estimation and finger pose estimation, and used the comprehensive heatmap as a constraint for the feature extraction of the 2D depth image. And then the probability heatmap of each joint were obtained.

In RGB image-based methods, Zimmermann et al. [5] proposed a network consisting of two sub-networks: a hand segmentation network that detected the hand and segmented the image based on the predicted hand mask, and a 3D pose regression network that acquired a fractional map and predicted the canonical 3D joint positions and the transformation matrix from camera coordinates to world coordinates. To simplify Zimmermann's network, Iqbal [6] et al. proposed a 2.5D pose representation method for a single RGB image and then a 3D model was reconstructed. Panteleris et al. [9] proposed a deep learning method based on hand models. First, the authors used the detection network YOLO v2 [10] for hand detection. And then the pre-trained Open-Pose [11] network is used for 2D joint position prediction. At last, a geometric hand model with 26 joints and a geometric hand model with 21 joints are adopted respectively for 3D joint position prediction. Although previous model-based approaches have used hand models to constrain the predicted pose, the structure of the hand has not been fully utilized. For this reason, He et al. [12] proposed an adversarial approach in which the generator predicted a pose based on the MANO hand model, and then employs a Graph Convolutional Network (GCN) to further refine the priori pose. In particular, the GCN used the prior pose and image features as input and predicted a new pose.

In multimodal visual information-based method, Mueller et al. [4] created a colour depth map based on each paired RGB-D image, which was used by a CNN to extract features and output a 2D hand position heat map to localize the hand region. However, at present, most of the research focuses on the estimation of gesture pose for single-handed gestures, while the research on bi-handed gestures has not received sufficient attention. Meanwhile, the main problem in bi-handed gestures research is the occlusion between the hands and the occlusion of the hands by objects, which leads to the low accuracy of the algorithm in detecting the position of the keypoints of the gesture.

In depth image-based gesture recognition methods, the depth image is sensitive to ambient light and the diversity of industrial environments, which leads to a decrease in the accuracy of gesture keypoints detection. Multimodal visual information-based method needs to consider data synchronisation and calibration of various visual sensors. Certainly, the system complexity is high. In contrast, the RGB image-based method is suitable for large-scale application scenarios and has better real-time performance due to the RGB images are easy to obtain, have low processing costs, and are highly popular. Therefore, this paper finally chooses the RGB image-based gesture recognition method for hand keypoints detection.

3 Establishment of Industrial Manipulation Gesture Dataset

Existing manipulation gesture datasets mainly focus on daily life manipulation gestures. The industrial manipulation gesture dataset is still relatively few. Therefore, an industrial manipulation gesture dataset is established in this paper.

3.1 Experimental Platform for Gesture Acquisition

To acquire gesture data, an experimental platform is designed as shown in Fig. 1.

It mainly consists of a Realsense D435i depth sensor, a computer terminal (PC) and a sensor bracket.

3.2 Gesture Data Acquisition

The dataset contains a total of 12 gestures, including single-handed gestures and bi-handed gestures, as shown in Fig. 2.

High-quality datasets play a crucial role in the training of deep learning models. To improve the adaptability of the dataset, this paper conducted data collection under four different lighting conditions, including indoor lighting, natural diffused light, direct sunlight, and low-light environment as shown in Fig. 3.

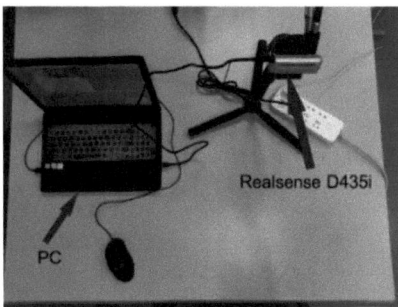

Fig. 1. Experimental platform

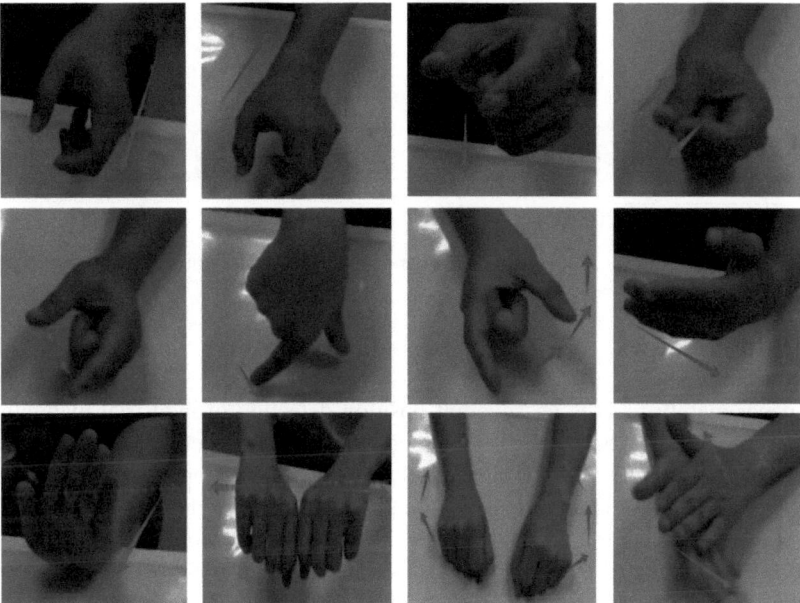

Fig. 2. Industrial manipulation gesture dataset

The impact of different person on the dataset was considered, and there were 28 participants in the collection process, of which 20 were male and 8 were female. There were 18 personnel with expertise related to industrial manipulation, while the others were general personnel. Each participant completed a full set of data collection tasks containing 12 different gestures. Of these, 300 samples were acquired for each gesture, for a total of 3600 640 × 480 RGB image sequences.

(a) Indoor lighting (b) Natural diffused light

(c) Direct sunlight (d) Low-light

Fig. 3. Gesture acquisition experiments under different lighting conditions

4 Methodologies

This paper mainly focuses on keypoint position detection of industrial manipulaiton gesture. And the flow chart of the keypoint position detection method is shown in Fig. 4. First, the image preprocessing is conducted to extract the motion region. And then, the BackboneNet network is used to detect the 2D coordinates of the gesture keypoints as well as to identify the left and right hands. Thirdly, the 3D coordinates of the gesture keypoints are estimated by using the PoseNet network according to the 2D heatmap. Finally, the filter is used for the data smoothing to reduce the trajectory jitter due to recognition extraction errors.

4.1 Image Preprocessing

In this paper, the frame difference method is applied to extract the motion regions, and the video frames are converted to grayscale frames according to Eq. (1), where R, G, and B correspond to the RGB pixel values of the original video frames respectively.

$$Gray = 0.2989 * R + 0.5870 * G + 0.1140 * B \qquad (1)$$

To extract the moving regions more accurately, Gaussian blur processing is implemented for the grayscale image by using the following formula (2). Gaussian blur is a common image smoothing technique that makes the grayscale value of each pixel in an image become closer to the average grayscale value of its surrounding pixels by applying

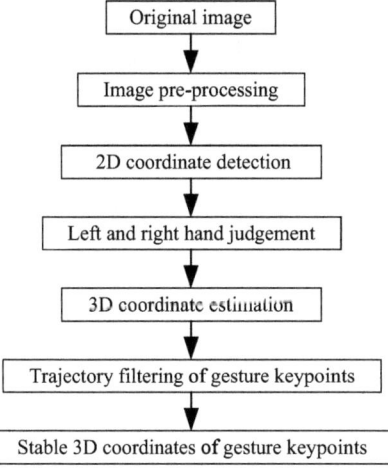

Fig. 4. Flowchart of keypoints position detection method

a weighted average to the image. Such a process effectively blurs out details and noise in the image, but at the same time preserves the overall structure of the image.

$$G(x, y) = \frac{1}{2\pi\sigma^2} e^{-(x^2+y^2/2\sigma^2)} \qquad (2)$$

where $G(x, y)$ is a Gaussian function, x and y are the coordinates of the pixel in the horizontal and vertical directions respectively and σ is the standard deviation of the Gaussian kernel.

After the Gaussian denoised video frames are obtained, they are processed by the frame difference method according to Eq. (3) for motion region extracting.

$$\text{diff}(x, y) = |I_1(x, y) - I_2(x, y)| \qquad (3)$$

where $I_1(x, y)$ is the pixel's grayscale value of the current frame image at (x, y) and $I_2(x, y)$ is the pixel's grayscale value of the previous frame image at (x, y). First, the grayscale frame image is converted to a binary image. And then, expansion and corrosion are used to the binary frame image to reduce noise. Consequently, the maximum rectangle of the moving object is drawn, and the maximum rectangle is mapped to the original video frame. Finally, the motion region is extracted and compressed to an 64 pixel × 64 pixel image, and the result is shown in Fig. 5.

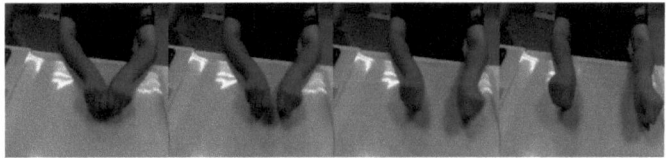

(a) Original Frames

(b) Frames extracted from the motion region

Fig. 5. Comparison of the effect of motion region extraction in the dataset

4.2 Gesture Keypoint Position Detection and Left/Right Hand Identification

The 2D coordinate detection of the keypoints of hand gesture based on RGB image has difficulties such as complex background interference, hand gesture diversity, etc. While BackboneNet network [13] has advantages such as deep network structure, effective feature extraction ability, etc., so it is used in this paper to detect the 2D coordinate of keypoint, and the structure of BackboneNet network is mainly composed of ResNet-50, which can identify left hand and right hand.

In some human-computer interaction, the 3D coordinate of the keypoints of hand gesture is usually required. In this paper, the PoseNet network [13] which is based on an encoder-decoder architecture is adopted to predict the 3D coordinates of keypoint. For the PoseNet network, the decoder is responsible for mapping the high-dimensional feature information extracted by the encoder back to the 3D space to reconstruct the 3D gesture of the hand. The features learnt by the network in this process are used to predict the 3D coordinates of each joint, and the design of the decoder ensures that the spatial information is recovered efficiently to achieve highly accurate gesture estimation.

4.3 Gesture Keypoint Trajectory Filter

The 3D coordinates of keypoints of hand gestures are detected based on the above deep learning model. However, the 3D coordinates cannot be directly used for human-computer interaction due to bias in the output results of the neural network, it can affect the continuity of the gesture trajectory. Therefore, to ensure the continuity of the gesture trajectory, a filter is used to smooth the position of the gesture keypoints. Savitzky-Golay filter is a filtering method that smoothes the data by local polynomial least-squares fitting in the time domain. Therefore, to achieve the effect of anti-jitter and jump, this paper chooses the Savitzky-Golay filter to optimise the 3D coordinates of keypoints of gestures. The flow of trajectory filtering is as following:

First, the information about the position of the hand keypoints detected in the first frame is stored into an array, the width of the filtering window is $n(n = 2m + 1)$, and the data in each length is taken as an interval, which is denoted as the H:

$$H = \{h_{n-m}, h_{n-m+1}, h_{n-m+2}, \cdots, h_n, \cdots, h_{n+m+1}, h_{n+m}\} \qquad (4)$$

where x is the coordinates of all keypoints of a frame image and m is the number of selected frames.

A $k - 1$ polynomial was used to fit the data points:

$$f = a_0 + a_1 h + a_2 h^2 + a_3 h^3 + \cdots + a_{k-1} h^{k-1} \tag{5}$$

The parameter A is then determined by least squares fitting method according to linearly equation system with k unknown numbers composed of n equations.

$$F_{(2m+1) \times 1} = H_{(2m+1) \times k} \cdot A_{K \times 1} + E_{(2m+1) \times 1} \tag{6}$$

The least squares solution of A is:

$$A = \left(H^T \cdot H \right)^{-1} \cdot H^T \cdot F \tag{7}$$

The model predicted or filtered value of F is:

$$\hat{F} = H \cdot A = H \cdot (H^T \cdot H)^{-1} \cdot H^T \cdot F \tag{8}$$

The filtered keypoint position can be obtained to achieve the smoothing of the gesture movement trajectory.

5 Experimental Results and Analysis

To verify the effectiveness of the proposed method, three different experiments are performed. The first experiment is carried out to evaluate the detection accuracy of keypoint on the InterHand 2.6M public dataset. The second experiment is aimed to evaluate the effectiveness of the gesture trajectory filtering. Finally, as the third experiment, the method proposed in this paper is applied on the industrial manipulation gesture dataset to verify its feasibility.

For the experiments, the main software environment used consists of the Ubuntu 18.04 operating system, the PyTorch deep learning framework, the OpenCV image processing library and several necessary Python libraries. The hardware environment, on the other hand, consists of an NVIDIA GeForce GTX 1050 graphics card, an i5-7300HQ central processing unit (CPU), and 16 GB of operating memory.

5.1 Keypoint Detection Accuracy Evaluation

In this section, the comparative experiments are conducted between the discussed method in this paper and the state-of-the-art methods on the InterHand 2.6 M public dataset to evaluate the keypoint detection accuracy.

The mean joint position error MPJPE is used as an evaluation index, as shown in Eq. (9).

$$MPJPE = \frac{1}{N} \sum_{i=1}^{N} \left\| J_i - J_i^* \right\|_2 \tag{9}$$

where N is the number of predicted joints, the predicted joints are J_i, the true joints are J_i^*.

Comparison is made with the methods proposed by Zimmermann [5], Spurr [14] and DIGIT et al. [15] and the results of the comparison experiments are shown in Table 1. Among them, the MPJPE of Zimmermann's method reaches 36.36 mm, the MPJPE of Spurr's method reaches 15.40 mm and the MPJPE of DIGIT's method reaches 16.75 mm, and the MPJPE of the method discussed in this paper is 14.04 mm, so the experimental results show that the method discussed in this paper has a higher accuracy than the other methods.

Table 1. Comparison experiments results

Methods	MPJPE(mm)
Zimmermann et al. [7]	36.36
Spurr et al. [8]	15.40
DIGIT et al. [5]	16.75
ResNet-50 + PoseNet	14.04

5.2 Gesture Trajectory Filtering Experiment

In order to evaluate the effectiveness of trajectory filtering, the detection results of ten consecutive frames are extracted for analysis in this paper while keeping the gesture unchanged. The keypoint detection results without filtering are shown in Fig. 6(a). The results after filtering by using Savitzky-Golay filter are shown in Fig. 6(b). The comparative results show that the noise at the keypoint of the gesture can be filtered out by using the filtering method to improve the accuracy of the gesture position detection and ensure the continuity and stability of the gesture trajectory.

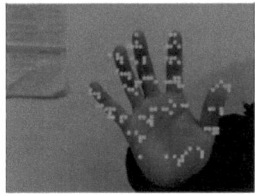
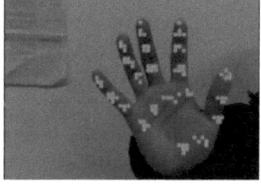

(a) Not filtered   (b) Filtered

Fig. 6. Comparison of results before and after filtering

5.3 Keypoint Position Detection of Industrial Manipulation Gesture

To verify the effectiveness of the proposed method in keypoint position detection of industrial manipulation gesture, experiments are performed on the industrial manipulation gesture dataset established in this paper. The detection results of some industrial manipulation gestures are displayed in the Visualization window as shown in Fig. 7.

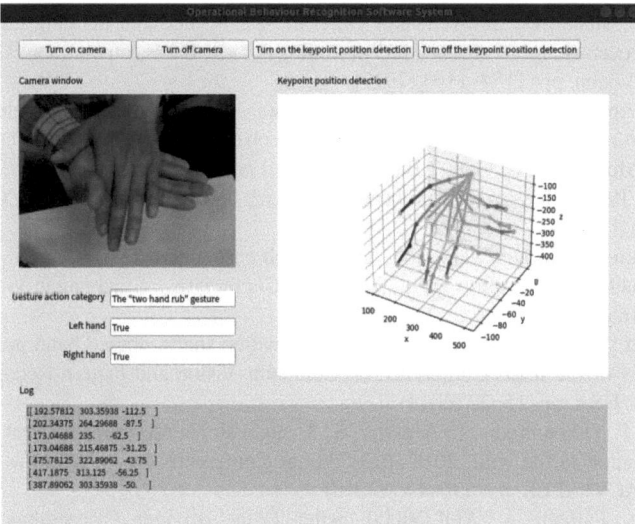

Fig. 7. Keypoint position detection results of the industrial manipulation gestures

The experimental results show that the keypoint position detection method proposed in this paper can detect the keypoint position of industrial manipulation gestures effectively and can be adaptive to the gesture occlusion.

6 Conclusion

This paper presents a method based on deep learning for hand keypoints detection of industrial manipulation gestures. We aim at solve the problems of low accuracy and incorrect keypoints detection of industrial manipulation gesture caused by the mutual occlusion of hands, the occlusion of objects on the hands and the similarity between left and right hands. In addition, an industrial manipulation gesture dataset is established in this paper to verify the effectiveness of the proposed method and the keypoint detection experiments as well as the gesture trajectory filtering experiments are conducted. The experimental results demonstrate that the proposed method is able to obtain the 3D coordinates of the gesture keypoint with high accuracy and perform well for keypoints detection of industrial manipulation gestures.

References

1. Guo, L., Lu, Z., Yao, L.: Human-machine interaction sensing technology based on hand gesture recognition: a review. IEEE Trans. Hum. Mach. Syst. **51**(4), 300–309 (2021)
2. Amaral, P., Silva, F., Santos, V.: Recognition of grasping patterns using deep learning for human-robot collaboration. Sensors **23**(21), 8989 (2023)
3. Tompson, J., Stein, M., Lecun, Y., et al.: Real-time continuous pose recovery of human hands using convolutional networks. ACM Trans. Graph. (ToG) **33**(5), 1–10 (2014)

4. Mueller, F., Mehta, D., Sotnychenko, O., et al.: Real-time hand tracking under occlusion from an egocentric rgb-d sensor. In: Proceedings of the IEEE International Conference on Computer Vision. pp. 1154–1163 (2017)
5. Zimmermann, C., Brox, T.: Learning to estimate 3d hand pose from single rgb images. Proceedings of the IEEE international conference on computer vision. pp. 4903–4911 (2017)
6. Iqbal, U., Molchanov, P., Gall, T.B.J., et al.: Hand pose estimation via latent 2.5 d heatmap regression. Proceedings of the European Conference on Computer Vision (ECCV). pp. 118–134 (2018)
7. Zhou, Y., Lu, J., Du, K., et al.: Hbe: hand branch ensemble network for real-time 3d hand pose estimation. Proceedings of the European Conference on Computer Vision (ECCV). pp. 501–516 (2018)
8. Du, K., Lin, X., Sun, Y., et al.: Multi-task information sharing based hand pose estimation. Proceedings of the IEEE Conference on Computer Vision and Pattern Recognition, Long Beach, CA, USA. pp. 15–20 (2019)
9. Panteleris, P., Oikonomidis, I., Argyros, A.: Using a single rgb frame for real time 3d hand pose estimation in the wild. 2018 IEEE Winter Conference on Applications of Computer Vision (WACV). IEEE, pp. 436–445 (2018)
10. Redmon, J., Farhadi, A.: YOLO9000: better, faster, stronger. Proceedings of the IEEE Conference on Computer Vision and Pattern Recognition. pp. 7263–7271 (2017)
11. Cao, Z., Simon, T., Wei, S.E., et al.: Realtime multi-person 2d pose estimation using part affinity fields. Proceedings of the IEEE Conference on Computer Vision and Pattern Recognition. pp. 7291–7299 (2017)
12. He, Y., Hu, W., Yang, S.F., et al.: 3D hand pose estimation in the wild via graph refinement under adversarial learning. Proceedings of the IEEE/CVF Conference on Computer Vision and Pattern Recognition (2020)
13. Moon, G., Yu, S.I., Wen, H., et al.: Interhand2. 6m: a dataset and baseline for 3d interacting hand pose estimation from a single rgb image. Computer Vision–ECCV 2020: 16th European Conference, Glasgow, UK, August 23–28, 2020, Proceedings, Part XX 16. Springer International Publishing, pp. 548-564 (2020)
14. Spurr, A., Song, J., Park, S., et al.: Cross-modal deep variational hand pose estimation. Proceedings of the IEEE Conference on Computer Vision and Pattern Recognition. pp. 89–98 (2018)
15. Fan, Z., Spurr, A., Kocabas, M., et al.: Learning to disambiguate strongly interacting hands via probabilistic per-pixel part segmentation. 2021 International Conference on 3D Vision (3DV). IEEE, pp. 1–10 (2021)

Development of Static Calibration Device for Eddy Current Sensors

Ling Zhang[1], Xiang Xu[2], Yang Liu[2], Mao Zheng[1], Qingping Wang[1], Jinjiang Han[1], Jun Wang[1], Bin Lei[2], and Chengbo Yang[1(✉)]

[1] Hongta Tobacco (Group) Co., Ltd., Yuxi 653100, Yunnan, China
973340521@qq.com
[2] Yuxi Cigarette Factory, Hongta Tobacco (Group) Co., Ltd., Yuxi 653100, Yunnan, China

Abstract. Eddy current sensors, as a non-contact detection device, are widely used in the production process of cigarette products. However, during the use of eddy current sensors, there may be significant errors or even errors in the indicated values due to aging or the influence of objective environment. Therefore, it is necessary to regularly perform static calibration of eddy current sensors based on their performance, and timely detect and deal with the problems existing in eddy current sensors. By analyzing the working principle and static characteristics of eddy current sensors, and based on the technical indicators and requirements stipulated in the national metrological verification regulations, the technical indicators of the calibration device are proposed, and the overall structure of the calibration device is designed. The induction disk, fixture, driving component, control system, etc. for static calibration of eddy current sensors are designed, and the design and installation of the static calibration device are completed. Completed the installation of multi-scale sensor fixtures and the installation and debugging of the drive control system. The development of the static calibration device for eddy current sensors was ultimately completed. Through experimental verification, the static calibration device for eddy current sensors can achieve a calibration stroke of 50 mm, with a position control accuracy of better than 5 μm, a position measurement accuracy of better than 3 μm, and a voltage measurement accuracy of better than 0.1%. The design and production of the static calibration device meet the requirements for use.

Keywords: eddy current sensor · static characteristics · static calibration · grating feedback · FPGA

1 Introduction

Eddy current sensors can non-contact measure the relative displacement between the tested metal conductor and the surface of the sensor probe. They are a non-contact linearized measuring tool. The non-contact measurement method avoids damaging the quality of the surface of the tested object when in contact with the surface. On the other hand, if the sensor is installed on the surface of the tested object, it is equivalent to adding a load on the surface of the tested object, which will reduce the accuracy of the test. In addition, in some high-speed rotating situations, using non-contact eddy current sensors for testing is more convenient than using contact sensors. The research on static calibration devices for eddy current sensors in China initially focused on manual calibration and data recording. Up to now, many domestic manufacturers and universities are still developing these manual calibration devices, including Beijing Vibration Instrument Factory, Southeast University and other enterprises and universities. In recent years, China has gradually begun to develop towards automatic calibration. Wang Tianna from Beijing University of Chemical Technology proposed an automatic static calibration method for eddy current sensors, which uses a stepper motor to drive the rotation of the micrometer to achieve the displacement of the induction disk [1]. Master Ding Meiying from Beijing University of Chemical Technology added an encoder to the stepper motor based on the device designed by Wang Tianna, allowing displacement readings to be directly read from the encoder, taking the development of an automatic static calibration device for eddy current sensors one step further [2]. However, although the open-loop control of stepper motors has achieved a certain degree of automation, the accuracy of position control is not high, especially the repeated accuracy of position control is not high, and the error is relatively large.

2 Design of Static Calibration Device for Eddy Current Sensors

The overall design concept of the automatic static calibration device for eddy current sensors is to replace manual operation with computer control to achieve automatic measurement, recording, processing, and storage of data. Data measurement includes measurement of displacement data and measurement of the output signal of the eddy current sensor. So the overall design idea is to first set certain parameters in the upper computer software by the user based on the technical indicators of the eddy current sensor. Secondly, the upper computer software generates and sends corresponding instructions to the lower computer measurement and control system based on the interface parameter settings. Then, the lower computer measurement and control system generates corresponding commands based on the instructions, controls the movement of mechanical components, reads displacement data and eddy current sensor signal data, and returns the processed data to the upper computer software. Finally, the upper computer software processes and saves the read data, completing the entire automatic calibration process [3–5]. Based on the above design ideas, the automatic static calibration device for eddy current sensors is divided into three parts for design: mechanical structure design, measurement and control system design, and upper computer software design. The overall structure of the automatic static calibration device for eddy current sensors is shown in Fig. 1.

3 Mechanical Structure Design

Based on the motion characteristics of the mechanical structure and the required functional characteristics, the design of the mechanical structure mainly aims to achieve relative linear motion between the induction disk and the sensor probe, as well as accurate installation of the eddy current sensor. Therefore, a motion mechanism and sensor

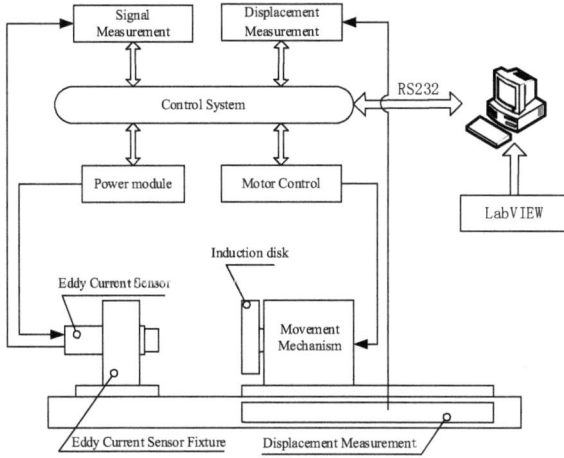

Fig. 1. System diagram of static calibration device for eddy current sensors

installation mechanism need to be designed. At the same time, it is necessary to design an adjustment mechanism for the zero position of the eddy current sensor to facilitate the correct selection of the zero position. When adjusting the zero position, a locking mechanism needs to be designed to prevent the sensor from sliding during the movement of the moving mechanism.

3.1 Drive Components

With the rapid development of digital technology, stepper motors, as one of the key products of mechatronics integration, have been widely used in various automated control systems. A stepper motor is an open-loop control element that converts pulse signals into angular displacement. The motion of the stepper motor is rotational motion, and the driving components required in this design ultimately need to complete linear motion. Therefore, it is necessary to design and select another mechanism to convert rotational motion into linear motion. In order to meet the requirements of high precision, a pre pressed ball screw is selected as the transmission mechanism.

The selection of stepper motors mainly considers parameters such as torque, speed, starting frequency, inertia torque, and step angle. Below, we will select the stepper motor based on the characteristics and requirements of the entire system during operation. Determine parameters such as torque, speed, starting frequency, inertia torque, and step angle separately.

Firstly, select the torque. During normal operation of the device, the stepper motor accelerates to a certain speed, then runs at a constant speed for a period of time, and finally decelerates to a stop. From this, the maximum torque TK required by the stepper motor during acceleration can be obtained. The maximum torque TK includes the friction torque T1 caused by external loads, the preloading torque T2 of the ball screw, and the required torque T3 during acceleration.

Assuming that the maximum resistance Fa caused by external friction and other loads can reach 100N, the lead Ph is 2mm, and the efficiency of the ball screw is 0.9. In addition, due to the coupling connection between the motor and the screw, there is no reducer, i.e. the reduction ratio r is 1, the friction torque caused by external loads and friction is obtained as

$$T_1 = \frac{F_a \times P_h}{2\pi \times \eta} \times r \tag{1}$$

Substituting data: $T_1 = 0.035 \text{ N} \cdot \text{m}$.

According to the parameter characteristics provided by BNK1402, the maximum preloading torque T2 of this model of ball screw is 0.049 N · m.

The required torque T3 for acceleration is $J \cdot \alpha$, where J is the inertia torque and α is the angular acceleration. The total mass of the moving component can be obtained from the three-dimensional modeling of the components, m = 6 kg, and the inertia torque of the ball screw is $J_s = 3.62 \times 10^{-6} \text{kg} \cdot \text{m}^2$, Then the moment of inertia is

$$J = m \left(\frac{P_h}{2\pi}\right)^2 \cdot 10^{-6} + J_s \tag{2}$$

Substituting data: $J = 4.2 \times 10^{-6} \text{kg} \cdot \text{m}^2$.

Assuming the angular acceleration of the motor at startup is $\alpha = 100 \text{ rad/s}^2$, the required torque for acceleration

$$T_3 = J \cdot \alpha \tag{3}$$

Substituting data: $T_3 = 0.00042 \text{ N} \cdot \text{m}$.

So the maximum torque during device operation is

$$T_t = T_1 + T_2 + T_3 \tag{4}$$

Substituting data: $T_1 = 0.085 \text{ N} \cdot \text{m}$.

In the design of this device, due to the high speed, stepping out can be more serious. Due to the small stroke, low speed can also achieve better dynamic characteristics of the device. Therefore, the operating speed should be selected as low as possible. However, the speed should not be too low, as low speed can cause issues such as running vibration and noise. Therefore, considering all factors, the initial speed requirement is set at 60 r/min.

For stepper motors with a speed above 1000 r/min, it is necessary to consider the issue of acceleration during startup. However, since the selected speed in this device is not very high, the selection of the starting frequency parameter is not very important in this design.

Next, consider another important parameter, inertia torque. According to the commonly used calculation formula, the inertia torque of the stepper motor can be obtained as $J_m = \frac{J}{C}$. C is a coefficient determined by the stepper motor and driver, Generally, it takes 3–10. If the value of C here is 3, then the inertia torque of the stepper motor is

$$J_m = \frac{J}{C} \tag{5}$$

Substituting data: $J_m = 1.53 \times 10^{-6} \text{kg} \cdot \text{m}^2$.

In order to improve resolution, when selecting a stepper motor, try to choose a smaller step angle. Common step angles are 1.8° and 0.9°. Based on the above parameter requirements and considering the rationality of the design, we have chosen the SST42C1065 stepper motor from Shinano Company, as well as the corresponding XNQ240MA stepper motor driver. The main parameters of the stepper motor are: step angle of 0.9°, inertia torque of 3.3×10^{-5} kg·m², holding torque of 0.157 N·m, and the motor is a two wire four wire system. Main parameters of the driver: maximum fine fraction 64, output current can be adjusted between 0-1.5 A, that is, the output torque size can be adjusted. Because the lead of the screw is 2 mm, the minimum resolution of linear motion when the subdivision of the driver is set to 64 is δ

$$\delta = \frac{0.9}{360} \times 2 \text{ mm} \div 64 \approx 0.078 \text{ μm} \tag{6}$$

Meet the minimum resolution requirement of 5 μm control accuracy.

3.2 Design of Eddy Current Sensor Fixture

According to the working principle and calibration principle of the sensor, the focus of the fixture design is to ensure that the surface of the sensor probe and the surface of the sensing plate are parallel after installation; In addition, it is necessary to design a multifunctional fixture to facilitate the clamping and installation of eddy current sensors of different shapes and sizes [6, 7].

The sensor bracket in this device can be used to install eddy current sensors of different shapes, suitable for sensors with cylindrical and planar mounting surfaces. For the installation of two different types of sensors, in order to facilitate the alignment of the central axis of the eddy current sensor probe and the central axis of the sensing disc, the sensor bracket can be moved vertically during the design; After the two axes are coaxial, the sensor bracket can be fixed by a locking mechanism. This locking mechanism includes locking screws, locking slides, screw fixing blocks, as well as sensor brackets and fixing brackets. The locking screw is installed on the screw fixing block, which is then installed on the sensor bracket, and the locking slide is also stuck inside the screw fixing block; When the sensor bracket slides up and down, it can drive the locking screw, locking slide, and locking fixing block to slide together. When the locking screw rotates, it can drive the locking slide to approach or move away from the fixed bracket. When the locking slide approaches and adheres tightly to the fixed bracket, it plays a locking role. In this design, locking screws are not directly screwed onto the fixed bracket, but are indirectly used to lock the bracket through the locking slide. This is because the contact area between the locking slide and the fixed bracket is larger, making it less likely to slide, which is more conducive to locking. The schematic diagram of the installation fixture for eddy current sensors is shown in Fig. 2.

The installation of cylindrical eddy current sensors is achieved by clamping the outer cylindrical surface. For different eddy current sensors, a series of liners have been designed here. The inner diameter of the liner can precisely accommodate small diameter eddy current sensors, and the outer diameter of the liner is consistent with the mounting hole of the fixture. This way, small diameter eddy current sensors can also be installed on the fixture through the liner. For planar eddy current sensors with different plane sizes

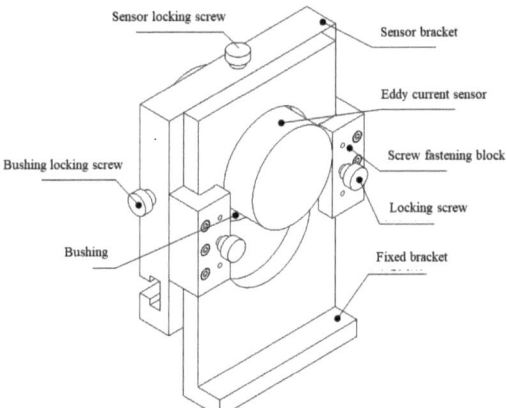

Fig. 2. Fixture of eddy current sensor

and installation hole positions, this design solves the installation problem of such eddy current sensors by opening a T-shaped groove on one side of the sensor bracket.

3.3 Zero Point Adjustment Mechanism Design

After the installation of the eddy current sensor, it is necessary to adjust the zero position. When adjusting the zero point position, the probe of the eddy current sensor should be tightly pressed against the end face of the sensing plate with a small force. If the contact force between the sensor and the sensing plate is too strong when the eddy current sensor is installed at the zero point position, the sensor bracket or the supporting components of the sensing plate will undergo elastic deformation, which will affect the accuracy of measurement calibration [8, 9]. However, due to the difficulty of manually installing eddy current sensors tightly, it is necessary to design a small displacement platform with rated thrust to adjust the zero position of the eddy current sensor. The zero adjustment mechanism includes a sliding table, cross roller guide rail, fixed torque knob, fixed nut, screw, etc. When the sensor comes into contact with the induction disk, continue to rotate the fixed torque knob. When the resistance exceeds the rated torque, a sound will be emitted to avoid excessive contact force between the sensor and the induction disk. The schematic diagram of the zero point adjustment mechanism is shown in Fig. 3.

After adjusting the zero position, in order to prevent the vibration generated by the stepper motor during movement from causing the sliding table to slide and affecting measurement accuracy, it is necessary to fix the sensor mounting bracket. Therefore, a locking mechanism is designed on the side of the sensor mounting sliding table. The locking mechanism is divided into three parts: the base, knob screw, and locking slide. The schematic diagram of the zero point locking mechanism is shown in Fig. 4.

The designed mechanical device structure diagram is shown in the following figure. The external structure diagram of the entire device is shown in Fig. 5, and the internal structure diagram of the entire device is shown in Fig. 6.

Development of Static Calibration Device for Eddy Current Sensors 35

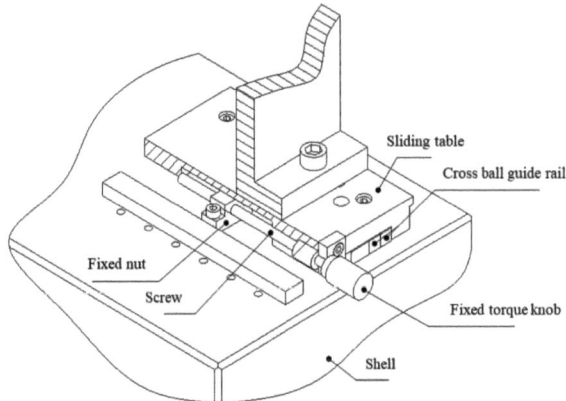

Fig. 3. Diagram of zero point adjustment mechanism

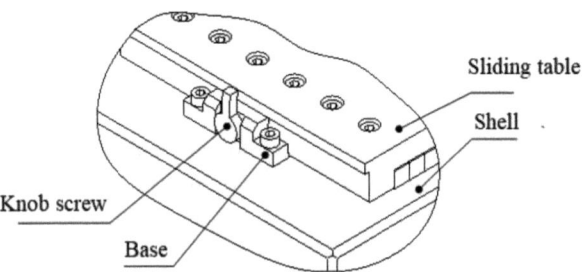

Fig. 4. Diagram of locking mechanism

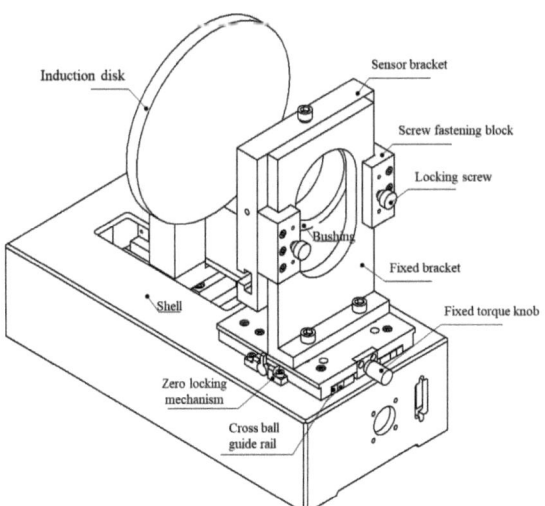

Fig. 5. The external structure diagram of the entire device

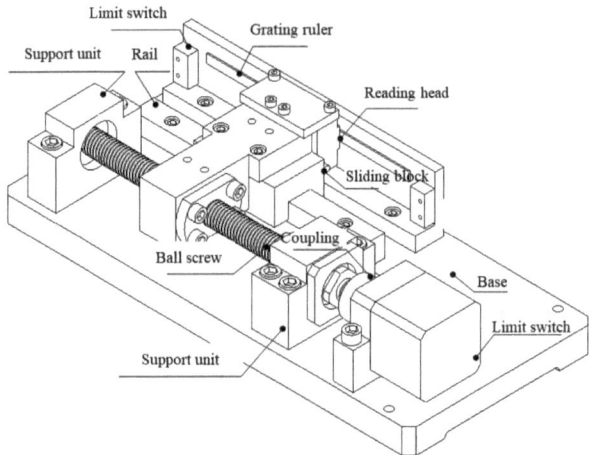

Fig. 6. The internal structure diagram of the entire device

3.4 Static Analysis of Mechanical Structures

After completing the design of the static calibration mechanical system for eddy current sensors, considering that the correct installation of the induction disk has a significant impact on the calibration accuracy of the eddy current sensor, the static analysis of the tilt angle of the disk surface under the influence of its own gravity after the installation of the induction disk is carried out. ANSYS software is used to establish the model, define material properties, divide the unit grid, and perform simulation calculations to obtain the relative axial deformation of the upper and lower end faces of the induction disk surface relative to the center of the disk surface [10]. As show in Fig. 7, it can be seen that due to gravity, the induction disk has tilted to a certain amount, and the relative axial deformation of nearly 0.028mm occurs at the upper and lower end faces of the induction disk. The actual and theoretical axes of the end faces can be calculated based on the actual and theoretical axes. A 23″ angle deviation occurred, resulting in an error of 0.011%. The deviation introduced by this angle will not have a significant impact on subsequent measurements and can be ignored. Therefore, the installation of the induction disk meets the design requirements.

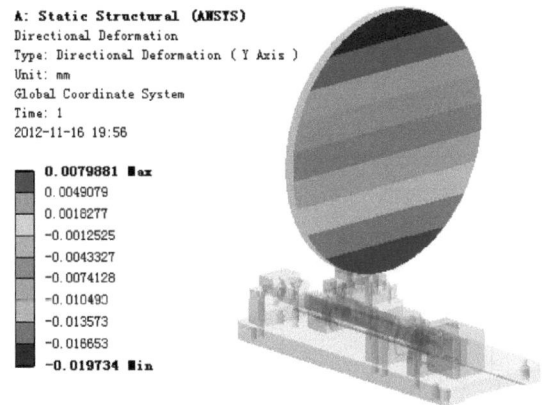

Fig. 7. Schematic diagram of static analysis of induction disk

4 Stepper Motor Control Module

In the design of this module, the main task is to complete the design of the frequency divider, counter, timer, and counter comparator [11, 12]. The function of the frequency divider is to divide the clock frequency according to different speed sizes, and generate pulse signals of corresponding frequencies. The design of the counter is to count the number of movements per 10% of the range in measurement mode. When the counter reaches a certain value, it will change the direction signal to change the direction of movement. After reaching the maximum count value, it will stop working in measurement mode and complete the measurement of the range. The timer is mainly designed to pause the operation of the motor. When the motor moves to every 10% range, the timer starts working according to the clock frequency. The FPGA internal trigger signal will start the sensor measurement module to work. When the timing time reaches the set value of 1 s, the FPGA will first stop the data conversion and processing of the sensor measurement module. Secondly, the voltage signal and displacement signal are sent to the communication module, and then the communication module is started to work. At the same time, the timer is reset and a new displacement value is assigned to the counting comparator. Finally, the motor continues to work. The displacement command of the upper computer is sent to the counting comparator through the communication module, which serves as a reference. The counting comparator compares the measured displacement data with the reference value, and determines whether to resend pulse signals, direction signals, and the number of pulse signals based on the nature of the deviation. The feedback of closed-loop control is completed through this counting comparator. The signal flow diagram of the stepper motor control module is shown in Fig. 8.

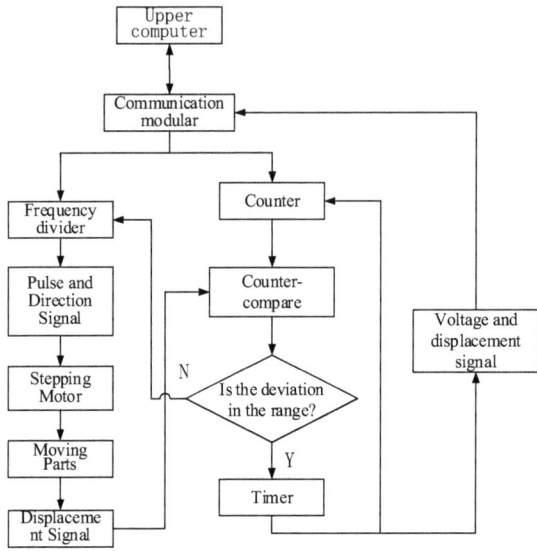

Fig. 8. Signal flow chart of stepper motor control module

5 Experimental Verification

In order to obtain the position control accuracy and displacement measurement accuracy of the device, this experiment used OPTODYNE's MCN-5005 laser interferometer to measure the operating displacement of the motion mechanism. Table 1 shows the measurement data of the moving components in auxiliary mode with a displacement of every 10mm of walking. The first ten rows show the displacement setting values for the forward motion of the motion mechanism, while the last nine rows show the displacement setting values for the return motion of the motion mechanism; The second column is the displacement value measured by the laser interferometer, which is the actual displacement value of the motion mechanism during operation; The third column is the displacement value measured by the grating system in the calibrator; The fourth column represents the displacement difference between the laser interferometer and the set displacement value, which is the absolute displacement error or control accuracy error. The fifth column represents the displacement difference between the laser interferometer and the calibrator, which is the measurement error of the calibrator. From the table, it can be seen that all the data is correct and the control accuracy is within 10 μm, and the measurement accuracy is within 5 μm, meeting the expected technical specifications. The definition of controlled displacement is the difference between the measured displacement value of the laser interferometer and the set displacement value; The definition of measurement error is the difference between the measured displacement value of the calibrator and the measured displacement value of the laser interferometer.

For the experimental research of the voltage measurement module, the main focus is on studying the measurement accuracy of the voltage measurement module, using the Agilent-34410 A digital voltmeter as the reference. The specific experimental approach is to first short-circuit the differential input terminal of the measurement module, with an

Table 1. Displacement values measured by laser interferometer and calibrator

Displacement (mm)	Laser interferometer (mm)	Calibrator (mm)	Control error (mm)	Measuring error (mm)
0	0.0000	0.0000	0.0000	0.0000
10	10.0003	10.0002	0.0003	0.0001
20	20.0004	20.0004	0.0004	0.0000
30	29.9998	30.0002	−0.0002	−0.0004
40	39.9994	40.0001	−0.0006	−0.0007
50	49.9994	50.0004	−0.0006	−0.0010
60	60.0006	60.0003	0.0006	0.0003
70	70.0006	70.0003	0.0006	0.0003
80	79.9999	80.0002	−0.0001	−0.0003
90	89.9994	90.0004	−0.0006	−0.0010
80	79.9997	79.9998	−0.0003	−0.0001
70	70.0002	70.0001	0.0002	0.0001
60	59.9988	60.0000	−0.0012	−0.0012
50	49.9988	49.9999	−0.0012	−0.0011
40	39.9992	39.9997	−0.0008	−0.0005
30	30.0001	29.9998	0.0001	0.0003
20	20.0000	19.9996	0.0000	0.0004
10	9.9999	9.9996	−0.0001	0.0003
0	0.0009	0.0002	0.0009	0.0007

input voltage of 0 V, and read the corresponding data in the upper computer. Next, input a 24 V stabilized voltage at the differential input terminal, read the corresponding data from the upper computer, and use an Agilent voltmeter to measure the magnitude of this voltage value. Then, the parameters are corrected in the upper computer software based on the measured data mentioned above. Finally, use a voltage measurement module and an Agilent-34410 A digital voltmeter to measure the voltage values from 1 V to 24 V every 1V. Table 2 shows the voltage data measured by the voltage measurement module and the Agilent-34410 A digital voltmeter. The error values of both are less than 0.1%, indicating that the measurement accuracy of this voltage measurement module meets the predetermined technical specifications and accuracy requirements.

After completing the experimental research of the above functional modules, the entire calibration device was calibrated using the Bentley 330709 eddy current sensor. The experimental data is shown in Table 3. The upper computer sends instructions to the calibration system, which controls the operation of the stepper motor. The stepper motor drives the motion mechanism to move one position every 10% of the range. The calibration system measures displacement and sensor signals, and obtains the relevant

Table 2. Voltage measurement table for Agilent-34410A and measurement module

Voltage(V)	Agilent(V)	Measuring module (V)	Relative error %	Voltage(V)	Agilent(V)	Measuring module (V)	Relative error %
1	1.0087	1.0082	0.050	13	13.0036	13.0029	0.005
2	2.0030	2.0035	0.025	14	14.0034	14.0027	0.005
3	3.0063	3.0045	0.060	15	15.0047	15.0039	0.005
4	4.0043	4.0016	0.067	16	16.0040	16.0029	0.007
5	5.0076	5.0046	0.060	17	17.0089	17.0085	0.002
6	6.0053	6.0059	0.010	18	18.0068	18.0072	0.002
7	7.0032	7.0037	0.007	19	19.0068	19.0075	0.004
8	8.0030	8.0032	0.002	20	20.0034	20.0052	0.009
9	9.0022	9.0020	0.002	21	21.0016	20.9999	0.008
10	10.0074	10.0071	0.003	22	22.0047	22.0037	0.005
11	11.0028	11.0025	0.003	23	23.0036	23.0032	0.002
12	12.0042	12.0038	0.003	24	24.0034	24.0039	0.002

characteristics of the eddy current sensor through the calculation formulas of static sensitivity. From the experimental data, it can be concluded that the calibration device can automatically complete the static calibration of the eddy current sensor, achieving the expected goals.

Table 3. Voltage measurement table for Agilent-34410A and voltage measurement module

Number	Displacement (mm)	voltage CH1 (V)	voltage CH2 (V)	Displacement (mm)	voltage CH1 (V)	voltage CH2 (V)
1	0	0.626	0.624	0	0.630	0.627
2	0.6	1.655	1.654	0.6	1.656	1.658
3	1.2	4.034	4.030	1.2	4.038	4.034
4	1.8	6.512	6.510	1.8	6.516	6.513
5	2.4	9.005	9.007	2.4	9.007	9.002
6	3	11.493	11.497	3	11.486	11.510
7	3.6	13.973	13.978	3.6	13.986	13.983
8	4.2	16.417	16.420	4.2	16.436	16.426
9	4.8	18.880	18.887	4.8	18.878	18.889
10	5.4	21.356	21.354	5.4	21.363	21.356
11	6.0	23.521	23.519	6.0	23.524	23.520

Based on the measured displacement value L_i and the corresponding signal output value U_i of the eddy current sensor, the sensitivity S in the linear regression equation can be obtained using the least squares method

$$S = \frac{\sum_1^n L_i U_i - \overline{L} \sum_1^n U_i}{\sum_1^n L_i^2 - \overline{L} \sum_1^n L_i} \tag{7}$$

Substituting data: S = 3.979 V/mm, consistent with the nominal value of 4 V/mm.

6 Conclusion

Combining the research status at home and abroad, the paper proposes a fully automatic static calibration method for eddy current sensors, which compensates for the small range of foreign calibration devices and the low measurement accuracy of domestic calibration devices. The main research work includes:

(1) The overall scheme of an automatic static calibration device for eddy current sensors has been designed. The mechanical structure design for automatic static calibration of eddy current sensors has been completed. Specifically designed the motion mechanism, eddy current sensor installation mechanism, zero point adjustment mechanism, and zero point locking mechanism.
(2) A measurement and control system for automatic static calibration of eddy current sensors based on FPGA has been designed. Specifically designed a stepper motor control module, displacement measurement module, eddy current sensor signal measurement module, communication module, and some auxiliary modules with FPGA as the core. Accurate control of stepper motors, precise measurement of displacement and voltage, and communication with upper computer software have been achieved.
(3) We have completed experimental research on the displacement measurement module and signal measurement module of the static calibration device for eddy current sensors, and finally conducted experimental tests on the entire system to obtain the experimental parameters and technical indicators of this device. The experimental results indicate that the system device has achieved the expected technical indicators and precise requirements.

References

1. Wang, T.: Research on Calibration System for Eddy Current Sensors. Beijing University of Chemical Technology, BeiJing (2018)
2. Wang, T.: Static Auto Calibration and Experiment Research of Displacement sensor. Beijing University of Chemical Technology, BeiJing (2020)
3. Chen, S., Peng, X.: Automatic calibration device for displacement sensor based on laser interferometer. Instrum. Tech. Sensor **4**, 28–33 (2021)
4. Yang, Y.: Research on automatic calibration technology of high precision displacement sensor of paper machine. Paper Sci. Technol. **41**(2), 85–87 (2022)

5. Song, Y., Xie, Y.: Research on wide scale and high accuracy calibration technology of linear displacement sensor. Aeronaut. Manuf. Technol. **62**(8), 93–97 (2019)
6. Yang, M., Cai, C., Liu, Z.: Calibration method of low frequency vibration sensor based on guideway bending correction of long stroke shaker. J. Vibrat. Shock **41**(1), 116–120 (2022)
7. Wang, H.: Research on High-acceleration Vibration Calibration Technology Based on Laser Interferometry. China Jiliang University (2021).
8. Cheng, L.: Research on self-calibration technology of acceleration sensor with integrated MEMS micro-vibration platform. Hangzhou Dianzi University (2023).
9. Weijinhe. Research on Key Technology of Fiber Bragg Grating Strain Sensor Calibration. TianJin: TianJin university, 2021.
10. Kuang, C., Li, J., Hu, J.: Optimal design of the connecting rod of vibration grinding mills based on Ansys workbench. J. Mech. Transmiss. **47**(6), 57–64 (2023)
11. Zhao, P., Li, S, Qian, M.: Design and implementation of stepper motor control system. Process Autom. Instru. **43**(11), 87–90, 94 (2022).
12. Kong, X., Wang, R., Zhou, F.: Research on adaptive dynamic programming control algorithm based on FPGA. Instrum. Technique Sensor (10), 100-106, 126 (2023).

Prediction of Landing Spare Parts Consumption Based on Multiple Linear Regression

Feng Guo[1(✉)], Hongwei Zhu[2], Shusong Yu[3], Hailu Liu[4], and Bin Tan[4]

[1] Naval Aviation University Qingdao Campus, Qingdao 266041, China
gf536149@163.com
[2] CHRDI, Jingdezhen 333001, China
[3] Academy of Industrial Internet, Ocean University of China, Qingdao 266100, China
[4] Naval Equipment Department Maintenance Team, Beijing 100084, China

Abstract. The factors affecting the consumption of landing spare parts are difficult to determine, which affects the accuracy of consumption prediction. This article explores the main influencing factors of landing spare parts consumption and uses multiple linear regression methods to predict the consumption of landing spare parts based on these factors. The calculation results show that the two factors of flight time and takeoff and landing frequency have a significant impact on the consumption, and the linear significance is significant. The multiple linear regression prediction results are in line with the actual situation, and the prediction effect is good. The research method in this article can be extended and applied to predict the consumption of various landing spare parts.

Keywords: Landing spare parts · Multiple linear regression · Consumption prediction

1 Introduction

In practical work, there are many factors that affect the consumption of aviation spare parts, such as fleet size, flight time, takeoff and landing times, aviation spare partsreliability, pilot driving ability, repair shop repair ability, etc. [1–5]. However, if modeling and prediction are to be carried out, it is necessary to screen out the main influencing factors, eliminate secondary influencing factors, ensure model accuracy, simplify the model, reduce model complexity, and improve model applicability [6, 7]. At present, there is a lack of literature on the use of multiple linear regression methods for in-depth research on the influencing factors and consumption prediction of landing spare parts, some literature has not taken into account the frequency of takeoff and landing, which to some extent affects the accuracy of predicting the consumption of landing equipment. Regression analysis prediction method is one of the most commonly used prediction modeling techniques [8–10], which is the core of data science and machine learning. It helps to make wiser decisions in important situations and can better solve the problem of predicting landing equipment consumption. This article mainly studies the impact of flight time, landing frequency, and consumption on landing spare parts consumption, based on three factors, combined with practical examples, using multiple linear regression method to verify the impact of flight time and landing frequency on landing spare parts consumption, and analyze the predictive effect of this method.

2 Models

2.1 Equation

If the research object is influenced by multiple factors $x_1, x_2, \cdots, x_m$, its multiple linear regression model is

$$y_i = \beta_1 + \beta_2 x_{2i} + \cdots + \beta_m x_{mi}, i = 1, 2, \cdots, n \tag{1}$$

If expressed in matrix form, it is

$$Y = XB \tag{2}$$

wherein,

$$Y = \begin{bmatrix} y_1 \\ y_2 \\ \vdots \\ y_n \end{bmatrix}, X = \begin{bmatrix} 1 & x_{21} & \cdots & x_{m1} \\ 1 & y_{22} & \cdots & x_{m2} \\ \vdots & \vdots & & \vdots \\ 1 & y_{2n} & \cdots & x_{mn} \end{bmatrix}, B = \begin{bmatrix} \beta_1 \\ \beta_2 \\ \vdots \\ \beta_m \end{bmatrix}$$

2.2 Formula for Calculating Parameter Vectors

The estimated value of the regression coefficient vector B is

$$\hat{B} = (X'X)^{-1} X'Y \tag{3}$$

2.3 Testing Formula

In the process of establishing a multiple linear regression model, in order to further analyze whether the relationship between the variables reflected in the regression model conforms to objective reality and whether the introduced influencing factors are effective, it is necessary to test the regression model. The commonly used testing methods include R-test and t-test.

The R-test is a method of testing the linear correlation between a set of independent variables $x_1, x_2, \cdots, x_m$ and the dependent variable y through complex correlation coefficients, also known as the complex correlation coefficient test. It can be used to measure the degree of linear correlation between the dependent variable y and the independent variables $x_1, x_2, \cdots, x_m$. This article studies two independent variables, and the formula for calculating the complex correlation coefficient in the binary case is as follows

$$R = \sqrt{1 - \frac{\sum y_i^2 - \hat{\beta}_1 \sum y_i - \hat{\beta}_2 \sum x_{2i}y_i - \hat{\beta}_3 \sum x_{3i}y_i}{\sum y_i^2 - n\bar{y}^2}} \quad (4)$$

R-test is to examine the linear correlation and regression effect between all independent variables as a whole and the dependent variable. The t-test is to test the hypothesis for each coefficient of the regression model using the t-statistic.

2.4 Prediction Formula

The given value of the independent variable is substituted into the regression model, and the predicted value is the point estimate value. The prediction interval is a range of intervals that includes the future true values of the predicted object, calculated using mathematical statistical methods at a certain level of significance. The advantage is that when various factors change, it can avoid significant deviation between predicted values and actual values.

In a multiple linear regression model, by substituting the given values of each variable into the regression model, a corresponding regression prediction value, namely the point estimate value, can be obtained.

If the predicted point is $X_0 = (1, x_{20}, \cdots, x_{m0})$, the predicted value is

$$\hat{y}_0 = \hat{\beta}_1 + \hat{\beta}_2 x_{20} + \cdots + \hat{\beta}_m x_{m0} \quad (5)$$

Among them, $\hat{B} = (\hat{\beta}_1, \hat{\beta}_2, \cdots, \hat{\beta}_m)$ is the estimated parameter value. If the above equation is represented by a matrix, it is

$$\hat{y}_0 = X_0 \hat{B} \quad (6)$$

The sample variance of prediction error $e_0 = y_0 - \hat{y}_0$ is:

$$S_0^2 = S_y^2 [1 + X_0(X'X)^{-1} X_0'] \quad (7)$$

Among them, S_y is the estimated standard error.
When the significance level α of the predicted value $\hat{y}_0$ is, the prediction interval of the predicted value $\hat{y}_0$ is:

$$\begin{cases} \hat{y}_0 \mp t_{\alpha/2}(n-2)S_y, & n < 30 \\ \hat{y}_0 \mp z_{\alpha/2}S_y, & n \geq 30 \end{cases} \quad (8)$$

Among them, z represents following a normal distribution, the larger n, the closer t distribution is to a normal distribution.

3 Example Analysis

The consumption, takeoff and landing frequency, and flight hour data of a certain type of brake disc from 2010 to 2019 are shown in Table 1. Try to use a multiple linear regression model to predict the consumption of this aviation spare parts in 2020, requiring a significance test to estimate the predicted range of the consumption of this aviation spare parts. The expected number of takeoffs and landings for this aircraft spare parts in 2020 is 220, with a flight hour of 420.

Table 1. Consumption, takeoff and landing frequency, and flight hour data of a certain type of brake disc from 2010 to 2019

Annual	consumption	number of takeoffs and landings	flight hours
2010	18	14	32
2011	21	36	58
2012	19	32	84
2013	49	56	102
2014	68	89	123
2015	92	112	232
2016	88	126	155
2017	138	134	287
2018	145	165	256
2019	188	210	412

The scatter plot of consumption with landing frequency and flight hours is shown in Fig. 1, where the horizontal axis represents consumption and the vertical axis represents number of takeoffs and landings and flight hours. It can be seen that there is a clear linear relationship betweennumber of takeoffs and landings andconsumption, as well as betweenflight hours andconsumption. Therefore, multiple linear regression can be considered for prediction.

Solution:

1) Assuming a linear relationship between takeoff and landing times x_2, flight hours x_3, and consumption y.
2) Establishing regression equations
    Let the binary linear regression equation be $\hat{y} = \beta_1 + \beta_2 x_2 + \beta_3 x_3$.
3) Calculate regression coefficients

The estimated value of the regression coefficient is $\hat{B} = \begin{bmatrix} -6.3704 \\ 0.5454 \\ 0.2059 \end{bmatrix}$.

The required regression prediction equation is $\hat{y} = -6.3704 + 0.5454 x_2 + 0.2059 x_3$.

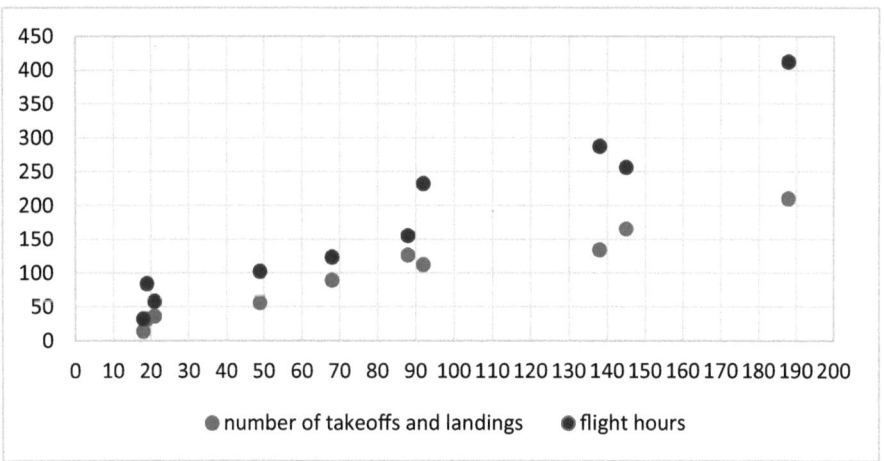

Fig. 1. The scatter plot of consumption with landing frequency and flight hours.

4) Testing the significance of linear relationships

Due to $R = 0.9901 > 0.697 = R_{0.05}(7)$, at the level $\alpha = 0.05$ of significance, the test passed, indicating a significant correlation.

As above, since the default constant x_1 value is 1, there is no need to conduct a significance test on the impact of this variable on consumption. Below, only the coefficients of t_2 and t_3 will be tested. $t_2 = 3.5237$, $t_3 = 2.5079$.

At the level $\alpha = 0.05$ of significance, $t_{0.05/2}(10 - 3) = 2.365$. Because the absolute values of t_2 and t_3 are both greater than $t_{0.05/2}(7)$, it can be asserted that the number of landings and flight hours have a significant impact on the consumption of aircraft spare parts.

Based on the above model estimates and various test results, it can be concluded that the established regression model is relatively good and can be used for prediction.

5) Prediction

Assuming the prediction point is $x_0 = [1\ 220\ 420]$, the estimated value $\hat{y}_0$ of the point obtained by substituting it into the regression equation is $\hat{y}_0 = 200.0989$, The prediction interval is 200 ± 22.

Therefore, with a takeoff and landing frequency of 220 and flight hours of 420 in 2020, it is estimated with 95% confidence that the consumption of this aircraft spare parts will be 178–222 pieces.

When making predictions, it is even more critical for the accuracy of prediction results to deeply analyze the development law of things and clarify the importance of main influencing factors than to simply pursue the progressiveness of methods. To verify this point, the above case data will still be used as an example, with takeoff and landing times and flight hours selected as independent variables, and the dependent variable unchanged. A univariate linear regression model will be established, and its predictive performance will be compared. The predicted values of univariate and multivariate linear regression are shown in Table 2, and their trend with observed consumption values is shown in Fig. 2.

Table 2. Predicted values of univariate and multivariate linear regression

Annual	The consumption observation value	The univariate linear regression prediction value		The multiple regression prediction value
		The independent variable only considers the number of takeoffs and landings	The independent variable only considers flight hours	
2010	18	6.4344	14.3746	7.8542
2011	21	26.5270	26.8572	25.2065
2012	19	22.8738	39.3398	28.3788
2013	49	44.7930	47.9816	45.1745
2014	68	74.9319	58.0637	67.4965
2015	92	95.9378	110.3946	102.4851
2016	88	108.7240	73.4269	94.2651
2017	138	116.0304	136.8001	125.8090
2018	145	144.3427	121.9170	136.3326
2019	188	185.4412	196.8126	192.9977

From this trend chart, it can be seen that the fitting effect of multiple linear regression prediction results is the best; From the perspective of variance, the variances of only considering takeoff and landing times and only considering flight hours in univariate linear regression prediction are 117.9701 and 172.3588, respectively. The former has a smaller variance, indicating that compared to flight hours, takeoff and landing times have a greater impact on aircraft spare parts consumption; The variance predicted by multiple linear regression is 62.1393, which is the smallest among these three cases. Based on the above analysis, it can be determined that the multiple linear regression prediction has the highest accuracy. Both single linear regression predictions did not fully consider the two factors that have a significant impact on aircraft spare parts consumption (i.e. takeoff and landing times, flight hours), so their prediction results are not as accurate as the multiple linear regression prediction method.

In addition, if one time exponential smoothing method is used to predict consumption, considering the significant increase in consumption trend, the weighting coefficient is set to 0.6, and the initial smoothing value is the average of the first two periods, then the predicted value is about 166, which is not within the prediction interval of multiple linear regression, and the prediction results of single exponential smoothing are generally lower than those of multiple linear regression (see Fig. 3). That is because the factors considered in exponential smoothing are too few, number of takeoffs and landings, flight hours and the future flight plans that affect consumption are not taken into account, this method cannot accurately reflect the impact of the above factors on

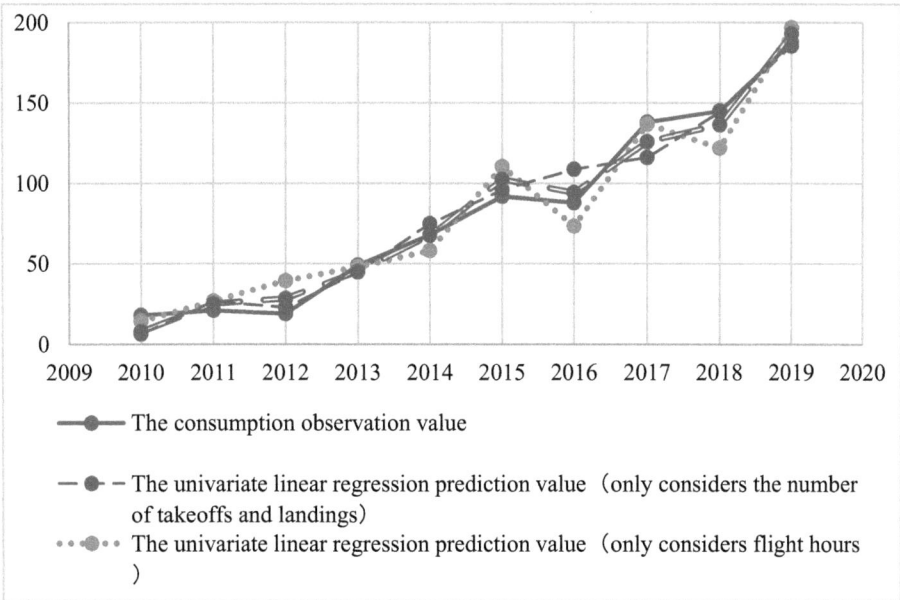

Fig. 2. The trend chart of observed consumption values and predicted values of univariate and multivariate linear regression methods.

consumption. Therefore, compared to one time exponential smoothing and univariate linear regression, multiple linear regression predicts more accurately.

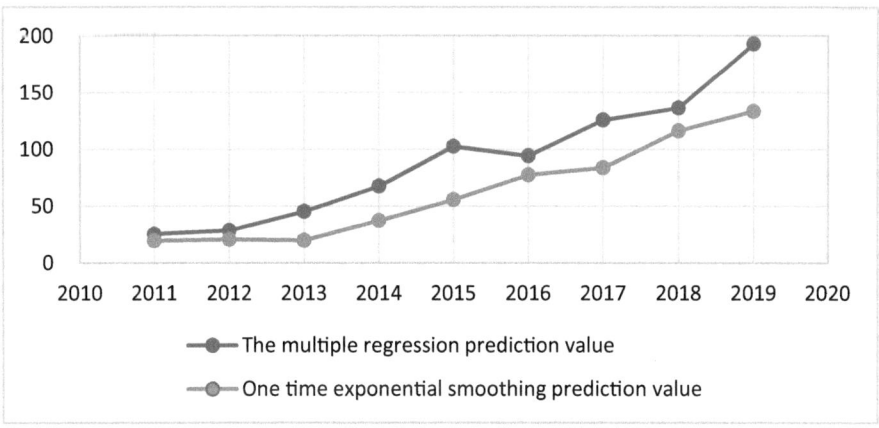

Fig. 3. The trend chart of predicted values of multivariate linear regression and one time exponential smoothing methods.

4 Conclusion

This article mainly focuses on the issue of landing spare parts consumption, exploring the influence of flight time and landing frequency on landing spare parts consumption, and how to use multiple linear regression method to predict the consumption of landing spare parts using the above three factors. The calculation results show that the two factors of flight time and landing frequency have a significant impact on consumption, and the linear significance is significant. The multiple linear regression prediction results are in line with the actual situation, and the prediction effect is good. It can be applied to the consumption prediction of various landing spare parts.

References

1. Zhang, R.C., Zhao, S.Z.: Study to optimize and distribute the cost of air spares support. J. Beijing Univ. Aeronaut. Astronaut. **31**(1), 102–104 (2005)
2. Chen, G., Sun, H.M.: Efficiency evaluation model of multi-echelon support system for radar spare parts. J. Air Force Radar Academy **25**(4), 272–275 (2011)
3. van Wingerden, E., Basten, R.J.I., Dekker, R., Rustenburg, W.D.: More grip on inventory control through improved forecasting: a comparative study at three companies. Int. J. Product. Econ. **157**, 220–237 (2014)
4. Sherbrooke, C.C.: Optimal Inventory Modeling of Systems Multi-Echelon Techniques (Second Edition), pp. 30–31. Kluwer Academic Publishers, Norwel (2008)
5. Zhang, L., Cui, C.L., Ben, X.W., et al.: Prediction model of the aviation materials consumption based on PCA of influencing factors. Ordnance Ind. Autom. **35**(8), 50–54 (2016)
6. Li, W., Xiao, S.C., Wang, J.H., et al.: Aviation material consumption prediction of army aviation training based on linear regression analysis. Ordnance Ind. Autom. **40**(4), 65–68 (2021)
7. Kang, Z.L., Xu, K.H., Yang, C.Q.: Application of ANFIS in Aviation material spare parts requirement prognostication. J. Ordnance Equipment Eng. **36**(1), 84–87 (2015)
8. Li, W., Xiao, S.C., Wang, J.H., et al.: Aviation material consumption prediction of army aviation training based on linear regression analysis. Ordnance Indust. Autom. **40**(4), 65–68 (2021)
9. Yang, Y., Sun, L., Guo, C.: Aero-material consumption prediction based on linear regression model. Procedia Comput. Sci. **131**, 825–831 (2018)
10. Zhang, L.H., Shao, W.D., Wang, D.C., et al.: Equipment maintenance material consumption prediction based on multivariable linear regression. J. Beijing Technol. Bus. Univ. (Nat. Sci. Ed.) **28**(6), 71–74 (2010)

Navigation Fuel Consumption Prediction Based on Improved LSTM Network

Xiaohu Lu[1], Nan Ye[1], Kang Bai[1,2(✉)], Jie Shi[2], and Qijin Tan[1,2]

[1] CSSC PRIDe (Nanjing) Atmospheric and Oceanic Information System Co., Ltd., Nanjing 211100, China
495172992@qq.com

[2] Ocean College, Jiangsu University of Science and Technology, Zhenjiang 212001, China

Abstract. Ship fuel consumption prediction is a crucial basis for ship navigation optimization. To enhance the accuracy of ship fuel consumption predictions, we proposed a prediction framework based on the fusion of channel and spatial information, which combined the long short-term memory network (LSTM) to capture temporal dynamic features with the convolutional neural network (CNN) feature extraction. Additionally, it incorporated the channel and spatial attention mechanism (CBAM) to improve feature representation and prediction performance. Compared to the benchmark LSTM network model, the convolutional neural memory network (Conv-LSTM-CBAM) with integrated attention mechanism increases the determination coefficient R^2 of the prediction results by 11%, and reduces the root mean square error (RMSE) and mean absolute percentage error (MAPE) by 4.25% and 5.9%, respectively.

Keywords: Ship fuel consumption prediction · LSTM · Conv-LSTM · CBAM attention mechanism.n

1 Introduction

As the global shipping industry rapidly develops, ships consume substantial amounts of fuel during operation. Ship navigation optimization plays an important role in resource conservation and environmental protection. Predicting ship fuel consumption is essential for navigation optimization.

The fuel consumption prediction method used physical principles such as fluid mechanics and dynamics to establish the overall resistance model of the ship. Young et al. [1] proposed a method including data preprocessing for ship resistance estimation and propulsion efficiency. The fuel consumption prediction method utilized historical data to build regression models or use neural networks to analyze and model future fuel consumption trends [2]. Ye et al. [3] used artificial neural networks to construct a fuel consumption black box model to predict the ship fuel consumption. YAN et al. [4] employed a BP neural network obtained speed and fuel consumption. Among neural network approaches, the LSTM performs well in processing time series data and is suitable for predicting ship fuel consumption on specific routes [5].

The ship navigation environment is complex, with many factors affecting fuel consumption [6]. To further improve prediction accuracy, we introduce a CNN and a CBAM mechanism into the LSTM network. The CNN can extract local features from the data, while the CBAM attention mechanism helps the model focus on more important features [7]. Finally, a Conv-LSTM-CBAM model integrating the attention mechanism was constructed and compared with the LSTM. The determination coefficient R^2 increased by 11%, and the RMSE and MAPE were reduced by 4.25% and 5.9%, respectively. These results indicate that the designed network model improves the performance of ship fuel depletion prediction.

2 Construction of Fuel Consumption Prediction Model

2.1 Overall Framework of Prediction Model

We present a deep architecture for ship fuel prediction, consisting of a Conv-LSTM module and a CBAM attention mechanism module as shown in Fig. 1.

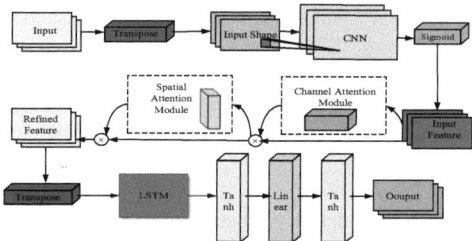

Fig. 1. Ship fuel consumption prediction model based on Conv-LSTM-CBAM.

The Conv-LSTM module consists of a CNN and an LSTM network. In the fuel consumption prediction, the input data is a time series containing wind, waves, and currents information. Through convolution operations, the spatial features in the data can be captured. The extracted features are analyzed using the LSTM to predict the changing trend of the input features over time and the cumulative impact of wind, waves, and currents on fuel consumption.

Additionally, CBAM integrates channel attention and spatial attention mechanisms. By adjusting the weights of different channels and spatial positions, the model's attention to key channels and key position information can be enhanced, improving its focus on important features and enhancing prediction accuracy.

2.2 Conv-LSTM Module Framework

Considering the spatial and temporal features extracted by CNN and LSTM, we integrate a CNN into an LSTM network [8]. Ship fuel consumption is influenced by the complex ocean environment, including wind, waves, and currents. The convolutional layer captures spatial patterns of wind speed, direction, wave characteristics, and current flow across different sea regions. This improvement enhances the accuracy of fuel consumption prediction in various sailing environments.

The Conv-LSTM module is the main component of the model proposed, which aims to extract the local and temporal characteristics of ship fuel consumption, as shown in Fig. 2.

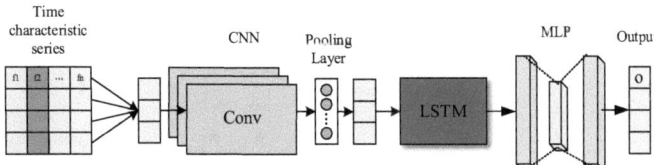

Fig. 2. Conv-LSTM module.

2.3 Conv-LSTM-CBAM Algorithm

CBAM combines channel and spatial attention mechanisms. As shown in Fig. 3, channel attention adjusts the weights of different channels to focus on key information, while spatial attention adjusts the weights of different spatial locations to focus on important location information.

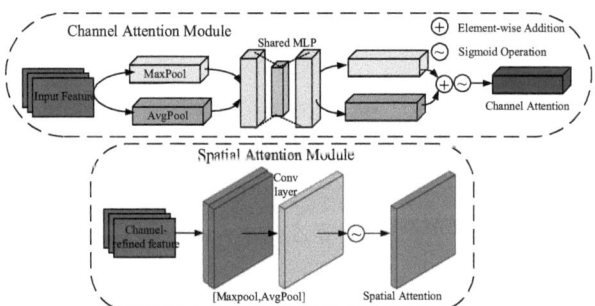

Fig. 3. Channel attention and Spatial attention in CBAM.

2.4 Kolmogorov-Arnold Networks

Multilayer Perceptron (MLP) was one of the first models applied to prediction problems and has shown great potential in nonlinear data modeling. However, the number of parameters in MLP does not scale linearly with the number of layers, and the model often lacks interpretability.

Liu [9] proposed Kolmogorov-Arnold Networks (KAN) to replace the MLP. KANs rely on the Kolmogorov-Arnold representation theorem. The theorem shows that any continuous function f defined in n-dimensional space can be represented by 2n+1 one-dimensional continuous functions Φ_i and $\Psi_{i,j}$:

$$f(x_1, x_2, \ldots, x_n,) = \sum_{i=1}^{2n+1} \Phi_i \left(\sum_{j=1}^{n} \Psi_{i,j}(x_j) \right) \quad (1)$$

The application in neural networks means that we can use a network architecture with a shape of [n, 2n+1, 1] to approximate any continuous function. The MLP and KAN are shown in Fig. 4. Unlike MLP, KAN do not represent weight parameters as real numbers but as B-spline functions that directly connect two neurons. Therefore, while MLP has fixed activation functions on nodes, KAN has learnable activation functions on edges. KAN is a combination of splines and MLP, allowing them not only to acquire features but also to optimize these acquired features with high accuracy.

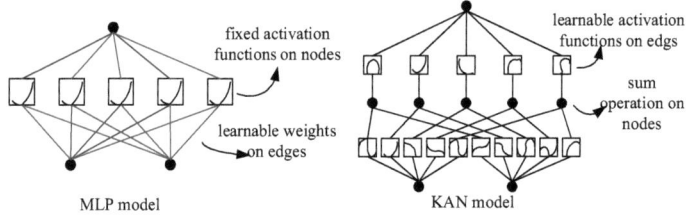

Fig. 4. MLP model and KAN model.

3 Experimentation and Analysis of Results

3.1 Analysis of Experimental Data

The data comes from actual voyages. This paper uses the method summarized by Jiang et al. [10] to reasonably process the data, including data segmentation and feature variable selection.

The RMSE, MAPE, and R^2 are used as indicators to evaluate the predictive performance of the model. The calculation formulas are shown in Eqs. (2)–(4).

$$RMSE = \sqrt{\frac{1}{n} \sum_{i=1}^{n} (\hat{y}_i - y_i)^2} \quad (2)$$

$$MAPE = \frac{1}{n} \sum_{i=1}^{n} \left| \frac{\hat{y}_i - y_i}{y_i} \right| \cdot 100\% \quad (3)$$

$$R^2 = 1 - \frac{\sum_{i=1}^{n} (y_i - \tilde{y}_i)^2}{\sum_{i=1}^{n} (y_i - \hat{y}_i)^2} \quad (4)$$

In the above formula, y_i and $\hat{y}_i$ represent the actual and predicted data of fuel consumption at the i-th moment, respectively. $\tilde{y}_i$ denotes the average value of the actual fuel consumption data, and n represents the number of samples.

3.2 Model Training Parameters and Methods

In the model training, the initial learning rate is 0.01, batch size is 256, training iterations are 100, and LSTM neurons are 16. A 0.01 dropout rate is used to prevent overfitting and enhance generalization. The loss function is mean squared error (MSE). Minimizing MSE through backpropagation and optimization updates the model parameters, improving prediction performance. The loss function is defined as follows:

$$Loss = MSE = \frac{1}{n}\sum_{i=1}^{n}(y_i - \hat{y}_i)^2 \tag{5}$$

We employed the Adam optimization algorithm to optimize the model parameters, allowing for adaptive adjustment of the learning rate.

3.3 Comparative Analysis of Experimental Results

To evaluate the performance of the Conv-LSTM-CBAM model, we conducted comparative experiments with other classic models (LSTM and Conv-LSTM) using the same. Additionally, to assess the superiority of the KANs network, we replaced the MLP in the prediction model with KANs, resulting in the improved LSTM-KAN model and Conv-LSTM-KAN model.

As shown in Table 1, compared to the LSTM, the LSTM-KAN prediction increased R^2 by 2% and reduced MAPE by 4%. Incorporating convolution further enhanced its predictive performance. This improvement stems from the KANs dual capability to acquire and optimize features with high precision. Next, we compared the Conv-LSTM-CBAM with other prediction models. Notably, compared to the LSTM model, R^2 improves by 11%. This enhancement is attributed to the model ability to extract spatiotemporal characteristics from data and leverage an attention mechanism to prioritize crucial features, thereby enhancing ship fuel consumption prediction.

Table 1. Comparison of performance indicators of different prediction models.

Index	LSTM	LSTM-KAN	Conv-LSTM	Conv-LSTM-KAN	Conv-LSTM-CBAM
R^2	0.8342	0.8533	0.8705	0.8851	0.9446
RMSE	0.0940	0.0812	0.0692	0.0782	0.0515
MAPE	13.1436%	9.4586%	8.3258%	8.5976%	7.2385%

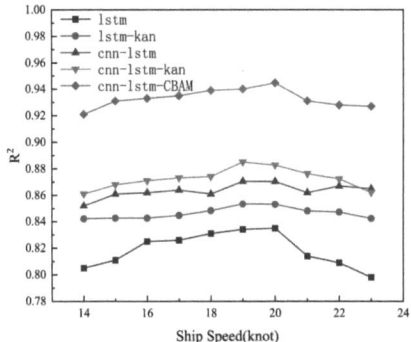

Fig. 5. Comparison of R^2 predicted by the model at different speed ranges.

To illustrate the impact of different speeds on prediction results, Fig. 5 presents the predictions of five networks models across various speeds. It is observed that R^2 initially increases and then decreases as speed varies. The highest prediction accuracy occurs within the speed range of 18–20 knots. Figure 6 shows that the Conv-LSTM-CBAM predictions closely align with the actual fuel consumption data curve, demonstrating intuitively that the model enhances the accuracy of ship fuel consumption prediction. Figure 7 shows the prediction error bands of the three models at time steps 30–60. The CNN-LSTM-CBAM model has the narrowest error band, indicating the highest prediction stability and reliability. The CNN-LSTM model is second, while the LSTM model has the widest error band and the greatest prediction uncertainty.

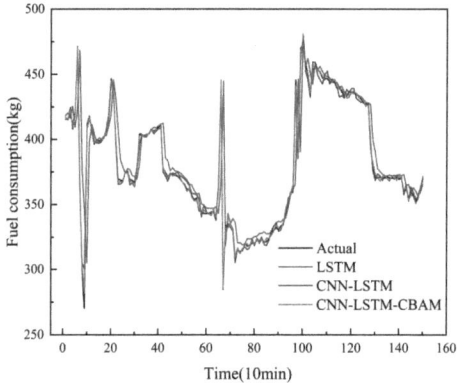

Fig. 6. Comparison between actual value and model prediction value.

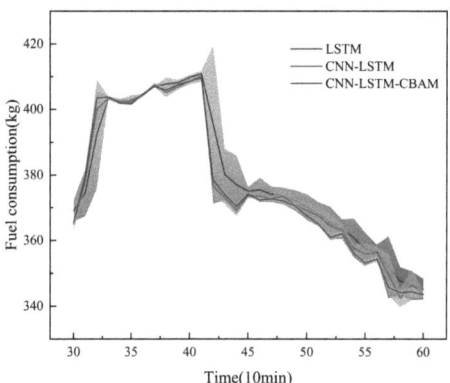

Fig. 7. Forecast error band plot for time steps 30–60.

4 Conclusion

This paper proposes a prediction model based on fused channels and spatial attention. The model leverages LSTM's capability to capture temporal dynamic features and is combined with CNN's feature extraction abilities. Additionally, the model introduces channel and spatial attention mechanisms. Channel attention identifies and enhances significant features while suppressing irrelevant ones. Spatial attention highlights crucial position, emphasizing key time steps. This dynamic adjustment allows the model to flexibly respond to various input data types and changes, thereby improving prediction performance and robustness. Simulation results demonstrate that compared to several other prediction models, the proposed model enhances ship fuel consumption prediction performance.

References

1. Kim, Y.R., Steen, S., Kramel, D., et al.: Modelling of ship resistance and power consumption for the global fleet: the MariTEAM model. Ocean Eng. **281**, 114758 (2023)
2. Fan, A., Yang, J., Yang, L., et al.: A review of ship fuel consumption models. Ocean Eng. **264**, 112405 (2022)
3. Ye, R., Xu, J.: Vessel fuel consumption model based on neural network. Ship Eng. **38**(3), 85–88 (2016)
4. Yan, X., Sun, X., Yin, Q.: Multiparameter sensitivity analysis of operational energy efficiency for inland river ships based on backpropagation neural network method. Marine Technol. Soc. J. **49**(1), 148–153 (2015)
5. Zhu, Y., Zuo, Y., Li, T.: Predicting ship fuel consumption based on LSTM neural network. In: 2020 7th International Conference on Information, Cybernetics, and Computational Social Systems (ICCSS), pp. 310–313. IEEE (2020).
6. Zhang, M., Tsoulakos, N., Kujala, P., et al.: A deep learning method for the prediction of ship fuel consumption in real operational conditions. Eng. Appl. Artific. Intell. **130**, 107425 (2024)
7. Woo, S., Park, J., Lee, J.-Y., et al.: CBAM: convolutional block attention module. In: Ferrari, V., Hebert, M., Sminchisescu, C., Weiss, Y. (eds.) Computer Vision – ECCV 2018: 15th European Conference, Munich, Germany, 8–14 Sep 2018, Proceedings, Part VII, pp. 3–19. Springer International Publishing, Cham (2018). https://doi.org/10.1007/978-3-030-01234-2_1
8. Borovykh, A., Bohte, S., Oosterlee, C.W.: Conditional time series forecasting with convolutional neural networks (2017). arXiv preprint arXiv:1703.04691
9. Liu, Z., Wang, Y., Vaidya, S., et al.: Kan: Kolmogorov-arnold networks (2024). arXiv preprint arXiv:2404.19756
10. Jiang, Y., Yin, S., Dong, J., et al.: A review on soft sensors for monitoring, control, and optimization of industrial processes. IEEE Sensors J. **21**(11), 12868–12881 (2020)

Research on a Radar Image Alignment Method

Yanbing Hu[✉] and Lingyu Wang

Chinese Flight Test Establishment, Xi'an, Shaanxi, China
h15339202045@sina.com

Abstract. In this paper, based on the framework of the Radiation Invariant Feature Transform (RIFT), we make innovative improvements from the perspective of feature computation, and then propose a multi-view radar image alignment method that integrates multi-feature description and shadow perception. In the prior art, most of the radar image alignment methods tend to rely on a single feature for description, which makes them show obvious limitations when facing complex nonlinear radial aberrations and multi-view changes. The method proposed in this paper, on the other hand, skillfully utilizes the spatial domain qualities of the real and imaginary parts of the log-Gabor filter in the specific stage of feature computation to accurately extract two types of significantly different features in the radar image. This multi-feature description breaks the constraints of the traditional single feature and is able to capture the information in the image in a more comprehensive and detailed way. In addition, the introduction of shadow perception mechanism is another major innovation of this method. By effectively identifying and analyzing the shadow region, the feature description is further supplemented and improved, thus making the alignment process more accurate and reliable. Shadow regions usually contain important structural and depth information, which is often neglected or mishandled by existing techniques. The present method, however, is able to fully utilize such information and effectively avoid alignment errors caused by shadows. This innovative initiative not only effectively avoids the adverse effects of single feature changes on the characterization, but also greatly improves the robust performance of the algorithm to cope with nonlinear radial aberrations. After a series of rigorous experimental validation, the method proposed in this paper shows significantly better performance than the existing algorithms in terms of root-mean-square error, probability of successful matching, and the number of correctly matched points, successfully realizing the high-precision alignment of radar images under multiple viewpoints. It provides valuable theoretical reference and practice for the development of related fields, and contributes to the progress of radar image alignment technology.

Keywords: Radar image alignment · Radiatively invariant feature transform · Multi-feature description · Shadow perception · Nonlinear radiative distortion · Feature extraction · Algorithm optimisation · High accuracy alignment

1 Introduction

In today's era of rapid technological development, radar technology has emerged as a cornerstone in various industries due to its ability to provide precise, long-range imaging in diverse environmental conditions. The advancement in radar systems has enabled their application in numerous fields such as military surveillance, weather forecasting, disaster management, automotive systems, and even geospatial mapping. Among the key processes in radar technology, radar image alignment plays a critical role, particularly in multi-view scenarios where precise synchronization of images from different perspectives is required.

Radar image alignment is vital not only in military operations, such as reconnaissance and missile guidance, but also in a broad range of civilian applications. For example, in automatic driving systems, accurate alignment of radar images ensures that the autonomous vehicle can detect obstacles and navigate complex environments safely. Similarly, in environmental monitoring and geographical mapping, properly aligned radar images are crucial for generating accurate representations of the terrain, detecting changes in landscapes, and monitoring the impacts of natural disasters.

However, the alignment of radar images presents significant challenges due to the intrinsic properties of radar systems and the complexities of the imaging environment. Radar systems often suffer from nonlinear radial aberrations, which can distort the captured images, making accurate alignment difficult. Additionally, variations in the viewing angles between different radar captures and inconsistent environmental factors, such as lighting, shadows, and weather conditions, can complicate the feature extraction process, leading to errors in image alignment. These factors necessitate the development of robust, adaptive alignment techniques that can handle such variabilities effectively.

In order to cope with these challenges, many scholars have devoted themselves to the research and development of new radar image alignment methods. The emergence of the Radiation Invariant Feature Transform (RIFT) framework has brought new ideas to this field. However, the existing methods based on the RIFT framework still have some limitations in practical applications [1]. The singularity of feature computation leads to insufficient robustness to nonlinear radial distortion, which makes it difficult to adapt to complex and changing practical scenes. Therefore, how to improve the feature calculation method under the RIFT framework to enhance the accuracy and reliability of radar image alignment has become the focus and hot issue of current research.

This paper presents a remarkable advancement in the domain of multi-view radar image alignment. The key innovation lies in the integration of multi-feature description and shadow perception. Unlike conventional approaches that rely on single or limited features for alignment, this paper's method utilizes the spatial domain properties of the real and imaginary parts of log-Gabor filters to extract multiple distinct features from radar images. This multi-feature extraction approach offers a more comprehensive and detailed representation of the image content, enabling a more accurate and robust alignment process.

The incorporation of shadow perception is another significant novelty. By precisely identifying and analyzing shadow regions, the method enriches the feature description and compensates for the potential errors caused by shadows, which are often overlooked or inadequately handled in existing techniques. This not only enhances the accuracy of the alignment but also increases the adaptability of the method to various imaging scenarios.

Therefore, how to improve the feature calculation method under the RIFT framework to enhance the accuracy and reliability of radar image alignment has become the focus and hot issue of current research.

In this context, this paper proposes a multi-view radar image alignment method based on multi-feature description and shadow perception. It aims to overcome the deficiencies of existing methods through innovative feature extraction and computation. We thoroughly investigate the spatial domain properties of the real and imaginary parts of log-Gabor filters and apply them to the extraction of radar image features. It is expected that this improvement can achieve significant enhancement in the key indexes such as root mean square error, successful matching probability and correct matching points, contributing new power to the development of radar image alignment technology and promoting better results in related application fields [2].

2 Improved RFIT Algorithm

Radiation-Variation Insensitive Feature Transform (RIFT) is an important method for processing image features.

The basic principle of RIFT is to achieve accurate matching and alignment of images by constructing a feature descriptor that is insensitive to radiation variations.

Mathematically, RIFT is usually based on the following key steps and formulas:

First, for a given image, its gradient information is computed. The gradient can be expressed as Eq. (1):

$$G = \sqrt{G_x^2 + G_y^2} \tag{1}$$

where G_x and G_y are the partial derivatives of the image in the x and y directions, respectively.

The feature description vector is then constructed by statistically analysing the gradient information. This usually involves computing the orientation histogram $H(\theta)$ of the gradient, where θ denotes the direction of the gradient [3].

In order to achieve radial invariance, RIFT normalises the feature description vectors to remove the effect of image radial differences. Through these steps and the corresponding mathematical calculations, RIFT is able to extract features that are robust to radiation variations, enabling effective matching and alignment of images taken under different radiation conditions.

In conclusion, RIFT uses mathematical models and image processing techniques to effectively solve the image alignment problems caused by radiation differences [4], providing strong support for applications such as multi-view radar image alignment.

For specific improvements, the method in this paper detects shadow regions in an image by marking shadow pixels by the method of image shadow detection and applying a mask to the feature vectors generated from subneighbourhoods that are severely affected by shadows, and retaining the feature vectors generated from other subneighbourhoods for subsequent matching. Due to the very low grey level of the shadowed region [5], after Gaussian filtering, the pixel grey level distribution curves of the radar images with shadows are significantly distorted in the low grey level region compared to those of the non-shadowed images. Inspired by this idea, it is found that when there are shadows in the radar image, the amplitude component sequence Ao(x,y) (normalised to [0,128]) obtained by 2D-LGF filtering is also distorted in the low grey area.

Then, the shadow pixels are marked by the method of image shadow detection, and a mask is applied to the feature vectors generated from the sub-neighbourhoods that are severely affected by shadows, and the feature vectors generated from the other sub-neighbourhoods are retained for subsequent matching [6].

For a given image I (x, y), the image first needs to be convolved with the 2D-LGF to obtain the responses e_{so} (x, y) and o_{so} (x, y) for the odd-symmetric log-Gabor wavelet and the even-symmetric log-Gabor wavelet; and then the responses obtained

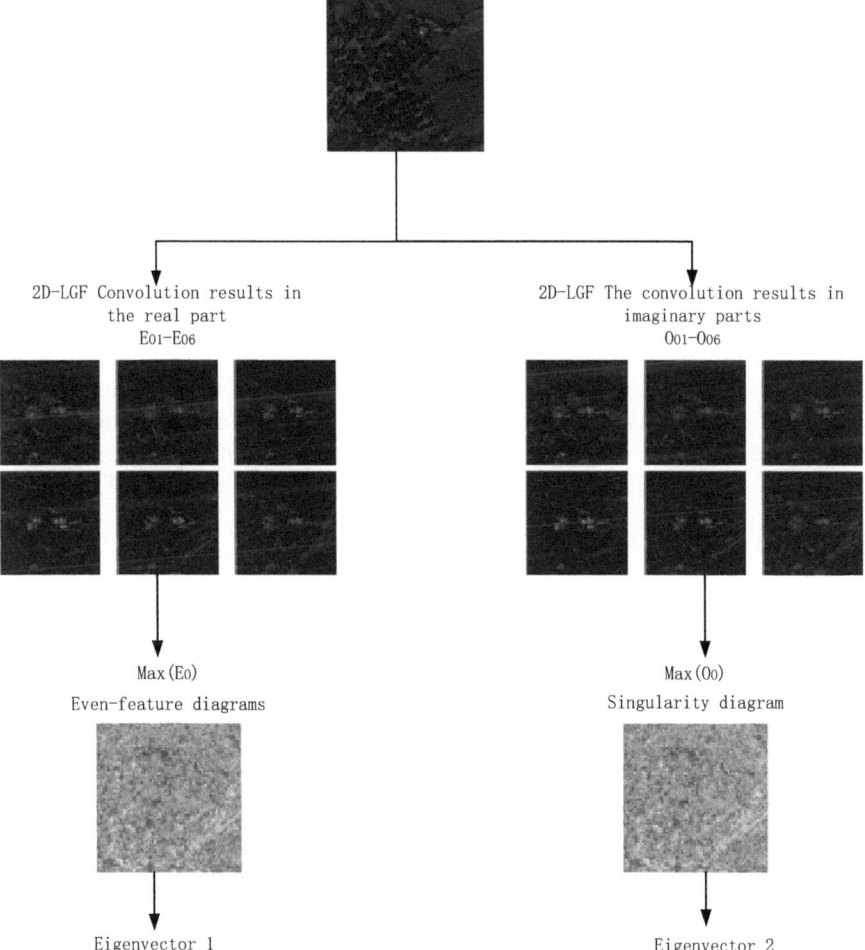

Fig. 1. Schematic flow of the improved RFIT algorithm for generating feature vectors

from all the scales are summed up in each direction o, respectively, to obtain the real convolution sequence E_0 (x, y) and the imaginary convolution sequence O_0 (x, y). Finally, the maximum values max (E_0) and max (O) found at each pixel position (xi, yj) of the two convolutional sequences are used to construct the "odd feature diagrams" and the "even feature diagrams", respectively, and generate two sets of feature vectors for different features in the two feature diagrams. Two sets of feature vectors are generated for different features in the two feature diagrams.

Finally, the retained feature vectors are used for multi-view radar image alignment to improve the alignment accuracy, and the flow diagram of the improved RFIT algorithm for generating feature vectors is shown in Fig. 1.

The experimental results show that the method can effectively improve the accuracy of multi-view radar image alignment, especially in the presence of shadowed regions. By applying a mask to the feature vectors generated from the subneighbourhoods that are seriously affected by shadows, and retaining the feature vectors generated from other subneighbourhoods for subsequent matching, the influence of the shaded regions on the multi-view radar image alignment can be reduced and the alignment accuracy can be improved. Instead of completely discarding the feature vectors of the sub-neighbourhoods affected by shadows, the method retains the feature vectors of other sub-neighbourhoods by applying masks [7], thus retaining more feature information, and the method can adaptively adjust the generation of feature vectors according to the results of shadow detection, which is highly adaptive to different shadow situations.

3 Data Description

In this study, in order to experimentally validate the proposed radar image alignment method, airborne SAR images from the Sichuan region of China were selected for alignment experiments [8]. The imaging data acquisition viewpoints are shown in Fig. 2, and the front and side views of the same area were imaged on three flight paths respectively, with the arrow direction in the figure clearly indicating the flight direction of the aircraft.

Fig. 2. Radar image acquisition viewpoint geographic map

The experiment uses the algorithm proposed in this paper to align four sets of images with typical different viewpoints from the data. The selected images are shown in Fig. 3. It should be noted in particular that the region selected for the experiment covers a large number of surface appendages such as houses and trees. These surface appendages have significant feature differences and shading differences in the images from different viewpoints, which makes the alignment of the images extremely difficult.

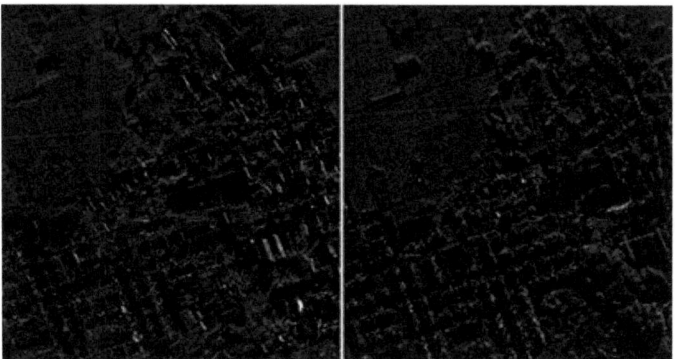

Fig. 3. Experimental radar image pair

In this study, to experimentally validate the proposed radar image alignment method, airborne SAR images from the Sichuan region of China were chosen for the alignment experiments. The images have a carrier frequency of 16.5 GHz. The imaging was conducted from three different flight paths (air line 1, air line 2, and air line 3), each capturing the front and side views of the same area at a 40° downward viewing angle. The pixel size is 1 m × 1 m, and the side-view direction is right.

The dataset is characterized by its diversity in image sizes, including 1000 × 1100, 500 × 500, and 1000 × 950, among others. The selected region for the experiment encompasses a large number of surface appendages such as houses and trees. These features present significant differences and shading variations in the images captured from different viewpoints, significantly increasing the complexity of image alignment. Details are shown in Table 1.

The imaging conditions involve factors such as weather conditions, flight altitude, and sensor characteristics, which contribute to the overall complexity of the dataset. The diversity and complexity of the dataset allow for a comprehensive assessment of the proposed alignment method's performance and its applicability in various real-world scenarios.

Table 1. SAR image parameters used in this paper

air line	carrier frequency	view from below	pixel size	sideways glance	image size
1	16.5 GHz	40°	1m × 1m	right lateral view	1000 × 1100

(*continued*)

Table 1. (*continued*)

air line	carrier frequency	view from below	pixel size	sideways glance	image size
2	16.5 GHz	40°	1m × 1m	right lateral view	1000 × 1100
3	16.5 GHz	40°	1m × 1m	right lateral view	500 × 500
3	16.5 GHz	40°	1m × 1m	right lateral view	1000 × 950

4 Radar Image Alignment Experiment

To assess the effectiveness of the improved RIFT algorithm for multi-view radar image alignment, a series of experiments was conducted using several carefully selected radar image sets. These images were captured from different viewpoints and included a variety of surface appendages such as buildings, trees, and other landscape features. This diversity in surface structures is crucial as it replicates the complexity often encountered in real-world radar imaging scenarios, making the experiment more robust and realistic.

To ensure fairness across all comparison algorithms, the nearest neighbor distance ratio (NNDR) method was uniformly applied to each alignment technique to determine the initial matching points between image pairs. The NNDR method is a well-established approach that identifies potential correspondences between features by calculating the ratio of distances between neighboring feature points. This allows for an initial selection of matching points based on their proximity in feature space, ensuring consistency in how the alignment process begins across all methods tested.

After the initial matching points were identified using NNDR, the fast sample consensus (FSC) method was employed to remove outliers from these matches. Outliers, or incorrect matches, can negatively impact the overall alignment process and reduce accuracy. The FSC method refines the matching process by filtering out these inaccuracies, ensuring that only valid, reliable correspondences are used in the final alignment. This step is critical in improving the robustness of the alignment results and ensuring that the comparison between algorithms is based on accurate data.

The final results of the improved RIFT algorithm were then quantitatively evaluated and compared against three leading algorithms: SIFT, SAR-SIFT, and the original RIFT. SIFT (Scale-Invariant Feature Transform) is a widely used algorithm for optical image alignment, known for its robustness in dealing with scale and rotation variations. SAR-SIFT is a variation of SIFT specifically adapted for synthetic aperture radar (SAR) images, designed to handle the unique properties of radar signals, such as speckle noise and surface reflections. The original RIFT algorithm, on the other hand, is aimed at aligning images under different radiation conditions, making it particularly useful in multimodal imaging scenarios.

Each algorithm was fine-tuned before the experiments to ensure that it performed optimally under the same conditions. This involved adjusting parameters such as feature detection thresholds and matching criteria to maximize their accuracy and reliability in the alignment process.

The feature point matching results from the various algorithms, illustrated in Figs. 4, 5, 6 and 7, demonstrated that the improved RIFT algorithm significantly outperformed the others. In particular, it showed better accuracy in terms of root-mean-square error (RMSE), a higher probability of successful matching, and a greater number of correctly matched points. These results confirm the superior capability of the improved RIFT algorithm in handling complex, multi-view radar image alignment tasks, offering clear advantages over existing methods.

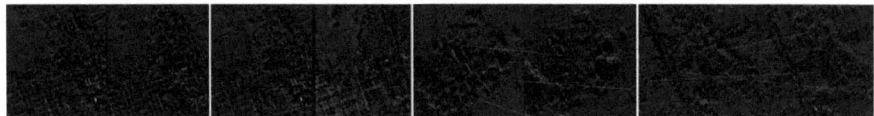

Fig. 4. SIFT algorithm

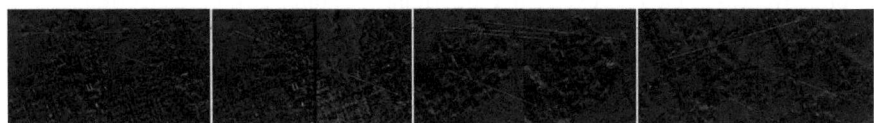

Fig. 5. SAR-SIFT algorithm

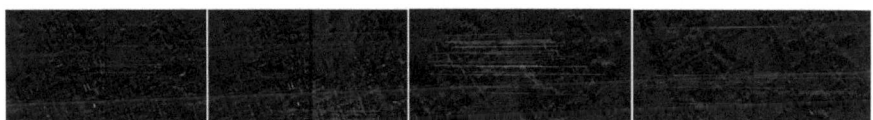

Fig. 6. RIFT algorithm

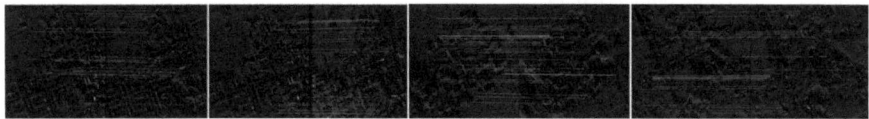

Fig. 7. Methodology of this paper

Table 2. Comparison of successful matching probability of this paper's method with other alignment algorithms

Area	Area 1	Area 2	Area 3	Area 4
SIFT	0%	0%	0%	0%
SAR-SIFT	0%	0%	0%	0%

(*continued*)

Table 2. (*continued*)

Area	Area 1	Area 2	Area 3	Area 4
RIFT	75%	55%	85%	90%
Methodology of this paper	100%	98%	100%	100%

The focus of this experiment is to verify the effectiveness of the improved RIFT algorithm in dealing with the multi-view radar image alignment problem. By selecting representative multi-group radar images and adopting a unified method of initial matching point selection and outlier removal, it is maximally ensured that different algorithms are compared under the same benchmark. The quantitatively evaluated metrics will be able to objectively and accurately reflect the performance of the individual algorithms in terms of alignment precision and accuracy [10], thus drawing reliable conclusions about the effectiveness of the improved RIFT algorithm. The three advanced algorithms in the comparison serve as references, which help to highlight the advantages and shortcomings of the improved RIFT algorithm more clearly, and provide valuable references for subsequent research and application.

The comparison algorithms used in this paper are SIFT, SAR-SIFT and RIFT, where SIFT is a classical optical image alignment algorithm, SAR-SIFT is an algorithm specially used for synthetic aperture radar (SAR) image alignment, and RIFT is an alignment method used for multimodal images. Before the experiment, the parameters of each algorithm have been adjusted to the optimal state.

The above table shows the experimental results of different algorithms in terms of multi-view radar image alignment performance metrics as shown in Tables 2 and 3.

Table 3. Comparison of the alignment performance of this paper's method with other alignment algorithms

Area	Area 1	Area 2	Area 3	Area 4
Number of matching points (RIFT)	19	16	34	35
Root Mean Square Error (RIFT)	6.465	9.366	4.535	4.643
Number of match points (methodology in this paper)	21	19	29	41
Root mean square error (methodology of this paper)	3.423	4.253	3.365	3.235

The method proposed in this paper has significant advantages in the multi-view radar image alignment problem. Compared with other comparison algorithms, the method performs well in both successful matching probability and root mean square error.

In the experimental results of region 1 and region 2, the method of this paper has significant improvement compared with other algorithms. This indicates that the method is better able to handle the case of small radial distortion and obtain a certain number of matched point pairs between images using the MIM feature description method.

Table 4 shows the performance evaluation of this algorithm and other algorithms in terms of the ability to handle shaded areas (A), the effect of feature extraction in shaded areas (B), the ability to adapt to light changes caused by shadows (C), the matching accuracy when there are many shaded areas (D), and the computational complexity (E), respectively.

Table 4. Performance evaluation of each algorithm on five major aspects.

algorithm	A	B	C	D	E
SIFT	So so	It can be difficult to extract valid features	Poor, susceptible to changes in light	Lower	High-er
SAR-SIFT	Better	It is designed according to the characteristics of SAR images, and can extract features well	Better, with some adaptability to the lighting changes of SAR images	Higher	High-er
RIFT	Better	Multi-modal image registration has a certain robustness to different features	Preferred, depending on the coverage of the multimodal data	Higher	High-er
this paper	It needs to be assessed on a case-by-case basis	It needs to be assessed on a case-by-case basis	It needs to be assessed on a case-by-case basis	It needs to be determined based on the results of the experiment	It needs to be assessed on a case-by-case basis

The differences shown by different algorithms in processing images with a lot of shadow areas mainly stem from the fact that they are designed on different principles and for different application scenarios.

The SIFT algorithm is designed for optical images. Shadows in optical images may lead to large changes in brightness and contrast, affecting the detection and characterization of feature points, and thus reducing their performance in shadow areas.

The SAR-SIFT algorithm is specifically designed for synthetic aperture radar (SAR) images, which are imaged differently from optical images and have some unique characteristics. The algorithm may be designed with common problems in SAR images in mind, such as shadows, noise, etc., so it performs better in dealing with SAR images with shadows.

The RIFT algorithm, as an alignment method for multimodal images, has the advantage of being able to handle different types of image features. It may cope with the feature changes and lighting differences brought by shaded regions by fusing multiple features or adopting a more robust feature description, thus achieving better results on such images, but the computational complexity is usually relatively high as well.The RIFT algorithm is used for multimodal image alignment, aiming at fusing the features of many different types of images. When confronted with shadowed regions, its multi-feature fusion strategy makes it adaptable to feature changes due to shadows. However, this adaptability also depends on the coverage of the multimodal data and the effectiveness of the algorithm in fusing different features. For the methods proposed in this paper, the reason for the difference in their performance may lie in the unique treatment of features in shaded regions, the characteristics of the feature descriptors employed, and the algorithm's ability to model and compensate for illumination variations. These factors work together to determine its different performance from other algorithms when dealing with images with more shaded regions.

5 Conclusion

In this paper, we propose a novel multi-view radar image alignment method that combines multi-feature description and shadow perception to enhance performance. This method builds upon the Radiation Invariant Feature Transform (RIFT) framework and introduces significant improvements in feature computation. By leveraging the spatial domain properties of the real and imaginary components of the log-Gabor filter, we are able to extract two distinct types of features from radar images. This dual-feature extraction process mitigates the negative impact of relying on a single feature type, which is often vulnerable to changes in the image content, particularly in complex environments. As a result, the robustness of the algorithm is significantly enhanced, allowing it to better handle challenges such as nonlinear radial distortion that frequently arises in radar imaging.

Through rigorous experimental validation, the proposed method has been shown to outperform existing algorithms in several key metrics, including root-mean-square error (RMSE), probability of successful matching, and the number of correctly matched points. These improvements make it possible to achieve high-precision alignment of radar images across multiple viewpoints, making this method highly effective in both controlled and dynamic environments. The approach not only serves as a valuable theoretical contribution to the field but also offers practical references for future applications, setting a new benchmark in radar image alignment technology.

The adaptability and stability of the method across various regions and scenarios highlight its potential for broad applicability. It is particularly effective in overcoming challenges posed by radiation distortion and complex scene structures. This adaptability makes it a promising solution for radar image alignment in diverse conditions, from military operations to civilian applications such as environmental monitoring and autonomous driving. Further improvements in the method's accuracy and reliability can be achieved by optimizing the feature extraction algorithms, utilizing more precise feature descriptors, and implementing advanced similarity measures. These refinements would further increase the effectiveness of the alignment process, especially in scenarios involving high variability in imaging conditions.

Moreover, the significance of root-mean-square error (RMSE) as a performance metric is underscored throughout this work. RMSE provides a critical measure of how closely the alignment results conform to the actual image structure, offering an essential tool for evaluating the precision and reliability of different alignment algorithms. By emphasizing the importance of this metric, the method introduced in this paper ensures that improvements in algorithmic performance are objectively quantifiable and meaningful.

In conclusion, the proposed method offers a fresh perspective on multi-view radar image alignment, blending cutting-edge techniques with practical considerations. It introduces new concepts and methods that advance the field of radar image processing, contributing to the ongoing progress in this rapidly evolving technology domain. This work is expected to inspire further innovations and improvements, benefiting both theoretical research and practical implementations in a wide array of radar-based applications.

References

1. Schmid, L., Medic, T., Collins, B.D., et al.: Georeferencing of terrestrial radar images in geomonitoring using kernel correlation. Int. J. Remote Sens. **44**(21), 6736–6761 (2023)
2. Garcia, P.L., Pallotta, L., Clemente, C., et al.: A cross-cross-correlation based method for joint coregistration of rotated multitemporal synthetic aperture radar images. IET Radar, Sonar Navi. **18**(1), 198–209 (2023)
3. Zhou, P., Zhang, G., Yang, W.: A review of ISAR imaging technology. In: 2020 IEEE International Conference on Information Technology, Big Data and Artificial Intelligence (ICIBA), pp. 664–668. Chongqing, China (2020). https://doi.org/10.1109/ICIBA50161.2020.9277180
4. Xu, T., Hao, C., Guo, Q., Yin, K., Hu, T., Yang, L.: An efficient alignment method for scanning data of 77 GHz mmWave imaging radar. In: 2022 IEEE 22nd International Conference on Communication Technology (ICCT), pp. 1859–1863. Nanjing, China (2022). https://doi.org/10.1109/ICCT56141.2022.10072903
5. Wang, Z., Li, H., Wang, Z., et al.: An improved synthetic aperture radar-scale invariant feature transform algorithm for interferometric imaging radar altimeter image registration. IET Image Process. **16**(7), 1866–1879 (2022). https://doi.org/10.1049/ipr2.12453
6. Chunjing, Y., Hongchao, M., Wenjun, L., et al.: A precisely one-step registration methodology for optical imagery and LiDAR data using virtual point primitives. Remote Sens. **13**(23), 4836 (2021)
7. Yu, J., Ma, L., Tian, M., et al.: Registration and fusion of UAV LiDAR system sequence images and laser point clouds. J. Imag. Sci. Technol. **65**(1), 010501-1–010501-9 (2021). https://doi.org/10.2352/J.ImagingSci.Technol.2021.65.1.010501
8. Xu, J., Jia, B., Pan, X., et al.: Hydrographic data inspection and disaster monitoring using shipborne radar small range images with electronic navigation chart. PeerJ Comput. Sci. **6**, e290 (2020). https://doi.org/10.7717/peerj-cs.290
9. Yu J, Ma L, Tian M, et al. Registration and fusion of UAV LiDAR system sequence images and laser point clouds. J. Imag. Sci. Technol. (2020)
10. Ullah, R., Saied, I., Arslan, T.: Multistatic radar-based imaging in layered and dispersive media for biomedical applications. Biomed. Signal Process. Control **82**, 104568 (2023). https://doi.org/10.1016/j.bspc.2023.104568

One-Shot Talking Head Generation with Audio-Aware Identity Compensation

Ruihong Yuan and Zhiguang Wang(✉)

China University of Petroleum, Beijing, China
2022216041@student.cup.edu.cn, cwangzg@cup.edu.cn

Abstract. The primary goal of talking head generation is to synthesize realistic and expressive videos of a person speaking, given an input audio signal and a source image of the person. This involves creating a dynamic, lip-synced, and visually convincing representation of the person in the image as they articulate the provided audio content. But artifacts are shown in generated videos such as blurring of the mouth area, distorted facial features and unstable head and lip motions. The above deficiencies can be attributed to unsync lips and insufficient facial representation and will tremendously diminish the quality of the generated talking head video. To address this issue, we propose a one-shot audio-aware talking head generation architecture, called AaICNet, which is compensated by the learned global facial feature. We use AaICNet to attain lip-sync audio embedding from a random given audio and then drive the portrait to speak, along with the input audio. Specifically, we first develop a audio decoder and face decoder to extract audio feature and face feature and concatenate them into a mixed-feature code. In order to morph the lip movements accurately, we learned a powerful lip-sync discriminator to produce driving video. After the intermediate speaker training stage, we select the person with the highest LSE-C score as the driving image for the next stage of training. Then we introduce an effective compensation module which calculates the global facial structure and prior to enrich the warped source image for the later generation. Extensive experiments demonstrate that our architecture can stably handle the one-shot portrait talking head generation task and can balance the visual quality and the lip-sync accuracy of the generated video.

Keywords: talking head · Compensation · audio-aware

1 Introduction

In this paper, we address the challenge of generating a lifelike talking head video from a single static source image combined with a dynamic driving video. This task involves developing an audio-driven model that can accurately replicate realistic facial expressions and precise lip movements, which is a crucial factor for creating photorealistic talking heads [11]. One of the primary challenges is the one-to-many mapping problem inherent in creating a one-shot portrait that accurately responds to various audio inputs. The field has seen considerable progress, with numerous studies achieving significant advances in precise lip synchronization, largely driven by the high demand for effective talking head generation [1, 2].

Some approaches [3] have focused on directly generating images using speech and face representations learned within a 2D framework. Meanwhile, more recent research has explored the use of 3D facial prior models [4] combined with decoupled expression codes [5]. These methods integrate audio features to produce lip-synced talking heads. However, such strategies often transfer facial information on a frame-by-frame basis, which may not effectively capture the temporal dynamics of audio and video sequences. This can result in generated videos that lack smooth transitions [13].

Additionally, the challenge is compounded by the scarcity of sufficiently large datasets, making it difficult to train models on a wide variety of voices and identities. Therefore, there is a pressing need for a model capable of dynamically adapting to diverse lip shapes from random inputs, while generating stable, identity-preserved, and accurate talking head videos. Such a model would contribute significantly to advancements in fields requiring high-quality, lifelike video synthesis, including virtual reality, film production, and interactive media applications.

We are excited to propose a novel one-shot Audio-aware Identity Compensation Network, which we have termed AaICNet. This innovative framework is designed to effectively learn temporal features from both audio and video inputs, enabling the generation of high-quality visual content. To enhance the quality of the portraits generated by our network, we have incorporated a well-designed global facial feature compensation module, which plays a crucial role in refining the final output. Specifically, our work builds upon the initial methodologies utilized for lip-sync talking head generation. These earlier approaches often relied on pixel-to-pixel reconstruction loss, which serves to evaluate and differentiate the quality of the generated output during the training process. Additionally, these techniques employed a lip-sync discriminator, which is instrumental in producing talking heads that exhibit vivid and precise lip synchronization, thus improving the overall realism of the generated animations. Despite these advancements, we recognize that the process of warping the source image can lead to diminished image quality, primarily due to artifacts introduced by motion flow. This limitation can adversely affect the visual fidelity of the generated portraits. To mitigate this issue, we propose an identity-preserving feature compensation module. This module is designed to adjust and enhance the generated images automatically, ensuring that they maintain their original identity characteristics despite the transformations applied. The identity-preserving feature compensation module operates by leveraging unsupervised key-point estimations derived from the source image. By conditioning on these estimated key-points, the module can effectively align and compensate for any distortions, leading to a more coherent and visually appealing final product. Through extensive experiments and rigorous evaluations, we have demonstrated the capability of our AaICNet to produce photorealistic talking heads with accurate lip movements. Importantly, our method showcases a robust ability to perform one-shot generation, which significantly reduces the computational resources and time typically required for such tasks.

Extensive experiments have showcased the capacity of our method to produce photorealistic talking faces with precise lip movements and a robust ability for one-shot generation. Our contributions can be outlined as follows:

- Our proposal introduces a highly innovative audio-lip synchronization network that revolutionizes the generation of accurate and synchronized talking faces. This network not only enhances the quality of synthetic speech but also facilitates natural communication through visual cues.
- To further enhance the audio-visual synchronization, we introduce an intermediate speaker selection module that automates the process of selecting an intermediate speaker possessing the most outstanding audio-visual synchronization features. This module eliminates the need for manual intervention and ensures optimal performance in real-time scenarios.
- Moreover, we propose a global facial feature compensation module that can be seamlessly adjusted based on the source image. This module allows for precise adjustments to facial features, ensuring a high degree of realism and authenticity in the generated talking faces. It effectively captures the nuances of facial expressions and matches them with the corresponding audio clip, enhancing the overall speaking experience.
- Crucially, our identity compensation module enables one-shot portrait speaking with an audio clip, transforming this approach into a speaker-agnostic method. This innovation allows for seamless integration of any individual's voice and facial expressions, irrespective of their identity, making it possible to create highly personalized and realistic talking faces. Our method opens up new avenues in areas such as virtual assistants, video games, and film production, where realistic talking faces are crucial for creating immersive experiences.

2 Related Work

2.1 Talking Head Video Generation

Talking Head Video Generation is an exciting and constantly evolving field in computer graphics and machine learning. It can be predominantly classified into two methods: image-driven and audio-driven. Image-driven methods rely on visual information from source videos to generate the talking head content. They typically involve capturing facial expressions, movements, and other visual cues from real or pre-existing videos. This approach requires extensive data collection and often results in highly detailed and realistic videos.

On the other hand, audio-driven techniques are becoming increasingly popular due to their ability to generate talking head videos based solely on audio input. This method is particularly useful when there is limited or no visual data available. Within the realm of audio-driven techniques, there exist two distinct categories: person-specific and person-agnostic methods.

Person-specific approaches typically focus on creating structured 3D facial animations tailored to a specific individual. They often involve capturing the facial geometry, texture, and motion data of a particular person to generate realistic talking head videos. These methods often require a pre-defined 3D model or mesh and use advanced rendering techniques to create highly detailed and realistic videos [6].

Person-agnostic methods, on the other hand, aim to generate talking head videos without requiring specific 3D models or extensive data collection for each individual.

Instead, they focus on learning the general patterns and characteristics of facial movements from audio input and use these patterns to generate videos of any face. Initial methods in this category focused on creating synchronized and accurate lip motions by learning a mapping between the audio clip and the corresponding lip landmarks [7]. Recent advancements in this field have shifted the focus to generating more natural and realistic facial expressions and movements. One recent work [7] concentrates on using 3D facial parameters such as expression, shape, pose, etc., to generate more accurate and dynamic talking head videos. These methods utilize deep learning techniques to learn the intricate relationships between audio and facial movements, resulting in more natural and convincing videos.

However, despite these advancements, current methods still face challenges in generating one-shot talking heads with satisfying lip-sync mouth and solid video quality. There is still a need for further research and innovation in this area to achieve truly convincing and realistic talking head videos from audio input only.

2.2 Memory Bank

In the context of contrastive learning, there is a coupling issue between dictionary size and batch size in an end-to-end setting. To address this, a memory bank approach is employed. This method involves saving the dictionary and updating the corresponding representations for each batch. The memory bank stores representations of all training data after encoding through a key encoder, showcasing its powerful performance in various domains such as image processing, face Recognition and video object detection. Deng et al. [8] established a memory bank to store historical facial features. In the computation of the softmax-based loss, there is an integration of historical facial features with classification weights through a weighted fusion process. This process results in dynamically variable classification weights, referred to as Variational Prototypes [9]. Essentially, it combines pair-based matching and class-based optimization within a single classification layer.

It contains three main modules: (i) Intermediate speaker module learns lip-sync motion from the input audio and face image. (ii) Optimal intermediate speaker selection module automatically choose an intermediate speaker with the best audio-visual synchronization features. (iii) Face feature compensation module learns a global facial memory bank and the motion flow between the source image and the target image [10]. Then it concatenates the warped feature and the facial memory bank to compensate the warped source image. After extracting the features of the source video and source audio and concatenating them, the synchronised driving video and a source image will be sent in the keypoint detector [14, 15]. After generating keypoints, the motion flow field is calculated, which is the basis for the pixels of the source image to move to the desired position. After the warp operation, a relatively rough facial feature map is obtained [16]. The rough human face is compensated for details by the compensation module, and then restored to a facial image with synchronized lips and audio and rich details.

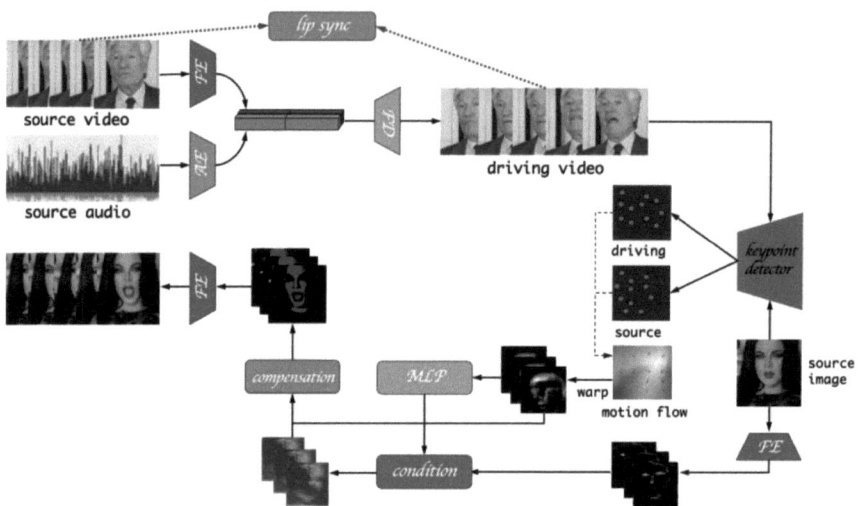

Fig. 1. Pipeline of our proposed AaICNet architecture.

3 The Proposed Approach

3.1 Overview

An overview of the Audio-aware Identity Compensation Network, as depicted in Fig. 1, presents a complex yet highly effective framework for generative tasks. The network can be introduced in three primary parts:(i) Intermediate speaker generation module. This module serves as the backbone of the entire system. Its primary function is to generate an intermediate speaker's video that is synchronized with a segment of audio. To achieve this, it takes as input a combination of audio and images of an automatically pre-selected identity. By utilizing deep learning techniques, it manages to create a video that seamlessly blends the audio with the selected identity's facial features. (ii) Optimal intermediate speaker selection module. This module functions as a filter, selecting the most suitable intermediate speaker from the generated pool. It evaluates the quality and coherence of each generated speaker video based on multiple factors, ensuring that the final output aligns not only with the input audio but also maintains a level of authenticity and naturalness. (iii) Facial feature compensation module. Once an intermediate speaker is selected, this module comes into play. It takes the generated intermediary video as input and uses it to drive an arbitrary image, effectively creating a talking head portrait. This module incorporates advanced techniques to compensate for any discrepancies in facial features, ensuring that the final output is a high-quality, convincing portrait. During the inference stage, the intermediate speaker generation module generates a lip-sync intermediate speaker's video by inputting a segment of audio and images of an automatically pre-selected identity. Then, the face compensation module takes the generated intermediary video as input to drive an arbitrary image, thus achieving one-shot portrait talking head generation.

3.2 Network Architecture

The whole network can be introduced as three parts: (i) Intermediate speaker generation module. Inspired by Wav2Lip [1], this module inputs a sequence face frame W with lower part masked, which then will be concatenated with the same length of unmasked face sequence as the face encoder input. This unmasked face sequence is to provide pose prior to guide later reconstruction process. The module is mainly a generator-discriminator architecture. Within this model are a facial encoder, an audio encoder, and a facial decoder, each composed of a series of convolutional layers. Specifically, the audio encoder encodes the input audio clip and the face encoder encodes a random reference frame R. Our distinguishing loss function is a combination of cosine similarity and binary cross-entropy loss [17]. Then we calculate the dot product between the face embedding f and audio embedding a, which indicates the sync probability of the audio-lip embeddings:

$$Psync = \frac{f \cdot a}{\max(\|f\|2 \cdot \|a\|2, \varepsilon)} \quad (1)$$

Then we concatenate the audio embedding and the face embedding as the decoder input. (ii).

Optimal intermediate speaker selection module. After extensive training on facial data, the intermediate speaker generation module will produce numerous speaker avatars driven by audio[18]. However, not all of these avatars are necessary for us. In the optimal intermediate speaker selection module, we calculate images with the best lip sync error confidence (LSE-C) and retain this image as the driving avatar for our next module. (iii) Face feature compensation module. This module first receives optimal intermediate speaker selection module's generated image (only receive one at a time) as a driving image D and a source image S. The keypoint detector first detect K pairs of key-points, i.e. $\{x_{s,t}, y_{s,t}\}_{t=1}^{K}$ and $\{x_{d,t}, y_{d,t}\}_{t=1}^{K}$ one the D and S, respectively. Then the pairs of key-points will be used to estimate the motion flow $A_{S \leftarrow D}$ between the S and D. And the motion flowed is leveraged to warp the encoded source face feature F_e^i in the i-th channel and generate the warped feature F_w^i. The key-points of the source image S are fattened and concatenated with the warped source feature and then are fed into the MLP to produce an implicit identity representation S_{id}. We extract features with half the number of channels from the warped feature and perform convolutional transformation to produce the projected feature F_{proj}^i. We train a global face memory bank [19] which can be conditioned by the S_{id} as query. Drawing inspiration from the style injection technique in StyleGANv2, we modify the identity representation S_{id} to tailor a 3×3 convolutional layer and condition the memory bank:

$$\omega'_{ijk} = si * \omega_{ijk} \quad (2)$$

$$\omega''_{ijk} = \omega'_{ijk} \sqrt{\sum_{i,k} (\omega'_{ijk})^2 + \varepsilon} \quad (3)$$

where the ω represents the weight of the convolution kernel; ε is a small constant to mitigate numerical instabilities; si is the i-th element in the learned implicit identity representation S_{id}, while i and k iterate over the output feature maps and spatial dimensions of the convolution, respectively[20].

Such mechanism provides flexible memory compensation feature to help generate more vivid image. During the training phase, the memory bank is updated automatically by the optimization gradients from training data. Here, we use L_{con} to enforce the consistency between the projected feature F^i_{proj} and the source face image:

$$L_{con} = \left\| F^i_V - de\left(F^i_{proj}\right) \right\|_1 \quad (4)$$

Furthermore, we utilize a cross-attention mechanism to compensate for the distorted source feature. The memory produces the Key F^i_k and Value F^i_v to condition on the projected feature F^i_{proj}.

Meanwhile, we perform a non-linear projection by mapping F^i_{proj} to a query feature F^i_Q through a 1 × 1 convolution layer, which is then followed by a ReLU layer. Subsequently, we apply cross-attention to reconstruct a more robust feature F^i_{ca} as follows:

$$F^i_{ca} = C_{1\times 1}\left(\text{softmax}\left(F^{iT}_Q \times F^i_K\right) \times F^i_V\right) \quad (5)$$

Then we employ it to the soft-max layer and then the 1 × 1 convolution layer so that we get the compensated feature F^i_{cpt}:

$$F^i_{cpt} = \text{Concat}\left[F^i_{ca}, F^{i,0}_w\right] \quad (6)$$

In decoding process, we pass the compensated feature F^i_{cpt} through a convolution layer and a sigmoid layer to produce the final face image I_{out}.

3.3 Optimization Losses

Sync Loss *Lsync*. We employ sync loss that minimizing the cosine similarity between the audio embedding and the face embedding to penalize inaccurate lip from the generator. The sync loss is defined as follows:

$$L_{sync} = \frac{1}{N}\sum_{i=1}^{N} -\log(P^i_{sync}) \quad (7)$$

Perceptual Loss *Leq*. We employ perceptual loss Lp in the training stage. Specifically, we downsample the generated image and the ground truth to four different resolutions (i.e. 256 × 256, 128 × 128, 64 × 64, 32 × 32) respectively as R_1, R_2, R_3, R_4 and G_1, G_2, G_3, G_4. Then we employ a pre-trained VGG network to extract those features and measure the L1 distance between G_i and R_i. The Perceptual loss is defined as follows:

$$L_p = \sum_{i=1}^{4} L1(G_i, R_i) \quad (8)$$

Equivariance Loss *Leq*. We utilize equivariance loss to guarantee the stability of the estimated keypoints in images after undergoing various augmentation operations.

In accordance with FOMM, when provided with an image I and its detected keypoints {Xi}, we initiate the process by applying a predetermined spatial transformation T to both the image I and keypoints {Xi}. This results in the transformed image IT and the corresponding transformed keypoints {XiT}. Following this, we identify key-points on the transformed image IT, equivalent to {XIT,i}. Subsequently, we apply equivariance loss to both the source image and the target image, defined as follows:

$$L_{eq} = \sum_{i=1}^{K} \left\| X_i^T - X_{I_T,i} \right\|_1 \quad (9)$$

Keypoint distance loss L_{dist}. We employ the keypoint distance loss to penalize the model when the distance between any two keypoints falls below a specified threshold. Consequently, the key-point distance loss effectively alleviates the crowding of keypoints within a small neighborhood. For a given image, considering every pair of keypoints X_i and X_j, the formulation is as follows:

$$L_{dist} = \sum_{i=1}^{K}\sum_{j=1}^{K} \left(1 - sign(\left\| X_i - X_j \right\|_1 - \alpha)\right), i \neq j \quad (10)$$

Consistency loss L_{con}. As discussed before, we ensure the consistency between the projected feature F_{proj}^i from the current training face image and the feature value FiV from the global meta-memory:

$$L_{con} = \left\| F_V^i - de\left(F_{proj}^i\right) \right\|_1 \quad (11)$$

We divide the training into two stages: the intermediate speaker training stage and the facial feature compensation stage. During the intermediate speaker training stage, the loss is:

$$L_i = L_{sync} \quad (12)$$

During the compensation training stage, the loss is:

$$L_c = L_p + L_{eq} + L_{con} \quad (13)$$

4 Experiments

We conduct quantitative and qualitative experiments to confirm the efficacy of our AaICNet.

4.1 Datasets and Metrics

Dataset. We evaluate our AaICNet on VoxCeleb1 and HDTF, which are respectively low visual quality dataset and high visual dataset. VoxCeleb1 has 1251 talking face videos and HDTF has 430 talking face videos with high-resolution. We trained our AaICNet on VoxCeleb1 and tested it on HDTF.

Metrics. We utilize structured similarity (**SSIM**), peak signal-to-noise ratio (**PSNR**), and learned perceptual image patch similarity (**LPIPS**) metrics to assess both low-level similarity and perceptual similarity. Meanwhile, to validate whether our architecture can generate accurate lip motion, we also use lip sync error distance (**LSE-D**) and lip sync error confidence (**LSE-C**) as our metric.

Table 1. Comparisons with state-of-the-art methods on HDTF.

Model	SSIM↑	PSNR↑	LPIPS↑	LSE-D↓	LSE-C↑
Wavlip-192	0.8487	27.6561	0.1208	8.0912	6.9509
PC-AVS	0.6383	20.6301	0.1077	6.6137	8.8550
MakeitTalk	0.5969	19.8602	0.1592	11.4913	3.0293
DINet	0.8758	28.4395	0.0289	8.3771	6.8416
Ours	**0.9425**	**30.0082**	**0.1786**	**6.5301**	**7.6821**

4.2 Comparison with State of the Art Methods

In Table 1, we compare AaICNet with Wavlip-192 [1], LipGAN, PC-AVS, MakeitTalk and DINet [2].

The results indicate that our AaICNet achieves the best visual quality among Wavlip-192, LipGAN, MakeitTalk, and PC-AVS, particularly noted on the SSIM metric within the HDTF dataset. We exceeded all baseline models in lip-sync accuracy metrics, highlighting the robust audio-lip synchronization capabilities of our model. Moreover, we outperformed existing baseline models across various visual assessment metrics, which illustrates our model's strong ability to generate realistic human faces.

Many competing approaches focus on directly generating pixels in the mouth region of the source facial image, often resulting in blurry mouth movements. In contrast, our method tends to produce more accurate lip motion, achieving improvements of 8.2% and 9.1% on the LSE-D and LSE-C metrics[1], respectively. Although DINet creates more vivid talking faces, its deforming and inpainting strategy struggles to effectively discriminate the lip-sync generation process, leading to less precise synchronization in comparison to our approach. Overall, our findings affirm the effectiveness of AaICNet in both visual fidelity and synchronization accuracy, setting a new benchmark for talking head generation.

5 Conclusion

In this study, we thoroughly analyze the current methodologies for talking head generation, acknowledging the inherent difficulty in simultaneously achieving precise lip-sync alignment and high-definition output quality. Recognizing the need for improved accuracy in lip-sync mouth movements, we introduce the Audio-aware Identity Compensation Network (AaICNet). This network is designed to capture subtle nuances in mouth movements in synchronization with the audio, ensuring a seamless integration of voice and facial expressions. Furthermore, we identify deficiencies in previously generated facial expressions and propose a global facial feature memory bank. This memory bank stores and retrieves facial features from previous frames, allowing for a more natural and diverse range of expressions in the generated talking heads. By combining AaICNet with the facial feature memory bank, our framework demonstrates remarkable performance in creating one-shot portraits with precise lip movements, improved expression quality, and high-definition output. Extensive experiments conducted demonstrate the effectiveness of our proposed framework. It not only generates convincing talking heads with accurate lip movements but also maintains a high level of authenticity and detail, even in one-shot scenarios. Our approach sets a new benchmark for talking head generation, paving the way for more advanced and realistic applications in various fields such as film, animation, and virtual reality.

References

1. Mukhopadhyay, R., Namboodiri, V.P., Jawahar, C.V.: A lip sync expert is all you need for speech to lip generation in the wild. In: Proceedings of the 28th ACM International Conference on Multimedia (2020). https://doi.org/10.48550/arXiv.2308.09716
2. Zhang, Z., Hu, Z., Deng, W., Fan, C., Lv, T., Ding, Y.: DINet: deformation inpainting network for realistic face visually dubbing on high resolution video. Proc. AAAI Conf. Artific. Intell. **37**(3), 3543–3551 (2023). https://doi.org/10.1609/aaai.v37i3.25464
3. Chen, L., et al.: Talking-head generation with rhythmic head motion. In: European Conference on Computer Vision (2020). https://doi.org/10.1007/978-3-030-58545-7_3
4. Blanz, V., Vetter, T.: Face recognition based on fitting a 3D morphable model. IEEE Trans. Pattern Anal. Mach. Intell. **25**(9), 1063–1074 (2003). https://doi.org/10.1109/TPAMI.2003.1227983
5. Daněček, R., Black, M.J., Bolkart, T.: EMOCA: emotion driven monocular face capture and animation. In: 2022 IEEE/CVF Conference on Computer Vision and Pattern Recognition (CVPR), pp. 20279-20290 (2022). https://doi.org/10.1109/CVPR52688.2022.01967
6. Lahiri, A.; Kwatra, V.; Frueh, C.; Lewis, J.; and Bregler, C.2021. Lipsync3d: Data-efficient learning of personalized 3d talking faces from video using pose and lighting normalization. In Proceedings of the IEEE/CVF conference on computer vision and pattern recognition, 2755–2764
7. Feng, Y., Feng, H., Black, M.J., Bolkart, T.: Learning an animatable detailed 3D face model from in-the-wild images. ACM Transactions on Graphics (TOG) **40**, 1–13 (2020). https://doi.org/10.1145/3476576.3476646
8. Deng, J., Guo, J., Yang, J., Lattas, A., Zafeiriou, S.: Variational prototype learning for deep face recognition. In: 2021 IEEE/CVF Conference on Computer Vision and Pattern Recognition (CVPR), pp. 11901–11910. Nashville, TN, USA (2021),, https://doi.org/10.1109/CVPR46437.2021.01173
9. Xu, R., Guo, M., Wang, J., Li, X., Zhou, B., Loy, C.C.: Texture memory-augmented deep patch-based image inpainting. IEEE Trans. Image Process. **30**, 9112–9124 (2021). https://doi.org/10.1109/TIP.2021.3122930
10. Wang, X., Li, Y., Zhang, H., Shan, Y.: Towards real-world blind face restoration with generative facial prior. In: CVPR (2021)
11. Fei, Z.: Memory-augmented image captioning. In AAAI, 2021. 3 Aliaksandr Siarohin, Stephane Lathuili ́ere, Sergey Tulyakov, 'Elisa Ricci, and Nicu Sebe. First order motion model for image animation. NeurIPS, 2019. 2, 4, 6, 7, 8, 9, 10, 11

12. Soumya, T., Juho, K., Esa, R.: Facegan: Facial attribute controllable reenactment gan. In: WACV (2021)
13. Yao, G., Yi, Y., Shao, T., Zhou, K.: Mesh guided one-shot face reenactment using graph convolutional networks. In: ACM MM (2020)
14. Zakharov, E., Shysheya, A., Burkov, E., Lempitsky, V.: Few-shot adversarial learning of realistic neural talking head models. In: ICCV (2019)
15. Liu, P., et al.: Self-appearance-aided differential evolution for motion transfer (2021). arXiv preprint arXiv:2110.04658
16. Karras, T., Laine, S., Aittala, M., Hellsten, J., Lehtinen, J., Aila, T.: Analyzing and improving the image quality of stylegan. In: CVP (2020)
17. Pumarola, A., Corona, E., Pons-Moll, G., Moreno-Noguer. F.: D-nerf: Neural radiance fields for dynamic scenes. In: CVPR (2021)
18. Dosovitskiy, A., et al.: An image is worth 16x16 words: Transformers for image recognition at scale. In: ICLR (2021)
19. Lu, Y., Chai, J., Cao, X.: Live speech portraits: real-time photorealistic talking-head animation. In: TOG (2021)
20. Qiu, H., Gong, D., Li, Z., Liu, W., Tao, D.: End2end occluded face recognition by masking corrupted features. IEEE Trans. Pattern Anal. Mach. Intell. **44**(10), 6939–6952 (2022). https://doi.org/10.1109/TPAMI.2021.3098962

Lightweight End-To-End Enabled Joint Source-Channel Coding for Wireless AUV Image Transmission

Guang Liu[1], Zhenguo Zhang[2(✉)], Minghui Wang[1], Bo Chen[1], Zesheng Liu[1], and Xiaojie Zhang[1]

[1] Systems Engineering Research Institute, China State Shipbuilding Corporation Limited, Beijing 102600, China
[2] College of Control Science and Engineering, Zhejiang University, Hangzhou 310007, China
zhangzhenguo@zju.edu.cn

Abstract. The underwater communication environment poses significant challenges that constrain both the transmission efficiency and robustness of Autonomous Underwater Vehicles (AUVs). To address these limitations, this paper introduces a novel deep learning (DL)-based joint source-channel coding (JSCC) scheme tailored for AUV image transmission. The proposed framework is designed to optimize both computational and energy efficiency, crucial for AUV operations in such demanding conditions. Specifically, we present DeepUAC, a compact neural network developed for computation- and energy-limited AUVs. This network is optimized for faster inference speeds and improved performance in underwater environments, where efficient use of resources is essential. DeepUAC leverages its streamlined architecture to balance the trade-offs between communication efficiency and image quality, ensuring robust performance even under challenging conditions. For edge devices, where resource constraints are even more critical, we employ lightweight vision transformers (ViTs) as the backbone for image reconstruction. This variant, termed DeepUAC-L, capitalizes on the lightweight and efficient nature of ViTs to provide high-quality image reconstruction with minimal computational overhead. The use of ViTs introduces a novel approach to feature extraction and image processing in underwater communication, allowing for superior handling of complex data even with limited computational power. Simulation results demonstrate that our proposed method outperforms existing approaches in terms of reconstruction quality and model size across a wide range of signal-to-noise ratio (SNR) values. These results highlight the effectiveness of our JSCC-based system in overcoming the inherent challenges of underwater communication, offering a robust and scalable solution for AUV image transmission.

Keywords: deep learning · Joint source-channel coding · image transmission · underwater communication

1 Introduction

Maritime strategy is a crucial factor in economic development, and autonomous underwater vehicles (AUVs) have been used as a practical exploration tool for developing and protecting marine resources [1]. For a long time, separation-based underwater acoustic communication has been the predominant method for AUVs, especially in long missions [2]. The goal of a digital communication system is to maximize the accuracy of symbol transmission in complex channel environments. This form of communication does not consider the meaning behind the symbols but rather focuses on approaching the channel capacity limit through various methods to ensure error-free data transmission. Researchers achieve this by developing advanced channel coding techniques, such as low-density parity check (LDPC) codes [3] and polar codes [4]. However, due to the difference in the transmission medium of acoustic waves, underwater acoustic communication suffers from narrow available bandwidth and poor channel conditions. The limited lithium-chemistry-based batteries drive AUVs to accomplish various missions, restricting their computational and communication capacities [5]. However, separation-based digital communication schemes fail to meet the demands of underwater communication, especially given the rapid growth of underwater devices.

To address the challenges inherent in underwater communication, deep learning (DL)-based joint source and channel coding (JSCC) schemes [6–9] offer a novel transmission paradigm. These schemes alleviate the communication burdens faced by AUVs by leveraging neural networks to effectively extract and recover source information features [10]. The first image transmission approach utilizing JSCC was termed DeepJSCC [11]. Building upon the foundations laid by DeepJSCC, the study in [12] introduced a channel feedback scheme designed to enhance image reconstruction performance, thereby improving the overall quality of transmitted images. Further efforts to enhance the efficiency of underwater acoustic communication systems were made by [13], which proposed a convolutional autoencoder specifically aimed at addressing the complexities associated with underwater acoustic channels. While these advancements represent significant progress, they tend to overlook the unique characteristics of underwater images, which often degrade due to challenging lighting conditions and complex environmental factors [14]. The inability of these previous methods to adequately account for such specific features may limit their effectiveness in real-world underwater scenarios, where image quality is crucial for successful transmission and analysis.

Therefore, there is an urgent requirement for innovative solutions that not only harness DL techniques but also take into account the unique characteristics of underwater imagery. By integrating these specific attributes, we can significantly enhance the robustness and performance of communication systems operating in challenging underwater environments. Such advancements could involve developing specialized algorithms that effectively address issues like color distortion, low visibility, and the impact of varying light conditions, all of which are prevalent in underwater settings. Additionally, research should focus on creating models that can adaptively learn from the diverse and often unpredictable conditions encountered in aquatic environments. This could lead to improved feature extraction methods that maintain the integrity of underwater images during transmission and recovery processes. Ultimately, a comprehensive approach that merges DL capabilities with a deep understanding of underwater imaging challenges will be crucial for advancing the efficacy of communication systems in these demanding scenarios. This will not only optimize data transmission but also ensure that critical information can be accurately captured and interpreted in real time, paving the way for more effective underwater exploration and monitoring.

In this paper, our focus lies in developing an underwater image communication system. In such environments, the transmitter and receiver must be designed with differing complexities in feature extraction, tailored to the computational capacities and energy resources of the devices involved. We propose a DL-based lightweight image communication system, named DeepJSCC, specifically designed for deployment on AUVs. This system accommodates the diverse computational capacities of transmitters and receivers. We introduce DeepUAC for efficient source encoding and multiple DeepUAC-L decoders to reconstruct the original image. Numerical results demonstrate the superiority of our approach over state-of-the-art lightweight image transmission schemes in terms of reconstruction quality and model size.

In this paper, we concentrate on developing an effective underwater image communication system. In underwater environments, it is crucial for the transmitter and receiver to be designed with varying levels of complexity in feature extraction. This tailoring is essential to accommodate the computational capacities and energy resources of the devices involved, such as AUVs. To address these challenges, we propose a novel DL-based lightweight image communication system named DeepJSCC. This system is specifically designed for deployment on AUVs, enabling it to effectively handle the diverse computational capabilities of both transmitters and receivers. Our framework introduces DeepUAC for efficient source encoding, which optimizes the initial processing of image data. Additionally, we implement multiple DeepUAC-L decoders that facilitate the reconstruction of the original image from the encoded information. Numerical results from our experiments clearly demonstrate the superiority of our approach compared to state-of-the-art lightweight image transmission schemes. Our system not only outperforms existing methods in terms of reconstruction quality but also maintains a smaller model size, making it highly suitable for resource-constrained underwater applications. By integrating advanced deep learning techniques with a focus on efficiency and adaptability, our proposed system offers a robust solution for reliable underwater image communication.

2 Proposed Method

We consider the problem of underwater wireless image transmission over the physical channel to recover the source image at the decoder under constrained bandwidth, as shown in Fig. 1. Let $S \in R^{H \times W \times 3} = [S_1, S_2, \ldots, S_m]$ be image sequence, where S_m represents the m-th image in S, H, and W is the image width, height, respectively. Our goal is to perfectly recover the image $\hat{S}$ at the receiver.

2.1 Source Encoder

The lightweight source encoder is designed for deployment on Autonomous Underwater Vehicles (AUVs), enabling efficient extraction of feature information from original

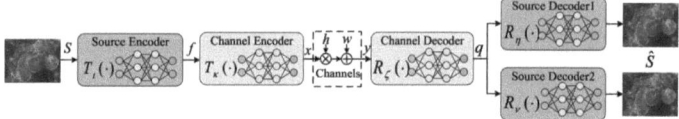

Fig. 1. The overall architecture of the proposed underwater image transmission system.

images with low computational complexity. To achieve this, we extend the mechanism introduced in [15] to optimize the encoder's performance for underwater communication scenarios. As shown in Fig. 2, the overall architecture of the source encoder is composed of three hierarchical stages. Each stage is carefully designed to reduce computational load while maximizing the encoder's ability to capture and process essential image features. This hierarchical design ensures that the encoder operates efficiently on the resource-constrained AUV devices, making it suitable for real-time underwater applications. The encoder's lightweight architecture allows for fast and accurate feature extraction, which is crucial for effective image transmission in underwater environments. Each stage includes a convolutional module (regular Conv 3×3 with stride 2), a FasterNet module (a FasterNet block, and regular Conv 1×1 with stride 1), and a noise attention (NA) module [16]. The FasterNet module, partitions the input features $F \in R^{\frac{H}{T} \times \frac{W}{T} \times c}$ into $F_1 \in R^{\frac{H}{T} \times \frac{W}{T} \times c_1}$ and $F_2 \in R^{\frac{H}{T} \times \frac{W}{T} \times c_2}$. Then, the features F_2 maps for computation with regular convolution. To preserve information integrity, it concatenates F_1 and F_2 and feeds them into a convolutional module.

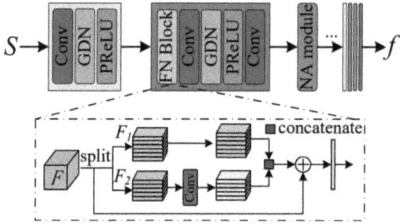

Fig. 2. Source encoder architecture of our method.

2.2 Channel Encoder and Decoder

The underwater acoustic channel is inherently complex, characterized by the superposition of multiple path components that result from the interaction between the ocean's surface and bottom. These path components vary significantly due to the irregular nature of underwater environments. Additionally, sound wave propagation in underwater channels faces various challenges, including the presence of unexpected reflectors such as rocks, vegetation, and marine life, which give rise to reflection and scattering phenomena. These reflections and scatterings distort the transmitted signal, leading to interference and signal degradation. As a result, the signal amplitude for each path in the underwater acoustic channel undergoes random variations, further complicating the communication process. This is primarily due to the time-varying nature of the underwater environment, where factors such as water temperature, salinity, and pressure can all influence the speed of sound and the way signals propagate. To model this scenario, we consider an underwater acoustic multipath channel model:

$$y = hx + w = \sum_{i=1}^{d} A_i \delta(\tau) x + w \qquad (1)$$

where h is the channel coefficients, d represents the number of symbols, A_i is the signal amplitude of the i-th voice line, $\delta(\tau)$ is the impulse function, and w is the ocean ambient noise distribution. Note that underwater acoustic channels suffer from short-time impulse noise, which is similar to Alpha stable distribution. Hence, ocean ambient noise w was given by

$$w = e^{\{jau - \gamma |u|^\alpha [1 + j\beta \mathrm{sgn}(u) v(u,\alpha)]\}}, \qquad (2)$$

$$v(u, \alpha) = \begin{cases} \tan\left(\frac{\alpha \pi}{2}\right), & \alpha \neq 1 \\ \frac{2}{\pi} \log |u|, & \alpha = 1 \end{cases} \qquad (3)$$

$$\mathrm{sgn}(u) = \begin{cases} 1, & u > 0 \\ 0, & u = 0 \\ -1, & u < 0 \end{cases} \qquad (4)$$

where α is the characteristic exponent ($0 < \alpha \leq 2$) to describe the heaviness level of the stable distribution, β is the symmetry parameter ($-1 < \beta < 1$), γ is a scale parameter ($\gamma > 0$), and a is the location parameter ($-\infty < a < +\infty$).

2.3 Source Decoder

We present a lightweight source decoder, referred to as DeepUAC-L, specifically designed for computation-limited devices operating in underwater communication scenarios. This decoder draws inspiration from the methodology described in [17] and is illustrated in Fig. 3. In our approach, the features q are initially processed by a standard convolutional layer, which lays the groundwork for subsequent feature extraction. Following this, we incorporate a 3 × 3 depthwise (DW) convolution combined with a squeeze-and-excitation (SE) layer. This combination is crucial for effectively learning the latent representations within the input data, enabling the model to better capture the intricate details inherent in underwater images. To further enhance the decoder's capabilities, we utilize residual networks to increase the depth of the neural network architecture. This depth is essential for capturing more contextual information, allowing the network to make more informed decisions during the reconstruction process. For upscaling the processed features, we implement the pixel shuffle operation, which rearranges the pixel values to improve the resolution of the output image. Additionally, the Non-local Attention (NA) module is integrated into the architecture to enhance the system's robustness. By enabling the network to focus on relevant contextual information from across the feature maps, the NA module improves the model's ability to reconstruct high-quality images, even in challenging underwater environments where clarity and detail are often compromised. Overall, DeepUAC-L effectively balances lightweight design and performance, making it well-suited for deployment in resource-constrained underwater communication systems.

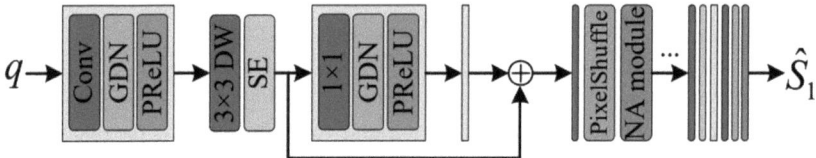

Fig. 3. The proposed lightweight source decoder.

As an upper bound for performance, we also introduce a more advanced source decoder, as depicted in Fig. 4. This decoder incorporates more complex computations and a larger model size to effectively address the specific characteristics of underwater images, such as color deviations and blurry details. To ensure robust performance in challenging underwater environments, it is imperative that the networks have sufficient generalization capacity. The interference caused by the water medium often leads to blurred image boundaries and distorted pixel distributions, which can significantly impact the quality of the transmitted images. To counteract these issues, we implement global and local feature fusion networks within our DeepUAC architecture to enhance visual representation. This dual approach allows the model to effectively integrate various levels of information, improving the overall clarity and detail of the reconstructed images. Additionally, we employ a mixed pooling module (MPM) to refine scene-parsing networks and enhance image boundaries, as referenced in [18]. This module contributes to better contextual understanding of the images, helping to mitigate the effects of distortion caused by underwater conditions. Following this, we utilize residual networks and the NA module as the backbone of our system, allowing for the extraction of detailed and contextually rich information from the input images. The extracted global and local features are then concatenated to reconstruct the input image at the receiver. This process is facilitated by the pixel shuffle module, which efficiently rearranges the pixels to enhance the resolution and quality of the final output. By integrating these advanced techniques, our proposed decoder significantly improves the ability to produce high-quality underwater images despite the inherent challenges posed by the aquatic environment.

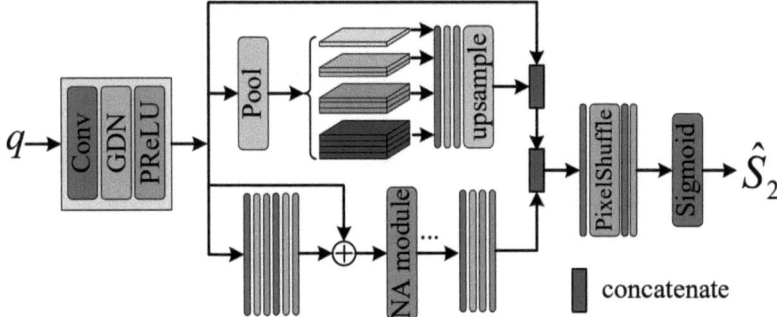

Fig. 4. The proposed enhanced source decoder.

3 Numerical Results

We conduct experiments on the EUVP dataset [19]. To improve the diversity of our training dataset, we randomly crop sections measuring 256 × 256 pixels from the images. We further augment the data by applying random transformations such as flipping, rotating, and altering the sequence of the triplets. We define the bandwidth ratio as $\rho = \frac{k}{3HW}$. The batch size is 8 and the downsampling factor t = 8. SNR values are randomly sampled from -5dB to 15dB in each batch. Previous studies [11–13] have demonstrated the superiority of DL-based wireless image transmission compared to traditional separation-based digital methods.

We compare the proposed method (DeepUAC and DeepUAC-L) with state-of-the-art DL-based schemes to exhibit its ability in underwater image transmission,

DeepJSCC: DL-based convolutional autoencoder directly maps the image pixel values to acoustic channel input symbols.

BDJSCC: The basic DeepJSCC-f structure achieves image compression and transmission.

LSSC: A lightweight UNet-enabled image transmission scheme, achieving better performance under limited resource devices.

The proposed JSCC-based scheme is trained end-to-end, specifically designed to operate efficiently under conditions of limited bandwidth and varying noise levels. By using an end-to-end training approach, the system can jointly optimize both the source encoding and channel transmission components, ensuring robust performance even in challenging underwater communication environments. The network learns to adapt to these constraints, maximizing image quality while minimizing resource use. In Table 1, we present the pseudocode for the method. The pseudocode outlines the key steps involved in the system's operation, from the input image processing and feature extraction to the reconstruction of the image at the receiver end. Each stage is carefully structured to account for bandwidth limitations and noise conditions, ensuring that the final system is capable of real-time deployment in underwater scenarios.

The underwater equipment needs to transmit image data to the dormant device within a short period while maintaining a certain level of computational capability. Shorter device latency indicates lower power consumption and more efficient communication. The average inference delay of different methods is shown in Fig. 5 for various devices.

Table 1. The program pseudocode of DeepUAC and DeepUAC-L.

Input: image S from EUVP dataset, $SNR_{train} = \{-5,\ldots,20\}$dB
1: **while** stop criterion is not met **do**
2: Generate normalized signal from input frames S
3: Output f from normalized frames S by the source encoder CNN block $T_l(\bullet)$
4: Output x from f by the channel encoder $T_k(\bullet)$
5: Transmit x over underwater physical with noise w and receive $\hat{y}$
6: Output q from y by the channel decoder $R_\xi(\bullet)$
7: Output $\hat{S}$ from q and by source decoder $R_{\eta/\nu}(\bullet)$
8: Compute l_{PSNR} or l_{SSIM} performance metrics
9: Update system parameters by SGD
10: **end while**
Output: Trained DeepUAC and DeepUAC-L

It can be observed that our DeepUAC-L achieves better latency performance than the baselines. Moreover, the architecture of the high-speed source decoder reduces the gap between DeepJSCC and DeepUAC-L. In particular, DeepJSCC exhibits the lowest CPU and GPU time latency, indicating that lower network complexity results in higher computational efficiency. However, it produces the poorest image reconstruction quality among all the solutions. The results suggest that improved computational and communication efficiency alone cannot meet system requirements. Meanwhile, the figure shows that DeepUAC has the highest time latency, both on CPU and GPU devices. This also indicates that the quality of underwater image communication is positively correlated with device time latency. In scenarios where energy is sufficient and time sensitivity is low, deploying more complex networks can achieve higher communication quality. In general underwater communication systems, it is crucial to strike a better balance between device latency and communication quality. The results demonstrate that the model is more suitable for neural network-accelerated devices.

Table 2 demonstrates that our proposed schemes outperform existing communication systems in terms of image reconstruction quality, while simultaneously requiring fewer floating-point operations (FLOPs). Specifically, with comparable recovered image quality, our low-complexity source encoder operates with only 19.45% of the FLOPs needed by the BDJSCC scheme. Similarly, the corresponding decoder, DeepUAC-L, utilizes just 7.72% of the FLOPs, making our approach significantly more efficient. Furthermore, it is worth noting that DeepJSCC achieves extremely low FLOPs and a reduced number of parameters in both the encoder and decoder. However, this reduction in complexity comes at the cost of image reconstruction quality, as DeepJSCC struggles to deliver satisfactory performance. This is primarily due to the model's insufficient network depth and width, which limit its ability to fully capture and explore the latent representations inherent in image pixels. Consequently, while DeepJSCC is efficient, it fails to provide the necessary capacity for high-quality image recovery.

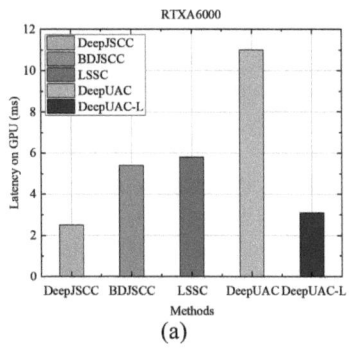
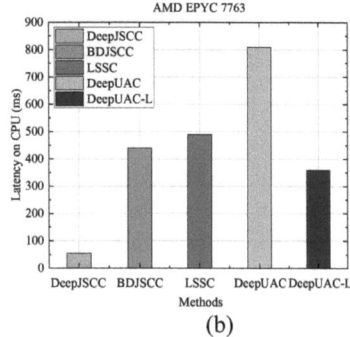

Fig. 5. Latency comparisons of different transmission methods with GPU and CPU.

Table 2. Reconstructed image performance by various compact models at SNR = 10dB.

Model	FLOPs		Parameters		Total		PSNR	SSIM
	Encoder	Decoder	Encoder	Decoder	FLOPs	Parameters		
DeepJSCC	0.22G	0.51G	0.07M	0.07M	0.73G	0.14M	27.13	0.774
BDJSCC	16.24G	44.4G	4.99M	4.99M	60.64G	9.98M	28.41	0.826
LSSC	6.13G	50.97G	2.4M	3.27M	57.1G	5.67M	27.39	0.786
DeepUAC	3.16G	90.57G	0.2M	12.1M	93.73G	12.3M	28.75	0.841
DeepUAC-L	3.16G	3.43G	0.2M	0.69M	6.59G	0.89M	28.23	0.819

Traditional separation-based digital communication schemes commonly use bit error rate (BER) as the primary metric to assess system performance, focusing on the accurate transmission of symbol sequences. In contrast, DL-based methods do not emphasize precise symbol-level transmission. Instead, they aim to optimize the overall quality of the reconstructed data. As a result, we employ alternative evaluation metrics such as Peak Signal-to-Noise Ratio (PSNR) and Structural Similarity Index Measure (SSIM). These metrics are more suitable for measuring the quality of image reconstruction and the system's robustness under various noise conditions, as they assess both the fidelity and perceptual similarity of the recovered images. This allows for a more comprehensive evaluation of the system's performance in real-world scenarios.

Figure 6(a) illustrates the performance of various methods in terms of PSNR as a function of the compression ratio. A clear trend emerges: as the compression ratio increases, the PSNR of all schemes improves, indicating better image reconstruction quality with more efficient compression. Among the methods, DeepUAC consistently achieves superior performance, outperforming BDJSCC by an average of 0.631 dB in PSNR, highlighting its effectiveness. In contrast, DeepUAC-L shows only a slight decrease of 0.025 dB in PSNR compared to DeepUAC, yet remains highly competitive. Additionally, DeepUAC-L demonstrates a significant advantage under challenging channel conditions, especially when the signal-to-noise ratio (SNR) falls below 10 dB. In these low-SNR scenarios, DeepUAC-L surpasses BDJSCC, proving its robustness and reliability in noisy environments, where maintaining image quality becomes increasingly difficult. This enhanced performance under poor channel conditions further emphasizes DeepUAC-L's suitability for practical applications in real-world communication systems.

We also evaluate the performance comparison of different schemes in terms of the SSIM under time-varying channels, as illustrated in Fig. 6(b). The results indicate that DeepUAC shows a notable increase of approximately 0.021 in SSIM compared to BDJSCC, reflecting its improved ability to maintain structural similarity in reconstructed images. In contrast, DeepUAC-L experiences a negligible decrease of just 0.0009 in SSIM, suggesting that it still performs competitively despite this slight drop. Furthermore, it is important to note that DL-based wireless image transmission schemes exhibit a significant advantage over traditional digital systems by effectively avoiding the "cliff effect." This phenomenon, often seen in conventional systems, results in abrupt degradation in image quality under adverse conditions. The ability of DL-based methods to mitigate this effect underscores their potential for more reliable performance in real-world applications, where channel conditions can be unpredictable and variable.

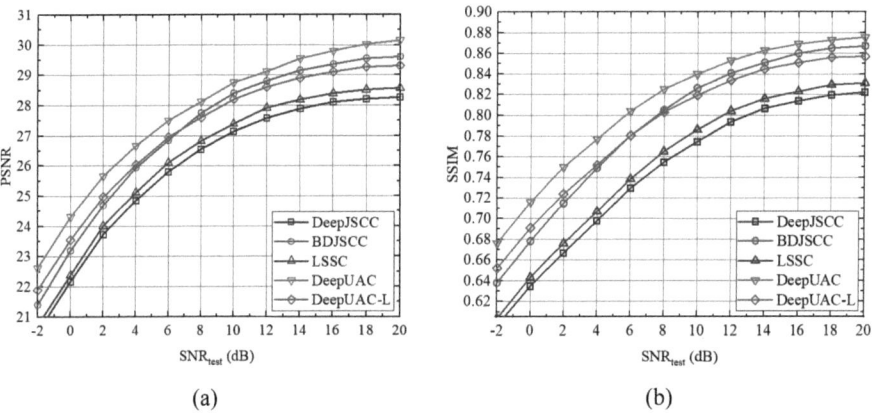

Fig. 6. Performance comparison of different approaches over the underwater acoustic channel for bandwidth compression ratio $\rho = 0.041$.

In Fig. 7, we present a visual comparison of various schemes at a signal-to-noise ratio for testing (SRNtest) of 10, with a bandwidth compression ratio of 0.041. The results clearly indicate that UASC significantly outperforms existing methods, providing a clearer and more detailed representation of the transmitted images while effectively mitigating underwater multipath disturbances. This advantage in clarity and detail highlights UASC's superior capability in handling challenging underwater conditions. Although DeepJSCC has the lowest FLOPs among all the methods evaluated, it suffers from visible blocking artifacts in the reconstructed images. This issue arises from the scheme's simplistic network architecture, which fails to adequately balance the various tasks involved in underwater wireless image transmission, such as feature extraction, bandwidth constraints, and noise interference. In contrast, UASC-L demonstrates better visual quality even when operating under limited computational resources. This resilience indicates that UASC-L effectively manages the complexities of underwater transmission, providing reliable performance without compromising image quality. Overall, the visual comparisons reinforce the advantages of UASC and UASC-L in scenarios with challenging conditions and resource limitations.

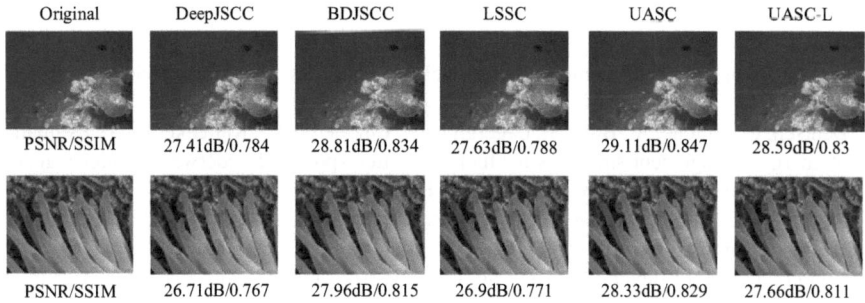

Fig. 7. Visualization comparison of various schemes at SNR = 10dB for bandwidth compression ratio $\rho = 0.041$.

4 Conclusion

In this paper, we proposed a novel deep learning-based JSCC system specifically designed for underwater wireless image transmission. Our framework integrates a lightweight encoder that significantly enhances the extraction of source features, optimizing the initial stages of the transmission process. To cater to diverse deployment environments, we designed two distinct decoders: DeepUAC and DeepUAC-L. This flexibility allows our system to be effectively implemented on a variety of devices, ensuring adaptability across different platforms. Our proposed JSCC system achieves an excellent trade-off between error protection and compression efficiency, enabling reliable image transmission in challenging underwater conditions. Experimental results clearly demonstrate that our method outperforms existing approaches in terms of computational complexity, requiring fewer resources while maintaining high-quality recovered images. This efficiency is crucial for underwater applications, where computational power and bandwidth may be limited. Moreover, our system effectively mitigates interference and overcomes the "cliff effect," a common issue in traditional communication systems where image quality degrades abruptly under adverse conditions. Looking ahead, we identify opportunities for further improvement in the coding efficiency of the proposed method. Future work may focus on incorporating multi-modal fusion from various AUV devices, which could enhance the system's robustness and performance. By leveraging diverse data sources, we aim to optimize the transmission process even further, paving the way for more effective underwater communication solutions.

References

1. Han, S., Zhang, T., Li, X., Yu, J., Zhang, T., Liu, Z.: The unified task assignment for underwater data collection with multi-AUV system: a reinforced self-organizing mapping approach. IEEE Trans Neural Netw. Learn. Syst. **35**(2), 1833–1846 (2024)
2. Cai, W., Liu, Z., Zhang, M., Lv, S., Wang, C.: Cooperative formation control for multiple AUVs with intermittent underwater acoustic communication in IoUT. IEEE Internet Things J. **10**(17), 15301–15313 (2023)
3. Gallager, R.: Low-density parity-check codes. IRE Trans. Inf. Theor. **8**(1), 21–28 (1962)
4. Arikan, E.: Channel polarization: a method for constructing capacity-achieving codes for symmetric binary-input memoryless channels. IEEE Trans. Inf. Theory **55**(7), 3051–3073 (2009)
5. Deutsch, C., Chiche, A., Bhat, S., Lagergren, C., Lindbergh, G., Kuttenkeuler, J.: Evaluation of energy management strategies for fuel cell/battery-powered underwater vehicles against field trial data. Energy Convers. Manage. X **14**, 100193 (2022)
6. Bao, J., et al.: Towards a theory of semantic communication. In: 2011 IEEE Network Science Workshop, pp. 110–117 (2011)
7. Gündüz, D., et al.: Beyond transmitting bits: context, semantics, and task-oriented communications. IEEE J. Sel. Areas Commun. **41**(1), 5–41 (2022)
8. Qin, Z., Tao, X., Lu, J., Tong, W., Li, G.Y.: Semantic communications: Principles and challenges (2021). arXiv preprint arXiv:2201.01389
9. Shi, Y., Zhou, Y., Wen, D., Wu, Y., Jiang, C., Letaief, K.B.: Task-oriented communications for 6G: Vision, principles, and technologies. IEEE Wirel. Commun. **30**(3), 78–85 (2023)
10. Zhang, Z., Yang, Q., He, S., Sun, M., Chen, J. (2022) Wireless transmission of images with the assistance of multi-level semantic information. In 2022 International Symposium on Wireless Communication Systems, pp. 1–6, Hangzhou, China
11. Bourtsoulatze, E., Kurka, D.B., Gündüz, D.: Deep joint source-channel coding for wireless image transmission. IEEE Trans. Cognitive Commun. Netw. **5**(3), 567–579 (2019)
12. Kurka, D.B., Gündüz, D.: DeepJSCC-f: Deep joint source-channel coding of images with feedback. IEEE J. Sel. Areas Inf. Theory **1**(1), 178–193 (2020)
13. Zhang, J., Sun, W., Zhao, Y., Du, H.: Semantic communication in underwater communication: advantage, problem and solution—a survey. In: 2023 8th International Conference on Intelligent Computing and Signal Processing, pp. 2120–2123, Xi'an, China (2023)
14. Fu, Z., Wang, W., Huang, Y., Ding, X., Ma, K.K.: Uncertainty inspired underwater image enhancement. In: European conference on computer vision, pp. 465–482. Springer, Nature Switzerland (2022)
15. Chen, J., et al.: Run, don't walk: chasing higher FLOPS for faster neural networks. In: Proceedings of the IEEE/CVF Conference on Computer Vision and Pattern Recognition, pp. 12021–12031, Vancouver, BC, Canada (2023)
16. Zhang, Z., Yang, Q., He, S., Chen, J.: Deep learning enabled semantic communication systems for video transmission. In: 2023 IEEE 98th Vehicular Technology Conference, pp. 1–5, HongKong (2023)
17. Wang, A., Chen, H., Lin, Z., Pu, H., Ding.: Repvit: Revisiting mobile cnn from vit perspective (2024). arXiv preprint arXiv:2307.09283

18. Hou, Q., Zhang, L., Cheng, M.M., Feng, J.: Strip pooling: rethinking spatial pooling for scene parsing. In: Proceedings of the IEEE/CVF conference on computer vision and pattern recognition, pp. 4003–4012, Seattle, WA, USA (2020)
19. Islam, M.J., Xia, Y., Sattar, J.: Fast underwater image enhancement for improved visual perception. IEEE Rob. Autom. Lett. **5**(2), 3227–3234 (2020)

Method for Predicting Impact Point of Trajectory Correction Projectile Based on IDBO-XGBoost

Dong Sun[1], Bo Zhang[2(✉)], and Feiyu Wang[1]

[1] College of Control Science and Engineering, Bohai University, Jinzhou, Liaoning, China
[2] Academic Development and Planning Division, Bohai University, Jinzhou, Liaoning, China
jzhzhb@sina.com

Abstract. In order to solve the problem of poor accuracy and real-time performance of the traditional numerical integration method in solving the projectile landing position, the XGBoost optimized by the improved Dung beetle optimizer (IDBO) is proposed to improve the accuracy and efficiency of the projectile landing point information prediction. Firstly, the six-degree-of-freedom ballistic equation is established, and the fourth-order Runge-Kutta method is employed to solve it. Subsequently, the flight characteristics of the projectile are analyzed and the dataset is constructed. Then, the data is preprocessed and the IDBO-XGBoost projectile drop point model is established. Meanwhile, XGBoost projectile impact point prediction models optimized by Sparrow algorithm (SSA), Particle swarm optimization (PSO), Dung beetle optimizer (DBO) and IDBO were compared. The simulation results show that the prediction error of IDBO-XGBoost model is significantly lower than that of other models, and the accuracy is improved by an order of magnitude, which provides support for the prediction of projectile impact point and the research of remote fire precision strike.

Keywords: ballistic correction · impact point prediction · dung beetle optimization algorithm · XGBoost algorithm

1 Introduction

In modern military conflicts, precision fire attack on long-range military targets has become a key factor affecting the outcome of military conflicts, and many countries regard long-range precision fire attack as an important development direction of ammunition technology [1]. In order to ensure that the projectile can hit the target at a long distance [2], it is necessary to predict the drop point information of the projectile.

Currently, scholars have proposed various methods for fast and accurate projectile drop prediction. The numerical integration method can be precise but relies heavily on computer performance and iteration size [3]. Neural network models like BP, WNN, and LSTM in literature [4, 5] approximate nonlinear trajectories, significantly improving prediction accuracy and efficiency, yet their application scope and accuracy can be enhanced.

This paper utilizes the fast convergence and high accuracy of the DBO algorithm, along with the efficiency and flexibility of XGBoost, to propose a method for fall point prediction by optimizing the XGBoost model with an improved DBO algorithm.

2 Algorithm

2.1 XGBoost Algorithm

The tree model is robust with strong generalization. The objective function $L^{(j)}$ in the XGBoost algorithm is shown in the formula.

$$L^{(j)} = \sum_{i=1}^{n} l\left(y_i, \hat{y}_i^{j-1} + f_j(x_i)\right) + \Omega(f_j) \tag{1}$$

where $l(\cdot)$ denotes the loss function, utilized to quantify the disparity between predicted values and actual values; $\hat{y}_i^{j-1}$ denotes the output of the $(j-1)^{th}$ tree.

2.2 IDBO Optimization Algorithm

Despite the DBO Algorithm's strengths in optimization and rapid convergence speed [6], it faces challenges such as imbalance between global exploration and local exploitation, vulnerability to local optima, and limited global exploration capabilities. To enhance the search performance of the DBO algorithm, this paper proposes improvements in three key areas: circle mapping strategy, embedded improved sine algorithm strategy, and adaptive Gauss-Cauchy mutation perturbation.

Circle Initializes the Chaotic Map. In optimization algorithms, the initial population significantly influences overall performance [7]. This study utilizes Circle chaotic mapping to generate initial individuals, thereby enhancing population diversity.

$$x_{i+1} = \mod(x_i + b - (\frac{a}{2\pi})\sin(2\pi x_i), 1) \tag{2}$$

where a and b are control parameters, the commonly used values are 0.5 and 0.2, and mod is the complementary function. Chaotic orbit state values range from (0,1).

Using Improved Sinusoidal Algorithm. In order to further improve the coordination ability of DBO algorithm in global exploration and local development, this paper introduces a sinusoidal guidance mechanism [8]. The improved formula is as follows:

$$x_i(t+1) = \begin{cases} x_i(t) + \alpha \times k \times x_i(t-1) + b \times \Delta x, \delta < ST \\ \omega_t x_i(t) + r_1 \times \sin r_2 \times [r_3 p_i(t) - x_i(t)], \delta \geq ST \end{cases} \tag{3}$$

where t is the number of current iterations, ω_t is the inertia weight, $x_i(t)$ is the ith position component of the individual in the tth iteration, $p_i(t)$ is the ith component of the best individual position variable in the tth iteration, r_1 is the nonlinear decline function, r_2 is the random number on the interval $[0, 2\pi]$, and r_3 is the random number on the interval $[-2, 2]$, $\delta = rand(1)$, $ST \in (0.5, 1)$.

Adaptive Gauss-Cauchy Hybrid Variation Perturbation. In the traditional DBO algorithm, individual dung beetles may converge to the local optimal solution too quickly. To address this issue, we introduce an adaptive Gauss-Cauchy hybrid perturbation strategy to enhance population diversity and facilitate escape from local optima. The formula is as follows:

$$X^r(t) = X_{best}(t) * (1 + \mu_1 * \text{Gauss}(\sigma) + \mu_2 * \text{Cauchy}(\sigma)) \tag{4}$$

where $X_{best}(t)$ is the optimal solution at the tth iteration, $X^r(t)$ is the position of X_{best} after perturbation, μ_1 and μ_2 are the weight coefficients of the mutation operator.

During algorithm iteration, beetles undergo mutation. Initially, with a scattered population, Cauchy distribution induces substantial mutations for diversification, aiding global exploration and rapid convergence [9]. Later, as beetle positions stabilize, Gaussian distribution is employed for perturbation to escape local optima and address high-dimensional challenges. Post-perturbation, a greedy rule ensures optimal positioning, as outlined below.

$$X_{best}(t) = \begin{cases} X_r(t), f_r \leq f_{best} \\ X_{best}(t), f_r \geq f_{best} \end{cases} \tag{5}$$

where f_r and f_{best} are the fitness value of the perturbed location and the fitness value of the optimal location respectively. By comparing the fitness values before and after the disturbance, we can choose whether to update the optimal position parameters.

3 Model

In this paper, PSO, SSA, DBO, and IDBO were employed to optimize the learning rate, maximum depth, and minimum leaf number of the XGBoost model. Four projectile impact prediction models—PSO-XGBoost, SSA-XGBoost, DBO-XGBoost, and IDBO-XGBoost—were constructed. The IDBO-XGBoost algorithm flow is shown in Fig. 1.

4 Simulation and Analysis

4.1 Generation Set

In this paper, the ballistic data employed for predicting the projectile impact point is acquired through MATLAB simulation. Firstly, the six-degree-of-freedom ballistic equation is established, and its form is presented in Formula 6. Subsequently, the fourth-order Runge-Kutta method is utilized to solve the equation under various initial firing angles, and the trajectory of the simulated projectile is depicted in Fig. 2. The range of the ballistic firing angle is set to commence from 5° and a trajectory is calculated every 2° until the firing angle reaches 51°. The integral step of the fourth-order Runge-Kutta method is set at 0.01s. The ballistic data was integrated into the training data of the landing point prediction model, with a total of 8370 samples.

The data simulation is based on the following basic assumptions.

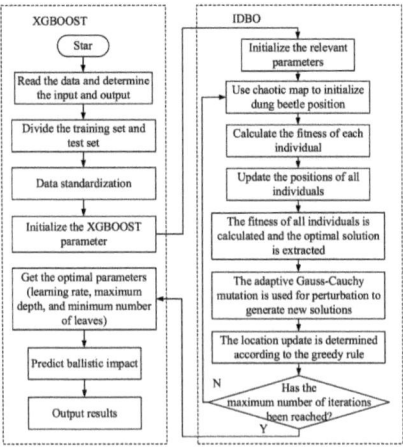

Fig. 1. Flow chart of IDBO-XGBoost projectile impact prediction

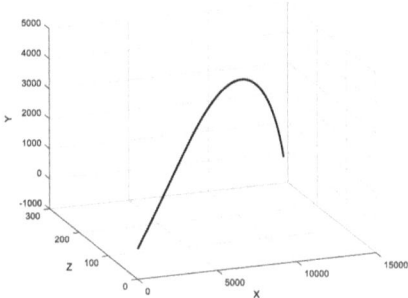

Fig. 2. Trajectory diagram of the projectile

① Model the Earth's surface as flat.
② Assume the nutation angle $\delta = 0$ throughout the entire projectile motion.
③ Standard meteorological conditions apply with no wind, rain, or snow.
④ Maintain a constant magnitude of gravitational acceleration ($g = 9.8$ m/s^2).

$$\begin{cases} dv_x/dt = -CH(y)G(v)v_x + \dfrac{v_x v_y}{R(1+y/R)} - 2\Omega[v_z \sin \Lambda + v_y \cos \Lambda \sin \alpha] \\ dv_y/dt = -CH(y)G(v)v_y - g + 2\Omega \cos \Lambda [v_x \sin \alpha + v_z \cos \alpha] \\ dv_z/dt = -CH(y)G(v)v_z - 2\Omega[(v_y \cos \Lambda \cos \alpha - v_x \sin \Lambda], \\ \dfrac{dx}{dt} = v_x, \dfrac{dy}{dt} = v_y, \dfrac{dz}{dt} = v_z, v = \sqrt{v_x^2 + v_y^2 + v_z^2}, \Omega = 7.292 \times 10^{-5} rad/s \end{cases} \quad (6)$$

In Eq. (6), the variable definition can be referred to reference [10] and will not be repeated here.

4.2 Training Results

The improved algorithm is used to predict the ballistic drop point, and the effect in the test set is shown in Fig. 3. In the whole validation set, the maximum absolute value of the range error of the ballistic drop point is 0.361 m, and the minimum absolute value is 0.001 m. The maximum lateral deviation is 0.0168 m, while the minimum is 0.0009 m. The overall error is small, and the accuracy can meet the actual requirements of ballistic fall point prediction.

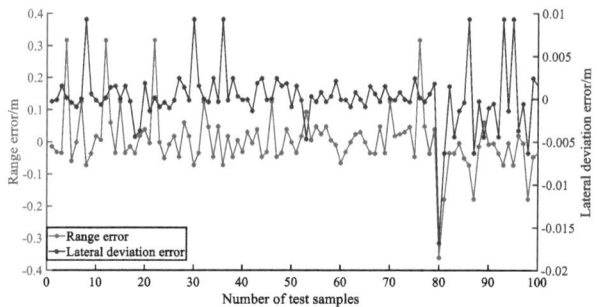

Fig. 3. IDBO-XGBoost trajectory drop prediction error.

4.3 Comparative Analysis of Predictive Performance

The study evaluated four models—XGBoost, SSA-XGBoost, PSO-XGBoost, and IDBO-XGBoost—on predicting ballistic drop points using a comprehensive performance evaluation. Analysis of Figs. 4 and 5 shows that the IDBO-XGBoost model exhibits stable error fluctuations and consistent trends in both training and test sets. It significantly improves prediction accuracy compared to the non-optimized XGBoost model and outperforms other intelligent optimization algorithms in reducing prediction errors, confirming its superiority in ballistic drop point prediction.

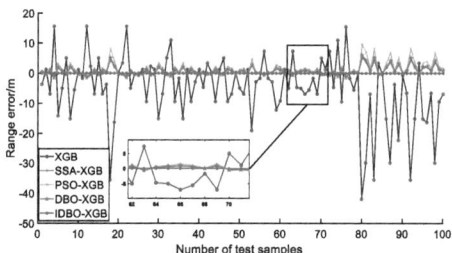

Fig. 4. The prediction error of range.

From the evaluation indexes of the prediction results of each model in Table 1, it can be seen that all the evaluation indexes of IDBO-XGBoost are optimal. It shows that the improved algorithm has strong accuracy and stability.

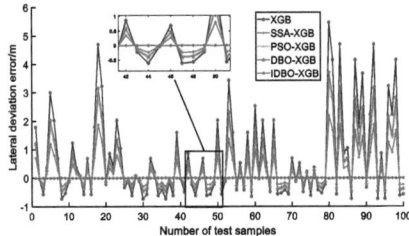

Fig. 5. The prediction error of lateral deviation.

Table 1. Evaluation indicators of prediction results of each model

Model	MAE_X	MAE_Z	MSE_X	MSE_Z	$RMSE_X$	$RMSE_Z$
XGBoost	7.564	1.112	119.174	2.652	10.918	1.629
SSA- XGB	0.863	0.442	1.737	0.421	1.318	0.649
PSO- XGB	1.6162	0.685	6.0628	1.006	2.462	1.003
DBO- XGB	0.482	0.442	0.446	0.42	0.668	0.648
IDBO- XGB	0.0532	0.00172	0.00726	0.000965	0.0852	0.00311

5 Conclusions

This paper proposes a projectile impact point prediction model based on IDBO-XGBoost. Through analysis with numerical examples using multiple sets of projectile trajectory data, the following conclusions are drawn.

1. The IDBO addresses several shortcomings of the original, including unbalanced global exploration and local exploitation capabilities, susceptibility to local optima, and weak global exploration ability.
2. Compared with XGBoost, SSA-XGBoost, PSO-XGBoost and DBO-XGBoost prediction models, the MAE of IDBO-XGBoost in range error and lateral deviation error are reduced by 7.51 m, 0.809 m, 1.563 m, 0.428 m and 1.1103 m, 0.44 m, 0.683 m, 0.44 m, and the evaluation index MSE and RMSE have different improvements. The IDBO-XGBoost model shows higher prediction accuracy than other models, making it more suitable for the complex engineering of projectile range prediction.

References

1. Gao, S.L., Fan, S.S., Yuan, C., et al.: An overview of foreign long-range precise air striking development. Aero Weaponry **30**(06), 11–17 (2023). https://doi.org/10.12132/ISSN. 1673-5048.2023.0115
2. He, Z., Zhang, B., et al.: Application of data fusion algorithm based on gray model combined with Kalman Filter in intelligent ammunition wireless sensor network. In: ICMLCA 2022. Shenyang.12636, 223 (2023). https://doi.org/10.1117/12.2675415

3. Shi, J.G., Liu, M., et al.: Research on method of falling point prediction for trajectory correction projectile. J. Ballistics **26**, 29–30 (2014). https:// doi.org/https://doi.org/10.3969/j.issn.1004-499X.2014.02.006
4. Hao, B., Liu, L.W., Gu, J.M.: Research on projectile range prediction based on SSA-BP algorithm. J. Gun Launch Control **45**(01): 10–15 (2024). https://doi.org/10.19323/j.issn.1673-6524.202308009
5. Roux, A., Changey, S., Weber, J., et al.: LSTM-based projectile trajectory estimation in a GNSS-denied environment. Sensors **23**(6), 3025 (2023). https://doi.org/10.3390/s23063025
6. Xue, J., Shen, B., et al.: Dung beetle optimizer: a new meta-heuristic algorithm for global optimization. Supercomputing **79**(9), 7305–7336 (2023). https://doi.org/10.1007/s11227-022-04959-6
7. Amezquita, L., Castillo, O., Soria, J., et al.: New variants of the multi-verse optimizer algorithm adapting chaos theory in benchmark optimization. Symmetry **15**(7), 1319 (2023). https://doi.org/10.3390/sym15071319
8. Luo, Y., Dai, W., Ti, Y.W.: Improved sine algorithm for global optimization. Expert Syst. Appl. **213**, 118831 (2023). https://doi.org/10.1016/j.eswa.2022.118831
9. Mao, Q.H., Zhang, Q.: Improved sparrow algorithm combining Cauchy mutation and opposition-based learning. J. Front. Comput. Sci. Technol. **15**(6), 1155–1164 (2021). https://doi.org/10.3778/j.issn.1673-9418.2010032
10. Qian, L.F.: The basic equation of particle trajectory and its solution. In: Lin, F.Q. (ed.) Gun Ballistics, Beijing Institute of technology Press, Beijing. p. 30 (2009). https://www.zhangqiaokeyan.com/book-cn/08150822343.html.

Research on Insulator Fault Detection Based on Improved YOLOv5

Lu Liao and Fenghua Jin(✉)

School of Business, Shanghai Dianji University, Shanghai 201306, China
jinfh@sdju.edu.cn

Abstract. In power systems, insulator fault detection is crucial for ensuring the safe operation of the grid. This paper proposes an improved YOLOv5 model for efficient insulator fault detection. The improvements primarily involve two aspects: replacing the backbone network of YOLOv5 with EfficientViT (Efficient Vision Transformer) and adding a SimAM (Simulated Attention Module) attention module to the neck of the network. EfficientViT, as an efficient vision transformer, significantly reduces computational complexity and parameter count while maintaining model performance. The SimAM attention module enhances feature extraction accuracy and model robustness by simulating the attention mechanism. In the experiments, we evaluated the improved model using a public dataset containing various types of insulator faults. The results show that the improved model achieves a 2.1% increase in mean Average Precision (mAP) and a 1.4% increase in recall rate under the same hardware conditions. Additionally, the model's parameter count is reduced by 4%, floating-point operations are reduced by 9%, and the final model size is decreased by 4.5%.

Keywords: Insulators · Object Detection · Multi-Scale Feature Extraction · Attention Mechanism

1 Introduction

In power transmission, insulators are primarily used to isolate electronic devices, overhead lines, cables, and other conductive components, preventing accidental current leakage and insulation faults [1]. Insulators are installed on outdoor transmission lines and operate under harsh conditions, being influenced by environmental factors such as high temperatures, lightning, strong winds, bird damage, rain, snow, or contamination. Additionally, insulators can be affected by material defects, mechanical aging, and mechanical stress, leading to faults such as self-explosion, skirt breakage, string drop, and surface flashover [2]. With the continuous development of deep learning, object detection has been increasingly applied in power systems Combining object detection with drones significantly improves the efficiency and accuracy of line inspections, reduces inspection costs, and plays a vital role in ensuring the safety and stability of the power system. [3].

2 Research Content

2.1 EfficientViT Model

EfficientViT adopts a hierarchical structure, dividing the image feature extraction process into multiple stages, each containing several Transformer blocks. By extracting and processing features layer by layer, EfficientViT can capture different levels of image information more efficiently, thereby enhancing the richness and accuracy of feature representation. To reduce computational load, EfficientViT introduces a simplified self-attention mechanism and feedforward network within each Transformer block [4]. By optimizing matrix multiplication operations and reducing redundant computations, EfficientViT significantly lowers the computational complexity of each block while retaining key attention mechanisms and feature transformation capabilities. EfficientViT also improves feature aggregation. It employs a more efficient feature fusion method, enabling faster aggregation and transmission of features from different stages, thus enhancing the overall processing speed and responsiveness of the model [5]. To further improve model efficiency, EfficientViT incorporates a design that combines convolution and attention mechanisms. By embedding lightweight convolution operations within Transformer blocks, EfficientViT can more efficiently handle local features while maintaining the advantages of the global attention mechanism. Compared to other similar algorithms, EfficientViT has higher accuracy and fewer parameters, as shown in Table 1.

Table 1. EfficientViT compared with similar algorithms

	Precision	Recall	mAP@0.5	GFLOPs	Parameters
SwinTransformer	91.5	88.9	92.5	18.6	7227720
ConvNextV2	92.1	89.3	93.0	18.0	7027720
NextViT	91.8	89.4	92.8	17.3	6905248
EMO	91.9	89.1	92.0	17.6	6585144
EfficientViT	92.1	89.3	93.2	18.0	6564304

2.2 SimAM Attention Mechanism

The design goal of SimAM is to maintain the effectiveness of the attention mechanism while significantly reducing its computational complexity. Compared to other complex attention mechanisms (such as SE modules or CBAM), SimAM adopts a simpler computational strategy by simulating the feature map to estimate the importance of each channel, thus alleviating the computational burden [6]. SimAM calculates the importance score of each channel by simulating its contribution within the feature map. Specifically, SimAM treats the feature map as a three-dimensional tensor and assesses each channel's impact on the final output by calculating the mean and variance across the entire feature map [7]. This process avoids complex matrix operations and high-dimensional computations, significantly improving computational efficiency. Using the importance scores obtained from the simulated attention mechanism, SimAM can perform weighting on each channel of the feature map. This weighting process involves simple scalar multiplication, making it very efficient without adding extra computational load. Moreover, this weighting operation effectively enhances the representation capability of important features while suppressing less important ones, thereby improving the overall performance of the model [8]. In object detection tasks, SimAM achieves a high level of accuracy while only slightly increasing computational and parameter loads. Compared to other algorithms, SimAM has higher accuracy and fewer parameters, as shown in Table 2.

Table 2. Attention Mechanism Comparison Table

	Precision	Recall	mAP@0.5	GFLOPs	Parameters
SE	91.2	88.5	91.5	16.3	7057720
ECA	91.5	88.6	91.7	16.5	7027720
CBAM	91.0	88.4	91.2	16.4	7157720
GAM	91.4	88.9	92.0	16.2	6857720
SimAM	92.0	89.4	92.5	16.5	6705248

2.3 EIOU Loss Function

EIOU (Efficient Intersection over Union) is a metric used to evaluate model performance in object detection tasks, aimed at improving the computational efficiency and accuracy of IoU (Intersection over Union) [9]. EIOU employs a dedicated weighting mechanism that enhances its evaluation capabilities when dealing with objects of different sizes and shapes. By weighting the geometric attributes of the boxes, EIOU reduces the performance drop observed with traditional IoU in such scenarios. The computation process of EIOU is optimized to significantly enhance computational efficiency while maintaining high accuracy. Compared to traditional IoU, EIOU demonstrates more stable performance for small objects and dense scenes, effectively improving the detection precision of the model [10]. The EIOU computation formulas are shown in Eqs. (1) and (2):

$$L_{EIOU} = L_{IOU} + L_{dis} + L_{asp} \quad (1)$$

$$= 1 - IOU + \frac{\rho^2(b, b^{gt})}{c^2} + \frac{\rho^2(w, w^{gt})}{c_w^2} + \frac{\rho^2(h, h)}{c_h^2} \quad (2)$$

In the equations, w and h represent the width and height of the minimum enclosing rectangle for the predicted and ground truth bounding boxes, and ρ denotes the Euclidean distance between two points.

3 Algorithm Promotion

The proposed insulator fault detection network based on YOLOv5 consists of three main components: the feature extraction network, the EfficientViT module, and the SimAM attention module. First, the feature extraction network is used to extract features from the original images. Then, the extracted features are input into the EfficientViT and SimAM attention modules for processing. Finally, the outputs from both modules are fused. The network structure before the improvement is shown in Fig. 1. The overall structure of the improved network is shown in Fig. 2:

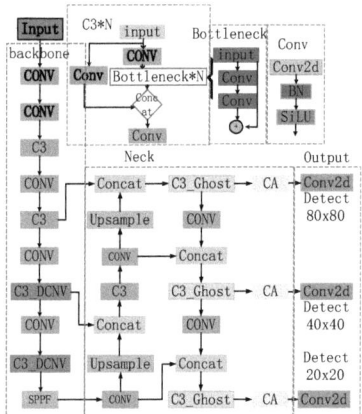

Fig. 1. Original Diagram   **Fig. 2.** Improvement Diagram

4 Experimental Results and Analysis

4.1 Experimental Environment and Training Settings

The experimental environment used in this study is Anaconda 4.12.0 and PyTorch 1.10. The experimental platform's CPU is an Intel(R) Xeon(R) Platinum 8260C CPU @ 2.30 GHz, and the GPU is an NVIDIA GeForce RTX 3090 (24 GB memory). The experimental setup included an input image size of 640 × 640, a batch size of 128, a total of 200 training epochs, and an initial learning rate of 0.01. Other settings followed the recommended parameters from the official YOLOv5 experiments.

4.2 Evaluation Metrics and Dataset Settings

To accurately demonstrate the detection precision and model complexity, the evaluation metrics used in this experiment include Precision, Recall, Mean Average Precision (mAP), and floating point operations (FLOPs), with GFLOPs $=10^9$ FLOPs. The 5,040 insulator images used in this study were all captured from transmission lines.

4.3 Ablation Study

To verify the independent effectiveness of the improved modules, seven sets of ablation experiments were conducted. Each experimental group used the same equipment and parameters to assess the impact of adding deformable convolutions and the attention mechanism on accuracy, as well as the effect of replacing C3 for lightweight implementation. The experimental results are shown in Table 3:

Table 3. Ablation Study

EfficientViT	SimAM	EIOU	Precision	Recall	mAP@0.5	GFLOPs	Parameters
			91.0	88.4	91.3	16.2	7027720
✓			92.1	89.3	93.2	18.0	6564304
✓	✓		93.8	89.6	93.2	16.2	7420000
✓	✓	✓	93.5	89.8	93.4	15.1	6649688

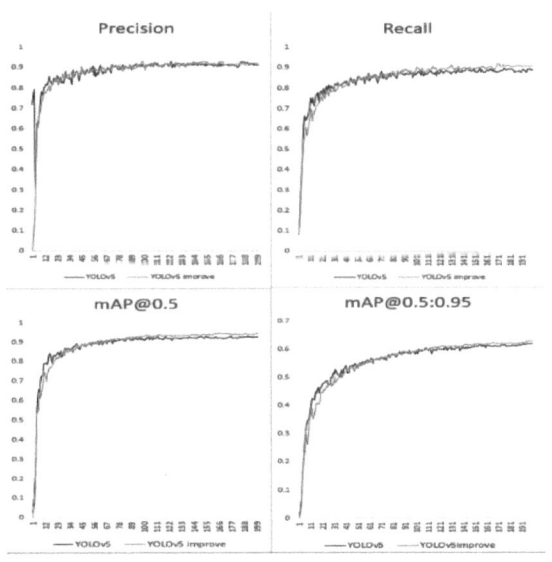

Fig. 3. Improved model performance metrics graph

From the results in Table 3, it can be seen that after replacing the backbone with EfficientViT, the model's accuracy, recall rate, and mAP@0.5 improved by 1.1%, 0.9%, and 1.9%, respectively, although the floating-point operations increased by 11.1%. This data indicates that the EfficientViT model has a significant effect. These results demonstrate that the attention mechanism enhances the model's feature extraction capabilities. Finally, when all the above improvements are applied simultaneously, mAP@0.5 increased by 2.1%, accuracy improved by 2.5%, and recall rate increased by 1.4%. These results show that all proposed modifications significantly enhance the network's performance and improve its ability to classify insulator faults. The performance metrics of the improved model are illustrated in Fig. 3.

5 Conclusion

To address the challenges of detecting insulators on transmission lines, such as difficulties in detection, occlusions, and complex backgrounds, this paper proposes an improved insulator fault detection method based on YOLOv5s. The backbone network of YOLOv5 was replaced with EfficientViT, enhancing its feature extraction capabilities and enabling the acquisition of more semantic information. The C3 module was integrated with an attention mechanism to replace the original C3 module, which strengthened the model's ability to process key information and improve detection accuracy. Finally, EIOU was utilized as the loss function for the model, further enhancing recognition precision.

Acknowledgement. Funding projects: Ministry of Education's Youth Fund for Humanities and Social Sciences Research (21YJC630047; 20YJCZH027); Shanghai Municipal Education Science Research General Project (C2022406).

References

1. Zhai, Y., Chen, R., Yang, Q., Li, X., Zhao, Z.: Insulator fault detection based on spatial morphological features of aerial images. IEEE Access **6**, 35316–35326 (2018)
2. Zhao, W., Xu, M., Cheng, X., Zhao, Z.: An insulator in transmission lines recognition and fault detection model based on improved faster RCNN. IEEE Trans. Instrum. Meas. **70**, 1–8 (2021)
3. Park, K.C., Motai, Y., Yoon, J.R.: Acoustic fault detection technique for high-power insulators. IEEE Trans. Industr. Electron. **64**(12), 9699–9708 (2017)
4. Liu, X., Peng, H., Zheng, N., Yang, Y., Hu, H., Yuan, Y.: Efficientvit: memory efficient vision transformer with cascaded group attention. In: Proceedings of the IEEE/CVF Conference on Computer Vision and Pattern Recognition (pp. 14420–14430) (2023)
5. Coccomini, D.A., Messina, N., Gennaro, C., Falchi, F.: Combining efficientnet and vision transformers for video deepfake detection. In: International conference on image analysis and processing, pp. 219–229. Springer International Publishing, Cham (2022). https://doi.org/10.1007/978-3-031-06433-3_19
6. Yang, L., Zhang, R. Y., Li, L., Xie, X.: Simam: a simple, parameter-free attention module for convolutional neural networks. In: International Conference on Machine Learning (pp. 11863–11874). PMLR (2021)
7. Mahaadevan, V.C., Narayanamoorthi, R., Gono, R., Moldrik, P.: Automatic identifier of socket for electrical vehicles using SWIN-transformer and SimAM attention mechanism-based EVS YOLO. IEEE Access **11**, 111238–111254 (2023). https://doi.org/10.1109/ACCESS.2023.3321290
8. Guo, M.H., et al.: Attention mechanisms in computer vision: a survey. Comput. Vis. Media **8**(3), 331–368 (2022)
9. Zhang, Y.F., Ren, W., Zhang, Z., Jia, Z., Wang, L., Tan, T.: Focal and efficient IOU loss for accurate bounding box regression. Neurocomputing **506**, 146–157 (2022)
10. Tong, Z., Chen, Y., Xu, Z., Yu, R.: Wise-IoU: bounding box regression loss with dynamic focusing mechanism (2023). arXiv preprint arXiv:2301.10051

Design of Attitude Calculation Algorithm Based on Kalman and Mahony Complementary Filtering

Feiyu Wang[1], Bo Zhang[2(✉)], and Dong Sun[1]

[1] College of Control Science and Engineering, Bohai University, Jinzhou, Liaoning, China
[2] Academic Development and Planning Division, Bohai University, Jinzhou, Liaoning, China
jzhzhb@sina.com

Abstract. For the industrial development trend of low cost and miniaturization of micro UAV, the accuracy and anti-interference of attitude calculation put forward more stringent requirements. an improved attitude calculation algorithm based on Kalman filter and mahony complementary filter is proposed. The gyroscope and accelerometer are used to estimate, predict and update the attitude angle through Kalman filter, suppress external disturbances such as motion acceleration and temperature drift. The attitude angle obtained by quaternion and the attitude angle calculated by Kalman are used to make a difference to obtain the angle deviation. The deviation angle is used to control the gyroscope angle. At the same time, the mahony complementary filter is used to correct the attitude of the gyroscope again, which greatly improves the anti-interference ability and accuracy of the system. The simulation results show that the improved fusion algorithm can effectively suppress external disturbances and enhance the stability of the system in both dynamic and static environments.

Keywords: kalman filtering · Mahony complementary filtering · quaternion · attitude algorithm

1 Introduction

In recent years, as MEMS (Microelectro Mechanical Systems) technology rapidly advances, the UAV industry undergoes significant changes. MEMS sensors are susceptible to temperature drift and other disturbances, necessitating enhanced accuracy in attitude angle through sensor data fusion. Currently, well-established algorithms include complementary filtering, neural networks, and gradient descent methods.

References [1–3] demonstrate the efficacy of Kalman filter, EKF, and Mahony complementary filter in reducing noise and mitigating heading angle drift. However, due to constraints of consumer-level microcontrollers, algorithmic advantages are often unrealized, and noise handling remains inadequate, thereby requiring improved accuracy solutions. References [4–6] considered the influence of Kalman filter algorithm on attitude calculation from the perspective of application and used extended Kalman filter algorithm to enhance the ability of anti-magnetic disturbance. In References [7–10], the PI feedback link is added for fusion filtering, and the solution ability of the algorithm is improved. But it needs to be improved in reducing the amount of calculation and the optimization of the solution process.

This study proposes an enhanced approach integrating Kalman filter with Mahony complementary filter. Furthermore, PI control is employed with Kalman filter and Mahony complementary filter to mitigate errors and enhance solution accuracy.

2 Attitude Angle and Rotation Matrix

The attitude is to describe the process of rotating from one coordinate system to another coordinate system. When the body coordinate system rotates around the X, Y and Z axes of the body, the corresponding attitude angles can be obtained as the roll, pitch and yaw. The attitude rotation matrix can be expressed by the quaternion, Let the quaternion be $Q = [q_0, q_1, q_2, q_3]$. which is expressed as follows:

$$C_n^b = \begin{bmatrix} q_0^2 + q_1^2 - q_2^2 - q_3^2 & 2(q_1 q_2 - q_0 q_3) & 2(q_1 q_3 + q_0 q_2) \\ 2(q_1 q_2 + q_0 q_3) & q_0^2 - q_1^2 + q_2^2 - q_3^2 & 2(q_2 q_3 + q_0 q_1) \\ 2(q_1 q_3 - q_0 q_2) & 2(q_2 q_3 + q_0 q_1) & q_0^2 - q_1^2 - q_2^2 + q_3^2 \end{bmatrix} \quad (1)$$

C_n^b represents the rotation equation from the navigation coordinate system to the body coordinate system. For example Eq. (2), Euler angle can be solved by quaternion.

$$\begin{bmatrix} \psi = \arctan\left[\dfrac{2(q_2 q_3 + q_0 q_1)}{q_0^2 - q_1^2 - q_2^2 + q_3^2}\right] \\ \theta = -\arcsin[2(q_3 q_1 - q_2 q_0)] \\ \phi = \arctan[\dfrac{2(q_1 q_2 + q_0 q_3)}{q_0^2 + q_1^2 - q_2^2 - q_3^2}] \end{bmatrix} \quad (2)$$

2.1 The Euler Angle is Obtained by Updating the Quaternion with Gyroscope and Accelerometer

The gravity vector is a fixed value [0,0, g] in the geodetic coordinate system. The three-axis acceleration in the carrier coordinate system at the current moment can be obtained by multiplying the rotation matrix and the gravity vector at this moment.

$$\begin{bmatrix} V_X \\ V_Y \\ V_Z \end{bmatrix} = \begin{bmatrix} q_0^2 + q_1^2 - q_2^2 - q_3^2 & 2(q_1 q_2 - q_0 q_3) & 2(q_1 q_3 + q_0 q_2) \\ 2(q_1 q_2 + q_0 q_3) & q_0^2 - q_1^2 + q_2^2 - q_3^2 & 2(q_2 q_3 + q_0 q_1) \\ 2(q_1 q_3 - q_0 q_2) & 2(q_2 q_3 + q_0 q_1) & q_0^2 - q_1^2 - q_2^2 + q_3^2 \end{bmatrix} \begin{bmatrix} 0 \\ 0 \\ -g \end{bmatrix} \quad (3)$$

The gravity vector is expressed as $B = [V_X\ V_Y\ V_Z]$, The three-axis acceleration component measured by the accelerometer can be expressed as $A = [a_X\ a_Y\ a_Z]$.

The error vector between the measured acceleration and the theoretical acceleration of the carrier can be obtained by cross producting the vector A and B, and the gyroscope data can be PI corrected by the error vector.

$$\omega_\Delta = \begin{bmatrix} \omega_X \\ \omega_Y \\ \omega_Z \end{bmatrix} = \begin{bmatrix} k_p e_x + k_i \int e_x \\ k_p e_y + k_i \int e_y \\ k_p e_z + k_i \int e_z \end{bmatrix} \quad (4)$$

At the same time, the first-order Runge-Kutta method is used to update the quaternion to obtain a more accurate quaternion, which is finally converted into Euler angle according to Formula (2).

3 Kalman Algorithm Flow

1) Priori estimation formula and error covariance matrix

$$\hat{X}_{\bar{k}} = A_k \hat{X}_{K-1} + B_k U_k \quad (5)$$

$$P_{\bar{k}} = A_k P_{k-1} A_k^T + Q \quad (6)$$

In the formula, $\hat{X}_{\bar{k}}$ is the estimation of state variable $\hat{X}_{K-1}$, U_K is the control input, A_K is the state transition matrix, and B_K is the control variable matrix. P_K is the estimation of the error covariance P_{K-1}, Q is the process noise of the angle and angular velocity of the gyroscope, and the two noises are independent of each other.

2) Kalman gain update and Modified estimation

$$K_k = \frac{P_{\bar{k}} H_k^T}{H_k P_{\bar{k}} H_k^T + R} \quad (7)$$

$$\hat{X}_k = \hat{X}_{\bar{k}} + K_k [Z_k - H_k \hat{X}_{\bar{k}}] \quad (8)$$

In the formula, R is the observation noise covariance matrix, H_K is the observation matrix and $P_{\bar{k}}$ is the error covariance matrix. The formula (13) is used to update the state, and the estimated value and the observed value are fused, where K_K is the Kalman gain.

3) Updating the state covariance

$$P_k = [I - K_k H_k] P_{\bar{k}} \quad (9)$$

The error covariance matrix is updated by Kalman gain KK and observation matrix HK.

4 Kalman Filtering and Mahony Complementary Filtering Algorithm Fusion

The Mahony complementary filter provides the current quaternion, which calculates the theoretical body attitude angle. The first error vector (ex, ey, ez) results from the difference between the theoretical attitude and the Kalman filter-calculated attitude angle. The second error vector (Ex, Ey, Ez) is formed through the cross product operation of the conventional complementary filter, resulting in two sets of error vectors.

These error vectors are then regulated using PI control to construct a more precise fusion filtering operation, enhancing the accuracy of attitude angle calculation. The flow chart of the complementary filtering of Kalman and mahony is shown in Fig. 1.

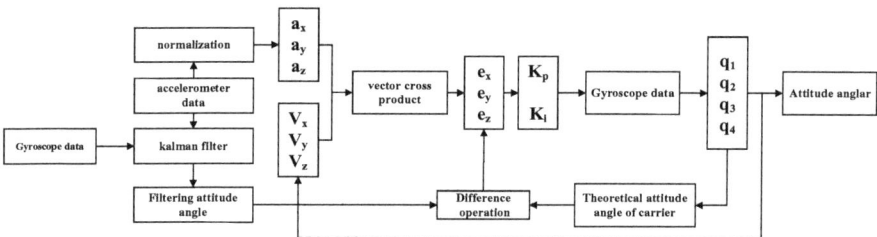

Fig. 1. Kalman and Mahony complementary filtering fusion algorithm flow chart

5 Experimental Simulation and Result Analysis

To assess the algorithm's feasibility and effectiveness, this experiment utilizes a high-performance microprocessor STM32F4 and a six-axis attitude sensor MPU6050, creating an attitude simulation system. The IMU module within the simulation system collects experimental data. Data is transmitted to the controller via I2C communication for processing, while serial communication links the controller to the host computer for real-time observation and analysis of experimental data and phenomena.

5.1 Static Experimental Analysis

The static experimental analysis is that the system is placed on the horizontal plane, and the data collected by the sensor is solved and analyzed. Figure 2a and b are the output data of the pitch angle and roll angle of the horizontal placement system when the system is stationary.

Figure 2 compares the static experiment. Theoretically, the attitude angle in a static state should be 0. However, as shown in the figure, when using the Mahony complementary filter alone to determine the roll and pitch angles, deviations occur due to sensor measurement accuracy and noise influence. In this paper algorithm, the Kalman filter is employed to filter noise and disturbances, effectively suppressing environmental noise and drift, thereby enhancing system stability.

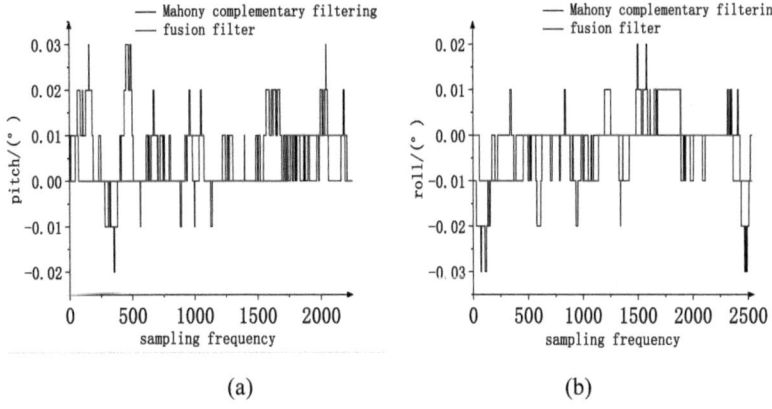

Fig. 2. (a) Static pitch angle; (b). Static roll angle

5.2 Dynamic Experimental Analysis

In the dynamic experiment, when the system is initially in the horizontal state, the system rotates at a certain angle. The influence of different algorithms on the angle is analyzed. Figure 3a and b are the output data of pitch angle and roll angle in dynamic experiment.

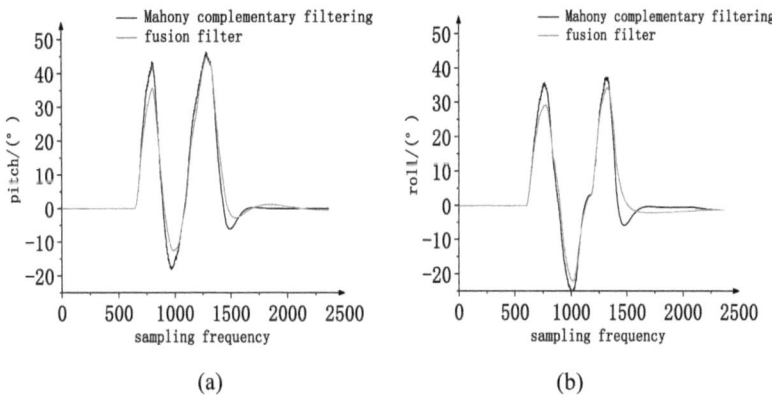

Fig. 3. (a) Dynamic pitch angle; (b) Dynamic roll angle

Through dynamic experimental comparisons, conventional complementary filtering is affected by noise, resulting in fluctuating angle changes and uncertain attitude angle errors. The system also shows significant overshoot and inadequate responsiveness. After algorithmic enhancements, the system exhibits more stable angle changes despite noise influence, achieving smoother transitions during peak periods. Furthermore, the system's anti-interference capability and stability performance are significantly improved.

As shown in Table 1, the mean square error and mean absolute error of the fusion filter are smaller than those of the Mahony complementary filter by comparing the roll angle error of the fusion filter and the Mahony filter under static state.

Table 1. Comparison of roll angle error

Algorithm	Max	Min	MSE	MAE
Mahony	0.02	−0.03	0.00805	0.0048
Ma-Kalm	0.01	−0.01	0.00581	0.0037

6 Conclusion

Based on the Kalman filter and Mahony complementary filter, this paper introduces a fusion complementary filter algorithm. It utilizes the Kalman filter to mitigate gyroscope integral drift and employs feedback control from the complementary filter to suppress accelerometer noise disturbance, thereby achieving more accurate current attitude angle determination. Experimental results demonstrate the algorithm's reliability in estimating attitude angle changes. Ultimately, the algorithm is simulated and validated through static and dynamic experiments, confirming its feasibility.

References

1. Liu, C., He, M., Dai, L.: Attitude solution method based on Mahony and improved Kalman fusion. J. Electron. Measur. Instrum. **09**, 64–71 (2022). https://doi.org/10.13382/j.jemi.B2205566
2. Zhu, P., Chen, W.P., Shi, Y., He, L.B., Xie, W.W., Yu, C.: Attitude solution method based on Mahony filtering and EKF fusion. Transducer Microsyst. Technol. **12**, 160–163+168 (2023). https://doi.org/10.13873/J.1000-9787(2023)12-0160-04
3. Liu, M., Cai, Y.L.: attitude calculation method of portable mobile robot based on complementary filtering. The 22nd China Academic Conference on System Simulation Technology and Its Applications (CCSSTA22nd 2021) Selected Essays (pp.376–380) Department of Electronics and Information, Xi 'an Jiaotong University (2021). https://doi.org/10.3390/mi12113 1373;
4. Guan, X.C., Liu, Z.F.: The application of gyroscope in UAV inertial navigation system. Sensor World **07**, 6–10 (2023). https://doi.org/10.16204/j.sw.issn.1006-883X. 2023.07.002
5. Chen, S.Q., Liu, M.: Design of AGV attitude calculation system based on STM32F767IGT6. Electron. Des. Eng. **05**, 70–74+79 (2023). https://doi.org/10.14022/j.issn1674-6236.2023.05.015
6. Yu, H.B., Jian, J.S., Yin, H.H.: Research on an aircraft attitude fusion algorithm. Electron. Measur. Technol. **03**, 80–85 (2023). https://doi.org/10.19651/j.cnki.emt. 2210594
7. Lu, Y.J., Chen, Y.D., Zhang, T.N., Li, Y.L., Zhao, W.P.: A practical quadrotor attitude fusion algorithm electronics optics & control **08**, 84–89 (2020). https://doi.org/10.3969/i.issn.1671-637X.2020.08.017
8. Sheng, G.R., Gao, G.W., Zhang, B.Y.: Research on quadrotor attitude calculation based on quaternion. Mod. Electron. Tech. **14**, 8–12+16 (2020). https://doi.org/10.16652/j.issn.1004-373x.2020.14.003
9. Lu, C.S.: Improved method for the complementary filtering attitude ofthe four-rotor aircraft. Electron. Measur. Technol. **18**, 69–73 (2020). https://doi.org/10.19651/j.cnki.emt.2004619
10. Mo, L., long, S.Y., Huang, R., Chen, M.Y.: Design of attitude calculation algorithm for small aircraft based on quaternion combined PI filter. Autom. Instru. **05**, 31–33 (2023). https://doi.org/10.14016/j.cnki.1001-9227.2023.05.031

Robot Modeling and Automation Control

Research and Design of Terminal Logistics and Distribution Robots

Hongji Chen[1(✉)], Yansheng Zhang[1], Yonghuan Yan[1], Qianhua Luo[1], and Kaishun Su[2]

[1] Electronic Information Engineering, Zhuhai College of Science and Technology, Zhuhai 519041, China
3281334148@qq.com
[2] Mechanical Engineering, Zhuhai College of Science and Technology, Zhuhai 519041, China

Abstract. With the development and application of robot technology in the industrial field, terminal logistics and distribution robot technology plays an increasingly important role in the field of intelligent logistics. The purpose of this study is to explore the design and optimization of terminal logistics and distribution robot systems to improve logistics and distribution efficiency, reduce costs, and meet the growing demand for distribution. In terms of robot navigation and perception, the safe and efficient movement of robots in complex environments is realized through the realization of panoramic calibration, automatic navigation, path planning and other technologies. Experimental verification shows that the designed terminal logistics distribution system can achieve effective autonomous distribution and stable and reliable operation, which will provide a reference for the development of terminal logistics and promote the intelligent and efficient development of logistics system.

Keywords: Automatic navigation · ROS · logistics and distribution · end-of-line logistics

1 Introduction

The mature development of the logistics market cannot be separated from the good end of the logistics distribution support [1]. With the increasingly mature development of the domestic logistics market, the quality of logistics services, logistics timeliness and so on put forward higher requirements, this project is to solve the problem of the end of the distribution, improve the quality of logistics services and logistics efficiency. Domestic logistics industry has been trapped in the "last kilometer" of the end of the distribution problem, some logistics enterprises end of the network investment is insufficient, management chaos, consumer complaints, service quality is worrying, difficult to meet the logistics market scale is increasing on the reality of the demand for end of the logistics distribution. The end of the logistics market is increasing in size [2].

In this paper, for the current end of the logistics distribution efficiency is insufficient, research and design of an end of the logistics distribution robot, the robot has a visual obstacle avoidance [3], automatic navigation [4], accurate placement, and other characteristics, can be in the courier site and express cabinets between the automatic delivery and loading and unloading of the intelligent logistics distribution robot. Mainly used in cities, campuses, and other express delivery environment, instead of the traditional courier personnel delivery of express delivery, reduce the end of the distribution cost at the same time also improve the efficiency of distribution, prompting the end of the delivery of intelligent and convenient, to solve the end of the problem of artificial distribution, to meet the growing scale of the logistics market for the distribution of the end of the distribution of logistics needs.

2 Robot Overall Structure Design

2.1 Mechanical Modelling

The mechanical structure of the end logistics delivery robot is an integrated intelligent service robot consisting of a chassis part composed of McNamm wheels, a robotic arm robotic arm part, and a express storage part. Enable robots to have strong flexibility and utilize the advantages of chassis to accurately and quickly pick up parcels for delivery. After multiple iterations and calculations such as motion simulation and finite element analysis, the improved model theoretically combines the advantages of mechanical structure strength, high precision in gripping express delivery, lightweight, easy maintenance, strong delivery ability, good stretchability, flexibility, and beautiful appearance. The overall mechanical structure of the robot is shown in Fig. 1.

Fig. 1. Overall structure diagram of the robot.

2.2 Chassis Structure

The chassis structure uses Mecanum wheel and the omni-directional intelligent mobile platform is capable of panning and rotating in place in any direction for great maneuverability [5]. As shown in Fig. 2, this innovative design allows the omnidirectional intelligent mobile platform to move freely in any direction, including translation and rotation in place. This versatility is crucial for navigating complex environments and tight spaces, making it particularly suitable for applications that require precise movement and positioning. With its ability to move smoothly across various terrains, the platform can easily adapt to different operational demands, enhancing its overall functionality.

In addition to the advanced wheel design, the platform is equipped with a sophisticated shock absorption system utilizing a cross-arm independent suspension. As illustrated in Fig. 2, this suspension mechanism significantly enhances the stability of the chassis by evenly distributing the platform's weight, improving its performance on uneven or rough surfaces. By effectively reducing vibrations and shocks, this system ensures a smoother ride, which is essential for maintaining the integrity of sensitive equipment installed on the platform. Together, these features create a robust and reliable mobile platform capable of efficiently and accurately handling a variety of tasks.

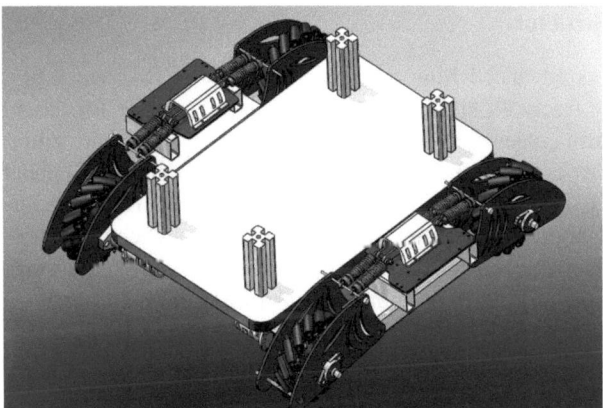

Fig. 2. Robot chassis structure.

2.3 Courier Storage Structure

The express storage area is a meticulously designed space with high functionality. Its storage cabinet is intelligently divided into eight compartments, capable of holding at least 80 packages simultaneously, ensuring each parcel is organized and easily accessible. Additionally, the area is equipped with advanced sensors that can instantly recognize the status of the packages and provide relevant recipient information and instructions through a display screen, significantly enhancing management efficiency.

Moreover, the express storage area features powerful front lights that automatically illuminate in low-light conditions, allowing staff to easily locate and retrieve packages even in dim environments. This comprehensive design not only improves operational safety and efficiency but also greatly enhances the user experience, making the package handling process smoother overall, as depicted in Fig. 3.

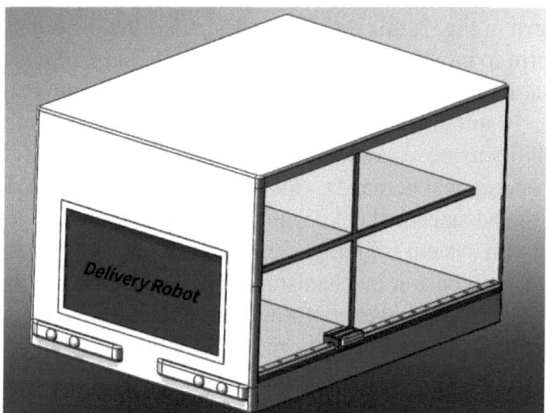

Fig. 3. Robot storage structure.

2.4 Chassis Structure

The base adopts advanced Motorized rails technology [6], which gives the arm the ability to move freely on specific axes, increasing the space for the arm-manipulator to move. The arm consists of 6 degrees of freedom, which greatly improves flexibility and stability. The arm has excellent telescopic performance and is capable of gripping couriers up to two times taller than the robot. The transmission design of the robotic arm extension adopts the structure of incomplete gears, when the robotic arm grips the courier, it realizes the self-locking function, preventing the phenomenon of dropping and damage in the process of gripping, as illustrated in Fig. 4.

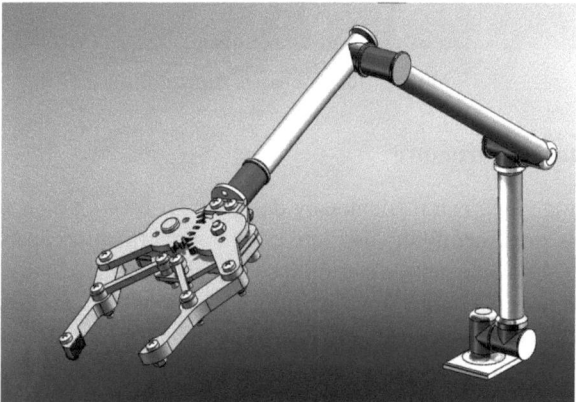

Fig. 4. Robot arm structure.

3 Robot Hardware System Design

The hardware system design of the end-to-end logistics and distribution robot includes a positioning and navigation system, a data processing system, a perception system, a motion control system and a human-machine interaction system. The positioning and navigation system uses GPS and Bei Dou hardware modules to determine the robot's position, the sensing system includes LIDAR and depth camera for environment mapping and obstacle avoidance, the motion control system consists of IMU attitude sensors, the power supply system, the motor drive module and 3508 brushless motors, the data processing system consists of the industrial computer and STM32F4071GH6 microcontroller, and the human-machine interactive system The interaction between the user and the robot is realized through the console APP.s shown in Fig. 5.

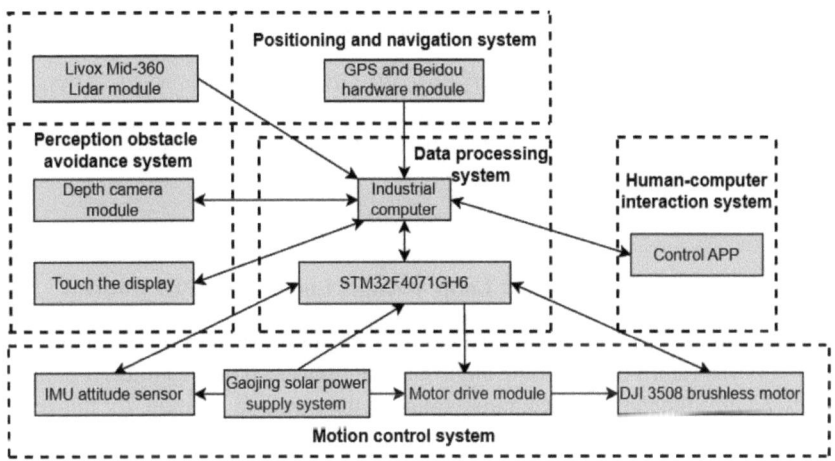

Fig. 5. Hardware System Design Diagram.

4 Motion Control Algorithm Design

The traditional classical PID as a reliable closed-loop feedback control algorithm is widely used in the direction of motor control [7], in the motor control of end-of-line logistics and distribution robots, which is mainly divided into two aspects:1. Chassis control; robotic arm control, and based on the classical PID for series-parallel level algorithm improvement.

4.1 Incremental Current Loop PID Control of Chassis Motor

Wheel chassis consists of four brushless motors with speed value feedback, in the absence of feedback, measured once the input current, that is, directly out of control to full-speed rotation, very dangerous, the force is enough to damage the entire chassis of the mechanical structure, that is, the proposed use of this improved incremental PID, the following is the incremental current-loop PID details:

Simulate the PID algorithm expression:

$$u(t) = K_P\left[e(t) + \frac{1}{T_1}\int_0^t e(t)dt + T_D\frac{de(t)}{dt}\right] \quad (1)$$

u(t): output of the PID system.

e(t): : The error generated by the PID system, i.e. the error between the set value r(t) and the measured feedback value y(t);

K_P, T_1, T_D: They are the proportional, integral, and differential coefficients of the regulator, respectively.

Analogue PID can not be directly used in practice, so it needs to be improved to incremental PID, incremental PID algorithms using weighted processing, do not need to accumulate. Secondly, the robot control modes are various, and the mode switching can be done with little impact, thus achieving disturbance-free switching[8].

Improved incremental PID algorithm expression:

$$u(k) = K_k[(e(k) - e(k-1) + T_i e(k) + T_d(e(k) - 2e(k-1) + e(k-2))] \quad (2)$$

K_k: Incremental controller proportional amplification factor;
T_i: Points time;
T_d: Differential time;

4.2 Robotic Arm Motor Current Loop + Angle Loop Series PID Control

Robotic arm consists of multiple gimbal motors with hollow shaft design, such precision type motors can return the real-time angle and rotation speed of the motor, robotic arm synergy requires the motor to accurately rotate to the specified position, for this reason, the robot is controlled by a current loop + angle loop string level PID. The following is a detailed explanation of the current loop + angle loop string level PID:

The basic equations for the control of the robot arm are not very different from the above, the special item to note is that this part of the control uses a series PID, which uses the target angle quantity to pull the velocity quantity, thus realizing the series loop control [9]. The schematic diagram of the cascaded PID control for the robotic arm is shown in Fig. 6.

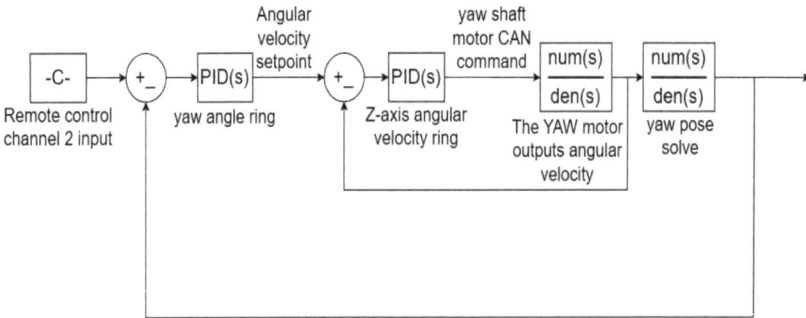

Fig. 6. Block diagram of serial PID control of robotic arm.

5 Automatic Navigation System Design

5.1 Positioning Map Building Algorithm

The construction of 3D information maps is crucial in path planning, and the localization and map building algorithm adopts SLAM (Simultaneous Localization And Mapping) technology, i.e. simultaneous localization and map building. The framework diagram of the localization and mapping algorithm is shown in Fig. 7. The algorithm first performs feature extraction based on the LiDAR scanning data, splits the high-precision 3D point cloud data into some local regions, and extracts SURF feature descriptors for each local region, and then uses these feature descriptors for matching and tracking, so as to obtain the robot's trajectory, and constructs the map in the process.

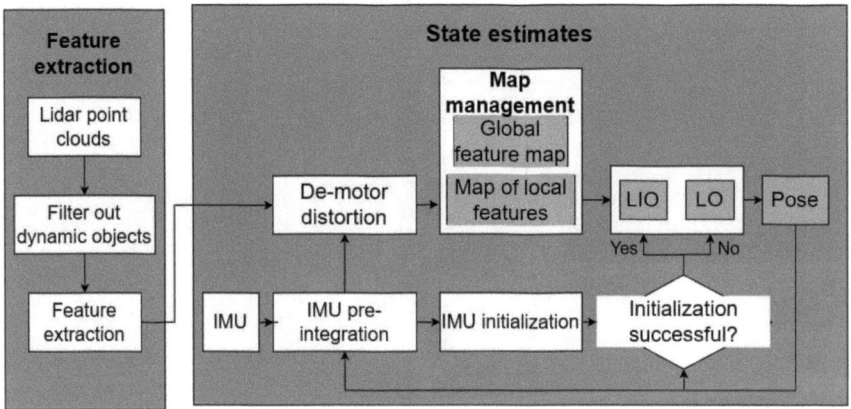

Fig. 7. Framework diagram of the algorithm for positioning map building.

5.2 Positioning Map Building Algorithm

In the development of autonomous driving technology, 360-degree panoramic calibration is a key process to ensure vehicle safety and precise operation. This process combines 3D lidar with depth cameras to achieve real-time perception of the surrounding environment through comprehensive data collection and processing. First, the system collects raw information from the lidar and camera. This data is then preprocessed to remove noise and format it properly to ensure accuracy in subsequent analyses. The feature extraction step identifies key features from the processed data to facilitate the joint calibration of the camera and lidar. Effective joint calibration integrates information from both sensors, forming a high-precision environmental model that provides accurate positioning for the vehicle. At the same time, the calibration of visual-inertial sensors further enhances the system's stability, allowing the vehicle to navigate more precisely in complex environments.

To ensure the reliability of the autonomous driving system [10] in various conditions, the calibration process must undergo thorough testing and validation across different road and weather scenarios. This includes various lighting conditions, rain and snow, as well as different road surfaces, all of which can impact sensor performance. Depending on the type of vehicle and system, the calibration methods and parameter settings may vary. For instance, heavier vehicles may require adjustments to sensor sensitivity to accommodate higher centers of gravity and different dynamic responses. Validating the results of real-time calibration is also essential for ensuring the system functions correctly; this process not only detects potential errors but also allows for optimization adjustments to enhance overall performance. The real-time calibration results for the designed road surface are illustrated in Fig. 8, demonstrating the application effects of this process in autonomous driving technology.

Fig. 8. Panoramic calibration effect.

5.3 Positioning Map Building Algorithm

The two algorithms with the most applications and better results are Dijkstra's algorithm [11] Aster's algorithm [12]. Star's algorithm has the characteristics of fast computing speed and strong inspiration, and it can find a shortest path in a very short time to achieve global path planning.

The core estimation function of the Aster algorithm:

$$f(n) = g(n) + h(n) \tag{3}$$

Among them:

h(n) is an estimate of the cost of getting from the initial state to the goal state via state n.

g(n) is the actual cost of getting from the initial state to state.

f(n) is the estimated cost of the best path from state n to the goal state.

When the distribution robot carries out the distribution task, the A* algorithm can search for the optimal path from the starting point to the end point more efficiently in the complex environment, dynamically adjust the path planning, and quickly converge to the optimal solution using the heuristic function, so that the distribution robot can complete the logistics and distribution task more safely and efficiently. The experimental simulation results are shown in Fig. 9.

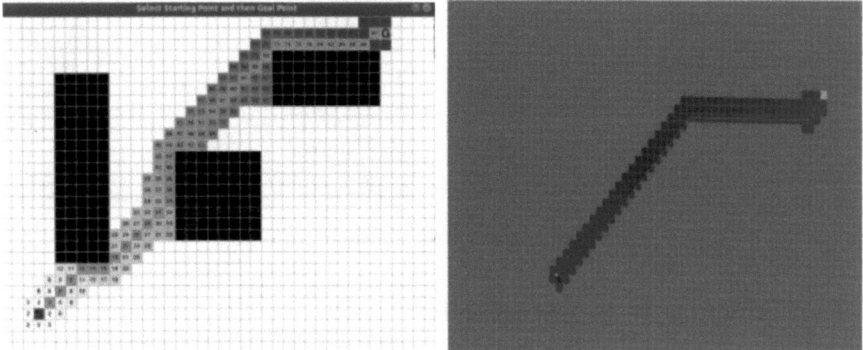

Fig. 9. Simulation of A* algorithm.

5.4 Positioning Map Building Algorithm

When the map is constructed, the end-of-pipe delivery robot achieves automatic navigation through global path planning and local path planning algorithms path planning algorithms, usually in the following steps:

a. Global path planning: generates a rough path using the Aster algorithm based on the start and end points.
b. Local cost map generation: a local cost map is generated in the area around the robot using sensor data to record information such as the location and size of obstacles in the area.
c. Local path planning: a local path is generated using a local path planning algorithm (e.g. DWA algorithm) based on a local cost map. The local path planning algorithm takes into account dynamic factors such as the robot's current speed, acceleration, etc. and controls the local path according to the planned local path [13].
d. Path tracking: the robot performs trajectory tracking based on the velocity and angular velocity output from the local path planning algorithm. The robot constantly compares itself with the local path and re-runs the path planning if it finds that the local path is no longer feasible.
e. Repeat the previous steps: The robot will constantly update its state and sense changes in the environment during its actual movement, and it is necessary to constantly repeat the above steps to ensure that the robot can move safely and efficiently.

The global and local planning results are shown in Fig. 10.

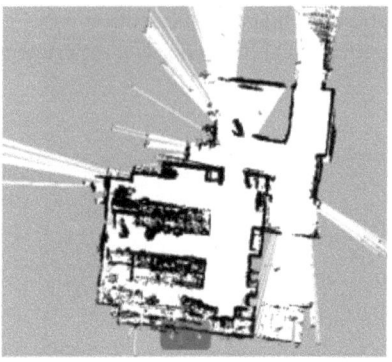 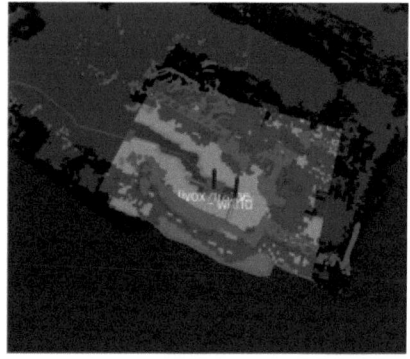

Fig. 10. Global and local planning effects

6 Experimental Tests and Results

The end distribution robot combines the ability of local path planning algorithms and the efficient global path planning ability of A* algorithms to achieve a multi-point navigation system with real-time sensing and path planning capabilities. The system is able to intelligently plan the optimal path to complete the delivery task, and can avoid obstacles in the dynamic environment to achieve efficient and flexible multi-point delivery making the delivery robot more adaptable to diversified delivery needs and able to intelligently plan the optimal path to complete the complex task of delivering to multiple destinations.

We build a simulated distribution scene inside the lab, including setting up obstacles, target points and robot movement areas to ensure that the experimental environment can simulate a real distribution scene. The designed multipoint navigation system was finally deployed to the robot for experimentation and successfully achieved multipoint navigation to deliver the goods to the three specified destinations, and the experimental test results are shown in Fig. 11.

Fig. 11. Experimental test effect diagram

7 Conclusion

Under the new situation, low-risk logistics and distribution is the trend, and the end-of-life logistics and distribution robots have a strong potential for market development. In this paper, according to the existing problems of the "last kilometer" end distribution link, a multi-sensor fusion end logistics distribution robot is designed, which uses LiDAR and depth camera module to sense the environment, and coordinates the work of each module through STM32 to accurately deliver the goods to the destination and put the courier into the courier cabinet through the robotic arm. Into the courier cabinet. At the same time, we have built a multi-dimensional scene of distribution robots and explored the functional architecture of intelligent unmanned delivery vehicles under the user demand, which greatly reduces the risk of the current urban logistics in the "last kilometer" end of the intelligent distribution, and improves the efficiency of the express "last kilometer" distribution. I believe that the unmanned express delivery vehicle will create more convenience for people's life, and better enhance the user experience.

Acknowledgments. This project is supported by the 2023 National College Student Innovation and Entrepreneurship Program, with project number S202313684004.

References

1. Shuo, W.: Research on the terminal delivery model of community logistics in the E-commerce environment in China. Mod. Mark. **5**, 54–57 (2021)
2. Sishi, G.: Research on the last mile delivery issues in E-commerce logistics. Logistics Eng. Manage. **43**(2), 81–84 (2021). https://doi.org/10.3969/j.issn.1674-4993.2021.02.023
3. Nascimento, M., Vicente, P., Bernardino, A.: 2D visual serving meets rapidly-exploring random trees for collision avoidance. In: 2020 IEEE International Conference on Autonomous Robot Systems and Competitions (ICARSC), Ponta Delgada, Portugal, pp.227–232 (2020). https://doi.org/10.1109/ICARSC49921.2020.9096133
4. Chenbeixi, Z., Zhiqiu, H.: An overview of automated guided vehicle (AGV) development. China Manuf. Inf. **39**(01), 53–59 (2010)
5. Jia, Q., Wang, M., Liu, S., Ge, J., Gu, C.: Research and development of mecanum-wheeled omnidirectional mobile robot implemented by multiple control methods. In: 2016 23rd International Conference on Mechatronics and Machine Vision in Practice (M2VIP), Nanjing, China, pp. 1–4 (2016). https://doi.org/10.1109/M2VIP.2016.7827337
6. Peijie, Z., Haojian, J.: Lean improvement research on the assembly line of automotive seat slide rails. Manuf. Autom. **44**(04), 40–44 (2022)
7. Keviczky, L., Bányász, C.: On the robustness of classical PID regulators: 2017 12th IEEE Conference on Industrial Electronics and Applications (ICIEA), Siem Reap, Cambodia, pp. 750–756 (2017). https://doi.org/10.1109/ICIEA.2017.8282940
8. Yan, Y., Zeng, R., Huang, Z., Chen, J., Xu, G., Ling, L.: Research on automotive balance chair posture control based on cascade PID. 2023 4th International Conference on Mechatronics Technology and Intelligent Manufacturing (ICMTIM), Nanjing, China, pp. 339–342 (2023). https://doi.org/10.1109/ICMTIM58873.2023.10246739
9. Baogang, H., Hao, Y.: A review of research and development on fuzzy PID control technology and some important issues it faces. Acta Automatica Sinica **04**, 567–584 (2001). https://doi.org/10.16383/j.aas.2001.04.011

10. Hailei, R.: Research on panoramic synthesis method based on multi-camera calibration. [Dissertation]. Xidian University (2019). https://doi.org/10.27389/d.cnki.gxadu.2019.002877
11. Bozyiğit, A., Alankuş, G., Nasiboğlu, E.: Public transport route planning: Modified dijkstra's algorithm. In: 2017 International Conference on Computer Science and Engineering (UBMK), Antalya, Turkey, pp. 502–505 (2017). https://doi.org/10.1109/UBMK.2017.8093444
12. Hart, P.E., Nilsson, N.J., Raphael, B.: A Formal basis for the heuristic determination of minimum cost paths. IEEE Trans. Syst. Sci. Cybern. **4**(2), 100–107 (1968). https://doi.org/10.1109/TSSC.1968.300136
13. Wang, H., Zhang, Z., Huang, X.: Improve the robot path planning based on the integration of A* and DWA. In: 2022 2nd International Conference on Algorithms, High Performance Computing and Artificial

Research and Implementation of Anti-Pinch Function for Car Windows Based on Microcontroller

Zhiguo Zheng[1,2], Zhujun Jiang[1], Xiaowei Zhao[1(✉)], and Jie Chen[1]

[1] School of Information Engineering, Hainan Vocational University of Science and Technology, Haikou, China
626486436@qq.com

[2] School of Information and Communication Engineering, Hainan University, Haikou, China

Abstract. In daily travel, there are numerous instances of car windows causing injuries through pinching. Based on this, this article proposes a study on the anti-pinch function of car windows using a microcontroller. This study uses the CC2530 microcontroller as the main control chip, employing a pressure sensor to detect the pressure on the car windows, and periodically collecting data. When the detected pressure exceeds a preset value, the car window is controlled to retract appropriately. Additionally, a coordinator node is used to connect to a WiFi communication module to enable remote control of the car window. This design allows for intelligent control of the car window based on the pressure detected, and users can also remotely control the window raising and lowering through their smartphones. This achieves intelligent, wireless, and networked control of car windows, offering a very broad development prospect.

Keywords: Microcontroller · Anti-pinch Window · CC2530 · WiFi · Remote Control

1 Introduction

In light of incidents involving car windows injuring people, the United States enacted regulations in 2008 under FMSS18, which mandate that all car windows with electric functionality must automatically retract to release obstructions in the event of an accident. It explicitly requires that the pinching force must not exceed 100N to ensure that it does not cause harm to the human body. This also helps to prevent motor overload and serves a self-protection role [1]. Similarly, China issued the GB11552–2009 "Protrusions Inside Passenger Cars" regulation in 2009, which strictly limits and controls the anti-pinch function of electric car windows in our country [2].

This article utilizes the HX711 pressure sensor for real-time monitoring of the pressure on car windows. When it detects that the pressure exerted on the window exceeds a set threshold, the window automatically lowers to release the obstruction and emits an alarm sound through the buzzer. At the same time, data is transmitted to the OneNET cloud platform via a WiFi communication module. The OneNET cloud platform communicates with the mobile app through the HTTP protocol, enabling users to remotely control the raising and lowering of the car window via their smartphones, thus playing a protective role.

2 Related Work

2.1 ZigBee Technology

Zigbee is a low-power local area network communication protocol that complies with the IEEE 802.15.4 standard. Technologies developed according to this standard primarily support short-range, low-power wireless communication. Its advantages include short-range communication, simple architecture, self-organizing networks, energy efficiency, low transmission rates, and low cost. It is mainly used in automation and aggregated control fields and can be integrated into various devices [3]. In this paper, Zigbee is primarily used to complete the internal communication of the system, allowing the coordinator and terminals to quickly establish connections and thus transmit data.

2.2 WiFi Wireless Communication Technology

In the IoT environment, WiFi communication technology has been continuously evolving and improving. This technology has low development costs, fast transmission rates, long transmission distances, and a wide coverage area. It plays a crucial role in enabling real-time data transmission and communication between car windows and cloud platforms.

2.3 Sensor Technology

Sensors, as a crucial means of information acquisition, along with communication technology and computer technology, constitute the three pillars of information technology. The HX711 pressure sensor selected for this article, with its high sensitivity, can accurately detect pressure changes between the car window and any obstacles. It plays an important role in this system.

2.4 Pressure Detection Module

The function of the pressure detection module is to detect the real-time pressure exerted on the car window and send the pressure data to the coordinator through the ZigBee network. After receiving the data, the coordinator uses the WiFi module and MQTT protocol to upload the data to the OneNET cloud platform. Therefore, the main functions of the pressure detection module include collecting pressure data and uploading data to the cloud platform.

2.5 Automatic Window Lowering Module

The hardware required for the window raising/lowering module is a stepper motor. The main function of this module is when the pressure sensor located at the terminal detects pressure exceeding a set value, the terminal calls the corresponding function to drive the motor in a clockwise direction, thereby opening the window.

3 System Principles and Composition

3.1 System Working Principle

This article provides a research design for anti-pinch technology for car windows, centered around a microcontroller. This technology involves elements such as terminal devices, coordination devices, remote control, and wireless network communication modules. The terminal nodes are responsible for collecting pressure data and intelligently controlling the lowering of the windows and the activation of the buzzer alarm. Using a ZigBee network, this data is transmitted to the coordinator node [4]. Subsequently, the coordinator node forwards the data to a WiFi communication component. This component uploads the data to a cloud server using the MQTT protocol. On the cloud server, the HTTP protocol is used to communicate with applets and to send commands to the WiFi component.

Thus, users can issue commands through the remote control module (composed of the cloud platform and applets). These commands are first sent to the WiFi communication component and then transmitted to the coordinator node. Ultimately, the terminal nodes carry out the corresponding actions based on the received commands, thereby achieving networked control of the car windows. The system composition diagram is shown in Fig. 1.

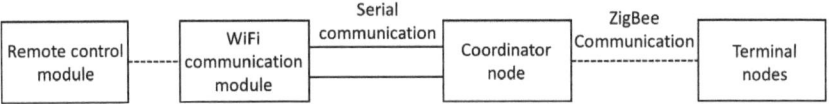

Fig. 1. System architecture diagram.

3.2 System Operating Mode

The HX711 pressure sensor is installed at the lower end of the car window glass to detect any external forces that may obstruct the window from rising, and it is connected via circuit to the CC2530 main control board. The CC2530 main control board continuously monitors the status of the HX711 pressure sensor and is connected to the stepper motor driver board to control motor rotation. It is also connected to a buzzer to manage the alarm function. Additionally, a WiFi module is connected to the CC2530 main control board to enable remote control of the window. The motor, which is connected to the window glass, facilitates the upward or downward movement of the glass. A schematic diagram showing the integration of the hardware with the window is shown in Fig. 2.

3.3 Working Principle

The terminal node is responsible for collecting pressure data and intelligently controlling the window by driving the motor. Using a ZigBee network, this data is transmitted to the coordinator node. Upon receiving the data, the coordinator node makes a decision

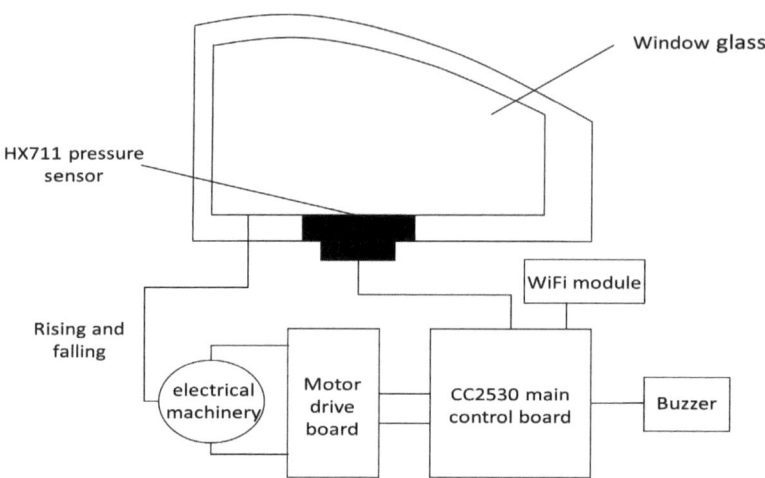

Fig. 2. Schematic Diagram of Hardware Integration with Car Window.

on whether to activate the buzzer. Subsequently, the coordinator node sends the data through a serial port to the WiFi communication component. This component uploads the data to the cloud server using the MQTT protocol. On the cloud server, the HTTP protocol is used to communicate with the mini-program and send instructions to the WiFi component.

Therefore, users can issue commands through the remote control unit, which consists of a combination of the cloud platform and the mini-program. These commands are first sent to the WiFi communication component, then forwarded to the coordinator node. Ultimately, the terminal node executes the corresponding operation based on the received instructions, thus achieving networked control of the car windows.

3.4 Key Technologies

1. Internet of Things(IoT) Technology.

Internet of Things (IoT) technology refers to a network technology that connects physical objects and the Internet by using information sensing devices such as Radio-Frequency Identification (RFID), infrared sensors, and laser scanners based on set protocols. This enables the exchange of information between physical objects and the Internet, facilitating intelligent recognition, positioning, and monitoring. IoT relies on current Internet network technology and serves as an expansion and extension of Internet technology. It not only allows Internet users to interact with tangible objects but also effectively enables communication and information exchange between objects.

Regarding the application of the Internet of Things, it involves three core elements: the perception layer, the network transmission layer, and the application layer. In the perception layer, the main responsibility is to collect information about the surrounding environment, including various physical quantities, sound, images, etc. The network transmission layer effectively transmits the collected information through various communication methods such as WiFi, Bluetooth, Ethernet, etc. The application layer transforms the collected information into visual and operational information through data analysis and processing techniques, making it easy for users to use and make decisions. The structured system of the Internet of Things helps developers to have a clearer understanding of its operational logic and practical application scenarios.

2. WIFI Wireless Communication Technology.

The full English name for WiFi wireless communication technology is Wireless Fidelity. The initial foundation of WiFi wireless communication technology protocols was based on the IEEE 802.11 standard, with the highest transmission rate reaching only 2 Mbps [5]. However, with the continuous development and exploration of wireless communication technology, different versions have emerged. In September 1999, the international community established two standards, 802.11a and 802.11b. At that time, projects based on 802.11a were relatively few, and the landscape of wireless local area networks was fundamentally changed with the introduction of 802.11b. After several years of research, 802.11 g was released in June 2003. This standard's working frequency band could reach 2.4 GHz, effectively improving the transmission rate of WiFi wireless communication technology, which gradually made WiFi wireless communication technology more widely known and utilized. The detailed development history of WiFi wireless communication technology is shown in Table 1.

Table 1. Development History of WIFI Wireless Communication Technology

WiFi Version	WiFi Standard	Release Date	Maximum Speed	Operating Frequency Band
WiFi 0	IEEE 802.11	1997	2 Mbps	2.4 GHz
WiFi 1	IEEE 802.11a	1999	54 Mbps	5 GHz
WiFi 2	IEEE 802.11b	1999	11 Mbps	2.4 GHz
WiFi 3	IEEE 802.11g	2003	54 Mbps	2.4 GHz
WiFi 4	IEEE 802.11n	2009	600 Mbps	2.4 GHz,5 GHz
WiFi 5	IEEE 802.11ac	2014	1 Gbps	5 GHz
WiFi 6	IEEE 802.11ax	2019	11 Gbps	2.4 GHz,5 GHz
WiFi 7	IEEE 802.11be	2022	30 Gbps	2.4 GHz,5 GHz, 6 GHz

With the continuous deepening exploration of wireless WiFi communication technology, WiFi communication technology is gradually integrating into various aspects of human life. Its simple and convenient operation allows for network connectivity over short distances, making it widely adopted by users and manufacturers, rapidly capturing the market. Compared with infrared technology, WiFi communication technology has a wider bandwidth and stronger penetration, making it highly favored in the field of smart homes. Consumers can use WiFi communication technology to freely control devices in remote rooms from places like bedrooms and kitchens. Additionally, the easy installation and operability of WiFi significantly reduce labor costs. Therefore, WiFi is widely used due to its low development costs, long transmission distances, relatively stable signals, and many other advantages.

To date, WiFi communication technology has been widely adopted globally. In the Internet of Things environment, WiFi communication technology has continuously evolved and improved over the long term. This technology has low development costs, fast transmission rates, long transmission distances, and wide coverage areas. Additionally, information is transmitted under low energy consumption conditions, so there is no need to worry about adverse effects on human health. WiFi devices are highly ubiquitous and widely used in various devices such as smartphones, tablets, and laptops. In this research paper, choosing WiFi communication technology as the communication method may be more readily accepted.

3.5 System Hardware Composition

The hardware used in this article primarily includes: two main control units, the CC2530 microcontrollers (divided into terminal and coordinator), the car window lifting control hardware ULN2003 stepper motor, the car window pressure detection hardware HX711 pressure sensor, the alarm hardware buzzer, and the WiFi communication hardware ESP-12F. The hardware composition is shown in Fig. 3.

Fig. 3. Hardware Components.

The system contains the following hardware modules.

1. Hardware Boards

CC2530 is a low-power wireless integrated processor chip introduced by Texas Instruments (TI), consisting of a microprocessing unit based on the 8051 core, a 2.4 GHz IEEE 802.15.4/Zigbee wireless transceiver, and various connectivity components. It features advantages such as low power consumption, strong reliability, and long-distance communication, making it widely used in IoT devices, including smart homes, industrial automation, smart security, and other fields.

Given that this chip itself possesses excellent data processing capabilities, equivalent to a strengthened 51 core, coupled with its built-in ZigBee short-range wireless communication technology, it can effectively assist in achieving wireless control of various window switches. Additionally, the outstanding scalability of the ZStack protocol stack makes it a choice for selecting this chip. To more effectively achieve the required performance, it is necessary to build an expansion baseboard to form a simple development board. The core board and baseboard of the hardware circuit are shown in Fig. 4.

Fig. 4. Core Board and Baseboard

2. Pressure Sensor

The working principle of the HX711 pressure sensor is as follows: When the power pin is connected to a 5 V voltage, the sensor starts collecting data on the pressure applied to the car window. It senses the strain caused by pressure changes and converts this strain into an electrical signal. This electrical signal is a small voltage change that is received through the differential input channels (A+, A-) of the HX711. Inside the HX711 chip, this voltage signal is converted into a digital signal through a 24-bit Σ-Δ analog-to-digital converter (ADC). This conversion process provides high-precision weight measurements. To adapt to various sensors and application scenarios, the HX711 offers multiple gain and offset calibration options, allowing adjustments to gain and offset to accommodate different ranges and accuracies of sensor outputs.

3. Stepper Motor

The stepper motor, as a type of closed-loop control system, converts electrical signals into angular or linear movements. Typically, its rotation speed and final braking position are determined by the frequency and quantity of input pulse signals. Whenever the driver receives a pulse, it guides the motor to rotate a constant angle in a predetermined direction, which is why it is called a "stepper" motor. Compared to DC motors with speed control, stepper motors are easier to control and meet design requirements, making them a common choice. When controlling a stepper motor, a driver module must be equipped, and using a circuit unit with a ULN2003 (featuring high voltage tolerance and capable of handling large currents in a Darlington configuration) as the driver is a common choice.

4. ESP-12 Module

The main function of the wireless network communication component is to receive remote control instructions transmitted from the cloud and then distribute them to hub nodes via a serial interface, which then forwards them to end devices, enabling remote control operation of end devices. When selecting a wireless network communication module, the ESP-12F module can be considered. Developed by Ai-Thinker Technology, this module contains the ESP8266 microcontroller from Espressif Systems. This processor integrates an advanced Tensilica Xtensa L106 ultra-low-power 32-bit MCU into a compact package, capable of running in a 16-bit energy-saving mode and operating at frequencies of 80 MHz or 160 MHz. The module supports a real-time operating system (RTOS) and integrates the Wi-Fi media access control layer (MAC), baseband (BB), radio frequency (RF), power amplifier (PA), and low-noise amplifier (LNA) together, along with an onboard antenna.

3.6 System Software Composition

The software part mainly includes the core code for the stepper motor driver, the core code for buzzer triggering, the core code for pressure detection, and the core code for cloud platform integration.

4 Results

Test Scenario 1: During the slow upward movement of the car window, without any external pressure, the anti-pinch function is not triggered. Test Scenario 1 is shown in Fig. 5.

Test Scenario 2: During the slow upward movement of the car window, external pressure is applied, but the pressure does not reach the triggering threshold. In this case, the anti-pinch function is not triggered. Test Scenario 2 is shown in Fig. 6.

Test Scenario 3: During the slow upward movement of the car window, external pressure is applied, and the pressure reaches the triggering threshold. In this case, the anti-pinch function is triggered. The stepper motor rotates clockwise to retract the window, and the buzzer sounds an alarm. The user can choose to control the window remotely through their smartphone. Test Scenario 3 is shown in Fig. 7.

After the code is uploaded, real-time data on the pressure exerted on the car window can be viewed on the OneNet cloud platform, and historical data can also be accessed. In

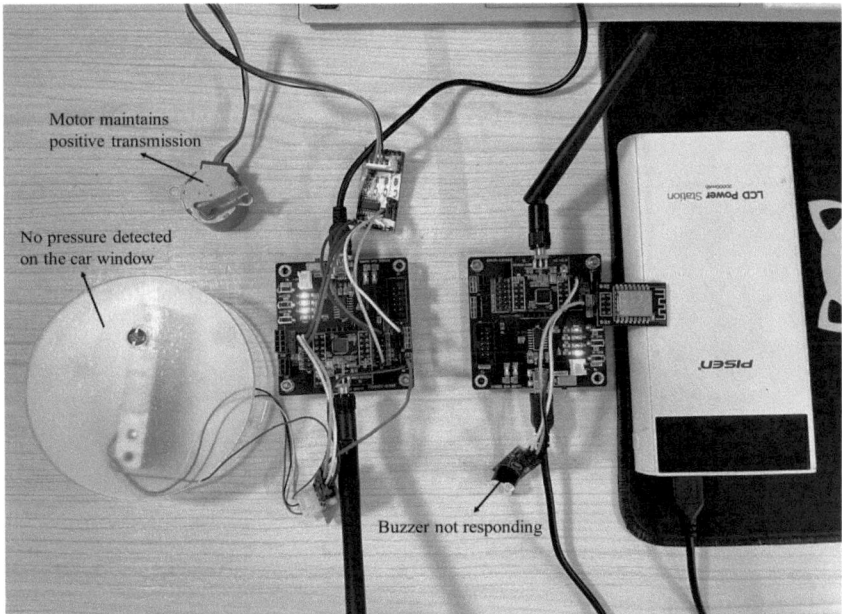

Fig. 5. Test Scenario 1.

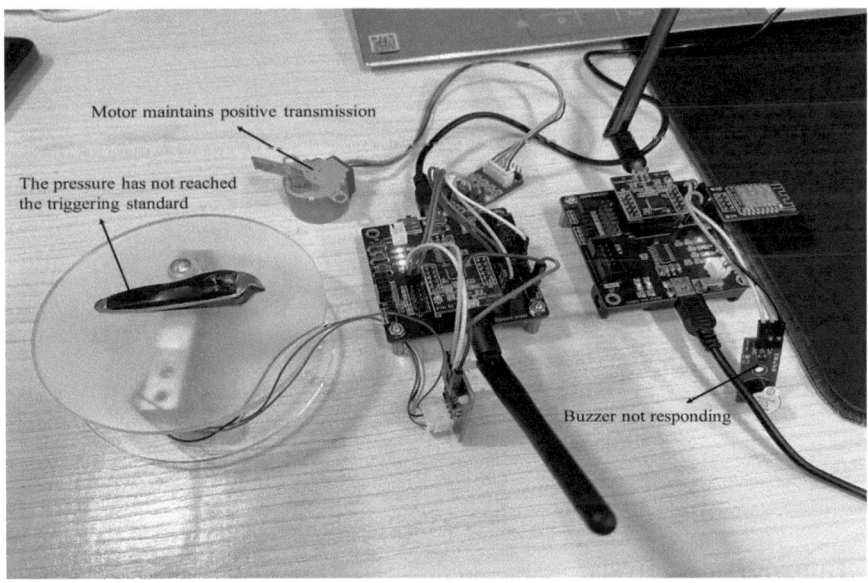

Fig. 6. Test Scenario 2

practical application scenarios, if the pressure exceeds the set threshold, the car window

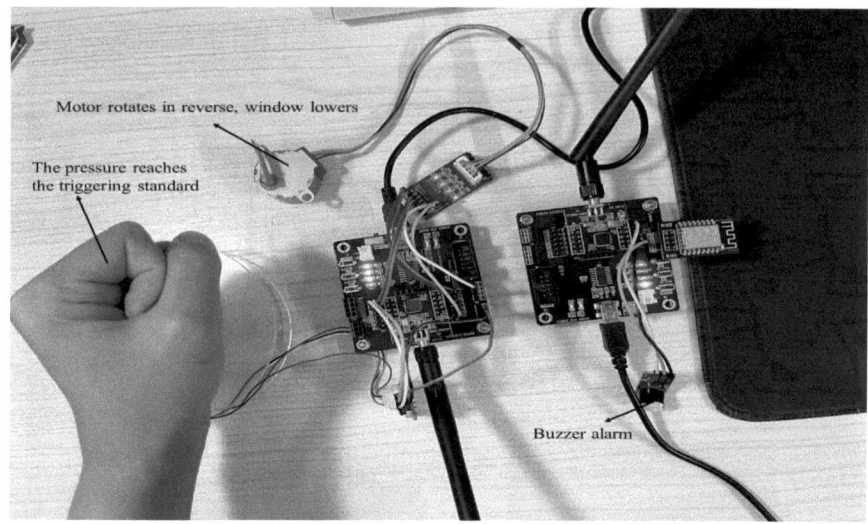

Fig. 7. Test Scenario 3

will automatically retract and the buzzer will start to alarm. The data flow of the car window pressure is shown in Fig. 8.

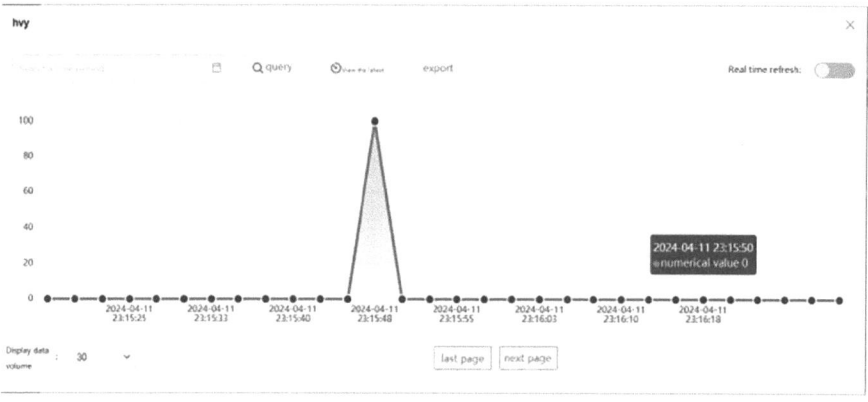

Fig. 8. Car Window Pressure Data Flow

5 Innovative Analysis

5.1 Compared to the Hall Sensor Solution

The Hall sensor solution, due to its simple design, convenient implementation, and straightforward mathematical modeling methods, as well as its self-learning capabilities, has found wide application in the market. However, it has a higher cost compared to other solutions because it inherently includes Hall sensors and requires motors with circular Hall sensors. Additionally, it requires high installation precision as it must be aligned vertically with the circular Hall sensors, resulting in higher overall development costs [4].

5.2 Compared to the Current Ripple Solution

For the current ripple solution for motors, this approach is based solely on the general characteristics of the motor. While this solution can reduce costs, its main technical challenge lies in eliminating interference spikes during current ripple detection. These spikes are related to the contact between the motor brushes and commutator, as well as the electrochemical corrosion conditions. Over time, these issues can gradually worsen, affecting the reliability of window anti-pinch systems [6].

Compared to the above two anti-pinch solutions, this paper uses the HX711 pressure sensor to determine the triggering of the anti-pinch function for car windows. This effectively solves the issues of high development costs and technical challenges. By connecting the pressure sensor to the car window, it can monitor the pressure changes during the window closing process in real-time. It can quickly react when the window encounters an obstacle, thereby effectively preventing pinching injuries.

6 Discussion

In the automotive field, this design can also be applied in multiple scenarios, such as the widespread use in automatic opening and closing systems of electric car doors, automatic parking assistance systems, lane keeping, collision warning, tire pressure monitoring and automatic inflation, and more. Further optimizations can be made to the anti-pinch function of car windows, enhancing the system's reliability and safety. For instance, further refinement of the pressure threshold that triggers the anti-pinch function could improve accuracy. Integrating other types of sensors could provide a more comprehensive perception of various conditions during the window closing process, enabling more accurate judgments and control, and further enhancing the system's sensitivity.

7 Conclusion

This article studies the anti-pinch mechanism of car windows controlled by microcontrollers and constructs an advanced car window control system that does not require wiring, featuring intelligent characteristics and networking capabilities. The system can automatically retract the window when it detects an obstruction and supports remote control operations through mobile devices. It employs ZigBee wireless communication technology for remote control and uses sensor technology to enhance the intelligence level of the window control system. Furthermore, the system is integrated with the Internet of Things technology for remote networked control. Capable of quickly integrating into a ZigBee network, the system has significant application potential and is expected to bring notable social benefits.

Acknowledgments. This research was supported by Hainan Provincial Natural Science Foundation of China (624RC528), Education Department of Hainan Province(Hnjgzc2023-82) and provincial high-level professional group "Computer Network Technology" in Hainan Province.

References

1. Cheng, A., Yang, Z., Yang, L., Sun, Y., Zhang, Z.: Design of anti-pinch control strategy for vehicle sunroof based on Hall motor. In: 2023 35th Chinese Control and Decision Conference (CCDC) (pp. 2607–2611). IEEE (2023)
2. Chi, Y.: Simulation analysis of electric window anti-pinch based on speed difference method. J. Eng. Mech. Mach. **8**(2), 36–43 (2023)
3. Komilov, D.R.: Application of zigbee technology in IOT. Int. J. Adv. Sci. Res. **3**(09), 343–349 (2023)
4. Nguyen, C.V., et al.: ZigBee based data collection in wireless sensor networks. Int. J. Inf. Commun. Technol. ISSN **2252**(8776), 213 (2021)
5. Mesquita, J., Guimarães, D., Pereira, C., Santos, F., Almeida, L.: Assessing the ESP8266 WiFi module for the Internet of Things. In: 2018 IEEE 23rd international conference on emerging technologies and factory automation (ETFA) (Vol. 1, pp. 784–791). IEEE (2018)
6. Yang, X., Chen, F.R., Li, C.: A design of window lifter system based on current detection. In: 2019 Chinese Automation Congress (CAC) (pp. 813–817). IEEE (2019).

Design of Non-standard Injection Mold with Hot Runner for Outdoor Measuring Cup of Electric Vehicle

Lijun Huang and Aldrin D. Calderon(✉)

School of Mechanical Manufacturing and Energy Engineering, Mapúa University, Manila, Philippines
adcalderon@mapua.edu.ph

Abstract. The outdoor measuring cup for electric vehicle is a kind of thin-walled deep-cavity plastic part, according to the structural characteristics of this plastic part, a non-standard two-platen hot runner injection mould is designed. The mould is opened twice and the plastic part is demoulded in three sequential steps. LKM conventional DI-type standard mould carrier is transformed into a two-plate non-standard mould carrier without ejector mechanism, which can effectively reduce the total height of the mould. Solve the problem that the maximum mould height of the injection moulding machine is not enough to accommodate the size of the mould. The mould release of the outer wall of the moulded part uses a kind of fixed mould half slider mechanism. The demoulding of the inner wall uses a kind of dynamic mould push plate mechanism; the two mechanisms are driven sequentially by the mould opening power through the T-type pull bar and fixed-pitch pull bar. Both can achieve the outer wall and inner wall demoulding in sequence, but also to ensure that the moulded part is completely demoulded. The setting of the positioning cone table and positioning components can effectively ensure the coaxially of the inner and outer wall moulding parts of the cylindrical thin-walled deep cavity moulding part, to ensure the quality of thin-walled moulding of the moulding part.

Keywords: Electric vehicle outdoor measuring cup · Thin-walled deep cavity · Mould frame modification · Half slider · Pusher mechanism

1 Introduction

The outdoor measuring cup for electric vehicle is a kind of plastic part with higher height and thinner wall thickness, which is generally called thin-walled deep-cavity plastic part. For the mould design of such plastic parts, there are two basic issues that must be dealt with, so as not to lead to the later mould manufacturing process of constantly changing and repairing the mould, resulting in unnecessary production waste [1]. Firstly, the coaxially of the outer and inner surfaces of the cylindrical thin-walled deep-cavity moulded parts must be well controlled, so as not to cause uneven wall thickness of the moulded parts, or even the lack of material in the local area, which may lead to the failure of moulding of the moulded parts. Secondly, for the demoulding of cylindrical thin-walled deep-cavity moulded parts, the inner wall is generally demoulded using a push plate, while the outer wall is demoulded using a Haff slide mechanism, to prevent demoulding deformation of the moulded parts [2, 3]. In the case of complete demoulding with a push plate, the design of the mould can be structurally simplified to make certain modifications, which can effectively save the cost of mould manufacturing.

Outdoor measuring cup plastic parts.

The shape of the plastic part of the outdoor measuring cup is shown in Fig. 1. It has a total height of 230 mm, a wall thickness of 1.8 mm, an outer diameter of 124 mm at the bottom, a slope of 2.5° on the outer wall of the cup, and a stem width of 18 mm. Additional features provided on the moulded part are 1 cup handle, 1 cup spout and 2 inner convex walls. The material used for the moulded part is polypropylene (PP) plastic which can withstand high temperatures of 130 °C and has a shrinkage rate of 1.1%–1.25%.

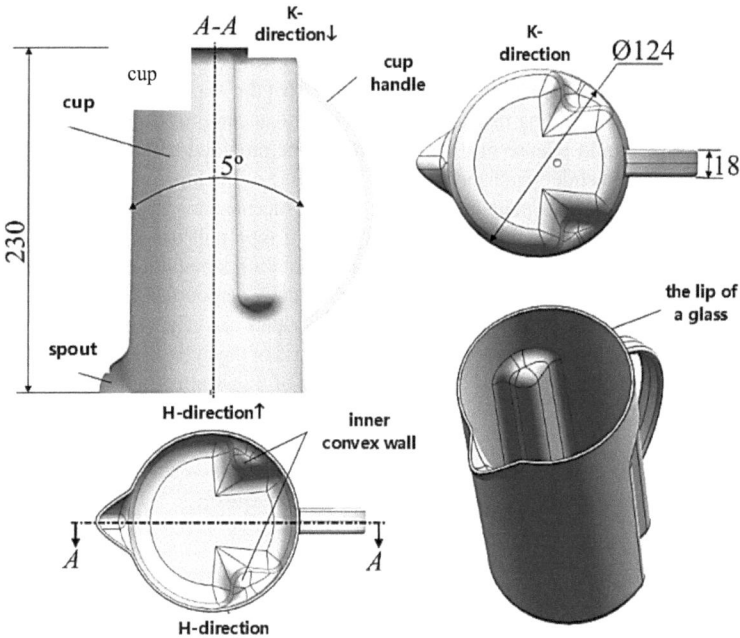

Fig. 1. Automotive outdoor measuring cup.

2 Mould Structure

The injection mould for the outdoor measuring cup is a simplified hot runner two-plate mould. Single-cavity layout, its structural arrangement is shown in Fig. 2. The mould is opened twice, the opening surface is Q1, surface, Q2 surface, and the plastic parts are demoulded in 3 sequential steps.

The mould cavities are cast directly using single point hot runner nozzles and cooled using 4 water circuits (W1–W4) for cooling.

Two mechanisms are designed to complete the demoulding of the part, one is the fixed mould half slider mechanism M1 and the other is the drawbar pusher mechanism M2. The mould does not have an ejector mechanism, instead, the moving mould pusher 18 is used to push out to complete the final demoulding of the part.

3 Non-standard Modifications of the Mould Carrier

In conjunction with the front view in Fig. 2, the conventional Lung Kee ((LKM) DI4545 standard mould carrier was dismantled and modified to simplify the structure of the mould and to facilitate the installation of the mechanism parts. Before the modification of the mould carrier, the specification of the original two-plate mould carrier was LKM DI4545-A290-B70-C 120. In conjunction with the actual need to install the mechanism on the mould, the parts in the original mould frame located between the moving template 19 and the moving mould seat plate 20 are removed. The removed parts include parts such as pads, ejector cover plates, ejector push plates and reset levers. In the modified non-standard mould carrier, the closing guidance of the mould plate is guided using 4 guideposts 3. The mould carrier can be opened at the opening faces Q_1 and Q_2. The opening of the Q_1 side of the mould is spaced by means of a spacing bar 15, and the opening of the Q_2 side is spaced by means of a T-bar 17.

The final demoulding of the moulded part is carried out using the moving mould pusher plate 18 pushed out for demoulding. Thus, four sets of positioning post assemblies 11 are mounted between the moving mould pusher plate 18 and the moving template 19 to ensure the accuracy of the reset when both are closed. Four sets of fine positioning assemblies 24 are mounted between the movable mould push plate 18 and the fixed mould plate 14 to ensure the accuracy of the reset when both are closed. To prevent heat dissipation, the fixed mould seating plate 2 is fitted with a heat-insulating plate 1 made of acrylonitrile-butadiene-styrene (ABS).

There are 3 reasons for the mould carrier to be modified. One is that it can effectively reduce the height of the mould and reduce the mould's opening stroke requirements for the injection moulding machine. Secondly, it saves mould frame material and reduces mould manufacturing cost. Thirdly, reduce the complexity of mould structure. After the structure of the mould frame is simplified, the moulding parts on the mould frame are easy to disassemble and adjust. To ensure that the outer wall moulding parts and inner wall moulding parts of the plastic parts have better coaxially after the mould cavity is closed. The uniformity of the wall thickness of the moulded part is ensured and the reliability of the mould action is improved [4, 5].

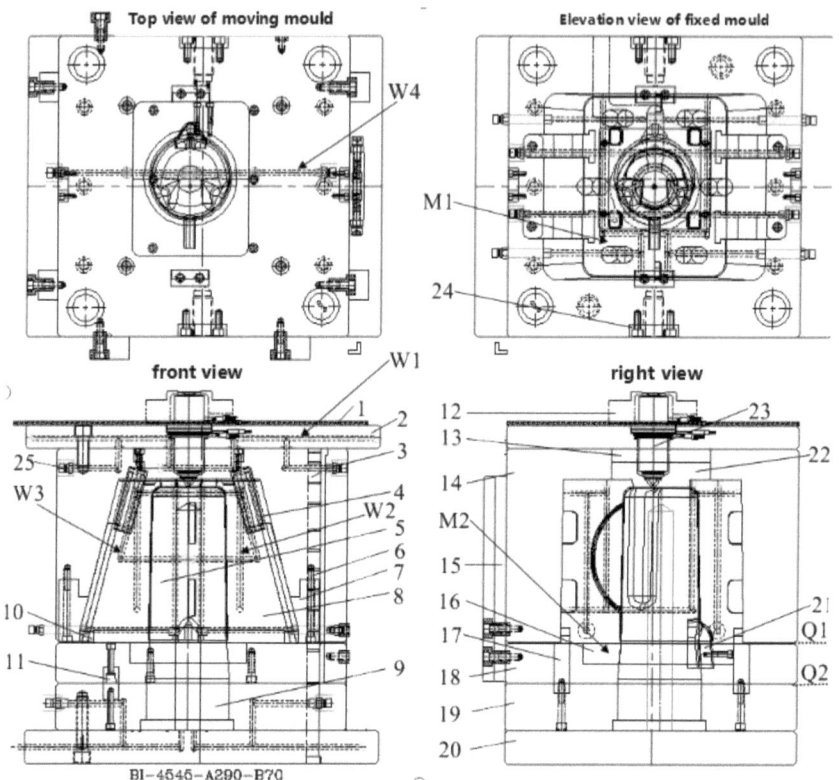

1-Heat insulation plate; 2-Fixed mould seat plate; 3-Guide pillar; 4-spring; 5-left slide; 6-screw; 7-T-guide; 8-right slide; 9-inner core insert; 10-limit block; 11-cylindrical positioning assembly; 12-hot nozzle collar; 13-spacer plate; 14-fixed template; 15-fixed distance pull plate; 16-pusher insert; 17-T-type tie rod; 18-dynamic mould pusher; 19-dynamic mould plate; 20-dynamic mould seat plate; 21-cup spout insert; 22-cup bottom outer wall insert; 23-Hot runner nozzle; 24-Fine positioning assembly; M1-Fixed mould half slider mechanism; M2-Tie rod pusher mechanism; $W_1 \sim W_4$-Cooling water circuit number; Q_1, Q_2-Mould opening surface.

Fig. 2. Mould structure.

4 Mould Cavity Parting Design

The mould cavity parting design is shown in Fig. 3, and the moulded part is placed in an inverted way in the mould cavity. The mould cavity is parted using 3 parting surfaces, the 3 parting surfaces are P_u, P_d and P_h. Since the outer wall of the moulded part can only be demoulded by side core extraction using a half slide, the parting surfaces P_u and P_d are provided for the first parting of the moulded part on the outer wall of the moulded part. In this way, the cup bottoms outer wall insert (part 22) of the moulded part at the bottom of the outer wall of the moulded part and the inner wall core insert (part 9) of the moulded part at the inner wall of the moulded part can be set up separately [6–9] for easy demoulding of the moulded part. Setting the parting surface P_u and P_d can also avoid the parting marks at the position of contour line L_1 and contour line L_2, which will affect the appearance of the moulded part. Since the outer wall moulded parts which are parted out from the parting surface Pu and Pd shall be set up as half sliders (left slider 5, right slider 8). Therefore, it is necessary to use the parting surface Ph of the haft slider to part the outer wall moulded parts of the plastic part for the second time. The parting surface Ph consists of three sub-parting surfaces S_1, S_2, S_3 on the same plane, and the parting line of the sub-parting surface S_2 is the minimum contour line L_3 inside the cup handle.

With the above parting setup, the mould cavity comprises 5 moulded parts. They are 1 cup bottom outer wall insert 22, 1 inner wall core insert 9, 2 half sliders left 5 and right 8, and 1 cup spout insert 21 as shown in Fig. 2. The cup spout inserts 21 is a partial moulding insert divided from the inner wall core insert 9, which is mainly for the convenience of machining the cup spout moulding part of the moulded part. Machining of plastic cup spout moulded parts. The gate of the mould cavity is provided on the cup bottom outer wall insert 22.

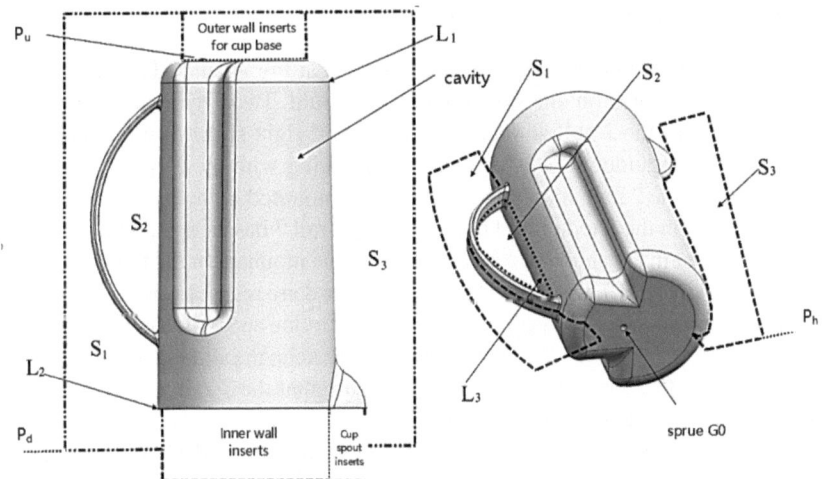

P^u, P_d, P_h-parting surfaces; L_1, L_2, L_3-contour lines; S_1, S_2, S_3-sub-parting surfaces; G_0-gate

Fig. 3. Setting of parting surface.

5 Pouring and Cooling

As shown in the right view in Fig. 2, the mould cavity is cast using a single hot runner nozzle 23 for casting [10, 11], with the location of the outlet at the lower end of this hot nozzle corresponding to the location of the gate G_0 in Fig. 3. For the cooling setup of the mould cavity, it is shown in the front view in Fig. 2. The outer wall insert 22 of the cup base is cooled using water circuit W_1. The inner wall core insert 9 is cooled using water circuit W_4. The left slide 5 is cooled using water circuit W_2 and the right slide 8 is cooled using water circuit W_3. The pipes of water circuit W_1–W_4 were set at Ø8 mm, and the surface roughness of the inner wall of the pipes was above $R_a = 6.3$ as far as possible to ensure the cooling effect [12–14]. The end of each water pipe is sealed with a brass plug. The sealing of the pipes between the mould plates is done with "O" rings. The fittings 25 of each water line are hidden as far as possible inside the formwork so that they are not damaged during the handling of the mould.

6 Removing Mechanism

As shown in the elevation view and the right view of the fixed mould in Fig. 2, the demoulding of the plastic part is divided into two parts: the demoulding of the outer wall and the demoulding of the inner wall [15]. The demoulding of the outer wall is done by using one set of fixed-mould Haff slider mechanism M_1. The demoulding of the inner wall is done by using a slat pusher mechanism M_2 to push out the mould. The structural design of the two mechanisms is as follows.

6.1 Fixed-Mould Half Slider Mechanism M_1

The fixed mould half slider mechanism M_1 is shown in Fig. 4, and M1 is a pop-up half slider mechanism located on one side of the fixed mould. Two T-type guide grooves are provided on each of the 2 half sliders left slider 5 and right slider 8 of the mechanism. Through the T-type guide grooves slidingly cooperating with the T-type rails of the T-type guide rails 7, the 2 half sliders are respectively mounted on both sides of the empty slots of the sliders in the fixed mould plate 14. The T-rail 7 has an upper end of the T-rail and a lower end set in the shape of a square cone and is mounted in the fixed template 14 with a screw lock. The left slider 5 and the right slider 8 are respectively provided with 2 springs 4. The springs 4 serve 2 purposes. One is to provide an auxiliary driving force for the slider to slide out along the T-rail. The second is to keep the slider at the final position of the sliding out after the slider is slid out, to ensure that the T-rail 7 can be accurately inserted into the T-guide groove of the slider when the mould is closed. The left slider 5 and the right slider 8 are provided with 2 limit slots, and the slider's sliding out stroke is limited by the limit block 10. The limit block 10 is mounted in the fixed template 14 with screw locking. The left slider 5 and the right slider 8 are provided with 2 tapers 1 for locking the two sliders by the cup bottom outer wall insert 22 in the closed state. The left slider 5 is provided with 4 taper 2. Correspondingly, the right slider 8 is provided with 4 taper table slots. When the left slider 5 and the right slider 8 are closed together, the 4 taper 2 cooperate with the corresponding taper table slots to ensure the accuracy of the closed reset of the two sliders on the Ph parting surface. The left slide 5 and the right slide 8 are provided with a push piece insert 16 underneath, which is fastened with screws. It is mounted on the moving mould push plate 18, and the material used is T8A steel, which has good wear resistance. When the left slider 5 and the right slider 8 are sliding out of the core along F_1 direction and F_2 direction respectively. The sliding drive power of each of the two sliders is composed of two forces at the beginning of the pulling force along the F_3 direction of the T-type tie bar 17 and the rebound tension of the spring 4. When the left slider 5 and the right slider 8 have completed a certain moving distance h in the movement sub-direction K_1 and K_2 respectively, the upper ends of the T-type drawbar 17 are out of contact with the left slider 5 and the right slider 8. Thus, the late slide-out driving force of the left slider 5 and the right slider 8 is provided only by the rebound tension of the spring 4.

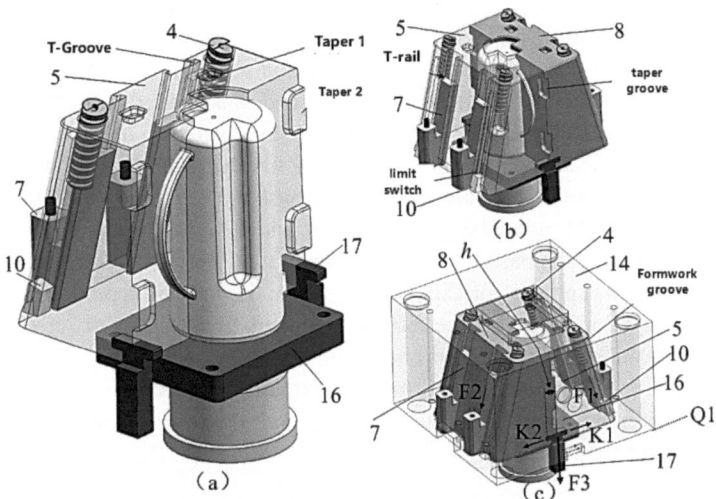

K^1, K_2 - side core pulling direction; F_1, F_2 - slider sliding out direction; F_3 - mould opening direction; h - side core pulling stroke the rest of the numbering is the same as Fig. 2 a- View of the mechanism after removal of the right slider; b- Panoramic view of the mechanism; c- Installation of the mechanism in the fixed template.

Fig. 4. Fixed mould half slider mechanism M1.

As shown in Fig. 4c, the mould release of mechanism M_1 works as follows. When the Q_1 side of the mould is opened, driven by the rebound tension assistance of the 4 springs 4, the 2 T-type drawbars 17 pull the left slider 5 and the right slider 8 downwardly according to F_3. The left slider 5 and the right slider 8 slide out from the empty slots of the slider in the fixed mould plate 14 along F_1 direction and F_2 direction respectively. When the left slider 5 and the right slider 8 complete the core pulling distance h in the respective side core pulling direction K_1 and K_2 respectively, they are detached from the 2 T-type drawbars 17. However, the left slider 5 and the right slider 8 can continue to be pushed out by the spring 4 until they are blocked by the limit block 10, thus completing the side core extraction of the outer wall of the plastic part. The resetting and closing process of the mechanism is opposite to the above process.

6.2 Drawbar Pusher Mechanism M_2

The composition of the drawbar pusher mechanism M_2 is shown in Fig. 5. The demoulding of the moulded part from the inner wall core inserts 9 and the cup spout insert 21 is accomplished by the moving mould pusher plate 18 pushing the pusher insert 16 thereon. During mould opening, the moving mould of the mould is opened in downward rows according to F_3. When the mould opening surface Q_1 is opened to a distance $d_2 = 250$ mm, the upper limit screw on the fixed template 14 pulls on the upper end of the fixed distance drawbar 15, and then pulls on the lower limit screw on the movable mould pusher plate 18 through the lower end of the fixed distance drawbar 15. Thereby, it stays motionless, and the Q_2 face is opened as the moving mould plate 19 continues to descend in the F_3 direction. When the moving plate 19 continues to travel with the inner wall core insert 9 and the cup insert 21 thereon for a distance of $d_1 = 5$ mm, the moulded part is blocked by the pusher plate 16 and is separated from the inner wall core insert 9 and the cup insert 21 which continue to travel. The inner wall of the part is thus demoulded. When the movable die plate 19 finally travels down to $d_1 = 13$ mm, the T-type tie bar 17 pulls down the movable die push plate 18, and the mould opening surface Q_2 of the mould cannot be opened further, and the mould opening is terminated.

In the assembly of the parts of the mechanism, the lower end of the T-type tie rod 17, after passing through the corresponding hole on the moving mould push plate 18, is then fastened and mounted on the moving template 19 by means of screws, and the raised parts at both ends of the upper end of the T-type tie rod 17 play a role in pulling the left slider 5 and the right slider 8 to slide out. At the same time, it also plays the role of controlling the separation distance d_1 between the moving template 19 and the moving mould pushing plate 18.

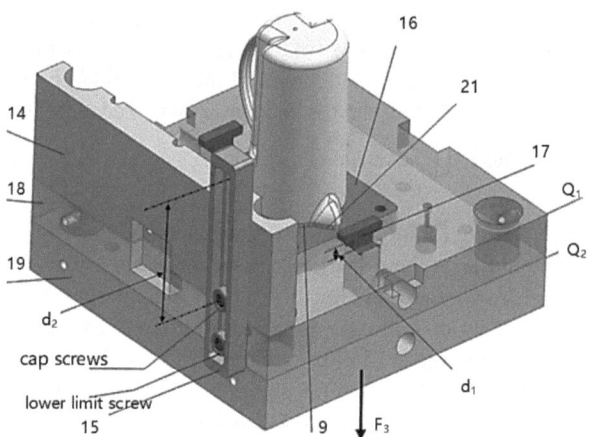

d_1, d_2 - fixed-pitch stroke; the rest of the numbering is the same as Figure. 2 and Figure. 4

Fig. 5. Drawbar pusher mechanism M_2.

7 Mould Working Principle

The working principle of the mould is shown in Fig. 6. The demoulding of the plastic part from the mould is done in the following steps.

(1) Separation at the P_u surface. When the moving mould of the mould moves in the direction of F_3, the mould will first open at the opening face Q_1 face. When it is just opened, the T-rod 17 pulls the left slider 5 and right slider 8 to slide out according to F_1 direction and F_2 direction respectively. The moulded part follows the inner wall core insert 9 and the cup spout insert 21 in the F_3 direction and first separates from the cup base outer wall insert 22 at the parting surface P_u.
(2) Half slider side core extraction to release the mould. The moving mould continues to move, and the moulded part continues to follow the inner wall core insert 9 and cup spout insert 21. The left slide 5 and right slide 8 separate at the parting surface P_h, and the two Half slides separate from the moulded part due to the movement in the K_1 and K_2 directions.
(3) The Q_2 side opens. The moving mould continues to move, and the fixed pitch drawbar 15 pulls the moving mould push plate 18 and push piece insert 16. Thus, the moulded part is pushed out of the inner wall core insert 9, the cup and spout insert 21 to achieve demoulding of the inner wall of the moulded part.
(4) Termination of mould opening. The moving mould continues to move, and the moving mould pusher plate 18 is pulled by the raised part of the T-type tie bar 17 on the moving template 19 and cannot continue to move any further. Mould opening of the mould is terminated.
(5) Reset. When resetting, the moving mould is moved in the reverse of the F_3 direction, and the Q_2 side is reset closed first. Then the four springs 4 of the two half sliders are compressed and the two half sliders are reset. Until Q_1 side reset closed, the mould is completely closed, waiting for the next injection cycle.

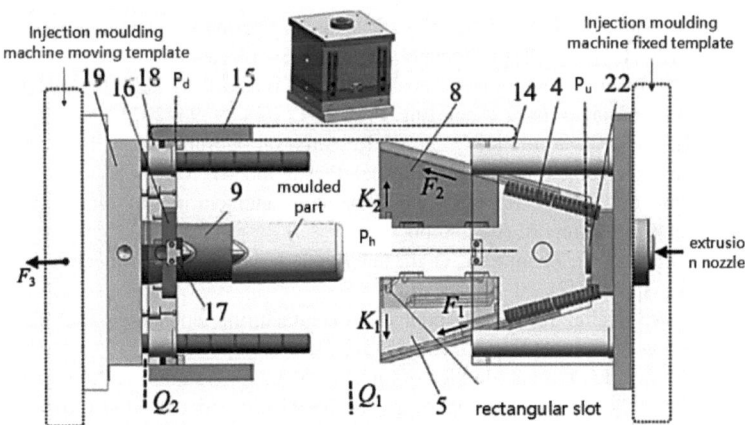

Part numbers are the same as Figure. 2, Figure. 3 and Figure. 4

Fig. 6. Working principle of mould. Part numbers are the same as Figs. 2, 3 and 4

8 Conclusion

A pair of hot runner two-platen moulds without ejector mechanism is designed for the injection moulding of cylindrical thin-walled deep-cavity plastic parts for outdoor measuring cups. The modified mould frame can effectively ensure that the outer wall moulded parts and inner wall moulded parts of the plastic parts have good coaxially after the mould cavity is closed. It ensures the uniformity of the wall thickness of the moulded parts, and at the same time avoids the limitation of the mould height design by the opening stroke of the injection moulding machine. For the demoulding of the outer wall of the moulded part, the fixed-mould haf slider mechanism is designed. For the demoulding of the inner wall of the moulded part, a moving mould pusher mechanism is designed. The two mechanisms are associated to control the mould release sequence through the T-bar and fixed-pitch puller. Not only can ensure that the mould release sequence of the outer wall first and then the inner wall, but also ensure that the simplified mould frame structure of the moving mould pusher can push out the moulded part smoothly and completely release the mould. The innovative design of the overall structure of the mould and the local modification design are good inspiration for the design of the mould structure of similar plastic parts.

References

1. Yonghui, C.: Design of aluminum profile extrusion mold for installation beam of new energy vehicle battery pack. Nonferrous Metal Process. **51**(06), 30–32 (2022)
2. Xinghui, Y., Zhenghua, L., Shangtao, L.: Design and load-bearing simulation analysis of injection mold for built-in steel pipe plastic tray. Appl. Eng. Plastics **52**(03), 103–111 (2024)
3. Chang, W., Kun, Z., Tonghui, L.: Flow analysis of bearing cover injection mold based on CAD/CAE technology. Plastic Technol. **49**(03), 103–106 (2021)
4. Ying, W., Kaiyuan, C., Jianping, C., et al.: Design of injection mold for internal threaded pipe joints with external grooves. Appl. Eng. Plastics **49**(04), 89–93 (2021)
5. Jizhan, H., Wei, C., Wenning, Q., et al.: Research on optimization of hot runner injection molding process for automotive audio panel. Plastic Ind. **47**(10), 81–85 (2019)
6. Gong Jiancong. (2024) Research on Flexible Manufacturing in New Energy Vehicle Production Car test report, (01):58–60
7. Jing, W., Laishui, Z., Zhenjie, L., et al.: Intelligent design system of injection mould inserts. Eng. Plast. Appl. **48**(7), 80–84 (2020)
8. Guiyong, W.: Digital design and intelligent manufacturing technology analysis of injection molds. China Equipment Eng. **10**, 45–47 (2023)
9. Mei, Y., Yan, T., Li, Y., et al.: Design of Injection Mold for Automotive Activity Contact Seat with Splicing Side Pull Core. Appl. Eng. Plastics **47**(05), 105–109+121 (2019)
10. Tiantian, Y., Qian, Y., Hui, L.: Design of a three-stage parting injection mold with multi-directional core pulling. Plast. Technol. **50**(10), 95–98 (2022)
11. Wang, X., Chuanlin, Z., Jingjie, H., et al.: Application of hot runner technology in plastic injection molds. Henan Sci. Technol. **35**, 65–67 (2019)
12. Chunxiao, Q., Kaiyuan, C., Xiaoming, H.: Design and optimization of runner system for front door sash based on Moldflow. Plastics **46**(2), 102–105 (2017)
13. Qin, X., Su, X.: Design and optimization of injection mould for PLC shell cover based on mouldflow. Plast. Sci. Technol. **46**(9), 115–120 (2018)

14. Zhai, L., Han, G., Hu, H., et al.: Structural analysis of injection molds based on mouldflow and abaqus softwares. China Plast. **32**(2), 128–133 (2018)
15. Feng, Z., Li, Y.: Design of precision mold manufacturing control based on industrial robots. Equipment Manage. Mainten. (13), 137–139 (2021).

Multi-objective Electric Vehicle Route Optimization for Low-Carbon Cold Chain Logistics Under Time-Dependent Networks

Pingping Zhao[✉], Meiyan Li, and Yanhua Yuan

Shandong University of Science and Technology, Qingdao, China
zhao0212112022@163.com

Abstract. This passage presents a study that addresses the issue of carbon emissions in electric vehicle cold chain logistics delivery within the context of the "dual carbon" strategic goals and the rapid growth of the fresh e-commerce industry. The research begins by utilizing polynomial functions to model vehicle speed and calculate energy consumption during delivery, which is then integrated into the cost function to determine electric vehicle power consumption costs. Given limited research on optimizing total costs and customer satisfaction as model objectives in time-varying road networks for cold chain logistics delivery, this paper develops a multi-objective electric vehicle routing optimization model. The optimization objectives include lowest total delivery cost and highest customer satisfaction. Total delivery costs encompass fixed costs for electric refrigerated vehicles, power consumption costs, refrigeration costs, carbon emission costs, and perishable product loss costs. Additionally, this paper introduces a non-dominated sorting genetic algorithm with an elite strategy (NSGA-II) to solve the proposed model. Finally, numerical experiments using data from a specific distribution network are conducted to validate both the model and solution algorithm's effectiveness with an aim to provide decision support for cold chain logistics companies regarding reasonable deliveries.

Keywords: time-dependent networks · customer satisfaction · cold chain logistics · NSGA-II

1 Introduction

In the global warming and extreme weather and other environmental problems are becoming more and more prominent today, the issue of carbon dioxide emissions has attracted more and more global attention. At the same time, China has also proposed a "dual-carbon" goal of "peaking carbon emissions by 2030" and "carbon neutrality by 2060." Relevant datas show that carbon emissions of China's transportation industry accounted for about 14% of the country's total emissions in 2021, which is one of the important areas of carbon emission reduction. At the same time, with the continuous improvement of people's living standards, consumers' demand for fresh products and quality requirements are also constantly improving, and cold chain logistics has also developed rapidly compared to the past. Therefore, the realization of energy saving and emission reduction in the field of cold chain logistics distribution has become a common concern and urgent need to solve the problem.

A large number of scholars have begun to study the Time-dependent Vehicle Routing Problem (TDVRP). For example, Shi et al. [1] analyzed the calculation method of travel time for time-dependent vehicle routing problem, established a path optimization model, and proposed an improved Tianying optimization algorithm to solve the model. Ren et al. [2] established a mixed integer programming model on the basis of considering the change of electric vehicle speed with time and the impact of time cost of money on depreciation cost. Wen et al. [3]constructed the travel speed function for all time periods throughout the day, and built the multi-temperature co-collocation path optimization model under various constraints. Fan et al. [4]established a path optimization model for simultaneous loading and unloading of vehicles under time-varying road speed and soft time window conditions. On the basis of the traditional vehicle routing problem, Jie et al. [5]added random factors such as time window and road traffic congestion, and proposed a hybrid algorithm combining scanning algorithm and improved particle swarm optimization algorithm to solve the problem. Aiming at the TDVRP problem, Lu et al. [6] used a three-level speed function to represent the constraints on vehicle speed during urban peak periods, and established an integer linear programming model. Cai et al. [7] established a mathematical model based on time-varying road network conditions considering the influence of road conditions in real life. Luo et al. [8] studied the time-varying green vehicle routing problem considering traffic congestion, and proposed a branch-pricing algorithm to solve the problem. Ceonhwa [9] applied road gradient and real-time traffic API, and proposed an efficient vehicle routing algorithm in the field of sustainable transportation to solve the model. Jin et al. [10] established a new dual-objective cash transport vehicle routing problem model that takes into account both economic and environmental objectives, and designed a neneighbor-first iterative local search algorithm considering special terrain to solve the model. Wang et al. [11] used segmentation function to describe vehicle speed, established a multi-objective mathematical model, and designed a single-parent genetic algorithm to solve small, medium and large-scale examples. Wang et al. [12] proposed a time-dependent road travel time path problem and designed an iterative local search heuristic algorithm to solve the model.

Based on a large number of research results, this paper has laid a good foundation for further research on TDVRP. In this paper, the term function is used to represent the continuous change of the speed of the electric refrigerated vehicle over time during transportation, to represent the continuous change of the vehicle speed, and on this basis, the driving power consumption cost and carbon emission cost of the electric vehicle are calculated. A multi-objective electric vehicle routing optimization model with the lowest total cost and the highest customer satisfaction under time-varying road network is constructed, and the non-dominated sequencing genetic (NSGA-II) algorithm is designed to solve the model. Finally, the effectiveness of the model and algorithm is verified by numerical simulation.

2 Problem Description and Model Construction

2.1 Problem Description

The multi-objective time-varying path optimization problem of electric refrigerated truck cold chain logistics considering carbon emissions can be expressed as that a cold chain logistics distribution center provides distribution services to multiple customer nodes. The goal of this problem is to minimize the total cost of vehicle distribution and maximize the customer satisfaction by planning the optimal vehicle route while meeting the customer's requirements on the quality of fresh products.

In order to facilitate the analysis and research, we make the following assumptions. 1. In the path optimization problem, there is a cold chain logistics distribution center. 2. The electric refrigerated truck starts from the cold chain logistics distribution center every time to provide customers with services in turn, and the electric refrigerated truck returns to the cold chain logistics distribution center after completing all the distribution tasks. 3. Electric refrigerated trucks in the entire transportation process, only need to consider delivery for customers, do not need to pick up goods. 4. Each electric refrigerated truck starts distribution for customers at the same time, and can be distributed at any time throughout the day. 5. The types of electric refrigerated trucks used in the distribution center are the same, the level of loss is the same, the load capacity, battery capacity and battery conversion rate are the same. 6. The demand, location, expected service time and service time of the distribution center for each customer node are known, and the customer demand will not change dynamically. 7. Each time the vehicle starts from the distribution center, the battery is fully charged, and the battery power supports the vehicle to complete a distribution and return to the distribution center. 8. The urban road is flat, and the distribution of pure electric refrigerated vehicles does not consider the resistance of the slope. 9. The maximum transport distance of each electric refrigerated truck is greater than the transport distance of the customer node. 10. There is only one electric refrigerated truck to serve each customer, but each electric refrigerated truck can serve multiple customer nodes.

2.2 Symbol Specification

The meanings of symbols, variables and sets required in this article are as follows. $K = \{1, 2, 3, ..., m\}$ is the collection of refrigerated trucks, and m is the number of refrigerated trucks that can be called by the distribution center. $N = \{0, 1, 2, ..., n\}$ is a collection of nodes, 0 is a distribution center, and the rest are customer nodes. h represents the fixed cost per electric refrigerated truck (¥). q_i represents the demand of customer node i (kg). G_{ij}^k represents the load capacity of the k vehicle from customer node i to customer node j (kg). p represents the average price per unit weight of fresh produce(¥/kg). θ_1 represents the spoilage rate of the product during its driving. θ_2 represents the rate of spoilage during the unloading of the product. t_{ij}^k represents the traveling time of electric refrigerated truck k from customer node i to customer node j in the distribution process(min). t_{si} represents the unloading time at customer node i (min). t_i^k represents the departure time of electric refrigerated truck k from customer node i. y_{ik} is variable 0–1, taking 1 when the vehicle is a node for distribution, otherwise 0. η_m represents the motor efficiency of the electric refrigerated truck. η_T represents the transmission efficiency of the transmission system of the electric refrigerated truck. η_v represents the conversion efficiency of the electric refrigerated truck inverter. g represents the acceleration of gravity with a value of 9.8 (m/s^2). f represents the coefficient of rolling friction, whose value is 0.01. C_D represents the air resistance coefficient, whose value is 0.28. A represents the area of the front of the vehicle (m^2). δ represents the conversion coefficient of vehicle rotating mass. v stands for vehicle speed (km/h). m_v represents the total mass of the vehicle (kg). a represents vehicle acceleration (m/s^2). η_1 represents the power consumption per unit time when the worker opens the door at the customer node when unloading ($\eta_1 = 4\,kW \cdot h/h$). η_2 represents the power consumption per unit time of the refrigeration unit during the running of the electric refrigerated vehicle when the door is closed ($\eta_2 = 2kW \cdot h/h$). c represents the cost per unit of power consumption(¥). b represents the cost per unit of refrigerant consumed per thousand calories absorbed by the vehicle during transportation(¥/kcal). x_{ij}^k is variable 0–1, taking 1 when the k car travels from node i to node j, otherwise 0. c_t represents the cost per unit of carbon emissions (¥). ρ represents the vehicle emission factor. κ represents that thermal power generation method accounts for the proportion of all power generation methods. s_k represents the actual load of car k (kg). Q_z represents the maximum load of the vehicle (kg). R represents the heat load generated by the vehicle per unit time during transportation (kg/h). E_{ik}^l represents the remaining power of the k car when it leaves the node (kW·h). E_{max} represents the amount of electricity when the vehicle is fully charged (kW·h). E_{min} represents the minimum amount of power required for the vehicle to run normally (kW·h). $[ET_i, LT_i]$ represents expected service time window of customer i. $[et_i, lt_i]$ represents acceptable service time window of customer i.

2.3 Model Construction

At present, most studies on time-varying road network use step function to represent the change of vehicle speed, but step function has certain limitations in describing the change of vehicle speed [13]. Therefore, polynomial function is used in this paper to represent the continuous change of vehicle speed with time during transportation of electric refrigerated truck, and its time speed function is shown in Fig. 1.

The objective functions of the multi-objective electric vehicle routing optimization model constructed in this paper are the lowest total distribution cost Z_1 and the highest customer satisfaction Z_2. The total cost includes the vehicles fixed cost C_1, the cargo damage cost C_2, the electricity consumption cost C_3, the refrigeration cost C_4 and the carbon emissions cost C_5. Whether the vehicle arrives early or late, it will reduce customer satisfaction and affect the service of the remaining customers.

$$C_1 = h \sum_{i=0}^{n} \sum_{j=0}^{n} \sum_{k=1}^{m} x_{ij}^k \qquad (1)$$

$$C_2 = \sum_{i=0}^{n} \sum_{j=0}^{n} \sum_{k=1}^{m} q_i p\left(1 - e^{-\theta_1 t_{ij}^k}\right) y_{ik} + \sum_{i=0}^{n} \sum_{j=0}^{n} \sum_{k=1}^{m} G_{ij}^k p\left(1 - e^{-\theta_2 t_{si}}\right) y_{ik} \qquad (2)$$

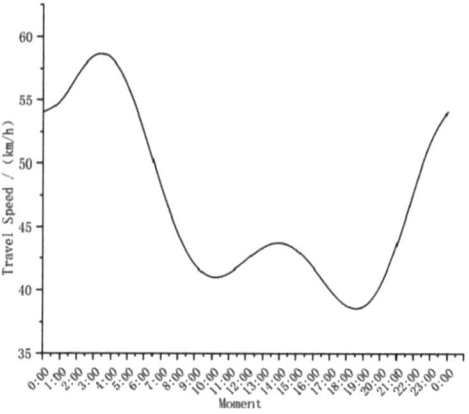

Fig. 1. Velocity time dependent function.

$$C_3 = c\sum_{i=0}^{n}\sum_{j=0}^{n}\sum_{k=1}^{m}\left(\frac{1}{3600\eta_T\eta_v\eta_m}\int_{t_i^k}^{t_j^k}v(t)\times\left[m_vgf+\frac{C_DAv(t)^2}{21.15}+\delta m_va\right]dt+\eta_1\sum_{i=0}^{n}\sum_{j=0}^{n}\sum_{k=1}^{m}\frac{t_{si}}{60}\cdot x_{ij}^k+\eta_2\sum_{i=0}^{n}\sum_{j=0}^{n}\sum_{k=1}^{m}t_{ij}^k\cdot x_{ij}^k\right) \quad (3)$$

$$C_4 = b\cdot R\left(\sum_{i=0}^{n}\sum_{j=0}^{n}\sum_{k=1}^{m}t_{ij}^k x_{ij}^k+\sum_{i=0}^{n}\sum_{j=0}^{n}\sum_{k=1}^{m}\frac{t_{si}}{60}\cdot x_{ij}^k\right) \quad (4)$$

$$C_5 = c_t\sum_{i=0}^{n}\sum_{j=0}^{n}\sum_{k=1}^{m}\rho\kappa\times\left(\frac{1}{3600\eta_T\eta_v\eta_m}\int_{t_i^k}^{t_j^k}v(t)\times\left[m_vgf+\frac{C_DAv(t)^2}{21.15}+\delta m_va\right]dt+\eta_1\sum_{i=0}^{n}\sum_{j=0}^{n}\sum_{k=1}^{m}\frac{t_{si}}{60}\cdot x_{ij}^k+\eta_2\sum_{i=0}^{n}\sum_{j=0}^{n}\sum_{k=1}^{m}t_{ij}^k\cdot x_{ij}^k\right) \quad (5)$$

$$F = \sum_{i=1}^{n}\begin{cases}0, t_i < ET_i', or, t_i > LT_i' \\ \frac{t_i - ET'}{ET - ET'}, ET_i' < t_i < ET_i \\ 1, ET_i < t_i < LT_i \\ \frac{LT' - t_i}{LT' - LT}, LT_i < t_i < LT_i'\end{cases} \quad (6)$$

In summary, this paper establishes a multi-objective route optimization model of low-carbon cold chain logistics for electric vehicles under the time-varying road network, as shown in Eq. (7)–(21):

$$\min Z_1 = C_1 + C_2 + C_3 + C_4 + C_5 \quad (7)$$

$$\max Z_2 = \max F \quad (8)$$

The constraints are as follows:

$$\sum_{j=1}^{n}\sum_{k=1}^{m}x_{ij}^k \le m, i = 0 \quad (9)$$

$$\sum_{j=1}^{n} x_{ij}^k = \sum_{j=1}^{n} x_{ji}^k \leq 1, i = 0, k \in K \tag{10}$$

$$\sum_{i=0}^{n} x_{ij}^k = y_{jk}, j \in N, k \in K \tag{11}$$

$$\sum_{j=0}^{n} x_{ij}^k = y_{ik}, i \in N, k \in K \tag{12}$$

$$s_k \leq Q_z, k \in K \tag{13}$$

$$\sum_{j=0}^{n}\sum_{k=1}^{m} x_{ij}^k = \sum_{j=0}^{n}\sum_{k=1}^{m} x_{ji}^k = 1, i \in N \tag{14}$$

$$\sum_{i=1}^{n}\sum_{k=1}^{m} y_{ik} = n \tag{15}$$

$$E_{0k}^l = E_{\max}, i \in N, k \in K \tag{16}$$

$$E_{ik}^l - E_t > E_{\min}, i, j \in N, k \in K \tag{17}$$

$$x_{ij}^k = 0, i = j, i, j \in N, k \in K \tag{18}$$

$$j \neq i, i \neq n \tag{19}$$

$$t_{j+1}^k = t_i^k + t_{sj} + t_{ij}^k, i, j \in N, k \in K, i \neq j \tag{20}$$

$$x_{ij}^k \in \{0, 1\}, y_{ik} \in \{0, 1\}, i, j \in N, k \in K \tag{21}$$

where, Eqs. (7) and (8) are objective functions. Formula (9) indicates that the number of paths is no greater than the number of vehicles. Formula (10) indicates that the electric refrigerated truck starts from the distribution center and should return to the distribution center after completing the distribution task. Formula (11) and formula (12) indicate that each electric refrigerated truck leaves after providing service to the customer. Formula (13) represents the maximum load limit of the vehicle. Formula (14) represents the constraint of vehicle access balance, and each customer only accepts the service once. Formula (15) indicates that every customer is served. Formula (16) indicates that the electric refrigerated truck is fully charged when it leaves the distribution center. Formula (17) indicates that the remaining power of the vehicle must be greater than the minimum driving power. Formula (18) indicates that there is no path between the same node. Formula (19) indicates that the subloop constraint is eliminated. (20) Indicates the continuity of time to ensure the continuity of delivery. Equation (21) represents the value constraint of the variable.

3 Algorithm Design

In this paper, the multi-objective cold chain logistics electric vehicle routing problem is studied. In general, in a multi-objective problem, the objectives are in conflict with each other, and it is impossible to achieve the optimal level of each objective at the same time. In addition, the search space of path optimization is very complex, and some conventional planning methods have been unable to find the optimal solution. However, NSGA-II algorithm introduces congestion degree, congestion comparison operator and elite strategy, so as to better solve the multi-objective optimization model, and is simpler and more effective than other algorithms in dealing with multi-objective optimization problems, and has obvious advantages. Therefore, this paper uses NSGA-II algorithm to solve the established model. The specific algorithm steps are shown in Fig. 2.

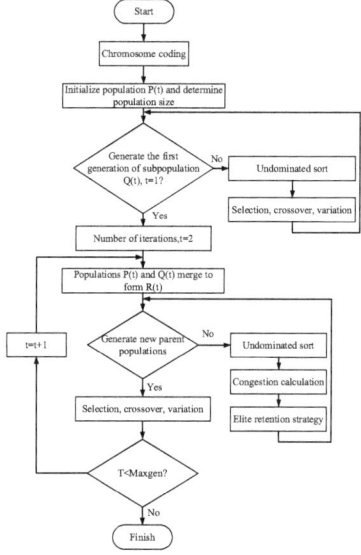

Fig. 2. Flowchart of NSGA-II algorithm.

(1) Integer coding

The vehicle distribution route optimization problem refers to the vehicle driving route obtained after the vehicle starts from the distribution center and passes through different customer nodes to provide distribution services. In this paper, integer coding is used, 0 is used to represent the distribution center, and other natural numbers represent the customers who need to carry out distribution services, where the order of each point in the chromosome represents the order of vehicle distribution. This coding method is more concise in expression, strong in extensibility, can reduce the complexity of the model and improve the efficiency of the model.

(2) Crossover operator

In this paper, individuals with higher fitness can be obtained by using partial matching crossover, which is a more commonly used method. In a partially matched crossover, the chromosomal parts of two parent individuals are exchanged to produce a new individual, and this crossover can introduce new diversity while retaining some favorable characteristics of the original individual.

(3) Mutation operator

The mutation operator can not only protect the diversity of individuals, but also prevent the algorithm from falling into the local optimal situation due to the fast convergence speed, and improve the global optimization ability of the algorithm. In this section, partial matching crossover is also adopted, and mutation probability is used to determine whether the algorithm needs to be modified. If the algorithm needs variation, exchange variation is carried out, that is, two loci are randomly selected on the chromosome, and then the genes at these two loci are exchanged. Through continuous random variation, the shortest path required for solving the problem is finally found.

(4) Elite retention strategy

The elite retention strategy in NSGA-II algorithm process can prevent the loss of outstanding individuals in the process of population evolution and improve the computational efficiency by merging the parent population with the offspring population, thereby generating a new population and performing a fast non-dominant ranking on it.

4 Example Analysis

4.1 Data and Parameter Settings

In order to verify the performance of the proposed algorithm, some data in a collocation network are selected for numerical experiments. The cold chain logistics distribution network includes 1 cold chain logistics distribution center and 45 customer nodes, whose location distribution diagram is shown in Fig. 3. On this basis, this paper gives the distribution center and customer node location coordinates, and customer demand data.

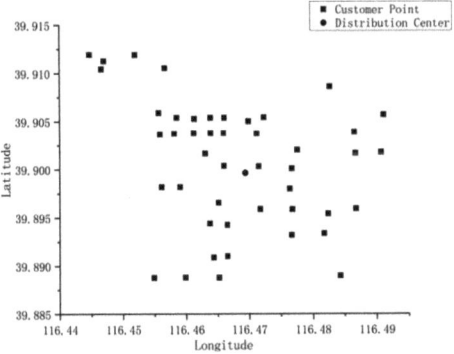

Fig. 3. Cross operator diagram.

4.2 Result Analysis

In this section, NSGA-II algorithm was used to solve the constructed model, in which the population number of the algorithm was set to 600, the number of iterations was set to 200, the crossover probability was set to 0.85, and the mutation probability was set to 0.2. Since the solution solved by NSGA-II algorithm is a set rather than a single solution, the Pareto optimal frontier solution set obtained by the final solution is shown in Fig. 4, and the vehicle path set under different indexes is shown in Table 1.

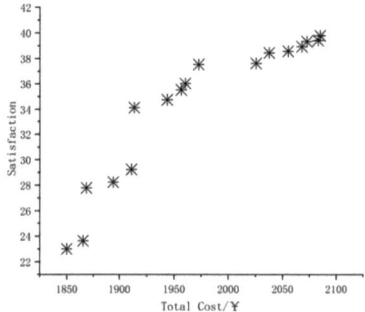

Fig. 4. Pareto optimal frontier solution set.

Table 1. Vehicle path collection under different indexes.

Index	Vehicle path set	Total cost/¥	Customer satisfaction
Optimal total cost	0—41—22—31—17—27—21—7—40—0 0—8—42—13—15—26—14—0 0—33—12—4—30—37—23—36—44—16—32—0 0—2—1—38—10—43—19—39—11—0 0—35—34—46—28—18—5—3—25—0 0—9—29—24—6—45—20—0	1 849.97	23
Optimal customer satisfaction	0—18—35—44—0 0—46—11—41—42—0 0—29—26—36—43—20—17—27—19—29—12—9—3—5—0 0—34—8—7—15—4—32—21—0 0—1—45—22—16—31—24—23—14—0 0—25—30—33—10—2—39—38—6—0 0—37—13—40—0	2 084.61	39.777 2

Since this paper optimizes two objectives at the same time, based on the Pareto optimal frontier solution set obtained, it can be known that the two objectives cannot be optimized at the same time. As can be seen from the data in Fig. 5, there is no solution set that makes the two objective functions reach the optimal simultaneously. When customer satisfaction increases, distribution cost also increases. In real life, making decisions needs to consider the influence of many factors, and compare the two goals, so as to choose the route that is more in line with the reality in the optimal solution. The optimal path of total cost and optimal path of customer satisfaction obtained by NSGA-II algorithm are shown in Figs. 5 and 6 respectively.

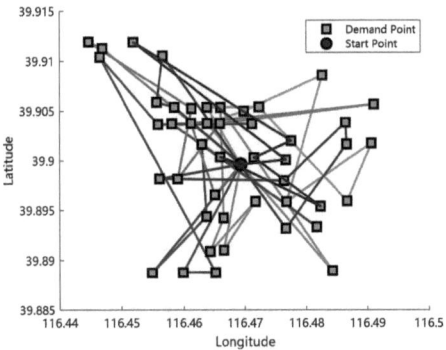

Fig. 5. The optimal distribution path for total cost optimal.

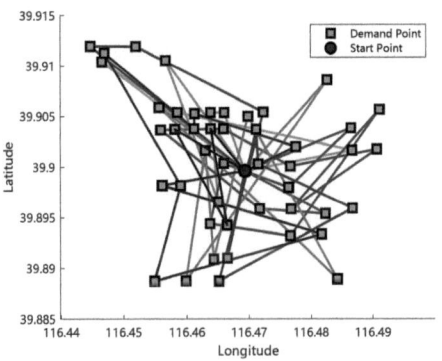

Fig. 6. The optimal distribution path for customer satisfaction.

Figure 5 shows that the solution with the lowest total cost in the Pareto solution set (Pareto solution set 1) can output the distribution route with the minimum total cost. The total distribution cost of this solution is 1 849.97¥, but the customer satisfaction rate is 23 of the lowest in the whole Pareto solution set. In this distribution roadmap, the distributor needs to deliver six times, which can save the cost to the maximum extent, but ignores the delivery time window required by customers, so this scheme has the lowest customer satisfaction.

Figure 6 shows that the solution with maximum customer satisfaction in the Pareto solution set (Pareto solution set 17) can output the distribution route with the highest customer satisfaction. The customer satisfaction of this solution is 39.777 2, but the total distribution cost is 2 084.61¥, which is the highest in the whole Pareto solution set. In order to achieve the highest customer satisfaction, the overall distribution process is carried out according to the time window required by the customer, and the goods are delivered as far as possible within the time window specified by the customer, but it also leads to the increase of the total distribution cost.

5 Conclusion

Based on the actual situation of cold chain logistics, aiming at the routing problem of electric vehicles in low-carbon cold chain logistics under time-varying distribution network, this paper established a multi-objective low-carbon vehicle routing model considering the total distribution cost and customer satisfaction, and used polynomial functions to describe the vehicle speed, reflecting the continuous change of vehicle speed, so as to get closer to the actual situation of cold chain distribution. And the solution model of NSGA-II algorithm is designed. The results show that there is no scheme that optimizes all the objectives. In actual decision making, decision makers should carry out different weights according to different situations.

Although the research results of this paper can provide a certain reference for fresh cold chain logistics enterprises, reminding enterprises to effectively reduce logistics distribution costs under the premise of ensuring customer satisfaction. However, the fresh products considered in this paper are all under the same temperature conditions when they are distributed. Therefore, in future studies, we can further study how to study the cold chain distribution of fresh products under different temperature conditions.

References

1. Shi, X., Zhao, X., Yan, L., et al.: Solving time dependent vehicle routing problem based on improved aquila optimizer algorithm. Comput. Eng. Appl. **60**(04), 355–365 (2024)
2. Ren, X.X., Fan, H.M., Bao, M.X., et al.: The time-dependent electric vehicle routing problem with drone and synchronized mobile battery swapping. In: Advanced Engineering Informatics (2023)
3. Wen, T., Li, K., Zhao, L., et al.: Research of route planning for electric vehicle cold chain distribution under time -varying road network. J. Dalian Univ. Tech. **62**(06), 641–649 (2022)
4. Fan, H., Tian, P., Lv, Y., et al.: Vehicle routing problem with simultaneous delivery and pickup considering temporal-spatial distance in time-dependent road network. J. Syst. Manage. **31**(01), 16–26 (2022)
5. Jie, K.W., Liu, S.Y., Sun, X.J.: A hybrid algorithm for time-dependent vehicle routing problem with soft time windows and stochastic factors. Eng. Appl. Artific. Intell. (2022)
6. Lu, J., Chen, Y.N., Hao, J.K., et al.: The time-dependent electric vehicle routing problem: model and solution. Expert Syst. Appl. (2020)
7. Cai, Y., Tang, Y., Cai, H.: Adaptive ant colony optimization for vehicle routing problem in time varying networks environment. Applic. Res. Comput. **32**(08), 2309–2312+2346 (2015)
8. Luo, H.Y., Mahjoub, D., Olivier, G.: A branch-price-and-cut algorithm for a time-dependent green vehicle routing problem with the consideration of traffic congestion. Comput. Indust. Eng. (2023)
9. Geonhwa, Y.: Sustainable vehicle routing problem on real-time roads: the restrictive inheritance-based heuristic algorithm. Sustain. Cit. Soc. (2022)
10. Jin, Y.Z., Ge, X.L., Zhang, L., et al.: A two-stage algorithm for bi-objective logistics model of cash-in-transit vehicle routing problems with economic and environmental optimization based on real-time traffic data. J. Indust. Inform. Integrat. (2022)

11. Wang, N., Hu, D., Xu, J., et al.: Time-dependent vehicle routing of urban cold-chain logistics based on customer value and satisfaction. China J. Highw. Transport **34**(09), 297–308 (2021)
12. Wang, Y., Wang, Z., Hu, X.P., et al. Truck–drone hybrid routing problem with time-dependent road travel time. Transport. Res. Part C (2022)
13. Fan, H., Zhang, Y., Tian, P.: Multi-depot electric vehicle routing problem with drones under time-dependent networks. J. Indust. Eng. Eng. Manage. **37**(02), 131–142 (2023)

Swin-MPGM: A Swin-Transformer Based Method for Content Separation in Challenging Environments

Yufeng Ding and Yan Feng(✉)

School of Mechanical and Electrical Engineering, Wuhan University of Technology Wuhan, Hubei 430000, China
283579@whut.edu.cn

Abstract. This study introduces Swin-MPGM, a novel scene text generation approach using GANs to separate text from complex backgrounds. It features a U-shaped architecture with a Swin-Transformer encoder for long-range dependencies and a CNN-decoder for image structure. The method addresses challenges like character recognition under wear, camera, and lighting variations. It innovatively generates image labels in real-time without pixel-level supervision, using text annotations and spatial info. It also includes an automatic multi-task loss balancing mechanism guided by homoscedastic uncertainty, optimizing training dynamically. Experiments on the Container Number datasets show improved generalization and robustness.

Keywords: Generative adversarial network · Separation of content and style · Textual reasoning

1 Introduction

Extracting text in real-world images is vital for applications like license plate recognition and manuscript identification. Despite advances in deep learning, challenges remain due to the complexity of natural images and the need for effective attention mechanisms. The human visual system tends to focus on text over background details, which is crucial when backgrounds are intricate and text features are less prominent.

Our study introduces a novel approach using a Generative Adversarial Network with an encoder-decoder architecture to separate text from backgrounds and restore text clarity. The generator extracts semantic text features and overlays them on a clean background. However, traditional CNN-based GANs struggle with long-range dependencies and feature resolution [1]. To overcome these, we incorporated Swin-Transformer blocks into our U-shaped generator [2] for better long-range dependency modeling and multi-scale input handling. This design captures both global and local dependencies, enhancing adaptability and generalization.

We also developed an on-the-fly image label generation strategy that eliminates the need for pixel-level supervision, using text annotations and spatial information to dynamically create labels. Additionally, we introduced an automatic multi-task loss balancing mechanism using homoscedastic uncertainty to optimize training by dynamically adjusting loss weights, improving generalization and robustness.

Our Swin-MPGM method addresses these challenges by:

1) Separating text from background using a Swin-Transformer-based generative network.
2) Generating image labels in real-time without pixel-level supervision.
3) Balancing multi-task losses automatically during training for better adaptability.

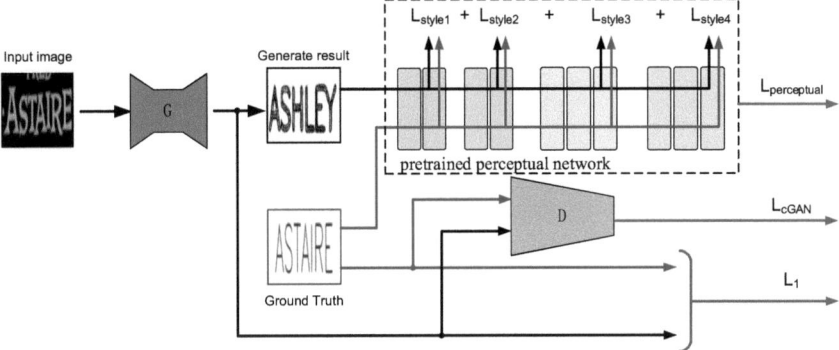

Fig. 1. Swin-MPGM network overview.

2 Swin-MPGM Network Overview

In this section, we have designed a framework to extract textual content from distracting background styles and transform the text style into a more recognizable font, employing a generative adversarial architecture, as illustrated in Fig. 1.

2.1 Objective

The objective of the proposed network can be expressed as.

$$\mathcal{L}_{\text{cGAN}}(G, D) = \mathbb{E}_{x,y}[\log D(x, y)] + \mathbb{E}_{x,z}[\log(1 - D(x, G(x, z)))] \quad (1)$$

where G tries to minimize this objective against an adversarial D that tries to maximize it, i.e. $G^* = arg\ \min_G \max_D \mathcal{L}_{\text{cGAN}}(G, D)$.

To achieve a less-blurred result, the L1 distance is incorporated into the objective function. Our final objective is.

$$G^* = arg\ \min_G \max_D \mathcal{L}_{\text{cGAN}}(G, D) + \lambda \mathcal{L}_{\text{L1}}(G) \quad (2)$$

2.2 Network Architecture Overview

The complete Swin-MPGM networks is made up of the generating network, discriminator network, and pretrained perceptual network (see Fig. 2).

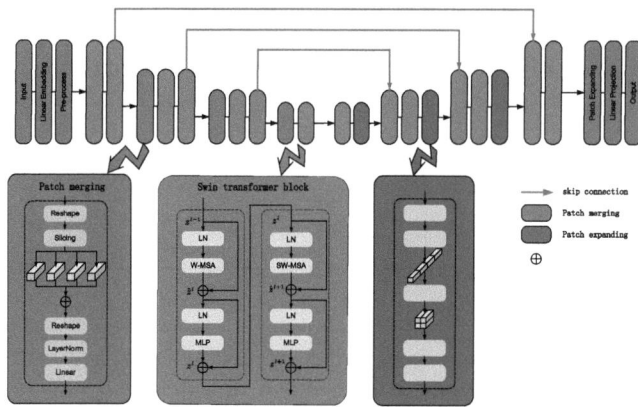

Fig. 2. Generative Network.

Generative Network: The generative networks' design was modified from [3], a U-shaped architecture that utilizes skip-connections and Swin-Transformer, which accepts an original image $z \sim \mathcal{N}(0, I)$ as input. The input image is initially split into non-overlapping patches with a patch size of 4×4 to obtain sequence embeddings. This allows the feature dimensions to be projected into an arbitrary number of dimensions represented by C, where the feature dimension becomes $4 \times 4 \times 3 = 48$. After that, a cascade of trans-former blocks make up a U-shaped encoder and decoder. The Swin Transformer blocks enable the learning of global and long-range semantic information interaction. Between each block layer in the encoder, down-sampling is achieved through a patch merging layer. This operation, performed without information loss, involves reducing the image resolution and adjusting channel numbers, facilitating a hierarchical design.

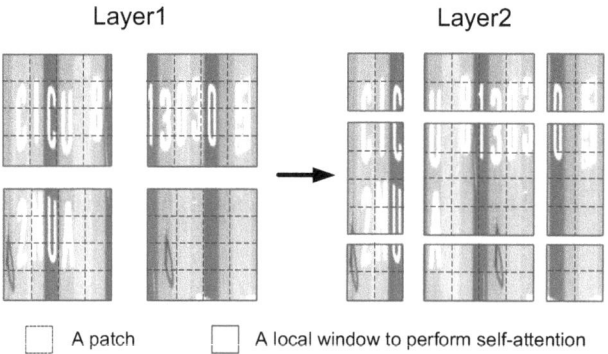

Fig. 3. Sifted window

In each basic building block as Fig. 3 shown, the received feature map is partitioned into non-overlapping windows. Subsequently, locally multi-head self-attention (MSA) is applied to each window. Sliding shifts between the windows are incorporated by the Swin-Transformer to guarantee interaction between neighboring windows for comprehensive global information modeling. More specifically, when receiving the input feature map $z^l \in \mathbb{R}^{H \times W \times C}$ of layer l, the calculation in Swin blocks is as follows:

$$\hat{z}^l = W - MSA(LN(z^{l-1})) + \tilde{z}^{l-1} \tag{3}$$

$$\tilde{z}^l = MLP(LN(\hat{z}^l)) + \hat{z}^l \tag{4}$$

$$\hat{z}^{l+1} = SW - MSA(LN(z^l)) + z^l \tag{5}$$

$$\tilde{z}^{l+1} = MLP(LN(\hat{z}^{l+1})) + \hat{z}^{l+1} \tag{6}$$

where W-MSA and SW-MSA refer to window-based multi-head self-attention under regular and shifted window partitioning. MLP represents a fully connected neural network, which can further refine the extracted features, and LN stands for layer normalization to ensure the stability and efficiency of the training process. By processing each window separately, the feature extraction block may leverage shifted windows to methodically collect the global structure and contextual information of a picture. This approach proves particularly effective in separating text from complex backgrounds during the style transfer process.

Discriminator Network: The discriminator network, which forms the basis of the Swin-MPGM model, is made up of a number of precisely crafted convolutional layers tasked with thoroughly examining the input image and enhancing its salient characteristics. LeakyReLU activation functions, which add nonlinearity and aid the network in successfully avoiding gradient disappearance, come after these convolutional layers and improve the model's expressiveness and generalizability. The network's internal activation is further stabilized, the training procedure is optimized, and the convergence speed is increased by the batch normalization layer that follows. The spatial resolution steadily drops as the network level deepens, focusing the network more on the image's high-level abstract and semantic information. Lastly, the network's confidence in the legitimacy of the image content is reflected in the pixel value of the single channel prediction map that the discriminator produces. This guarantees the effectiveness and precision of the model in challenging text recognition tasks. This architecture provides a strong basis for the performance of Swin-MPGM models in difficult text generation scenarios by enabling the discriminator network to efficiently recognize and assess the quality of the generated network output image.

Pretrained Perceptual Network: The pretrained perception network, utilizing a VGG16 model [2], takes two inputs: one from the ground truth and one from the generating network. By combining these inputs, the network can sequentially process the outputs of four convolutional blocks for both the generated and actual images in parallel. This approach ensures the visual authenticity and style consistency of the generated images, allowing for a deeper understanding of their internal structure and style, ultimately improving the quality of image production.

2.3 Label Generation

Our goal is to extract clean text from images without needing exact pixel-level labels.

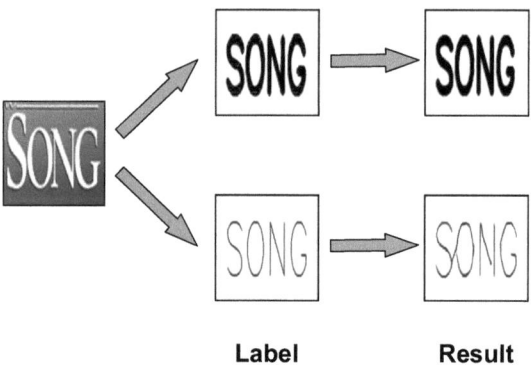

Fig. 4. The influence of labels on outputs

However, obtaining pixel-level aligned labels is impractical. Moreover, unsupervised image segmentation methods, such as clustering seg-mentation, may produce foreground text regions that are not entirely accurate and generate some incorrect labels. To obtain more realistic image labels for textual content, we generate the desired character content as labels on a white background using text content labels. During the testing of the network, we observed that the structural style of the reference labels, such as the thickness of character strokes (e.g., thicker or thinner), influences the feature representation generated by the generator. As shown in Fig. 4, labels with finer character strokes contain fewer pixels with effective information, leading to a reduced number of pixels corresponding to the original character structure in the image. This leads to the network not fully learning the corresponding structural information of characters, resulting in incorrect outputs, such as characters sticking. Initially, the image resolution and character count in the character generation process must be taken into account in order to compute labels with different thicknesses that match different picture scales.

We create realistic text labels on a white background based on text annotations. The thickness of these labels impacts the feature representation; thinner strokes can result in missing character details and merging issues. Thus, label thickness must be adjusted based on image resolution and character count to suit different scales.

$$\delta = \frac{W}{N \times tw_{min}} \tag{7}$$

where W is the width of the original image, N is the number of characters in the label, tw_{min} is the minimum character size, and δ is the character scaling ratio.

The stroke weight of the characters in the image label represents the proportion of pixels containing valid character content in the target style image. This is typical-ly related to the number of characters and the image resolution. When the image resolution is fixed, as the number of characters increases, the character strokes should become finer to achieve optimal readability in limited space, avoiding the occur-rence of sticking between generated image labels and preventing ambiguity in the generated results. Conversely, when the number of characters is small, the character strokes should be appropriately thicker to ensure that the generated image labels in-clude as many valid character content pixels as possible.

$$S = \begin{cases} W/0.15W_{min \times N} & \text{if } W/H \geq 1 \\ H/0.15H_{min \times N} & \text{if } W/H < 1 \end{cases} \tag{8}$$

where W and H represent the width and height of the image, respectively. W_{min} and H_{min} are the minimum image resolution and S is the setting for the stroke weight of characters in the generated images.

2.4 Loss Function

Specifically, the separation of text and background can be fundamentally viewed as a combination of two tasks: text content extraction and image style transfer. The objective is to make the generated image as close as possible to the target image, achieving a high level of image similarity. So, the GANs should learn a mapping from the real text image I to the label with black text on a white background, causing the generated result $G(I)$ to be similar to the label.

L1 Loss: To enhance the clarity and fidelity of character images generated by GANs, we opted for the L1 loss to refine the background. Unlike the L2 loss, which imposes strict penalties for large differences but diminishes penalties for small disparities, the L1 loss maintains a consistent focus on evaluating differences between results and labels. For this reason, we combine the GAN framework with the L1 loss to ensure that the generated character structures remain recognizable. This fusion prioritizes fidelity to the original content, thereby mitigating the impact of subtle variations in the background on the overall character generation.

$$\mathcal{L}_P(G) = \mathbb{E}_{x,y,z}\left[\|y - G(x,z)\|_1\right] \tag{9}$$

Then the objective changes to

$$G^* = \arg\min_G \max_D \mathcal{L}_{cGAN}(G, D) + \lambda \mathcal{L}_{L1}(G) \tag{10}$$

where $\mathcal{L}_{cGAN}(G, D)$ uses MSE Loss.

Perceptual Loss: Instead of relying on pixel-wise losses, we define the context loss based on a pre-trained VGG16 network described in [4] as φ. Then, we can get the context loss as the Euclidean distance between the feature representations of a reconstructed image $G(x,z)$ and the ground truth y. The perceptual loss can be described as follows:

$$\mathcal{L}_{content}(G) = \mathbb{E}_{x,y,z}\left[\|\phi(y) - \phi(G(x,z))\|\right] \tag{11}$$

Multi task loss: Combining cGAN loss with perceptual loss, the entire loss function has the following expression:

$$G^* = \arg\min_G \max_D \mathcal{L}_{cGAN}(G, D)$$

$$+ \lambda \mathcal{L}_{L1}(G) + \mu \mathcal{L}_{\text{content}}(G) \tag{12}$$

In the Swin-MPGM generator, the loss for text content extraction and image style transfer is computed separately. The weights λ and μ of the two sub-tasks need to be manually set during training, which consumes a considerable amount of time and computational resources to experiment with parameter values. This process may not necessarily achieve optimal result. As [5] noted, homoscedastic uncertainty may be used to quantify task-related uncertainty. In Swin-MPGM, the content generation loss is determined by the formula (8). We define the likelihood of these two tasks as Gaussian distributions, the their means given by the model outputs, along with an observation noise scalar σ. We define $f^W(x)$ as our sufficient statistics and obtain the following multi-task likelihood:

$$p(y_c, y_s | f^W(x)) = p(y_c | f^W(x)) \times p(y_s | f^W(x)) \tag{13}$$

where y_c and y_s are model outputs corresponding content extraction task and images style transfer task. Finally, above formula can be equal to:

$$\begin{aligned} L = & \frac{1}{2\sigma_1^2} \arg\min_G \max_D \mathcal{L}_{\text{cGAN}}(G) \\ & + \frac{1}{2\sigma_2^2} \mathcal{L}_1(G) + \frac{1}{2\sigma_3^2} L_{\text{content}}(G) \\ & + \log \sigma_1 + \log \sigma_2 + \log \sigma_3 \end{aligned} \tag{14}$$

where $L_{content}(G)$ corresponds to the content loss, $L_{cGAN}(G)$ corresponds to the style loss, while σ_i represents the observational noise of the model, capturing the amount of noise present in the output. When the noise σ_1 increases, the weight corresponding to L_{cGAN} decreases accordingly. Conversely, when the noise σ_1 decreases, the weight corresponding to L_{cGAN} increases accordingly. Therefore, introducing σ_i as a hyperparameter into the training process allows for optimizing the allocation of loss weights during network training. This significantly accelerates the rate of loss reduction and improves the accuracy of the generated results.

3 Experiment Result and Analysis

We implement our proposed model using the PyTorch1.8 platform on one RTX 4080 GPU. The initial learning rate lr and batch size are 0.002 and 24. We train our proposed model with the Adam optimizer for 1200 epochs. The Container Number dataset consists of 4849 images collected from various lighting environments, as shown in Fig. 5. This dataset includes scenarios with damaged, blurred, obscured, and overexposed text. Such diversity helps test the robustness and generalization capabilities of models under various lighting conditions.

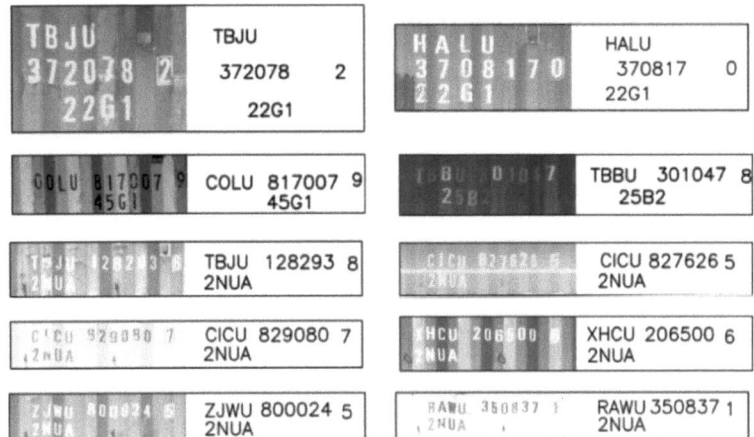

Fig. 5. Container Number dataset

In practical applications, due to the variability of environments, models need to adapt to varying light intensities and directions to ensure robust text generation in various scenarios. The inclusion of diverse scenarios in the Container Number dataset, such as damaged, blurred, and obscured text, enhances the dataset's ability to evaluate the model's performance under real-world conditions. This comprehensive consideration of diversity in dataset design contributes to the development of robust and reliable text recognition systems with practical application value.

Our approach involves training every model over 1000 iterations at a reduced resolution of 224 × 224 pixels in order to minimize the computational load. Initially, Swin-MPGM designed a generator based on the Swin-Transformer and a discriminator based on a 70 × 70 PatchGAN.

3.1 Comparing Multi-task Loss Training

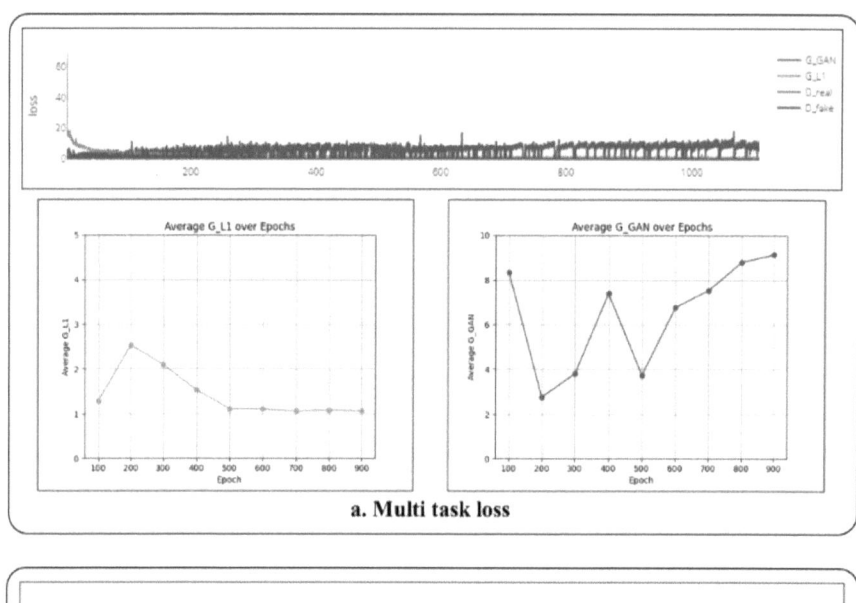

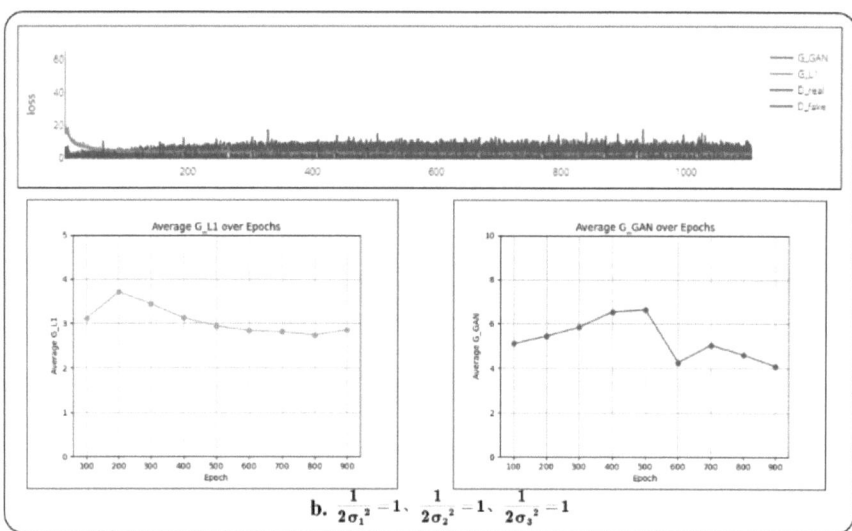

Fig. 6. Comparison of multi-task loss training.

The loss of multitasking is contrasted with not using it. The pictures in Fig. 6 make it clear that using multi-task loss produces much better generation result and faster iteration speed than when it is not used. Compared to training with manually set weights equal to one, lower L1 losses can be achieved using self-balanced multi-task weights, which means that the generated image has a higher similarity to labels at the pixel level.

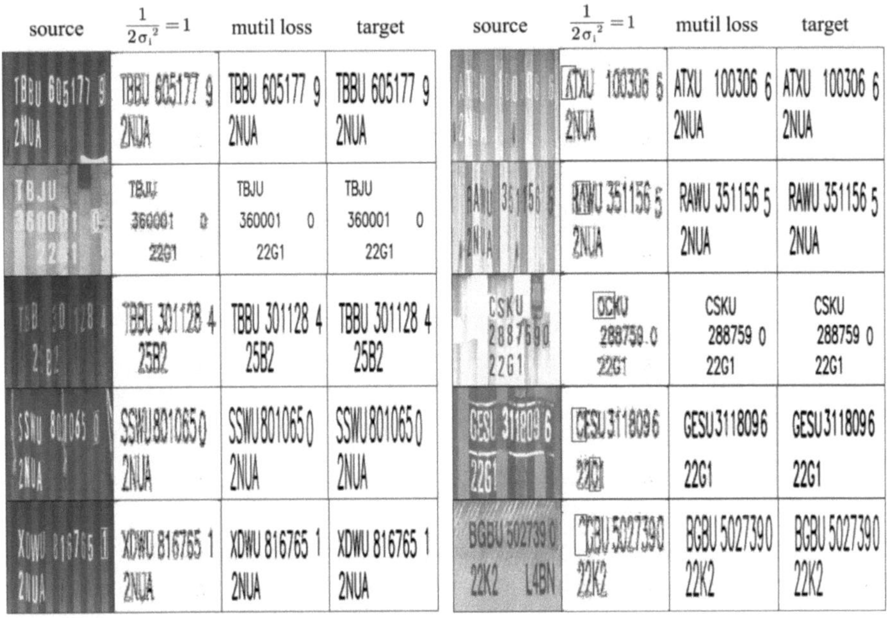

Fig. 7. Comparison of various loss weight.

More specifically, as Fig. 7 shows, when using mutil-task loss, Swin-MPGM is able to produce smoother text content instead of noisy results. At the same time, it is more accurate in the generated result, for example, when generating character "A" and "C", using mutil-task loss will not result in missing content.

3.2 Comparison of the Generated Results of Various Models

To demonstrate the efficacy of our proposed Swin-MPGM method, a thorough analysis of the outcomes from several models is provided. This analysis is crucial for highlighting the enhancements and distinctive advantages our approach provides compared to existing solutions in the fields of text-background separation and style transfer.

Comparing Swin-MPGM to other GAN-based method, including pix2pix [6] and Cycle-GAN [7], which have been extensively utilized for image-to-image translation tasks. The comparison reveals that while these methods show promise, they struggle with the nuanced requirements of text generation, often resulting in blurred or distorted character shapes.

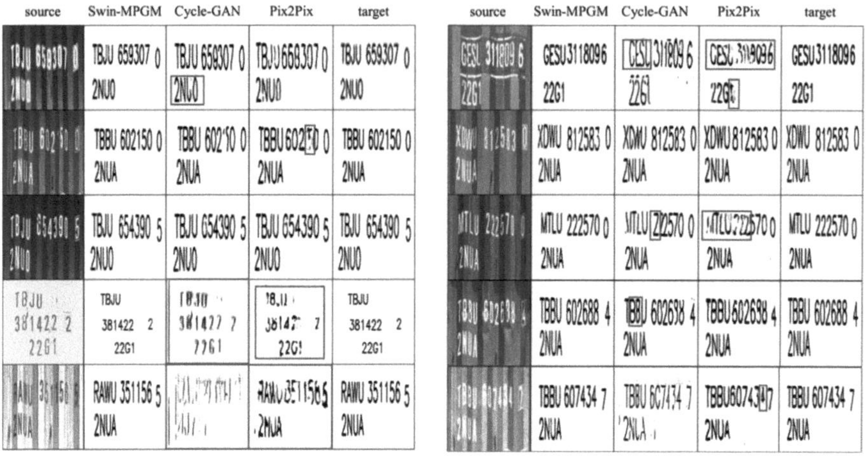

Fig. 8. Comparison of our Swin-MPGM model with using pix2pix and Cycle-GAN.

Comparing Swin-MPGM to other GAN-based method, including pix2pix and Cycle-GAN, which have been extensively utilized for image-to-image translation tasks, is illustrated in Fig. 8. The comparison reveals that while these methods show promise, they struggle with the nuanced requirements of text recognition, often resulting in blurred or distorted character shapes. The inability to handle complex text-background interactions limits their effectiveness in practical applications. The result of Cycle-GAN shows that the generated character "G" is partially missing and confuses the characters "Z" with "2", leading to an erroneous result. In the results of Pix2Pix, it is evident that the characters "8" and "9" are confused, and the character "W" is also partially missing.

We then introduce our Swin-MPGM method into the comparison, emphasizing the incorporation of the Swin-Transformer architecture and the automatic balancing mechanism for multi-task losses. The results are striking, with our model demonstrating a significant enhancement in the clarity and accuracy of the generated text images. The characters are well-defined, with sharp edges and correct proportions, even when placed against challenging backgrounds. As shown in Fig. 8, Swin-MPGM can fill in missing parts of characters while ignoring the effects of shadows and overexposure. The Swin-Transformer's ability to capture long-range dependencies is instrumental in maintaining the structural consistency of the text, while the multi-task loss balancing ensures that both the content and style of the text are accurately preserved.

4 Experiment Result and Analysis

The Swin-MPGM method is a major step forward in recognizing text in challenging environments. It uses a GAN framework with Swin-Transformer architecture to adeptly separate text from complex backgrounds. The U-shaped network, blending CNN and transformer strengths, excels at capturing and generating text while preserving character structure, crucial for real-world applications with cluttered backgrounds. A key innovation is the online label generation strategy that simplifies training and adapts to various text styles without needing pixel-level annotations. The automatic loss balancing mechanism, guided by homoscedastic uncertainty, optimizes training for efficient learning and consistent performance across datasets. Experiments confirm the method's effectiveness, generating clean backgrounds with accurately represented text, setting a new standard for robust text generation.

5 Conclusion

In conclusion, the Swin-MPGM method proposed in this study has made significant progress in complex text recognition environments. By integrating the Swin-Transformer architecture within a GAN framework, this method effectively separates text from complex backgrounds while maintaining the structural integrity of characters. Additionally, the online image label generation strategy simplifies the training process, and the automatic balancing mechanism enhances the model's learning efficiency and performance. Experimental results demonstrate that Swin-MPGM excels in generating text that closely aligns with real images, offering a new approach for future research in scene text recognition.

References

1. Luo, C., Lin, Q., Liu, Y., et al.: Separating content from style using adversarial learning for recognizing text in the wild. J. Int. J. Comput. Vis. **129**, 960–976 (2021)
2. Lyu, Q., Guo, M., Pei, Z.: DeGAN: mixed noise removal via generative adversarial networks. Appl. Soft Comput. **95**, 106478 (2020)
3. Cao, H., Wang, Y., Chen, J., et al.: Swin-unet: Unet-like pure transformer for medical image segmentation; In: European Conference on Computer Vision. Tel Aviv, pp. 205–218 (2022)
4. Ledig, C., Theis, L., Huszár, F., et al.: Photo-realistic single image super-resolution using a generative adversarial network. In: Proceedings of the Proceedings of the IEEE Conference on Computer Vision and Pattern Recognition. Hawaii, pp. 4681–4690 (2017)
5. Kendall, A., Gal, Y., Cipolla, R.: Multi-task learning using uncertainty to weigh losses for scene geometry and semantics; In: Proceedings of the IEEE Conference on Computer Vision and Pattern Recognition. Utah, pp. 7482–7491 (2018)
6. Isola, P., Zhu, J-Y., Zhou, T., et al.: Image-to-image translation with conditional adversarial networks; In: Proceedings of the IEEE Conference on Computer Vision and Pattern Recognition. Hawaii, pp. 1125–1134 (2017)
7. Zhu, J-Y., Park, T., Isola, P., et al.: Unpaired image-to-image translation using cycle-consistent adversarial networks; In: Proceedings of the IEEE International Conference on Computer Vision. Venice, pp. 2223–2232 (2017)

Flow Field Analysis and Structure Optimization of Silica Sol Shell Drying Chamber

Zhiqiang Hu[1], Fang Wang[2(✉)], Hongfang Qi[1,2], and Tao Chen[3]

[1] School of Mechanical Engineering, Wuhan Polytechnic University, Wuhan 430023, China
[2] School of Intelligent Manufacturing, Wuhan Huaxia Institute of Technology, Wuhan 430223, China
jyfrtwf@sina.com
[3] Xiangyang Liqiang Machinery Co., Ltd., Xiangyang 441000, China

Abstract. Introduction: This is an application-based article. Objectives: In order to solve the problem of uneven drying inside the drying chamber of the existing silica sol shells and improve the drying quality of the shells, the structural optimization is carried out by means of numerical simulation. Methods: Numerical simulation of the flow field in the drying chamber is carried out based on the standard k-ε model, according to the simulation results, the distribution characteristics of the flow field in the drying chamber of the two airflow organization schemes are compared and analyzed, and the structural optimization scheme of installing a deflector plate is put forward, and the parameter optimization test is carried out by applying the orthogonal test method to obtain the optimal design parameters of the deflector plate: width of the deflector plate is 225 mm, the angle is 30°, and the spacing is 150 mm. Resutts: The results show that the velocity and temperature distribution of the upper and lower air supply mode is more uniform than that of the upper and lower return mode, so we choose to add the deflector plate to the upper and lower air supply drying chamber to further improve its uniformity. After optimization of the structure, the velocity non-uniformity coefficient decreased by 16%, and the temperature non-uniformity coefficient decreased by 0.3%. Conclusion: The temperature distribution and speed distribution in the drying chamber optimized by the structure are more uniform, and it can be applied to the hot air drying of silica sol shell.

Keywords: silica sol shell · drying chamber · numerical simulation · deflectors · air supply method

1 Introduction

Silicone sol is a commonly used shell binder, which has the characteristics of high temperature resistance, creep resistance, no environmental pollution and high casting quality [1], and is widely used. In the process of silica sol shell preparation, shell drying is a crucial part [2], and the drying and hardening effect directly determines the quality and performance of silica sol shell. Shell drying relies on the flow of hot air in the drying chamber to take away the moisture on the surface of the shell, the current enterprise shell drying mainly relies on the fan blowing, drying efficiency is low, close to the fan position of the wind speed is fast, the temperature is high, the shell drying faster, away from the fan position of the wind speed is low, the temperature is low, the shell drying slower, overall drying is not uniform, prone to produce the surface of the shell rough burrs, the shell hole bridging and the surface layer of shell cracks and other defects. It is easy to produce Therefore, to ensure the uniformity of the flow field distribution in the shell drying chamber is very critical to improve the shell drying effect.

Aiming at the problem of non-uniformity of flow field distribution inside the drying chamber, scholars at home and abroad have done many researches. Sun Wei [3] simulated and analyzed the area of air inlet and wind speed in order to improve the flow field uniformity inside the drying box of herbs, and the results showed that the flow field uniformity inside the drying box was the best when the area of the air inlet was 0.96 m^2 and the wind speed was 3.0 m/s. Li Ruolan [4] studied the influence of three factors on the distribution of the flow field inside the drying chamber of wolfberry: the spacing of material trays, the tilt angle and the position of the air inlet, and determined the optimal structural design scheme. Luo Quanquan [5] in order to solve the problem of uneven airflow in the drying chamber, proposed to change the right-angle wall into a rounded arc angle, and add a baffle plate to divert the flow, the results show that the setting of three baffle plates can effectively improve the uniformity of the airflow in the drying chamber. Aktas [6] designed a new type of cylindrical drying chamber for drying mint leaves, the drying chamber consists of an air-source heat pump, a heat recovery device, and temperature controllers, and experiments have proved that cylindrical drying chamber can obtain a more uniform airflow, the drying chamber can obtain a more uniform airflow. The drying chamber can obtain a more uniform airflow to dry the product to prevent the spreading of light weight items such as mint leaves over the drying system. Babu AK [7] conducted an experimental study on a heat pump assisted tray intermittent drying chamber. This study proved that intermittent drying chamber with multiple trays is challenging to dry the fragile and thermally sensitive food materials in a thin layer and it is necessary to ensure good air distribution and reduced pressure drop over all the compartments of the drying chamber. It is necessary to ensure that the air in all compartments of the drying chamber is well distributed and the pressure drop is reduced to achieve uniform drying of the product.

Many scholars have studied the drying inhomogeneity of various material objects and proposed solutions, but there are fewer studies on the drying inhomogeneity of silica-sol shells. For the above problems, this paper establishes the silica sol shell drying chamber model, designs the airflow organization scheme and uses Ansys Fluent software to numerically simulate and analyze the flow field of drying chamber with different schemes, and further improves the uniformity by adding a deflector plate in order to achieve the purpose of improving the drying effect.

2 Numerical Simulation of Flow Field in Drying Chamber

2.1 Drying Chamber Model

According to the enterprise design requirements, in order to ensure the formation of uniform temperature field and velocity field, try to ensure the uniformity of the heat of the material being dried, the drying room is designed for the import and export in the same side, the hot air is sent by the fan into the air supply channel, it will be from the inlet of the drying room into the drying room, and then flow through the drying room in all areas, and in the surface of the material, the moisture will be taken away, and then discharged by the exhaust port on the same side.

In this paper, the drying chamber was modeled in 3D using UG software as shown in Fig. 1. The size of the designed drying chamber is 2000 mm × 2000 mm × 2000 mm, the size of the material trolley is 1500 mm × 500 mm × 1500 mm, and the spacing between the two trolleys is 250 mm.

The shells to be dried are placed on trolleys into the drying chamber. 8 groups of shell mold trees are placed on each trolley, and each drying chamber accommodates two trolleys for a total of 16 groups of shells. The external air is heated up to the required drying temperature of 28 °C by a heat pump device, and then the air supply fan sends this part of the hot air into the drying chamber through the air supply outlet at a speed of 5 m/s to dry the shells.

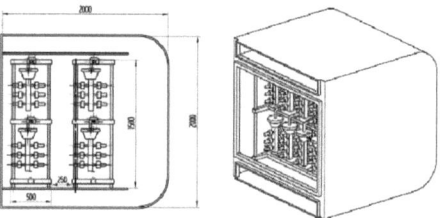

Fig. 1. Drying chamber model.

2.2 Airflow Organization Programme

In the drying process, a reasonable airflow organization scheme is also a key factor to ensure the quality of the dried product [8]. In the actual drying process, the situation is always complex and variable, it not only receives the influence of climate, geographic location and product characteristics and other factors, but also by a variety of factors together, such as temperature, humidity and wind speed will affect the drying rate of the product, and different ways of airflow organization scheme will have a different impact on the final drying effect, so the designed drying chamber of the airflow organization scheme must be guaranteed to be the most unfavorable position in the drying chamber can also obtain better drying. Therefore, the airflow organization scheme of the drying chamber must be designed to ensure that the most unfavorable position in the drying chamber can also obtain better drying. For this study, two different airflow organization schemes are proposed, namely, up-feeding and down-returning single-vent air supply and up-feeding and down-returning double-vent air supply, as shown in Figs. 2 and 3 below.

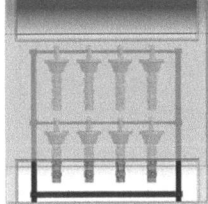
Fig. 2. Upper air supply and lower air return.

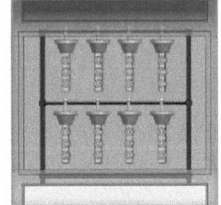
Fig. 3. Top and bottom air supply.

2.3 Mathematical Model

Fluent meshing provides two task-based workflows, Watertight and Fault-Tolerant, which cover most use cases. These workflows guide the user step-by-step through the meshing process, starting with geometry, importing and ending with volumetric mesh generation. These workflows are customizable and can be saved for reuse in future analyses. A sketch of the simulation flow is shown in Fig. 4 below.

From the relevant knowledge of fluid dynamics, it is known that the hot air in the drying chamber is a steady state viscous flow, and when the wind speed is small, the change in density is negligible, and the gas can be approximated as incompressible. Therefore, assuming that the air fluid is an incompressible ideal gas and its viscosity coefficient is constant, the control equations of the corresponding fluid motion are established according to the law of conservation of momentum and the law of conservation of energy [9].

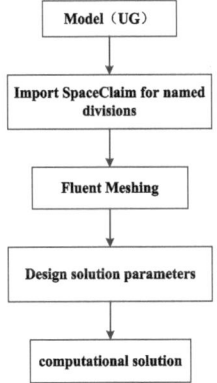
Fig. 4. Simulation flow sketch.

The continuity equation:

$$\frac{\partial u_i}{\partial x_i} = 0 \tag{1}$$

Momentum equation:

$$\frac{\partial(\rho u)}{\partial t} + \frac{\partial(\rho u_t u_j)}{\partial x_i} = -\frac{\partial P}{\partial x_i} + \frac{\partial}{\partial x_j}\left[(u+u_t)\left(\frac{\partial u_t}{\partial x_j} + \frac{\partial u_j}{\partial x_i}\right)\right] \tag{2}$$

Energy Equation:

$$\frac{\partial(\rho T)}{\partial t} + \frac{\partial(\rho u_i T)}{\partial x_j} = \frac{\partial}{\partial x_j}\left[\left(\frac{k}{c_P} + \frac{u_t}{\sigma_T}\right)\frac{\partial T}{\partial x_j}\right] + \frac{S_T}{c_P} \tag{3}$$

The k-ε model can provide good initial guesses, has a good convergence speed and relatively low memory requirements, and is commonly used in industry as it is easier to achieve convergence compared to other models. Considering that the state of indoor fluid flow is mainly turbulent and the flow line is curved with fewer vortices, the standard k-ε model is more applicable compared to the realizable k-ε model and the RNG k-ε model, so the standard k-ε model is chosen to solve the unconfined problem of the turbulence model and to consider the effect of gravity on it.

k-equation:

$$\frac{\partial(\rho k)}{\partial t} + \frac{\partial(\rho u_j k)}{\partial x_j} = \frac{\partial}{\partial x_j}\left[\left(\mu + \frac{\mu_t}{\sigma_k}\right)\frac{\partial k}{\partial x_j}\right] + G_k - \rho\varepsilon \tag{4}$$

ε-equation:

$$\frac{\partial \rho\varepsilon}{\partial t} + \frac{\partial(\rho u_j \varepsilon)}{\partial x_j} = \frac{\partial}{\partial x_j}\left[\left(\mu + \frac{\mu_t}{\sigma_\varepsilon}\right)\frac{\partial \varepsilon}{\partial x_j}\right] + C_{\varepsilon 1}\frac{\varepsilon}{k}G_k - C_{\varepsilon 2}\rho\frac{\varepsilon^2}{k} \tag{5}$$

In the above equation: ρ is the air density, kg/m^2; P is the air pressure, pa; $C_{\varepsilon 1}$ and $C_{\varepsilon 2}$ are empirical constants, taking the values of 1.44 and 1.92; σ_k is the Planck's number corresponding to the turbulent kinetic energy, k, taking the default value of 1.0; σ_ε is the Planck's number corresponding to the dissipation rate, ε, taking the default value of 1.3; G_k is the term of the generation of turbulent kinetic energy, k, due to the mean velocity gradient; μ is the hydrodynamic viscosity, N·S/m^2; μ_t is the vortex viscosity coefficient.

2.4 Boundary Conditions

In this paper, the task-based watertight workflow in ANSYS, i.e., Watertight, is used and its Fluent Meshing is used to mesh the drying chamber, and then the mesh is solved and computed by post-processing. All wall surfaces of the drying chamber are assumed to be standard wall surfaces. Firstly, the external air is heated, and its temperature is allowed to rise to about 28 °C, and then the air supply unit sends the hot air into the drying chamber at a speed of 5 m/s. In the simulation process, we use the velocity inlet, and the outlet is selected as the pressure outlet without reflux, so it is assumed that the outlet gauge pressure is 0. The dimensions and parameter settings of the air supply and return outlets are shown in Table 1.

Table 1. Design parameters of the air outlet.

Type of air outlet	upward air supply and downward air return	Upper and lower air supply, central return air
Number of air inlets	1	2
Number of air outlets	1	1
Air inlet size/mm	1800 × 400	1800 × 200
Air outlet size/mm	1800 × 400	1800 × 1300
air velocity/(m/s)	5	5
temperature/°C	28	28

2.5 Evaluation Indicators

In order to get a more accurate drying effect, we introduce two evaluation indexes, velocity inhomogeneity coefficient and temperature inhomogeneity coefficient [10], to investigate the performance of the drying chamber. The smaller the value is, the better the uniformity is indicated.

Velocity inhomogeneity coefficient:

$$S_v = \frac{\sigma_v}{\bar{v}} \times 100\% = \frac{\sqrt{\frac{1}{n}\sum_{i=1}^{n}(v_i - \bar{v})^2}}{\bar{v}} \times 100\% \qquad (6)$$

Temperature inhomogeneity coefficient:

$$S_t = \frac{\sigma_t}{\bar{t}} \times 100\% = \frac{\sqrt{\frac{1}{n}\sum_{i=1}^{n}(t_i - \bar{t})^2}}{\bar{t}} \times 100\% \qquad (7)$$

In the above equation, σ_v, σ_t are the standard deviation of velocity and temperature; $\bar{v}$, $\bar{t}$ are the mean values of velocity and temperature; v_i, t_i are the monitored values of velocity and temperature, and n is the number of monitoring points.

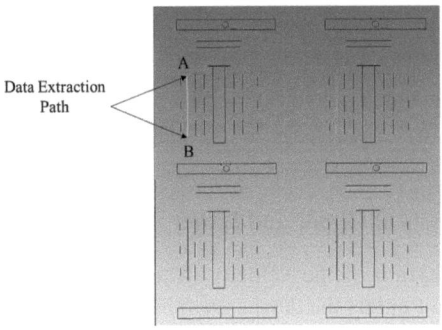

Fig. 5. Schematic diagram of the monitoring area setup.

Through the post-processing software CFD-Post create line function in the drying chamber of four different types of shell region to create a point line to realize the regional monitoring, monitoring area settings are shown in the following Fig. 5, in order to intuitively and accurately reflect the effect of the distribution of the flow field in the drying chamber, through the extraction of the velocity and temperature values on the path AB, and then plotted into a point line diagram for analysis.

3 Analysis of Simulation Results

3.1 Simulation Analysis of Upward Air Supply and Downward Air Return

Figure 6 is a cloud diagram of the velocity distribution of the airflow in the drying chamber when the hot air enters the drying chamber at a speed of 5 m/s. As can be seen from the figure, the hot air enters the drying chamber from the air inlet after being heated, and the speed is very fast at the beginning, and after reaching the first wall, the local flow rate decreases and the wind direction changes, and then it continues to go downward until it touches the second wall, and then a part of the airflow disperses upward to the left, and a part of the airflow is discharged directly by the air outlet. To the left upward dispersion of the airflow in the shell to travel and take away the moisture on the surface of the shell, but due to the airflow after a number of energy loss speed has decreased a lot, resulting in the shell area of the wind speed is too low to meet the requirements. Figure 7 is a cloud diagram of the temperature distribution of the airflow in the drying chamber when the hot air at about 28 °C enters the drying chamber. As can be seen from the figure, the hot air in the process of skimming the surface of the shell, close to the inlet and outlet of the shell temperature is slightly lower than away from the inlet and outlet of the shell temperature, the overall temperature change is not great, basically maintained at about 27 °C.

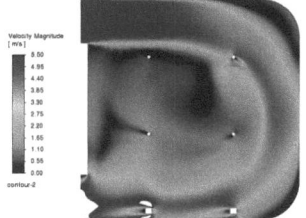 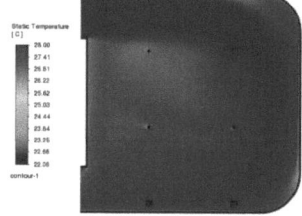

Fig. 6. Up-send-down-return velocity field cloud map.

Fig. 7. Up-send-down-return temperature field cloud map.

3.2 Simulation Analysis of Upper and Lower Air Supply and Middle Air Return

Figure 8 is a cloud diagram of the velocity distribution of the airflow in the drying chamber when the hot air enters the drying chamber at a speed of 5 m/s. As can be seen from the figure, the airflow is fed by double air supply ports and then meets in the middle of the drying chamber, then skims over the material area, and finally discharged by the exhaust port, which leads to a very obvious and regular stratification phenomenon of the air velocity in the material area, and the air velocity close to the middle of the chamber reaches up to 4.5 m/s, while the air velocity far away from the middle of the chamber reaches a minimum of only less than 1 m/s. Figure 9 is the temperature distribution cloud diagram of the airflow inside the drying chamber when hot air at about 28 °C enters into the drying chamber. The temperature distribution cloud diagram of the airflow inside the chamber. As can be seen from the figure, when the hot air passes through the surface of the shell, the temperature of the shell close to the air inlet and outlet is slightly higher than that of the shell far from the air inlet and outlet, and the temperature change is not big in general, which is controlled at about 27 °C.

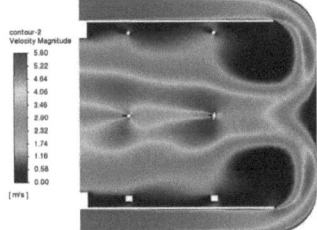 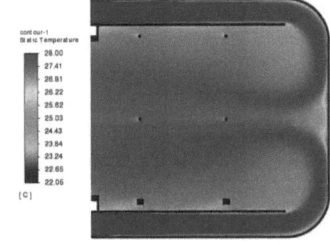

Fig. 8. Up and down air velocity field cloud.   **Fig. 9.** Up and down air temperature field cloud.

When we compare the simulation of the above two air supply methods, although the temperature distribution of the upward and downward air supply method is relatively uniform, the air velocity in the material area is very low and the distribution is uneven and irregular, so it is not easy for us to improve and optimize it. While the upper and lower air supply method although the speed distribution is not uniform, but we can find that the uneven distribution is regular by observing the airflow direction, so finally we choose the upper and lower air supply method and optimize the structure of the drying chamber to achieve better drying effect.

4 Optimization of Drying Chamber Structure

4.1 Design of Deflector Plate Structure

In the simulation process, we found that the velocity field distribution inside the drying chamber is inhomogeneous, and in order to improve this inhomogeneity, it is necessary to add a deflector [11], which is a special type of deflector to guide the airflow to different directions for the purpose of improving the distribution of the flow field inside the drying chamber. For the case of upper and lower double-air outlet air supply in the drying chamber, we designed downward and upward tilting [12] deflector plates for airflow guidance, and good drying can be obtained for the shells which are far away from the center. And in the middle of the two airflow junction design a top and bottom of the expanding deflector to facilitate the airflow better diffusion to the material area, as shown in Fig. 10.

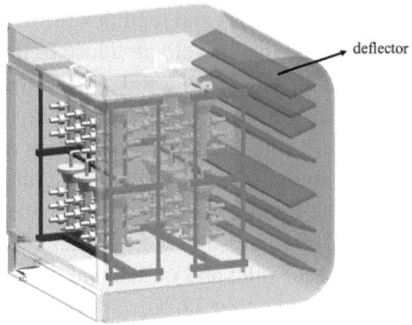

Fig. 10. Deflector plate structure diagram.

Orthogonal experimental method is a systematic and efficient experimental design method, which can consider the effects of multiple factors simultaneously and determine the optimal combination of factors to meet the experimental requirements through reasonable sample selection and factor combination. In order to find out the most reasonable design and arrangement of the deflector, we designed an orthogonal experimental scheme, in which the three factors are the width, angle and spacing of the deflector, which do not affect each other, based on the above considerations, the orthogonal experimental study is carried out by using the standard orthogonal experimental table of $L_9(3^3)$ and simulation is performed on it. The influencing factors and levels are shown in Table 2, and the orthogonal experimental scheme is shown in Table 3.

Table 2. Influencing factors and levels.

Level/Influence factor	Deflector width A/mm	Deflector Angle B/°C	Deflector spacing C/mm
1	175(A_1)	20(B_1)	120(C_1)
2	200(A_2)	25(B_2)	150(C_2)
3	225(A_3)	30(B_3)	180(C_3)

4.2 Optimization of Structural Analysis

The results of the polar analysis are shown in Table 4, from which it can be seen that the width, thickness and spacing of the deflector plate are effective influencing factors. From the results of the polar analysis, the larger the polar value R of the factor, the more significant the influence of the velocity inhomogeneity coefficient by the factor. As shown in Table 4, the order of factors affecting the speed non-uniformity coefficient is B (angle) > A (width) > C (spacing).

In Table 4, K_1, K_2 and K_3 are the sums of the corresponding velocity inhomogeneity coefficients of the experiments at each level. k_1, k_2 and k_3 are the average values of the corresponding velocity inhomogeneity coefficients of the experiments at each level, respectively. The smaller the velocity inhomogeneity coefficient is, the smaller the ki

Table 3. Orthogonal experimental protocol.

Experimental program	Deflector width A/mm	Deflector Angle B/°C	Deflector spacing C/mm	Horizontal Combination	Velocity inhomogeneity coefficient %	Experimental program
1	175(A_1)	20(B_1)	120(C_1)	$A_1B_1C_1$	34	1
2	175(A_1)	25(B_2)	150(C_2)	$A_1B_2C_2$	24	2
3	175(A_1)	30(B_3)	180(C_3)	$A_1B_3C_3$	16	3
4	200(A_2)	20(B_1)	150(C_2)	$A_2B_1C_2$	20	4
5	200(A_2)	25(B_2)	180(C_3)	$A_2B_2C_3$	21	5
6	200(A_2)	30(B_3)	120(C_1)	$A_2B_3C_1$	19	6
7	225(A_3)	20(B_1)	180(C_3)	$A_3B_1C_3$	18	7
8	225(A_3)	25(B_2)	120(C_1)	$A_3B_2C_1$	21	8
9	225(A_3)	30(B_3)	150(C_2)	$A_3B_3C_2$	9	9

value corresponding to the level of each factor is. k_3 of A factor is smaller, so A_3 is better; k_3 of B factor is smaller, so B_3 is better; k_2 of C factor is smaller, so C_2 is better; according to the k value of the level of each factor, the optimal parameter combination of $A_3B_3C_2$ was obtained, which corresponds to the experimental program 9, i.e., the width of the deflector plate is 225 mm, the angle of the deflector plate is 30 °C, and the spacing of the deflector plate is 150 mm.

Table 4. Range analysis results.

programmatic	A	B	C
K_1	74	72	74
K_2	60	66	53
K_3	48	44	55
k_1	24.6	24	24.6
k_2	20	22	17.6
k_3	16	14.6	18.3
Range R	8.6	9.4	7
Prioritize factors	B > A > C		
optimal value	A_3	B_3	C_2
Preferred combination	$A_3B_3C_2$		

By analyzing the velocity improvement maps of each test scheme in Fig. 11 below, it can be seen that: (1) Scheme No. 1, No. 2 and No. 4 have uneven wind velocity in the shell region because the width of the deflector plate is not wide enough, which leads to the intersection of the two hot air streams mainly in the middle, resulting in the high velocity in the middle and the uneven wind velocity in the shell region. (2) Scheme No. 6 and No. 8 because of the low spacing of the deflector plate, resulting in uneven wind speed in the shell area near the deflector plate and the shell area far away from the deflector plate. (3) No. 5 and No. 7 both have a region that does not dry well because the spacing of the deflector plates is too large. (4) No. 3 and No. 9 have better overall results, and No. 9 has a more uniform wind speed in the shell area than No. 3.

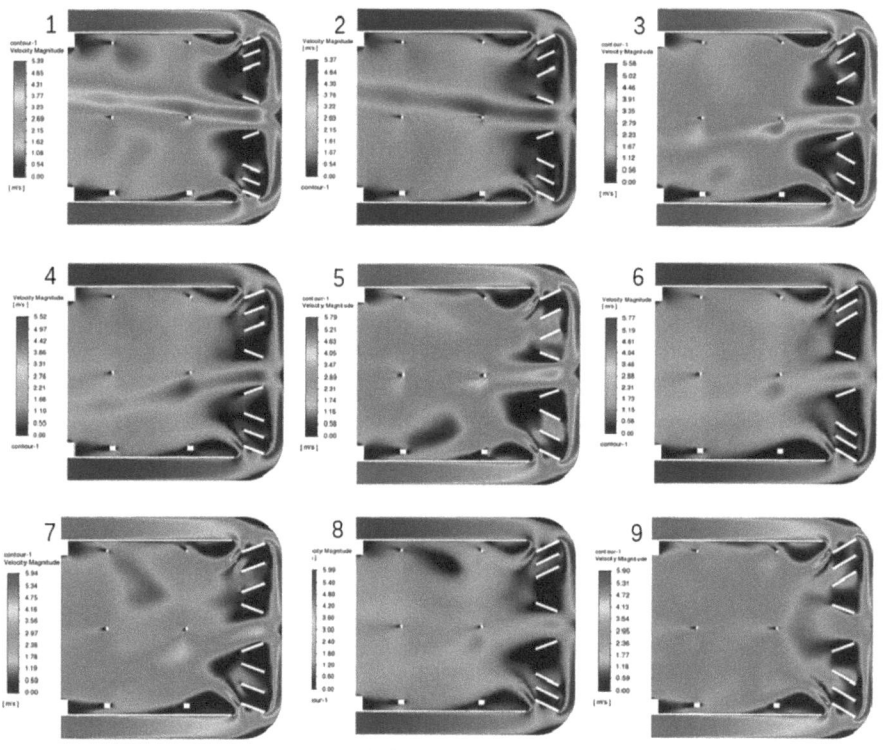

Fig. 11. Cloud view of velocity field improvement for experiments 1–9.

In order to get the drying effect of experiment 9 more accurately, we extracted and compared the data of 4 monitoring areas before and after the improvement. Figure 12 below shows the comparison of the quantitative analysis data of the velocity field before and after the improvement. From the data in the figure, it can be seen that the changes in the velocity field before and after the improvement are relatively obvious, and the velocity change before the improvement is extremely uneven, with the maximum wind speed of up to 5 m/s, and the minimum wind speed of less than 2 m/s. After the improvement, the wind speed is more uniform, and the wind speed is basically between 2.5 m/s and 3 m/s, which can meet the requirements of drying wind speed.

Figure 13 below shows the comparison of the quantitative analysis data of the temperature field before and after the improvement. From the data in the figure, it can be

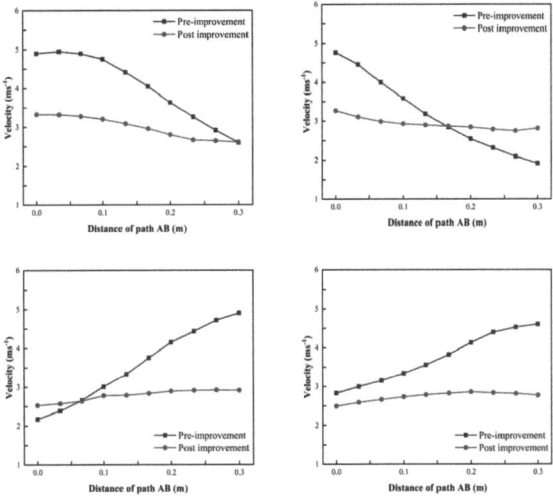

Fig. 12. Comparison of velocity field before and after improvement.

seen that the temperature distribution before the improvement has been more uniform, basically between 27 °C and 27.5 °C. After the improvement, the temperature distribution is more uniform than before, basically at 27 °C, the temperature fluctuation is only 0.1 °C.

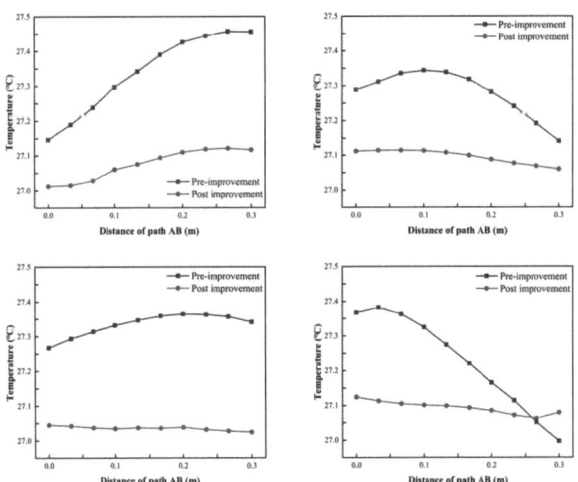

Fig. 13. Comparison of temperature field before and after improvement.

Tables 5 and 6 below show the mean, standard deviation and inhomogeneity coefficients of the velocity and temperature in the drying chamber before and after the improvement with the addition of the deflector. From the table, it can be seen that after the drying chamber was improved by adding the deflector plate, the velocity non-uniformity coefficient decreased by 16% and the temperature non-uniformity coefficient decreased by 0.3%. From the simulation results, it can be seen that after adding the special deflector plate in the drying chamber, the velocity and temperature of the hot air flowing through the surface of the material layer are improved, and the distribution of the flow field in the whole drying chamber is more uniform.

Table 5. Data comparison of speed before and after improvement

conditional	Velocity average $\bar{v}/\text{m} \cdot \text{s}^{-1}$	Velocity standard deviation $\sigma_v/\text{m} \cdot \text{s}^{-1}$	Velocity inhomogeneity coefficient $S_v/\%$
Pre-improvement	3.62	0.90	25
Post improvement	2.90	0.26	9

Table 6. Data comparison of temperature before and after improvement

conditional	Temperature average $\bar{t}/°C$	Temperature standard deviation $\sigma_t/°C$	Temperature inhomogeneity coefficient $S_t/\%$
Pre-improvement	27.29	0.10	0.4
Post improvement	27.07	0.03	0.1

5 Conclusion

In this paper, the air supply performance of silica sol shell drying chamber is studied, the flow field distribution law inside the drying chamber is simulated by establishing a model of the shell drying chamber, and the air supply effect of the drying chamber is compared and analyzed under two different air supply methods, and the following conclusions are obtained:

(1) Comparison and analysis of the distribution of the flow field under the two ways of air supply, although the temperature distribution is uniform, but the speed distribution is not uniform, and because of its energy loss in the flow process, resulting in the working area of the wind speed can not reach the drying requirements. While the upper and lower air supply mode although the velocity distribution is not uniform but its distribution characteristics are more regular, and the wind speed can meet the requirements, so we choose to use the upper and lower air supply mode and its unevenness to optimize the structure.

(2) Based on the non-uniformity of the flow field distribution in the drying chamber with upper and lower air supply, we choose to optimize and improve the structure of the drying chamber by adding a special deflector plate. The velocity inhomogeneity coefficient of the original structure after drying is 25%, and the temperature inhomogeneity coefficient is 0.4%; the velocity inhomogeneity coefficient after optimization of the structure is 9%, and the temperature inhomogeneity coefficient is 0.1%, i.e., the velocity inhomogeneity coefficient decreases by 16%, and the temperature inhomogeneity coefficient decreases by 0.3%. From the simulation results, it can be seen that the temperature distribution and velocity distribution in the drying chamber after structural optimization are more uniform, which can be applied to the hot air drying of silica sol type shell.

References

1. Jin, Z., Li, R., Chen, J.: Research and application of new technology of high strength silica sol shell. Modern Cast Iron **39**(6) (2019)
2. Zhao, L.J.: Analysis on the production of precision silica sol shell. Sci. Advice Sci. Technol. Manag. (2) (2023)
3. Sun, W.: Numerical Simulation and Characteristic Analysis of Flow Field in Heat Pump Drying Chamber, p. 69. Yunnan Normal University (2021)
4. Li, R.L.: Simulation Study on Flow Field Uniformity of Air Energy Hot Air Type Wolfberry Dryer, p. 66. Xi'an University of Science and Technology (2020)
5. Luo, Q.Q., Li, B.G., Yuan, C.H.: Optimization of airflow in drying chamber based on CFD. Packag. Food Mach. **36**(5), 27–31 (2018)
6. Aktaş, M., Khanlari, A., Aktekeli, B., et al.: Analysis of a new drying chamber for heat pump mint leaves dryer. Int. J. Hydrog. Energy **42**(28), 18034–18044 (2017)
7. Babu, A.K., Kumaresan, G., Antony Aroul Raj, V., et al.: Experimental investigations of thin-layer drying of leaves in a heat-pump assisted tray-type batch drying chamber. J. Mech. Eng. **66**(4), 254–265 (2020)
8. Zhao, N.: Development and Performance Test of Multi-heat Source Heat Pump Based Ginseng Drying Chamber. Dalian University of Technology (2022)
9. Dun, Z., Qin, Y., Guan, X.: Simulation optimization and evaluation analysis of the data center airflow distribution. Build. Energy Effic. **43**(3), 27 (2015)
10. Huo, P., Wang, Y.Z., Li, N.N.: Optimization of flow field uniformity in drying chamber based on CFD. China Ceram. **59**(6), 74–82 (2023)
11. Dong, L., Wang, S., Ouyang, R.L., et al.: Flow field simulation and structural optimization of mesh-belt pepper drying machine. J. Agric. Mach. **54**(S1), 373–380 (2023)
12. Zhang, J.H.: Design and Drying Chamber Simulation of Stevia Rebaudiana Drying System Based on Solar Energy Heat Pump. Dalian Ocean University (2020)

Design of Personalized and Lightweight Rehabilitation Fixators Based on nTopology

Yaohua Feng[1(✉)], Xuerong Yang[2], Siyuan Cheng[2], Zhengyang Chen[1], Bojian Fang[1], and Zhixi Chen[1]

[1] School of International Education, Guangdong University of Technology, Guangzhou, China
`735461252@qq.com`
[2] College of Mechanical and Electrical Engineering, Guangdong University of Technology, Guangzhou, China
`imdesign@gdut.edu.cn`

Abstract. To address the issues of inadequate therapeutic effects, side effects, poor fit, and aesthetic deficiencies associated with traditional external fixation for fractures, a personalized and rapid customization and optimization design method for rehabilitation fixators is proposed, based on reverse engineering and 3D printing technologies. Taking the wrist rehabilitation fixator as an example, a handheld scanner is used to scan the hand model, and the collected triangular mesh data is processed. The model reconstruction is completed using Geomagic Studio software to establish a CAD model. On this foundation, forward design work is carried out using nTopology additive manufacturing software in conjunction with Solidworks software. Concurrently, based on clinical symptom analysis and requirement inference, a lightweight design for the fixator is achieved. This approach proposes a convenient and effective method for the design and optimization of personalized rehabilitation fixators.

Keywords: Rehabilitation orthosis · Personalized · Lightweight · nTopology software

1 Introduction

Traditional medical immobilizers mainly use plaster fixation and plastic orthoses, which are effective in fixation but have problems such as non-breathable, easy to harbor bacteria, may cause skin allergy [1, 2], contraction after hardening is not conducive to rehabilitation [3], and the appearance problem may also lead to low self-esteem of the affected children and abandonment [4]. In recent years, some personalized medical rehabilitation immobilizer design methods based on reverse engineering technology have emerged in the continuous innovation in the field of medical rehabilitation [5–8].

The nTopology software is excellent in dealing with surface modeling, lightweight design and topology optimization, and its modular design is easy for clinicians to learn and use, which effectively simplifies the complexity of the forward design. Therefore, in this paper, a personalized and lightweight design process for medical rehabilitation devices is proposed by combining reverse engineering technology and nTopology software with a wrist immobilizer as an example, aiming to provide a simple and easy-to-learn rapid design method for people with non-engineering backgrounds.

2 Design and Optimization Process of Personalized Rehabilitation Fixator

Personalized rehabilitation fixator adopts a tailored approach and is designed according to the specificity of the injured site of the patient, aiming to improve the comfort of the patient and promote healing, and effectively prevent secondary injuries. In addition, the personalized design of the fixator meets the patients' needs for aesthetics and enhances psychological satisfaction, thus bringing positive effects to the patients' rehabilitation process. Therefore, the design of the personalized fixator needs to comprehensively consider the physical therapy effect and the emotional needs of the patient to support comprehensive rehabilitation. Generally, the customization process of the immobilizer consists of three-dimensional scanning to collect the data of the injured part of the patient, then reverse reconstruction to form a digital model, and finally forward design of customized personalized immobilizer, which is divided into four design stages. The specific process is shown in Fig. 1.

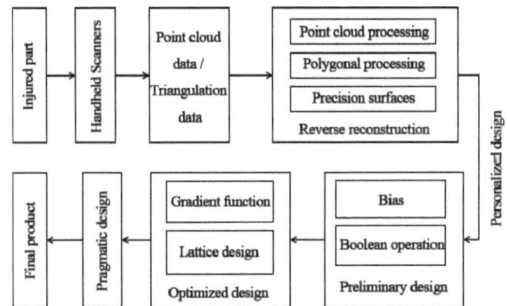

Fig. 1. Personalized rehabilitation fixator design flowchart.

1. Use a handheld or body scanner to quickly acquire human surface data to form point cloud data or triangular sheet data.
2. Import the point cloud data or triangulation sheet data into the Geomagic Studio software for reverse modeling. Specifically, three processing steps are included: point cloud processing, polygon processing, and precise surface processing to obtain a high-precision surface model. Among them, for simple human surface, such as legs, automatic surface processing [9] can be adopted; And complex areas, such as hands, need to manually draw contours and grid division, by simplifying the field skills such as approximating the graph to the basic shape to divide the contour area, to ensure the generation of high-quality surface models.

3. The generated surface model is imported into the nTopology software for forward design. The preliminary design can obtain the proper shape and size of the holder shell by biasing, Boolean operation and other functions. Secondly, based on the condition of the injured part and the doctor's opinion, the optimal design is carried out, and the gradient function and lattice module are used to design the fixator with good support, air permeability and light weight. In addition, if the patient has other wearing habits, the personalized demand design can be increased. Finally, the CAD format model is exported.
4. Use Solidworks software for practical design, mainly to solve the design of auxiliary parts of the fixer, including binding slots, adjusting knobs, etc., and finally realize the complete design model of the fixer.

3 Design Examples

3.1 Data Acquisition

Design a personalized, lightweight wrist retainer. The hand model is scanned with REVscan handheld scanner, and the method of two scans is adopted. First, the hand model is placed in stereo for a 360° surround scan, and then the flat hand model for a second scan of the palm surface. During scanning, VXscan software needs to be connected to the computer to confirm the normal operation of the red light and cross laser, and then the operator can scan the model. The operator should observe the surface data in the software window in real time and try to ensure that there is no omission in the scanning. The scanning results are shown in Fig. 2. After scanning, the STL file is exported by VXscan.

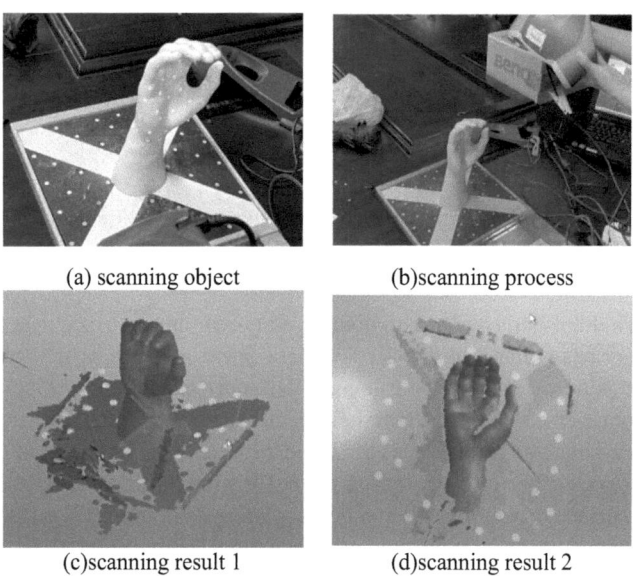

(a) scanning object   (b) scanning process

(c) scanning result 1   (d) scanning result 2

Fig. 2. Surface Data Acquisition

3.2 Reverse Modeling

Reverse modeling is the process of processing the scan data to obtain a digital model that differs no different from the surface features of the injured site, to facilitate the subsequent design of a fixation device that accurately matches the shape and size of the patient's injured site. In this design, the original data scanned by REVscan handheld scanner is directly triangular surface data, so the main processing work consists of polygon processing and accurate surface.

Polygon Processing. The main function of polygon processing is to build a digital model based on the original triangular surface data to reflect the characteristics of the physical object as much as possible. At the same time, the surface of the digital model is more detailed and smoother. In this way, the shape of the subsequent fixator can better fit the injured site, and facilitate the processing of accurate curved surfaces.

Import the original STL file into the Geomagic Studio software for polygon processing. Remove the obvious environment clutter first, and the detail clutter will be processed later. The two scan data files are then aligned and merged to form a roughly complete model. Next, the remaining flakes are removed and the voids are repaired. For the missing area of four fingers and missing area of thumb, the method of "bridge and internal hole" and the method of "internal hole" are used respectively, and the function of "fill by tangent line" is used to restore the features of the solid object. In the final stage of polygon processing, abnormal details are eliminated by removing unnecessary features, smoothing processing and mesh repair operations, to ensure that the digital model features are consistent with the entity as much as possible, and the bottom of the model is closed to form a closed body, as shown in Fig. 3.

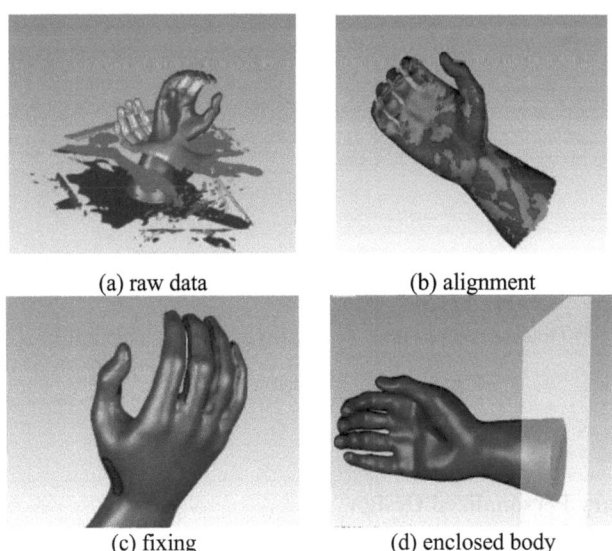

(a) raw data   (b) alignment

(c) fixing   (d) enclosed body

Fig. 3. Polygon Processing

Precision Surfaces. To process the polygon model from the previous part into a solid model with higher precision, which is convenient to import into the forward design software for subsequent processing, the precise surface function of the Geomagic Studio software is required to do this. Among them, the processing process mainly includes setting the contour line, setting the surface sheet, constructing the grating, and fitting the surface, as shown in Fig. 4.

According to the surface conditions of the complex hand model, the contours of the surface sheet are drawn manually, which reduces the difficulty of the regular surface sheet, reduces the curvature anomaly, reduces the fitting error, and makes the solid model fitting effect better. Specific division strategy: the five fingers are approximately a cylinder, the arm is approximately a cuboid, and the area of the palm and the back of the hand is divided according to the adjacent contour lines, as shown in Fig. 5. After the outline is drawn, a solid model capable of forward design can be obtained according to the above processing process.

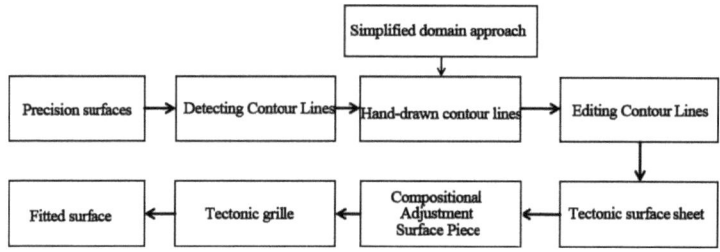

Fig. 4. Precise surface stage processing flowchart

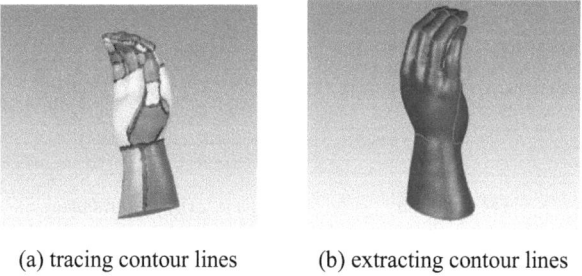

(a) tracing contour lines　　(b) extracting contour lines

Fig. 5. Counter division illustration

3.3 Preliminary Personalized Design

The most basic and important link in the personalized design of medical rehabilitation fixator is to establish a fixator shell whose inner surface shape and size can be completely fitted with the injured part of the patient. In order to achieve this goal, the initial personalized design mainly adopts the idea of thickening and Boolean operation to obtain the fixator shell that conforms to the above goal.

The STL file is imported into the nTopology software and converted into the implicit physical model of the software first (the software represents the imported surface model as a mathematical function, which facilitates the subsequent modeling of surface geometric features stably combined with the software's own algorithm). To optimize the subsequent lightweight lattice design, the width of the edge of the five fingers and wrist was reserved in the design to avoid friction between the rough edges of the lattice body and the skin. At the same time, 1 mm gap is reserved to increase comfort, and 2 mm thickness is set to ensure the strength and support of the fixer. The specific process is shown in Fig. 6.

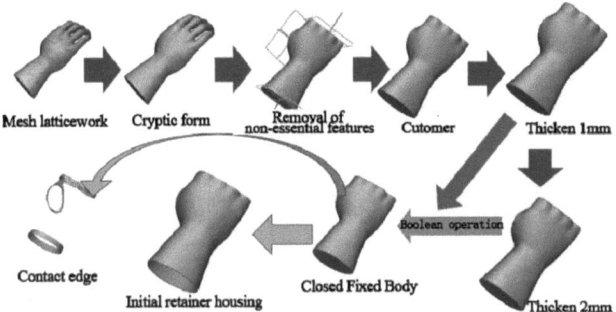

Fig. 6. Initial fixator design procedure

In the modeling process, cutting out non-essential features of implicit bodies, such as five fingers and arm edge. Subsequently, bias operations were carried out successively to obtain the offset body which was 1 mm and 3 mm thicker than the original implicit body. The two biasing bodies are then Boolean reduced to form a closed fixer body with gap size and thickness and sealing on both sides, as shown in Fig. 7. Then, the closed fixator body is bored with the cutting body to obtain the initial fixator shell that can meet the basic wearing requirements. Finally, using the above method to offset, Boolean reduction operations, to obtain the contact edge.

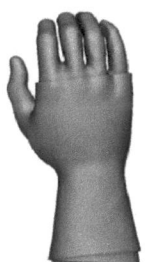

Fig. 7. Initial fixator

3.4 Optimization Design

The main ideas to achieve optimal design: consider the balance relationship between the support, permeability and weight of the fixer, and achieve lightweight design. Further, consider the wearing habits of human bones or patients, and carry out special design for individual parts to increase the comfort of patients.

Lightweight Treatment. For lightweight processing, the Tyson polygon lattice design module of nTopology software is used to achieve the goal of air permeability of the holder for the lattice hollow structure. The gradient function module is used to control the density and thickness arrangement of the hollow structure to achieve the optimization goal of both support and lightweight characteristics. The arrangement law of the hollow structure can be determined according to the clinical disease theory and demand reasoning method, adjust the lattice thickness of the injured area, enhance the support, while maintaining the permeability and lightweight of other areas.

The specific implementation method is shown in Fig. 8. First, the implicit body of the preliminary fixer is converted to the Mesh body. Secondly, the linear gradient function and number gradient function parameters are set. Meanwhile, set the Tyson polygon module based on the gradient function to generate the lattice body, as shown in Fig. 9. Finally, through Boolean operation, the lattice features are mapped to the initial fixer body to generate the final lightweight design, as shown in Fig. 10.

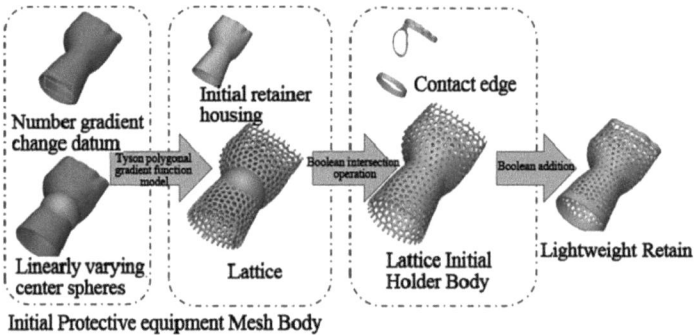

Fig. 8. Lightweight fixator design procedure

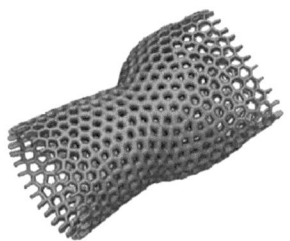

Fig. 9. Lattice effect image

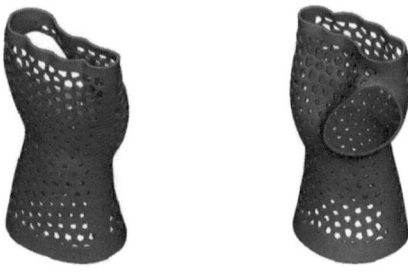

Fig. 10. Lightweight design effect image

Special Design. After the completion of lightweight design, for further consideration of wearing comfort. There is a radial styloid structure at the junction of the distal radius joint and the wrist joint. Pain caused by entrapment and friction between the styloid structure and the fixator may occur if the fixator is directly worn. For this reason, the circular hollow structure is adopted in this part of the area, and the radial styloid is exposed outside the fixator to avoid the discomfort of wearing for a long time. Since the hand model does not have this feature, it is necessary to establish a sphere to simulate the styloid structure of the radius. The sphere was moved to the approximate position point, and the final personalized and lightweight rehabilitation fixator with hollow completion was obtained by using Boolean operation, as shown in Fig. 11.

Fig. 11. Optimization comfort effect image

3.5 Practical Design

Finally consider the practical design and design the magic belt assembly port. The implicit body model designed in the previous part was converted into CAD format file (.igs), imported into SolidWorks software, divided the fixed frame into upper and lower two pieces, and designed assembly holes for easy assembly, as shown in Fig. 12.

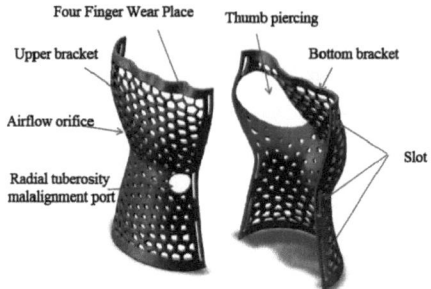

Fig. 12. Product assembly drawing

To facilitate doctors to make product iteration according to patients' wearing feelings. In terms of parameter management, the nTopology software extracts important parameters so that parameters can be adjusted according to patient evaluation to improve comfort, as shown in Fig. 13.

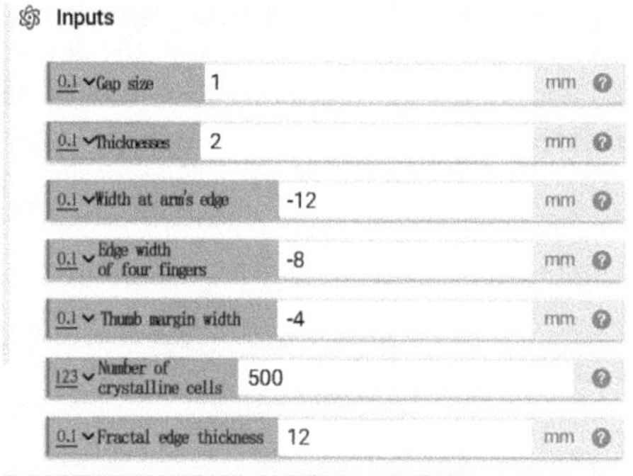

Fig. 13. Key parameter tuning block

4 Conclusion

The study proposes a design scheme for personalized and lightweight rehabilitation fixators using reverse engineering technology and nTopology software. The process involves data acquisition, reverse reconstruction, and forward design in nTopology, incorporating human anatomy to enhance comfort and personalization. The final design is then imported into SolidWorks for binding. Leveraging nTopology's capabilities, this method simplifies the operation and optimizes the fixator's support, weight, and air permeability. It is well-suited for students in clinical medicine and medical engineering to quickly master the design of personalized and lightweight rehabilitation fixators. For special cases, the fixator's shape can be adjusted for conditions like edema deformation to provide appropriate spacing. This approach offers valuable insights for similar medical device designs.

References

1. Zhang, P., Wu, Q., Xu, W.P., et al.: Optimum design and development of personalized fixation frame for fracture. Guizhou Sci. **35**(02), 89–91 (2017)
2. Fan, Q.Y.: Application of orthoses in the field of clinical rehabilitation in orthopaedics. Mod. Rehab. **25**(18), 5–7 (2001)
3. Kechang, P.: Biomechanical Study on Binding Force of Cloth and Thickness of Paper Pressure Pad in the Treatment of Distal Radius Fracture with Small Splint. Beijing University of Chinese Medicine, Beijing (2013). (in Chinese)
4. Russo, R.N., Atkins, R., Haan, E., et al.: Upper limb orthoses and assistive technology utilization in children with hemiplegic cerebral palsy recruited from a population register. Dev. Neurorehabil. **12**(2), 92–99 (2009)
5. Liao, Z.W., Mo, Y.X., Zhang, G.D., et al.: Design and manufacturing of customized rehabilitation orthosis using 3D printing. Chin. J. Med. Phys. **35**(04), 470–477 (2018)
6. Shi, H., Lian, Y.T., Pei, Y.J., et al.: Application progress of 3D scanning and its derivative technique in medical fie. Chin. Med. Equip. **17**(01), 163–167 (2020)
7. Su, H., Yang, X.R., Cheng, S.Y., et al.: Personalized medical brace design based on Geomagic Design X. Mach. Tool Hydraul. **47**(07), 94–97 (2019)
8. Guo, J.B.: Development of Intelligent Rehabilitation Brace for Distal Radius Fracture. Southeast University (2024). https://doi.org/10.27014/dcnki.Gdnau.2022.001099
9. Xie, W.L.: Design of Personalised Rehabilitation Brace Based on Three-Dimensional Scanning and 3D Printing. Guangdong University of Technology (2019). https://doi.org/10.27029/d.cnki.ggdgu.2019.001261

Study on the Profiling of the Header and the Method for Measuring Cotton Stalk Height

Kai Wu, Jianming Jian[✉], Xiuying Tang, Ziyang Tian, Kaihuan Ju, and Junming Yin

College of Engineering, China Agricultural University, Haidian, Beijing, China
jamesjian@126.com, txying@cau.edu.cn

Abstract. Profiling headers, agricultural machinery capable of automatically adapting to ground undulations, play a significant role in the recovery of cotton stalks. This study investigates the application of profiling headers in the cotton stalk recovery process, designs the structure and hydraulic system of the profiling system, and proposes two control strategies: PID control and fuzzy control. Comparative analysis reveals that fuzzy control outperforms in terms of stability, accuracy, and responsiveness, making it suitable for use in farmland environments with significant nonlinear disturbances. This paper also explores methods for measuring cotton stalk height, utilizing the Yolov5s object detection model combined with the SGBM stereo matching algorithm to achieve accurate measurement of cotton stalk height. Experimental results indicate that fuzzy control enables the header to intelligently respond to ground undulations, with system response times meeting the requirements for cotton stalk recovery. Additionally, the height measurement using a stereo camera reduces manual measurement time and provides valuable insights for header blade speed adjustment and blockage prevention. This research is of great significance for the intelligent development of cotton stalk recovery machine headers.

Keywords: stalk recovery · Fuzzy control · SGBM stereo matching · Height measurement · Yolov5s object detection

1 Introduction

In the process of cotton cultivation, a significant amount of cotton stalks is produced in addition to the primary product, cotton. As agricultural waste, if not properly handled, cotton stalks not only occupy farmland space but also potentially cause environmental issues. Therefore, effectively managing and utilizing cotton stalks has become a crucial topic in agricultural production. With technological advancements, cotton stalk recovery technologies and equipment have significantly improved [6]. The application of machinery such as cotton stalk shredders, balers, and recovery machines has greatly enhanced the efficiency of cotton stalk recovery and processing. Profiling headers, which can automatically adapt to ground undulations, play a significant role in the recovery of cotton stalks [5].

Profiling headers significantly enhance the efficiency and quality of harvest, reduce soil disturbance, lower labor intensity, and adapt to various terrains, thereby promoting the effective recovery and utilization of cotton stalks and supporting sustainable agricultural production [2]. Currently, profiling technology in China can be categorized into active profiling and passive profiling.

Active profiling, is becoming a trend, on the other hand, faces several challenges. The response sensitivity of hydraulic systems and various factors still exhibit lag issues, and precise and rapid control needs improvement. Furthermore, the sensors used in active profiling are mostly laser and angle sensors, which do not perform well in harsh field environments [7].

2 Materials and Methods

2.1 Profiling Header System Design

Structural Design. The structural design of the mechanical profiling device relies primarily on two profiling wheels that adhere closely to the ground. The height of the header above the ground is measured by the profiling structure. The profiling structure, as shown in Fig. 2, consists of a profiling wheel (1), a profiling sliding rod (2), an upper limit block (3), a lower limit block (4), a casing (5), and a telescopic spring (6). The casing of the profiling device is bolted to the sides of the header to prevent it from moving. The profiling sliding rod moves up and down within a defined range with the ground undulations. The telescopic spring provides pressure and shock absorption, preventing excessive terrain changes from damaging the header. The sliding length of the profiling sliding rod is measured using a highly reliable wire displacement sensor. In this design, profiling devices are installed on both sides of the header, with the overall structural layout shown in Fig. 1.

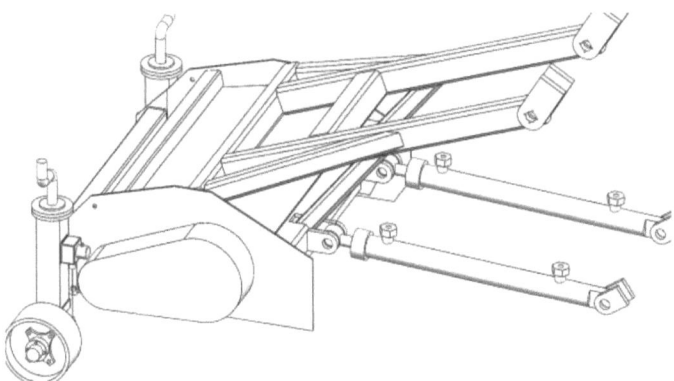

Fig. 1. General Assembly Drawing

Hydraulic System. The hydraulic system design of the header has been improved based on the previous generation's system. Initially, the header used a single-acting hydraulic

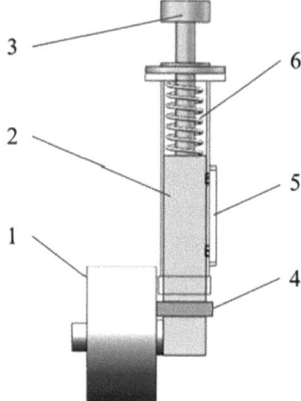

Fig. 2. Profiling Structure

cylinder, where the header was raised by hydraulic oil pressure and lowered by its own weight. To enable the profiling function in conjunction with the mechanical structure design, the hydraulic system has been modified. A three-position four-way proportional valve has been added, and the single-acting hydraulic cylinder has been replaced with a double-acting hydraulic cylinder. Additionally, a check valve has been installed before the proportional valve's oil inlet to prevent the hydraulic oil from flowing back due to the header's weight. A PLC (Programmable Logic Controller) has also been added as a new system controller, allowing the header to switch freely between manual adjustment mode and automatic profiling mode. The process is shown in Fig. 3 below.

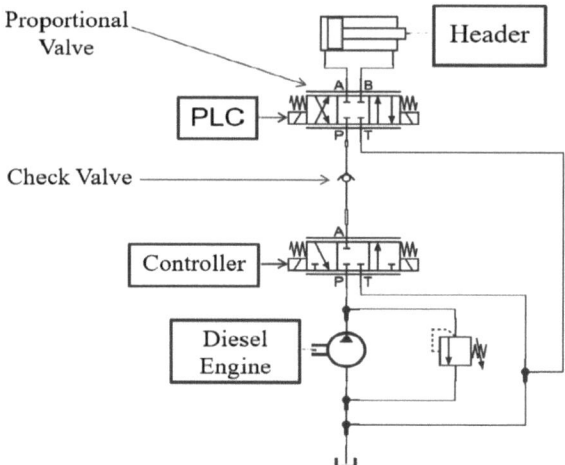

Fig. 3. Hydraulic System

During the operation of hydraulic systems, considering the instability of the O-type three-position four-way hydraulic valve in maintaining pressure, as well as the high reliability requirements for agricultural machinery during prolonged operation, a proposal is made to replace the O-type three-position four-way valve with a Y-type three-position four-way valve. It is important to note that the Y-type three-position four-way valve does not inherently possess pressure-holding capabilities; therefore, it must be paired with a check valve to achieve pressure maintenance in the hydraulic oil circuit. In practical applications, we utilize a dual-path hydraulic balance valve to meet the requirements for pressure compensation and unidirectional flow in the oil circuit. The dual-path hydraulic balance valve not only effectively regulates pressure within the hydraulic system but also ensures stable flow distribution under varying operating conditions, thereby enhancing the overall performance and reliability of the system. Through this modification, the hydraulic system can maintain optimal operating conditions under high loads and extended operational periods, ensuring the efficient functioning of agricultural machinery.

Control Strategy. Two control strategies, PID control and fuzzy control, are used in this design. Their stability, accuracy, and responsiveness are analyzed and compared to determine their respective advantages and choose one as the control strategy for the cotton stalk recovery machine. PID control (see Fig. 4), as a traditional control method, uses integral, proportional, and derivative transformations of the error to regulate the controlled object. Its main advantages are its simplicity, maturity, and high reliability in industrial applications.

Fuzzy control (see Fig. 5), on the other hand, is a control method based on fuzzy logic, used to handle systems with uncertainty and complexity [1]. It simulates human decision-making processes and controls the system through fuzzy sets and fuzzy reasoning. The input variables are first converted into fuzzy sets using membership functions. The knowledge base contains fuzzy rules and membership functions. Fuzzy reasoning applies these rules to map the fuzzy inputs to fuzzy outputs. Finally, the defuzzification process converts the fuzzy outputs into precise control outputs.

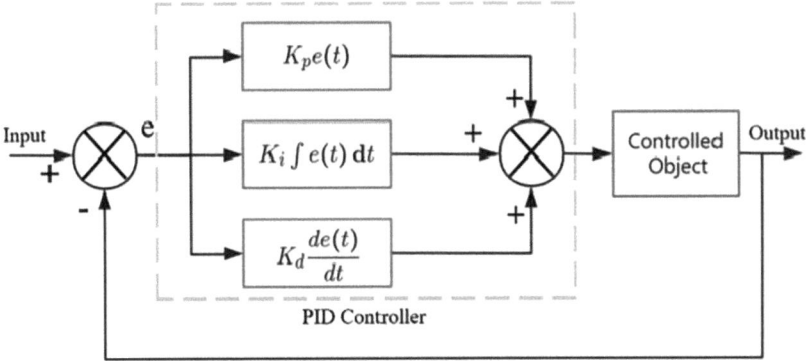

Fig. 4. PID control

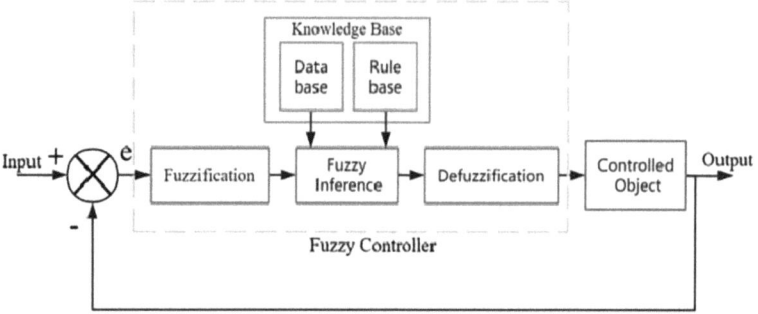

Fig. 5. Fuzzy control

In this design, Gaussian functions are selected as the membership functions, with five sets (NB, NS, Z, PS, PB) as the fuzzy sets. Based on the requirements, 17 fuzzy rules are established. Common fuzzy reasoning methods include Mamdani and Sugeno reasoning; Mamdani reasoning is used in this design. Each fuzzy set has a membership function, and the result of the membership function is the membership degree of the input corresponding to each fuzzy set. All output fuzzy sets specified by the rules are then combined. Table 1 lists the fuzzy rules.

Table 1. Fuzzy Rule

Fuzzy Rule	Error Variation					
	Fuzzy Set	NB	NS	Z	PS	PB
Error	NB		NB	NB	NS	
	NS		NB	NS	NS	
	Z		NS	Z	Z	Z	PS
	PS				PS	PS	PB
	PB				PS	PB	PB

In this paper, for Mamdani inference, each fuzzy set has a membership function, and the result of the membership function is the degree of membership of the input corresponding to each fuzzy set. Then, all the output fuzzy sets specified by the rules are combined.

$$\mu_C(y) = \max_{i=1}^{m} \mu_{B_i}(y) \qquad (1)$$

where $\mu_C(y)$ is the degree of membership of the aggregated output fuzzy set, and $\mu_{Bi}(y)$ is the degree of membership of output y corresponding to fuzzy set Bi. Finally, the defuzzification operation converts the fuzzy output into a precise control output. Common methods include the centroid method and the maximum membership method [13]. This paper uses the centroid method for defuzzification. The aggregated fuzzy set is converted into a precise value y* using the centroid method formula as follows:

$$y^* = \frac{\int y \cdot \mu_C(y) dy}{\int \mu_C(y) dy} \tag{2}$$

System Simulation Analysis. MATLAB is used for system simulation, with the hydraulic model built using AMESIM software and co-simulated with MATLAB. PID and fuzzy control models are built in MATLAB's Simulink. Input signals are set as shown in the Fig. 6, and the response of both models is observed. To better compare the two control methods, the input signal is designed in three stages, allowing for observation of accuracy, responsiveness, robustness, and other control response indicators for both models [12]. The response curves for PID and fuzzy control are shown in Fig. 7.

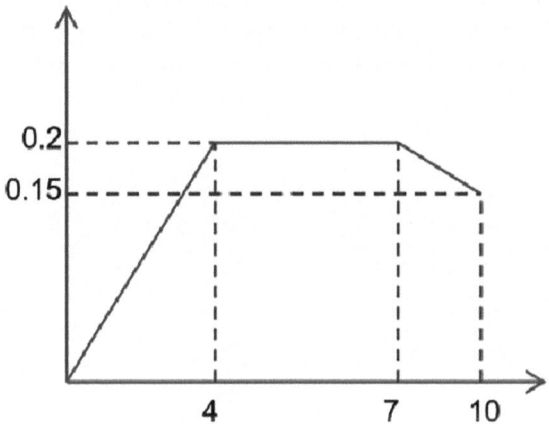

Fig. 6. Input signals

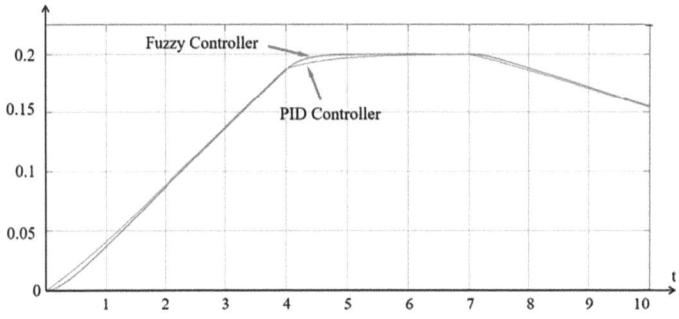

Fig. 7. The response curves

After detailed analysis of the system response data, the fuzzy control response curve and data set are smoother. Fuzzy control demonstrates higher stability and robustness for nonlinear control scenarios, which is beneficial in the presence of various nonlinear disturbances during the cotton stalk recovery machine's operation. Using a fuzzy control strategy will effectively enhance the stability of the header's operation.

2.2 Cotton Stalk Height Measurement Method

Principle of Convolutional Neural Networks. The diagram Fig. 8 below illustrates a simple CNN (Convolutional Neural Network) structure. The first layer inputs an image and performs convolution operations to obtain feature maps with a certain depth in the second layer. The feature maps in the second layer undergo pooling operations, resulting in feature maps with a similar depth in the third layer [9]. This process is repeated to obtain feature maps with an increased depth in the fifth layer. Finally, these feature maps (matrices) are flattened into vectors and passed into the fully connected layer, which is essentially a BP (Back Propagation) neural network. Each feature map in the diagram can be regarded as neurons arranged in a matrix form, similar to the neurons in a BP neural network [10].

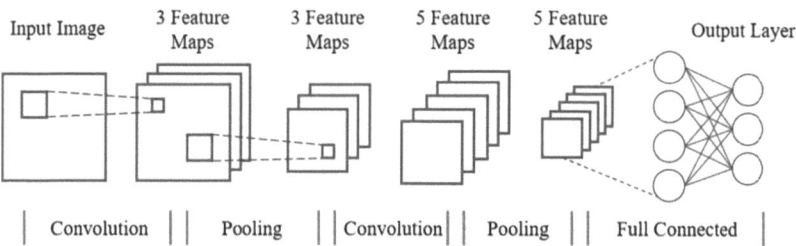

Fig. 8. Principle of Convolutional Neural Networks

Cotton Stalk Height Measurement Method. Using the principle of disparity maps from stereo cameras to construct the spatial coordinates of objects, this method involves two cameras capturing the same scene to generate depth information. In stereo vision, one commonly used stereo matching algorithm is SGBM (Semi-Global Block Matching) [11]. Compared to the traditional BM (Block Matching) algorithm, SGBM provides smoother and more accurate disparity maps, demonstrating greater robustness to noise and complex texture variations [3]. The implementation of the SGBM algorithm begins with the calculation of a cost function:

$$C(x, y, d) = |I_L(x, y) - I_R(x - d, y)| \qquad (3)$$

SGBM utilizes the idea of dynamic programming by accumulating costs in different directions (typically horizontal, vertical, and diagonal) to obtain a globally optimal matching path. It begins by initializing the cost at the first pixel of each row, then processes each pixel by updating the current row's cost based on the previous row's costs and the current pixel's cost. Finally, it aggregates costs in multiple directions, such as left to right and right to left, to consider different matching paths, resulting in a smoother and more consistent disparity map. Where I_L and I_R are the pixel values of the left and right images, respectively. To reduce local matching uncertainty, SGBM aggregates matching costs in multiple directions, including horizontal, vertical, and diagonal directions. The cumulative cost in each direction is given by:

$$S_P(x, y, d) = C(x, y, d) + \min(S_P(x - \Delta x, y - \Delta y, d), S_P(x - \Delta x, y - \Delta y, d - 1) \\ + P_1, S_P(x - \Delta x, y - \Delta y, d + 1) + P_1, \min_k S_P(x - \Delta x, y - \Delta y, k) + P_2) \tag{4}$$

where P represents the direction, Δx and Δy are the offsets in the current direction, P_1 is a constant penalty for small disparity changes, and P_2 is a constant penalty for large disparity changes. The cumulative costs are then aggregated over all directions:

$$S(x, y, d) = \sum S_P(x, y, d) \tag{5}$$

Finally, the disparity map is determined by finding the disparity ddd with the minimum total cost:

$$D(x, y) = \arg\min_d S(x, y, d) \tag{6}$$

This describes the SGBM algorithm for determining the final disparity map. The diagram below illustrates the principle of distance measurement using a stereo camera. u_{l0} and u_{r0} are the optical centers of the left and right cameras, f is the focal length, T is the baseline of the stereo camera, and P is a point in space. u_l and u_r are the projections of point P on the imaging planes of the left and right cameras, respectively [8].

This study uses the Yolov5s object detection model combined with the SGBM stereo matching algorithm to measure cotton stalk height. Due to the uncertain intrinsic parameters of the camera, approximate values are insufficient for distance measurement. We need precise intrinsic and extrinsic parameters of the camera, such as focal length, principal point, distortion coefficients, rotation matrix, and translation vector [3]. Therefore, manual calibration of the camera is necessary. This study uses MATLAB's Stereo Camera Calibrator for stereo camera calibration, and the calibrated intrinsic parameters of the camera are shown in the Table 2.

The Yolov5s model detects the cotton stalk and assigns a bounding box. The center of the bounding box is used to calculate the distance from the object to the baseline center of the stereo camera. The SGBM stereo matching algorithm determines the spatial coordinates P(X,Y,Z) of the point corresponding to the center of the bounding box. Knowing the focal length f in the y-direction of the camera and the height of the cotton stalk in the image (the difference between the highest and lowest y-coordinates), we can use the vertical length h of the bounding box as a proxy [4].

Table 2. Stereo Camera Calibration Intrinsic Parameters

Camera Parameters	Left Camera	Right Camera
Intrinsic Matrix	$\begin{bmatrix} 516.5 & -1.4 & 320.3 \\ 0 & 516.6 & 270.8 \\ 0 & 0 & 1 \end{bmatrix}$	$\begin{bmatrix} 511.8 & 1.3 & 317.3 \\ 0 & 513.1 & 269.6 \\ 0 & 0 & 1 \end{bmatrix}$
Distortion Coefficients	$\begin{bmatrix} -0.05 & 0.08 & 0.01 & 0 \end{bmatrix}$	$\begin{bmatrix} -0.06 & 0.12 & 0.01 & 0 \end{bmatrix}$
Rotation Matrix	$\begin{bmatrix} 1 & -0.004 & 0.013 \\ 0.004 & 1 & 0.013 \\ -0.013 & -0.013 & 1 \end{bmatrix}$	
Translation Matrix	$\begin{bmatrix} -120.4 & -0.189 & -0.662 \end{bmatrix}$	

3 Results

3.1 System Response Speed

The machine studied in this research underwent field trials in Binzhou City, Shandong Province, China, under the experimental conditions illustrated in the Fig. 9 below. The contouring structural components were installed on both sides of the cutting platform. In practical applications, we incorporated feedforward control into the contouring control system, enabling a faster descent speed when transitioning from the non-working position to the working position of the cutting platform. Moreover, prior to the experiments, a dead zone was defined for the contouring signals. This ensures that the cutting platform does not exhibit oscillations due to minor electrical current fluctuations within this dead zone, thereby enhancing the stability of the machine during operation. To validate the feasibility of the proposed research, we designed the following field trials, which primarily focus on testing the contouring speed and accuracy of the cutting platform.

A stopwatch was used to record the time taken for the header to stabilize from the start of movement. The response times for the header's ascent and descent are shown in the Table 3.

The cutting platform is elevated to its maximum position, which corresponds to the maximum extension of the hydraulic cylinder. A series of ten experiments are designed, where the platform is lowered to specified target heights. After each descent, the actual height of the cutting platform is measured, as shown in Table 4. This experimental setup aims to evaluate the performance of the hydraulic system in achieving the desired positions accurately. The data collected will help assess the system's precision and effectiveness in controlling the height of the cutting platform.

Fig. 9. Principle of Convolutional Neural Networks

Table 3. Response time of header in rising and falling

Experiment Number	Header Lift Height/cm	Response Time/s	Experiment Number	Lowering Height/cm	Response Time/s
1	5	0.4	6	5	0.4
2	10	0.9	7	10	0.8
3	15	1.3	8	15	1.1
4	20	1.8	9	20	1.5
5	25	2.2	10	25	1.9

Table 4. Feedback displacement of header in rising and falling

Experiment Number	target height/cm	Feedback displacement/cm	Experiment Number	target height/cm	Feedback displacement/cm
1	1	1.10	6	6	6.20
2	2	2.10	7	7	7.20
3	3	2.90	8	8	8.15
4	4	4.05	9	9	8.90
5	5	4.90	10	10	10.20

3.2 Cotton Stalk Height Detection

Due to the need to wait until November for this year's cotton stalk recycling, we used a previous dataset as a validation dataset to test the effectiveness of stereo matching. The results are shown in the Table 5.

Table 5. Response time of header in rising and falling

Experiment Number	Binocular height recognition	Actual height
1	71 cm	70.1 cm
2	69 cm	67.9 cm
3	75 cm	74.5 cm
4	80 cm	78.8 cm
5	74 cm	73.4 cm

4 Conclusions

The fuzzy control demonstrates excellent performance in achieving the contour-following effect of the header. Its superior adaptability and flexibility enable the header to intelligently respond to ground undulations. Through the fuzzy controller, the header can adjust its height in real time based on ground height data obtained from sensors, meeting the response time requirements for agricultural machinery operations during cotton stalk recycling. The preliminary implementation of cotton stalk height measurement using the Yolov5s model saves labor time for measuring cotton stalk height and provides reference value for adjusting header cutter speed and preventing header blockage. This research holds significant importance for the intelligent development of cotton stalk recovery headers.

Acknowledgments. This paper is one of the phased results of the following two projects: (1) Autonomous Region Key Research and Development Program Project – "Research and Development of Self-propelled Multi-functional Intelligent Residual Film Recovery Equipment Control System", Project Number: 2022B02022-4. (2) Central Guidance Local Science and Technology Development Special Fund Project – "Research and Application of Intelligent Upgrading for Residual Film Recovery Equipment in Cotton Fields", Project Number: ZYYD2023C08.

References

1. Craessaerts, G.D., Baerdemakeer, J., Missotten, B.: Fuzzy control of the cleaning process on a combine harvester. Biosys. Eng. **106**(2), 103–111 (2010)
2. Xie, Y., Alleyne, G., Greer, A.: Fundamental limits in combine harvester header height control. J. Dyn. Syst. Meas. Contr. **135**(3), 034–035 (2013)

3. Ma, H., Dong, K., Wang, Y.: Lightweight plant recognition model based on improved YOLOv5s. Trans. Chin. Soc. Agric. Mach. **54**(8), 267–276 (2023)
4. Zhang, L., Ding, G., Li, C.: DCF-Yolov8: an improved algorithm for aggregating low-level features to detect agricultural pests and diseases. Agronomy **13**(8), 2012 (2023)
5. Kim, G.S., Cho, J.: Vision-based vehicle detection and inter-vehicle distance estimation. In: 2012 12th International Conference on Control, Automation and Systems, pp: 625–629 (2012)
6. Jimenez, B., Jose, A.D.: High throughput determination of plant height, ground cover, and above-ground biomass in wheat with LiDAR. Front. Plant Sci. **9**(9), 237 (2018)
7. Zhang, J., Zhang, H., Wu, Z.: A review of vision-based systems for agricultural machinery automation. Comput. Electron. Agric. **183**, 105966 (2021)
8. Kumar, A., Singh, S.: Machine learning approaches for smart farming: a review. Agric. Syst. **176**, 102653 (2020)
9. Boehmler, D.F., Lentz, K.: A review of control techniques for precision agriculture and their impact on crop yield. Precision Agric. **20**(1), 41–58 (2019)
10. Gonzalez-de-Santos, P., Zubizarreta, A.: Autonomous robotic systems for precision agriculture: a review. J. Field Robot. **39**(3), 231–250 (2022)
11. Ali, M., Ali, A., Shafique, M.: Advances in agricultural robotics: a review of recent developments. Agric. Robot. **4**(1), 23–39 (2020)
12. Meyer, G.E., Maja, K.: An overview of computer vision applications in agriculture. Agric. Biol. Eng. Trans. **9**(2), 143–150 (2016)
13. Bashir, M.F., Ahmed, I.: A review of unmanned aerial vehicles (UAVs) in precision agriculture: applications and future perspectives. Int. J. Agric. Biol. Eng. **16**(2), 1–14 (2023)

Pump Equipment Fault Diagnosis Based on an Improved DenseNet Model

Chao He, Jiarula Yasenjiang[✉], Debo Wang, and Yang Xiao

School of Intelligent Manufacturing Modern Industry, Xinjiang University (School of Mechanical Engineering), Xinjiang, China
yasenjiang@xju.edu.cn, 107552204305@stu.xju.edu.cn

Abstract. Due to the often complex and harsh working environments of pump equipment, the signals collected are frequently marred by high-noise interference. Traditional Convolutional Neural Network (CNN) models struggle to adequately mine fault features under such interference, leading to subpar diagnostic performance. To address this issue, this paper proposes a pump equipment fault diagnosis method based on an improved Densely connected convolutional networks (DenseNet) model. This model incorporates the Depthwise Separable Convolution (DSC) algorithm, Self-Attention mechanism modules, the Gaussian Error Linear Unit (GELU) activation function, and Global Average Pooling (GAP). These enhancements are applied to the foundational DenseNet model to improve its diagnostic capabilities. Experiments conducted with pump equipment data collected by the authors show that the improved DenseNet model achieves a classification accuracy of 99.58% after sample denoising. Additionally, noise simulation experiments further demonstrate that the model proposed in this paper can achieve more effective pump equipment fault diagnosis compared to traditional DenseNet models.

Keywords: improved DenseNet · fault diagnosis · pump equipment

1 Introduction

Pump equipment, as an indispensable component in industrial production and daily life, plays a pivotal role in numerous fields such as water treatment, petrochemicals, maritime, and aerospace [1]. The stable operation of pump equipment is directly related to the safety, efficiency, and reliability of the entire system. However, due to the inevitable exposure of pump equipment to various complex and harsh environments over long-term operation, such as wear, corrosion, and impurity blockage, these factors can lead to a decline in pump equipment performance, and even failures. Once a failure occurs, it not only affects the production schedule but may also lead to severe safety accidents. Therefore, effective fault diagnosis of pump equipment is of significant importance for ensuring the safe and stable operation of the equipment, reducing unexpected downtime, and lowering maintenance costs [2].

With the rapid progress of deep learning technology and its widespread deployment in the industrial sector, deep learning methods such as convolutional neural networks (CNN) have gradually become one of the key technologies for pump equipment fault detection. Yang et al. [3] generated two-dimensional images from the vibration signals of an axial piston pump and input them into a convolutional network model to diagnose the hydraulic pump. To improve the diagnosis efficiency of piston wear faults, Du et al. [4] proposed a piston wear fault identification method based on sensitivity analysis and probabilistic neural networks. Wang et al. [5] proposed a new piston pump fault diagnosis method using a global attention residual shrinkage network (GARSN), which effectively improved the fault detection accuracy under complex noise environments. However, due to the complex and harsh working environment of pump equipment, the collected signals are often mixed with high-intensity noise, which makes it difficult for traditional CNN to effectively extract fault features, thus affecting the accuracy of diagnosis [2]. Based on this, this study proposes a new method for pump equipment fault diagnosis using an improved Densely connected convolutional networks (DenseNet) model. The model introduces the Depthwise Separable Convolution (DSC) algorithm, the Self-Attention module, the Gaussian Error Linear Units (GELU) activation function, and Global Average Pooling (GAP), and then improves the basic DenseNet model. Finally, the improved DenseNet model is used to experiment with self-collected pump equipment data, and the results show that the improved DenseNet model can achieve effective pump equipment fault diagnosis.

2 Related Methods

Currently, artificial intelligence technologies such as machine learning and neural networks are being used to diagnose faults in pump equipment, effectively identifying the type and specific location of failures. This adapts to the needs of pump equipment under varying working conditions and environments. However, many of these AI methods have not been fully tested under the complex and varied operational conditions found in actual industrial scenarios. Further experiments may be required to verify their stability and reliability in different settings. Additionally, data collection and processing may need more refined and scientific designs to enhance the model's generalizability and reduce dependency on specific datasets. Building on this foundation, this paper has conducted data collection and processing for pump equipment and proposes a fault diagnosis method for pump equipment based on an improved DenseNet, as introduced in the earlier section.

DenseNet is primarily composed of two main components: dense blocks and transition layers [6]. The dense blocks define the relationship between the inputs and outputs, adopting a concatenation approach where the feature maps from all the preceding layers are used as inputs to the next layer. This feature reuse mechanism allows DenseNet to effectively combine contextual information, thereby enhancing the efficiency of the network model. The transition layers are responsible for controlling the number of channels. Due to the accumulation of feature maps within the dense blocks as the layer depth increases, the dimensionality of the input feature maps can become very large. To address this, the transition layers employ 1 × 1 convolutions to perform channel-wise dimensionality reduction, thereby improving the computational efficiency. Currently, the DenseNet network has achieved promising results in the field of image recognition.

However, in the dense blocks of DenseNet, any given layer receives the output feature maps from all the preceding convolutional layers through a simple concatenation. This process does not consider the inter-channel correlations, and irrelevant information may affect the model's ability to make accurate predictions. Furthermore, when dealing with noisy data, the noise from one layer could propagate to the subsequent layers, leading to the network overfitting to the noise. Additionally, the increased input dimensionality due to the multi-channel data fusion to preserve more original feature information has led to a rise in computational cost. To overcome these drawbacks, we propose enhancements to the DenseNet model. By incorporating targeted modifications, we aim to improve the model's ability to efficiently capture relevant feature representations while maintaining robustness against noise and reducing the computational overhead.

2.1 GELU Activation Function

In the proposed improvements to the DenseNet model, we replace the activation function in the dense blocks and transition layers from the commonly used Rectified Linear Unit (ReLU) to the GELU. This change is aimed at enhancing the convergence speed and overall performance of the training process. Compared to the ReLU activation function, GELU is a more smooth and continuous activation function, with a continuous S-shaped curve positioned between the Sigmoid and ReLU functions. This effectively alleviates the problem of neuron deactivation caused by the ReLU function's constant output of zero for negative inputs, thereby enhancing the model's representational capacity. Furthermore, the GELU activation function has been shown to perform better in addressing the gradient vanishing problem in neural networks. This property supports the training and optimization of deeper neural network architectures, ultimately contributing to an improvement in the model's overall performance [7]. The mathematical expression for the GELU activation function is as follows:

$$GELU(x) = x * P(X \leq x) = x * \Phi(x) \tag{1}$$

where $\Phi(x)$ represents the cumulative distribution function of the standard normal distribution.

2.2 Depthwise Separable Convolution

In the transition layers, we introduce DSC, an efficient convolutional operation composed of two steps: depthwise convolution and pointwise convolution [8]. The depthwise convolution operates independently on each channel, focusing on capturing spatial features; the subsequent pointwise convolution then effectively combines these independently processed channels through 1 × 1 convolutions to extract channel features. This two-step processing approach not only significantly reduces the model's parameter count and computational load, thereby decreasing computational complexity, but also enhances the network's robustness to noise and improves model efficiency and performance by more finely processing spatial and channel information. Consequently, depthwise separable convolution, as a lightweight convolutional operation, provides an effective means to enhance network processing capabilities and achieve model lightweighting. The overall structure of DSC is shown in Fig. 1.

2.3 Self-attention Module

The Self-Attention mechanism, utilized within the Transformer model, is designed to capture dependencies between different positions within a sequence. This mechanism can handle input sequences of arbitrary lengths, unrestricted by the limitations of fixed or sliding window sizes [9]. The Self-Attention mechanism boasts high flexibility, dynamically allocating attention weights based on various parts of the input sequence. It effectively captures long-range dependencies between different positions in the sequence. Allowing the model to focus on both global and local information when processing the input sequence, the mechanism dynamically assigns weights between global and local attention. This enables the model to selectively suppress noise and highlight genuine signals. The following Fig. 2 illustrates the working principle of the Self-Attention module.

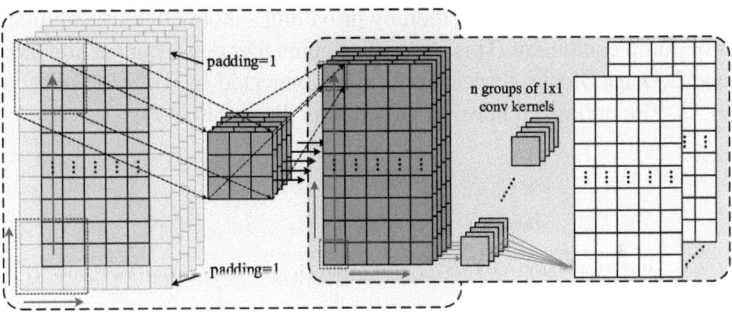

Fig. 1. The Architecture of DSC

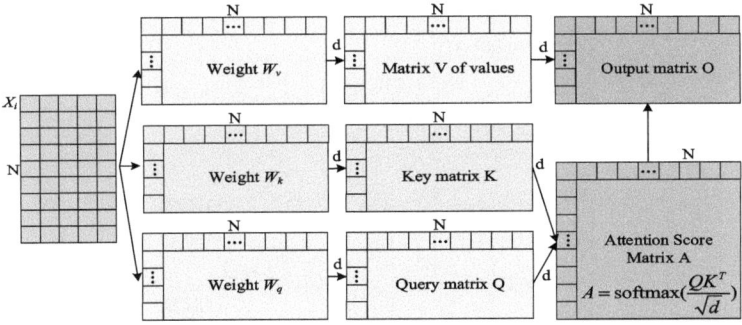

Fig. 2. The principle of Self-Attention

2.4 Global Average Pooling

In this paper, we have improved the classification layer of DenseNet by replacing the traditional fully connected layer with a GAP layer, which effectively reduces the number of model parameters and mitigates the risk of overfitting. The GAP layer compresses the spatial information of the feature maps into a single feature vector, providing an efficient feature representation for Softmax classification [10]. Additionally, the GAP layer introduced in this study is a specially designed, dimension-adaptive pooling structure that is primarily aimed at reducing the model's parameter count and enhancing the algorithm's operational speed, while adaptively matching the dimensional transformation between the last DenseBlock layer and the Softmax layer.

2.5 Model Architecture

Through the aforementioned structural optimizations to DenseNet, the aim is to enhance the model's feature extraction capabilities and computational efficiency, while reducing sensitivity to noise and strengthening its generalization performance. Such improvements make the model more suitable for practical fault diagnosis tasks, enabling more accurate identification of fault patterns and increased efficiency and accuracy in diagnosis. The optimized DenseNet structure is designed to better capture key features in the face of complex data and noise, thereby providing a more effective solution for fault diagnosis of pump equipment. This paper configures four dense connection blocks, with 1, 2, 3, and 3 DenseBlocks respectively, each connected by Transitions between two DenseBlocks. The optimized network structure is illustrated in Fig. 3.

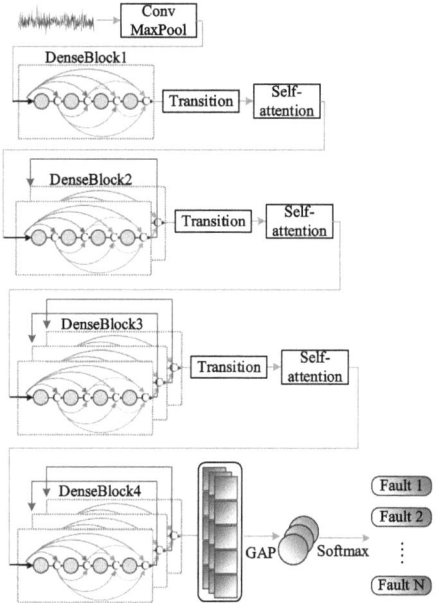

Fig. 3. Schematic diagram of the improved model structure

3 Experimental Validation

3.1 Description of Experimental Data

The data collected in this paper were obtained from a dry rotary vane screw pump, with the data acquisition device shown in Fig. 4. The sensor test points are depicted in Fig. 5. The sampling frequency was set to 25,600 Hz, with the pump's operating cycle at 1/150th of a second. Data were collected under both normal operating conditions and fault conditions, excluding periods of high fluctuation during the pump's cyclic aeration in the testing process. After the pump's stable operation, a 6-s data segment was sampled. By recording and disassembling the pump, various fault categories were identified. The sensor installation locations are indicated in the figure. Through data collection, we acquired time-series vibration data from five critical locations of the pump equipment, including the chamber side, two distinct bearing sides, the gear side, and the motor side.

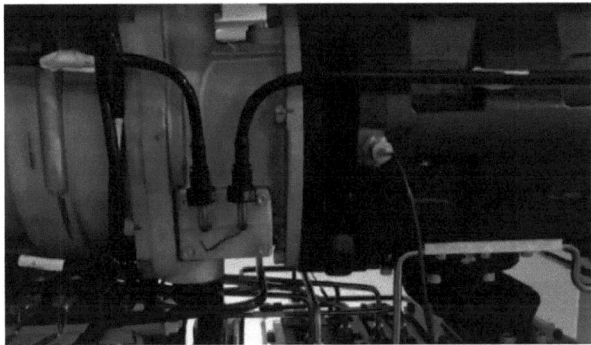

Fig. 4. Data acquisition device for dry rotary vane screw pump

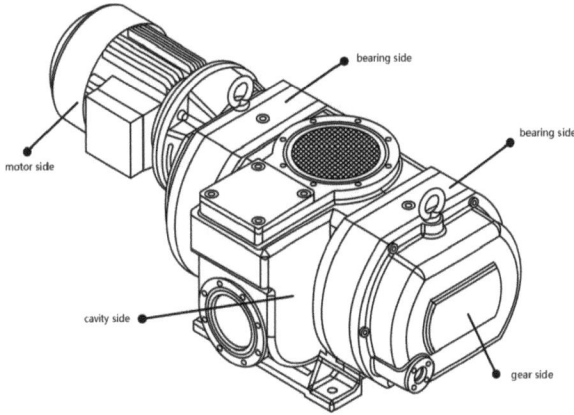

Fig. 5. Schematic of sensor placement

Given a pump operating cycle of 1/150 s and a sampling frequency of 25,600 Hz, it can be calculated that approximately 170 data points are sampled per cycle. To ensure the reliability of the data, under each operating condition, each channel's data is sampled ten times to reduce the impact of specific samples in the dataset. Each sampling lasts for 6 s, totaling 153,600 samples per single sampling event. The individual sample length is set to 850, resulting in approximately 1,800 samples collected per channel. From the five channels, 1,200 samples are randomly selected at corresponding positions for data fusion. The setup for the fused samples of the five fault conditions and the normal condition is shown in Table 1.

Table 1. Sample configuration for dry rotary vane screw pump

label	Fault types	Fault names	Number of samples
0	\	Normal condition	1200
1	Rotor	Spindle wear	1200
2	Impeller	Rotor imbalance	1200
3	Bearing	Bearing wear	1200
4	Bearing	Bearing cage breakage	1200
5	Gear	Gear wear	1200

3.2 Fault Diagnosis Process

The model structure parameters proposed in this paper are detailed in Table 2, with DenseBlock counts set to 1, 2, 3, and 3 layers, respectively, interconnected by Transition layers. The "−1" in the output size column indicates adaptability, corresponding to the number of batch_size. The training is set for 40 epochs, the optimizer selected is SGD, with a learning rate of 0.01 and a momentum of 0.9. The loss function chosen is the Cross-Entropy Loss.

To ensure rigorous scientific research, each experiment is conducted five times, under the same training hyperparameters, with the same samples, network model parameters, and experimental platform, and the mean of the results is taken. After obtaining the data, preliminary processing is performed first; one-hot encoding is used to label the samples. Subsequently, the samples are paired with their labels using the TensorDataset in PyTorch, and they are divided into training and testing sets in an 8:2 ratio. The training set is used to iterate model parameters and fit sample features, while the testing set is used to verify model accuracy. The model diagnosis process is illustrated in the following Fig. 6.

The dry rotary vane screw pump data, after preprocessing, were experimented upon along with the original dataset, which includes six operating condition samples: normal operation, main shaft wear, dynamic balance fault, bearing wear fault, bearing cage fracture, and gear wear, sequentially referred to as Fault 0 to Fault 5. The experiments

Table 2. Model structural parameters

Layer name	Network parameters	Output shape
Convolutional layer	7×7 conv, stride = 2, padding = 3	[−1, 64]
Max pooling layer	3×3 max pooling, stride = 2, padding = 1	[−1, 64]
DenseBlock1	$\begin{pmatrix} 1 \times 1 Conv \\ 3 \times 3 Conv \end{pmatrix} \times 1$	[−1, 32]
Transition Layer1	1 x 1 conv	[−1, 16]
	2×2 average pool, stride = 2	[−1, 16]
DenseBlock2	$\begin{pmatrix} 1 \times 1 Conv \\ 3 \times 3 Conv \end{pmatrix} \times 2$	[−1, 32]
Transition Layer2	1 x 1 conv	[−1, 16]

(*continued*)

Table 2. (*continued*)

Layer name	Network parameters	Output shape
	2×2 average pool, stride = 2	[−1, 16]
DenseBlock3	$\begin{pmatrix} 1 \times 1 Conv \\ 3 \times 3 Conv \end{pmatrix} \times 3$	[−1, 32]
Transition Layer3	1×1 conv	[−1, 16]
	2×2 average pool, stride = 2	[−1, 16]
DenseBlock4	$\begin{pmatrix} 1 \times 1 Conv \\ 3 \times 3 Conv \end{pmatrix} \times 3$	[−1, 32]
Classification layer	7×7 GAP	[−1, num_classes]
	Fc, Softmax	

were conducted to verify the fault diagnosis performance of the model, with 40 training epochs. Initially, the model was trained using the training set, employing a suitable learning algorithm and loss function for optimization. During training, the model's performance was monitored to adjust its hyperparameters, such as learning rate and batch size. Subsequently, the trained model was evaluated using the testing set to calculate performance metrics for the fault diagnosis task, including accuracy, confusion matrix, F1 score, etc. The model's performance was analyzed to assess its diagnostic capability across different fault types, and necessary adjustments and improvements were made.

3.3 Experimental Results and Analysis

By conducting comparative experiments using the original DenseNet and the improved DenseNet on the same sample set, the advantages of the model improvement were validated. The only difference between the samples was whether they had undergone denoising; all other settings, such as model parameters, network depth, and sample

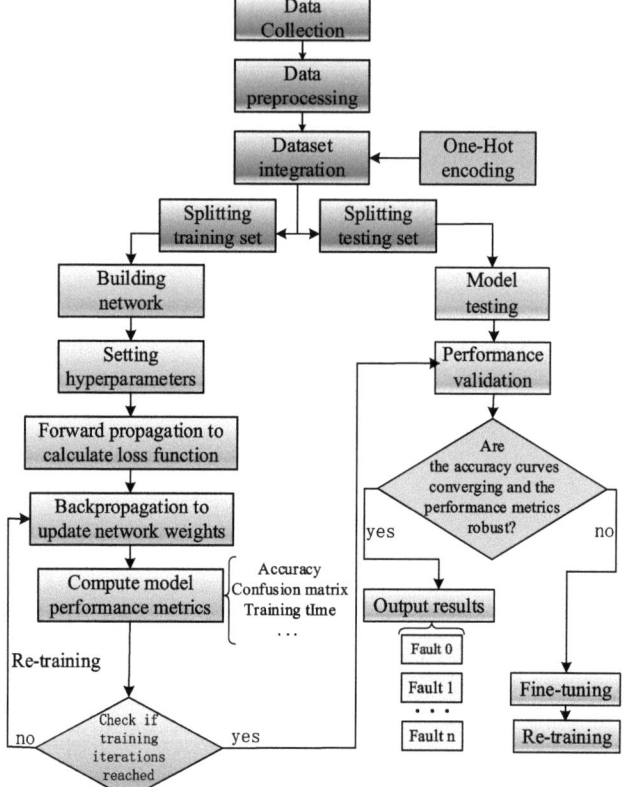

Fig. 6. Schematic diagram of the model diagnostic process

configuration, were the same. The results of the comparative experiments are shown in the following Table 3.

According to the data presented in Table 3, DenseNet demonstrates a significant increase in accuracy with datasets that have undergone denoising algorithm processing. Noise represents random and irregular data fluctuations, which are inherently unavoidable. Such noise can obscure true features, and the goal of denoising algorithms is to extract the genuine signals or features from these noisy datasets. After denoising, the sample features are more clearly delineated, allowing the model to fit the features more precisely and resulting in a notable enhancement in performance. Further analysis of the data in Table 3 indicates that the improved DenseNet outperforms the original DenseNet model in both raw and denoised data. This suggests that the proposed improved model has a significant performance advantage and also validates the effectiveness of the theoretical improvements in practical applications.

This paper evaluates the convergence rate and stability of the model through the accuracy curves of the training and testing sets. Figure 7 illustrates the trend of training and testing accuracy, from which it can be observed that the training accuracy reached over 97% after approximately 20 training epochs, while the testing accuracy, after a slight

Table 3. Model performance comparison

Model	Pre-Denoising sample accuracy	Post-Denoising sample accuracy
DenseNet	93.98%	97.41%
Improved DenseNet	97.38%	99.58%

fluctuation, consistently remained above 95%. This indicates that the model possesses a high level of accuracy in processing complex vibration signal fault classification tasks. Furthermore, this paper introduces a multi-class confusion matrix to analyze the misclassification instances during the fault diagnosis process with the improved DenseNet model. As shown in Fig. 8, the confusion matrix has the predicted labels on the y-axis and the true labels on the x-axis; the model achieved an accuracy rate of over 99% for the classification of six fault types of the pump.

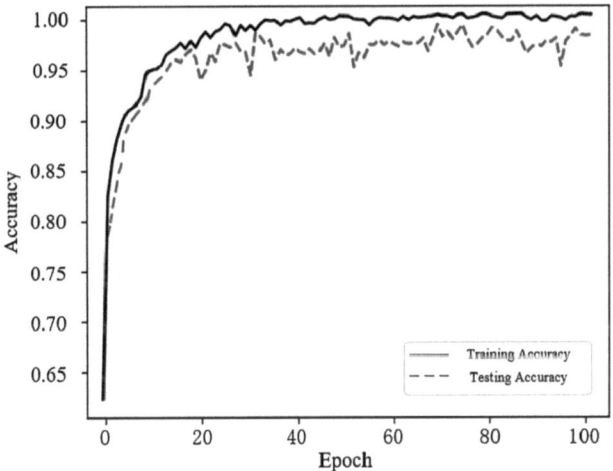

Fig. 7. Model accuracy convergence chart

The assessment results of the experimental outcomes are presented in Table 4, from which it can be observed that for the six fault conditions, the model achieved an average precision rate of 99.59%, a recall rate of 99.56%, and an F1-Score of 99.58%. These metrics reflect the model's classification performance across various operating conditions. Considering these performance indicators collectively, it can be concluded that the model demonstrates excellent overall classification performance under the six conditions, and it performs well in both positive and negative class prediction.

The t-SNE dimensionality reduction results are depicted in Fig. 9. In this diagnostic model, the predictive accuracy rate reaches 100%, and the t-SNE dimensionality reduction outcomes exhibit no overlap. This implies that the model is capable of accurately classifying each category when categorizing the test data, thereby demonstrating the model's exceptional performance and reliability for this specific task.

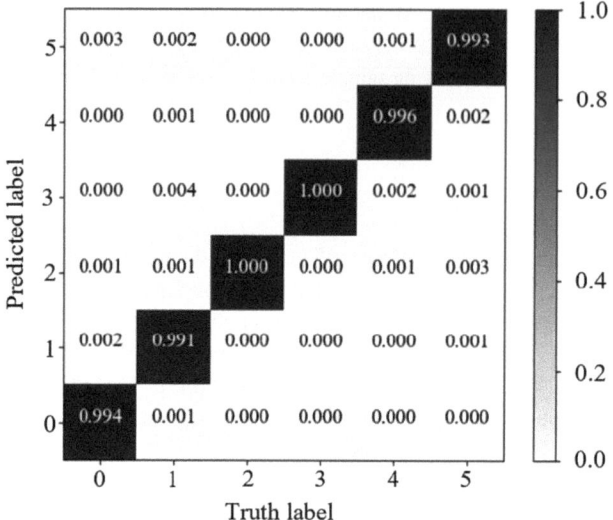

Fig. 8. Model diagnostic confusion matrix

Table 4. Model evaluation metrics

	Normal 0 (%)	Fault 1 (%)	Fault 2 (%)	Fault 3 (%)	Fault 4 (%)	Fault 5 (%)
Precision	99.42	99.14	100	100	99.64	99.33
Recall	99.82	99.73	99.45	99.32	99.63	99.42
F1-Score	99.67	99.41	99.74	99.75	99.63	99.32

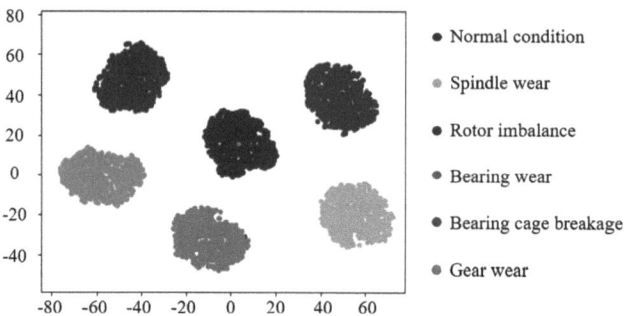

Fig. 9. t-SNE visualization

3.4 Additional Experiments and Results Analysis

The experimental results of this paper indicate that the improved DenseNet has good accuracy for the collected data of dry rotary vane screw pumps. However, this only represents a single scenario of noise contamination, and the model's performance under extreme conditions still lacks investigation. In experimental studies, researchers can selectively introduce noise to simulate the impact under specific conditions. This paper artificially adds noise at different SNR levels of −5, −2, 0, 2, 5, and 8 to simulate extreme environments.

In this section, the original signals, which include three types of data: normal operation, bearing roller wear, and dynamic balance fault, with 200 samples in each category, are polluted by adding noise at SNR levels of − 5, −2, 0, 2, 5, and 8 to simulate the operating conditions of equipment in real harsh environments, thereby verifying the performance of the model in this section. During the model training process, different noise data are allocated to the training set and the test set in an 8:2 ratio. The experimental results are shown in Table 5. The accuracy data show that when SNR ranges from 0 to 8, where noise pollution is more severe and data quality significantly degrades, the improved DenseNet still performs well. However, when SNR is less than 0, the data pollution reaches a more serious level, and the features of the original signal are more deeply buried by noise. The improved DenseNet, due to the role of DSC and the Self-Attention module, still has a fault diagnosis recognition rate of 83.13% under extreme noise environments, while the original DenseNet does not perform as well as the improved version.

Table 5. Model accuracy under different levels of noise pollution

Model	SNR = − 5	SNR = − 2	SNR = 0	SNR = 2	SNR = 5	SNR = 8
DenseNet	67.32%	71.73%	85.61%	87.24%	88.75%	90.34%
Improved DenseNet	83.13%	89.31%	94.22%	96.34%	97.23%	97.27%

4 Conclusions

This paper presents a fault diagnosis method for pump equipment based on an improved DenseNet model. By improving the original DenseNet model and experimentally validating it with data collected from pump equipment, the results demonstrate that this method can accurately classify faults, achieving high-precision fault diagnosis. Additionally, this study conducted experiments under simulated noisy conditions to further confirm the feasibility and effectiveness of the proposed approach.

References

1. Yang, H.Y., Zhang, B., Xu, B.: Development of axial piston pump/motor technology. J. Mech. Eng. **44**(10), 1–8 (2008)
2. Zhou, H.J., Wang, C.W., Zhou, G.J., et al.: Fault diagnosis of antifriction bearing of centrifugal pump based on random forest. Chin. J. Ship Res. **15**(3), 129–135 (2020)
3. Yang, X.: Fault diagnosis of plunger pump based on ICEEMDAN-GCNII. Hydraul. Pneum. Seals **44**(6), 21–29 (2024)

4. Du, Z., Zhao, J., Zhang, X.: A recognition method of plunger wear degree of plunger pump using probability neural network. Vibroeng. Procedia **14**, 45–50 (2017)
5. Wang, X.Q., Wu, K., Zhao, G.H., et al.: Fault diagnosis of piston pump based on global attention residual shrinkage network. Chin. J. Ship Res. (2025). https://doi.org/10.19693/j.issn.1673-3185.03739
6. Huang G., Liu Z., van der maaten L., et al.: Densely connected convolutional networks. In: Proceedings of the IEEE Conference on Computer Vision and Pattern Recognition. Honolulu, HI, USA, pp. 4700–4708 (2017)
7. Lee, M.: GELU activation function in deep learning: a comprehensive mathematical analysis and performance. arXiv: 12073, 2023
8. Wang, K., Yasenjlang, J.: Fault monitoring of process industry system based on DSC-DenseNet. Mach. Tool Hydraul. **52**(7), 226–230 (2024)
9. Gibbons, F.X.: Self-attention and behavior: a review and theoretical update. Adv. Exp. Soc. Psychol. **23**, 249–303 (1990)
10. Zhang, B., Zhao, Q., Feng, W., et al.: AlphaMEX: a smarter global pooling method for convolutional neural networks. Neurocomputing **321**(DEC. 10), 36–48 (2018). https://doi.org/10.1016/j.neucom.2018.07.079

Research on the Residual Controllable Robot Grinding Technology of 500 kV High-Voltage Cable Insulation Layer

Hai Zhu[1], Kailin Duan[1], Bo Yan[1], Mi She[2(✉)], Bo Wang[1], and Jingli Jia[1]

[1] Xiangjiaba Hydropower Plant, Construction and Management Center of Xiangjiaba Dam Power Station, Xuzhou District, Yibin, Sichuan, China
{zhu_hai,duan_kailin,yan_bo1,wang_bo3,jia_jingli}@ctg.com.cn

[2] Wuhan Digital Design and Manufacturing, Innovation Centre Co., Ltd., 5F, Wuhan Intelligent Equipment Park, No. 8 Ligou South Road, East Lake New Technology Development Zone, Wuhan, Hubei, China
shemi0618@163.com

Abstract. At present, the 500 kV high-voltage cable insulation layer in the industry is grinded by sand belt or sand belt grinder, the grind of the high-voltage cable insulation layer depends entirely on the feeling or experience of the operators, which results in the poor roundness and quality consistency of the grinded high-voltage cable insulation layer, the risk of breakdown of high-voltage cable is very easy to occur, which seriously threatens the safe and stable operation of high-voltage cable. On the other hand, a great deal of dust will be produced in the course of grind of high-voltage cable insulation layer, which will lead to bad working environment on site and indirectly affect the grinding quality. Therefore, in this paper, the robot and force-controlled grinding system are used to study the residual controllable grinding process for the high-voltage cable insulation layer, it is of great significance to improve the grinding quality of high-voltage cable insulation layer, improve the working environment and advance the intelligentized level of the grind of high-voltage cable insulation layer.

Keywords: 500 kV high-voltage cable insulation layer · robot · residual controllable grinding technology

1 Introduction

Along with the popularization of robot technology, the robot has the characteristic of high repeat positioning precision, which can guarantee the processing precision and consistency, more and more robots are used in the grinding field [1], compared with manual grind, industrial robot grind has the advantages of high precision, stable quality, low cost and high efficiency [2]. At present, the application of robot grind at home and abroad is mainly aimed at the aspects of edge deburring and surface polishing with the shape [3], the residual controllable grind of the workpiece, in particular, the residual controllable robot grinding technology of 500 kV high-voltage cable insulation layer basically has not been involved. In this paper, taking 500 kV high-voltage cable insulation layer robot grind as an example, we built a robot force-controlled grinding system platform, and tested the material removal amount of high-voltage cable insulation layer by single grind. The material removal amount prediction model was obtained, and the residual controllable grinding test was carried out on the high-voltage cable insulation layer sample, thus can provide solutions for the residual controllable robot grind of 500 kV high-voltage cable insulation layer.

2 Robot Force-Controlled Grinding System Platform

The robot force-controlled grinding system platform is composed of a robot, a force-controlled device, a sand belt grinder, a high-voltage cable insulation layer sample, fixtures and so on. The sand belt grinder is installed on the force-controlled device, which is installed at the end of the robot, and the high-voltage cable insulation layer sample is fixed on the workbench through the fixtures. The robot can control the track and moving speed of the sand belt grinder, and the force-controlled device can control the grinding force of the sand belt grinder applied on the high-voltage cable insulation layer sample. The robot payload is 14 kg, the maximum output force of the force-controlled device is 100 N, the stroke of the force-controlled device is 35.5 mm, the power of the sand belt grinder is 800 W, and the maximum speed of the sand belt grinder is 8.5 m/s. The robot force-controlled grinding system platform for grinding the high-voltage cable insulation layer sample is shown in Fig. 1.

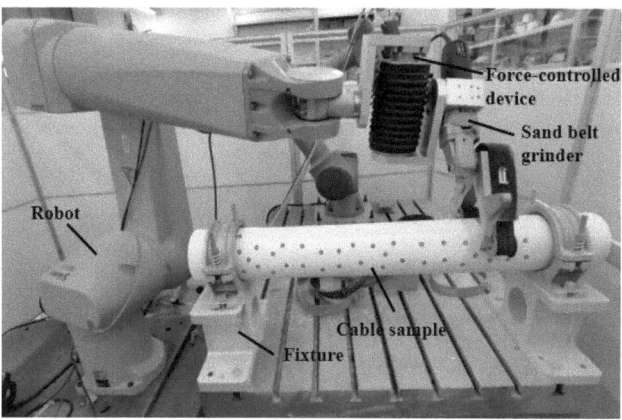

Fig. 1. Robot force-controlled grinding system platform for grinding the high-voltage cable insulation layer sample

3 Test of Material Removal Amount by Single Grind

The factors that affect the material removal amount by single grind are the grit number of sand belt, the grinding force, the moving speed of robot and the speed of sand belt, etc., for the high-voltage cable insulation layer sample, because of the less single material removal amount grinded by sand belt grinder, therefore, in the design of technological experiments, the speed of sand belt grinder is fixed and maximum speed is used, only the effects of the grit number of sand belt, the grinding force and the moving speed of the robot on the material removal amount are considered. In the test, the 320 grit sand, 400 grit sand and 600 grit sand are used according to the process requirements, the range of grinding force is 15N, 20N, 25N, 30N, 35N, the range of moving speed is 35 mm/s, 25 mm/s, 15 mm/s, 10 mm/s, 5 mm/s. The grinding process parameter groups for test of material removal amount by single grind designed are shown in table 1 below.

Table 1. Grinding process parameter groups for test of material removal amount by single grind

NO	Grit number	Grinding force (N)	Moving speed (mm/s)
1	320	35	5
2	320	30	10
3	320	25	15
4	320	20	25
5	320	15	35
6	400	15	25
7	400	20	15
8	400	25	10
9	400	30	5
10	400	35	35
11	600	15	15
12	600	20	10
13	600	25	5
14	600	30	35
15	600	35	25

As the single grinding material removal amount is less, in order to improve the precision of measurement, the average value after several times of grind is taken as the single grinding material removal amount of the corresponding process parameter group, the high-voltage cable insulation layer samples before and after grinding are scanned to obtain point clouds, and then the measurement of grinding material removal amount is carried out in the measurement software. The scan and measurement of the high-voltage cable insulation layer sample before and after grinding is shown in Fig. 2.

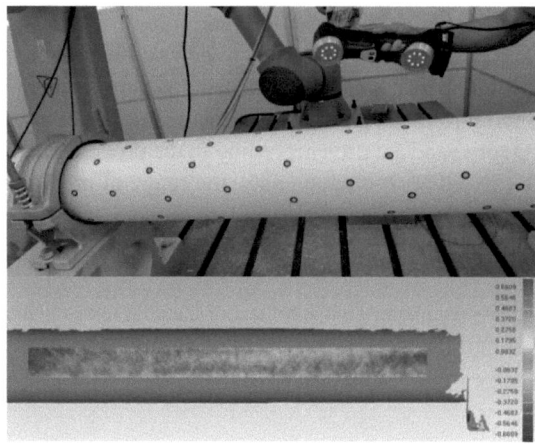

Fig. 2. Scan and measurement of the high-voltage cable insulation layer sample before and after grinding

The single grinding material removal amounts of 320 grit, 400 grit and 600 grit sand belt corresponding to each process parameter group are shown in the Table 2 below.

Table 2. Single grinding material removal amounts of 320 grit, 400 grit and 600 grit sand belt corresponding to each process parameter group

NO	Grit number	Grinding force (N)	Moving speed (mm/s)	Grinding times	Total material removal amount (mm)	Single material removal amount (µm)
1	320	35	5	20	0.265	13.25
2	320	30	10	60	0.4061	6.77
3	320	25	15	100	0.3145	3.15
4	320	20	25	100	0.2787	2.79
5	320	15	35	200	0.3364	1.68
6	400	35	35	200	0.293	1.47
7	400	30	5	100	0.343	3.43
8	400	25	10	100	0.2009	2.01
9	400	20	15	100	0.1767	1.77
10	400	15	25	200	0.1986	0.99
11	600	35	25	350	0.15	0.43
12	600	30	35	500	0.1038	0.21
13	600	25	5	120	0.2217	1.85
14	600	20	10	150	0.2255	1.50

(*continued*)

Table 2. (*continued*)

NO	Grit number	Grinding force (N)	Moving speed (mm/s)	Grinding times	Total material removal amount (mm)	Single material removal amount (µm)
15	600	15	15	250	0.1849	0.74

4 Construction and Validation of Material Removal Amount Prediction Model

4.1 Construction of Material Removal Amount Prediction Model

In order to select proper process parameters according to the residual distribution of the high-voltage cable insulation layer in the actual grinding process, it is necessary to have enough process parameter groups. Adding test process parameter groups to the test to obtain the corresponding material removal amount can increase the process parameter data set, however, it is difficult to cover all the process parameters needed by the actual high-voltage cable insulation layer and the test period is long, so the material removal amount prediction model can be established by using the test data of small samples, by acquiring the required process parameter group through the prediction model, the test times can be greatly reduced and the applicability of the process data set can be enhanced.

In this paper, the random forest algorithm is used to construct the material removal amount prediction model. The random forest algorithm is an integrated learning method based on decision tree [4], which can make regression prediction. It is widely used because of its high precision. Decision tree is an algorithm based on tree structure [5]. There are two important steps in constructing a decision tree: Establishment of decision tree and pruning. The pruning of decision tree can effectively prevent the over-fitting of decision tree, reduce the complexity of complex decision tree and improve the prediction precision. The structure of decision tree is divided into root node, non-leaf node and leaf node, one non-leaf node represents one attribute, the node is divided according to different attributes, and then extends to another new attribute node through branches, finally, the leaf node is reached, which represents a split result, and the above steps are repeated until every node on the decision tree can no longer split, that is, the decision tree is completed.

Random forest algorithm is based on random sampling a certain number of samples back in the original sample set, building a subset of samples, and then random sampling f features, node splitting, building a single decision tree, after repeating the above steps, k different decision trees were established to form random forest. After the random forest is set up, every decision tree is regressed and output. Finally, using the idea of integrated learning, the forecasting results of random forest are averaged as the forecasting results of random forest regression.

In simple terms, random forest regression is a combination model composed of a set of regression decision trees $\{h(x, \theta_n), n = 1, 2, 3, \ldots, N\}$, in which, θ_n is the random variable, x is the independent variable, N is the number of decision trees. After the random forest is established, we can know the result of regression prediction:

$$h(x) = \frac{1}{N} \sum_{n=1}^{N} \{h(x, \theta_n)\} \qquad (1)$$

According to the single grinding material removal amounts of 320 grit, 400 grit and 600 grit sand belt corresponding to each process parameter group, The random forest algorithm is used to construct the material removal amount prediction models for 320 grit, 400 grit and 600 grit sand belt, the material removal amount prediction model of 320 grit sand belt for grinding high-voltage cable insulation layer is shown in Fig. 3, the material removal amount prediction model of 400 grit sand belt for grinding high-voltage cable insulation layer is shown in Fig. 4, the material removal amount prediction model of 600 grit sand belt for grinding high-voltage cable insulation layer is shown in Fig. 5.

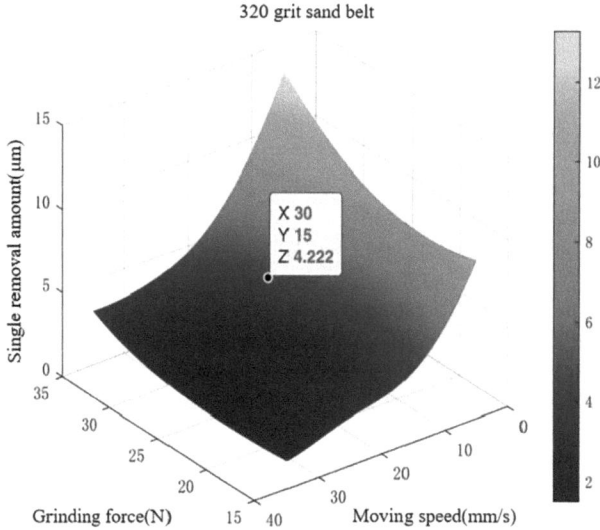

Fig. 3. Material removal amount prediction model of 320 grit sand belt for grinding high-voltage cable insulation layer

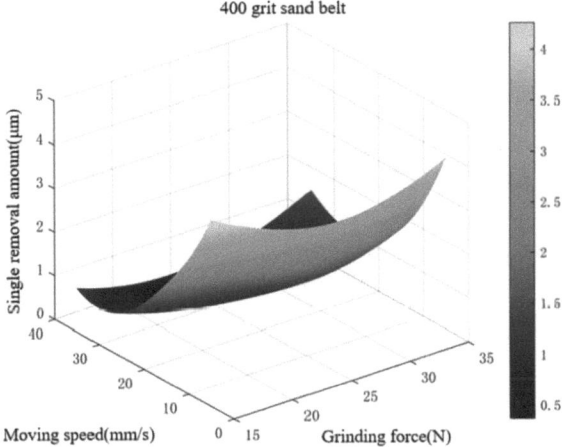

Fig. 4. Material removal amount prediction model of 400 grit sand belt for grinding high-voltage cable insulation layer

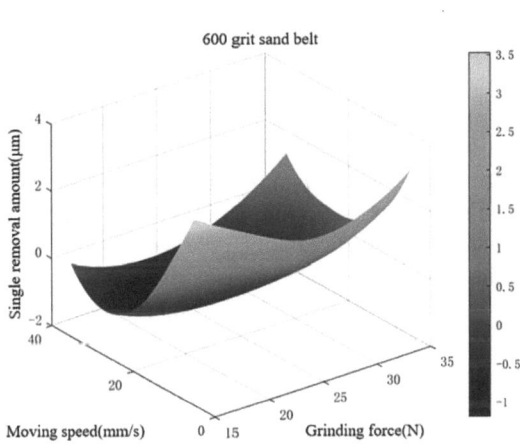

Fig. 5. Material removal amount prediction model of 600 grit sand belt for grinding high-voltage cable insulation layer

4.2 Validation of Material Removal Amount Prediction Model

On the material removal amount prediction model of 320 grit sand belt for grinding high-voltage cable insulation layer, select a point, the corresponding grinding force is 30N, moving speed is 15 mm/s, and the corresponding material removal amount prediction value is 4.222 μm. In the validation test, the grit number of sand belt is 320, grinding force is 30N, moving speed is 15 mm/s. The total removal amount is 0.1766 mm after grinding 40 times, the scanning measurement result of validation test of material removal amount prediction model of 320 grit sand belt for grinding high-voltage cable insulation layer is shown in Fig. 6. The average removal amount in single grind is about 4.415 μm, and the prediction value is 4.222 μm, the prediction error is 4.4%. The test result shows that the prediction model has high accuracy and can be used to predict the material removal amount.

Fig. 6. Scanning measurement result of validation test of material removal amount prediction model of 320 grit sand belt for grinding high-voltage cable insulation layer

5 Residual Controllable Grinding Test

Because the main purpose of the grind of high-voltage cable insulation layer is to improve the roundness of the insulation layer under the condition of the minimum material removal amount, the dynamic measurement-grind method is adopted, after each grinding, the grinding area is scanned, the point cloud after grinding is compared with the fitting cylinder to obtain the residual, and then the residual area is grinded to improve the roundness of the insulation layer through repeated grind.

Firstly, a scanner is used to scan the high-voltage cable insulation layer sample and the feature board which is installed on it, and point clouds are obtained. In the measurement software, the measuring coordinate system (Coordinate system 1) on the high-voltage cable insulation layer sample is established based on the feature board, as shown in Fig. 7. Then, the target cylinder is fitted to the area to be grinded on the high-voltage cable insulation layer sample by the cylinder fitting function, as shown in Fig. 8. Through analysis and comparison, the residual and its position on the high-voltage cable insulation layer sample in the measuring coordinate system are obtained, as shown in Fig. 9.

Fig. 7. Measuring coordinate system (Coordinate system 1) on the high-voltage cable insulation layer sample

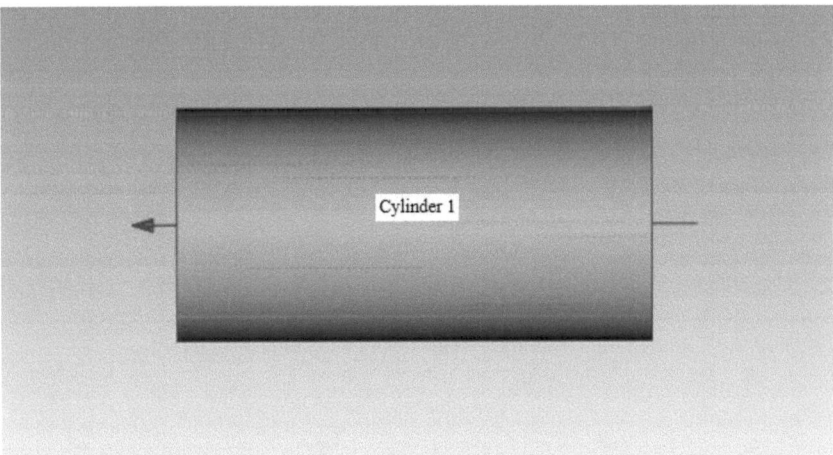

Fig. 8. Target cylinder fitted by the area to be grinded on the high-voltage cable insulation layer sample

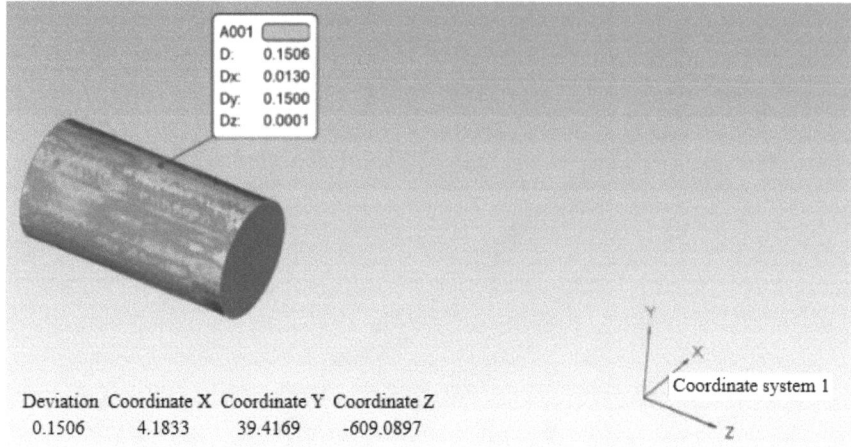

Fig. 9. Residual and its position on the high-voltage cable insulation layer sample in the measuring coordinate system

On the actual high-voltage cable insulation layer sample, the position of the residual is determined by the feature plate, and then the corresponding grinding process parameter group is selected for grind. After grinding, the high-voltage cable insulation layer sample is measured, and then the residual is grinded again according to the condition of the residual, to improve roundness by grinding several times. The maximum residual of the high-voltage cable insulation layer sample before grinding is 0.53 mm, as shown in Fig. 10, after grinding 10 times, the maximum residual of the high-voltage cable insulation layer sample is 0.18 mm, as shown in Fig. 11, and the Ra of surface roughness is 0.316 μm, as shown in Fig. 12.

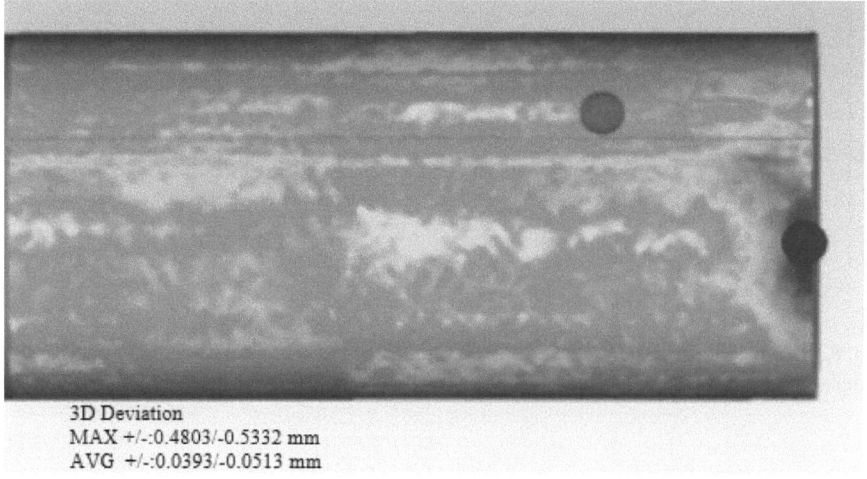

Fig. 10. Maximum residual measurement result of the high-voltage cable insulation layer sample before grinding

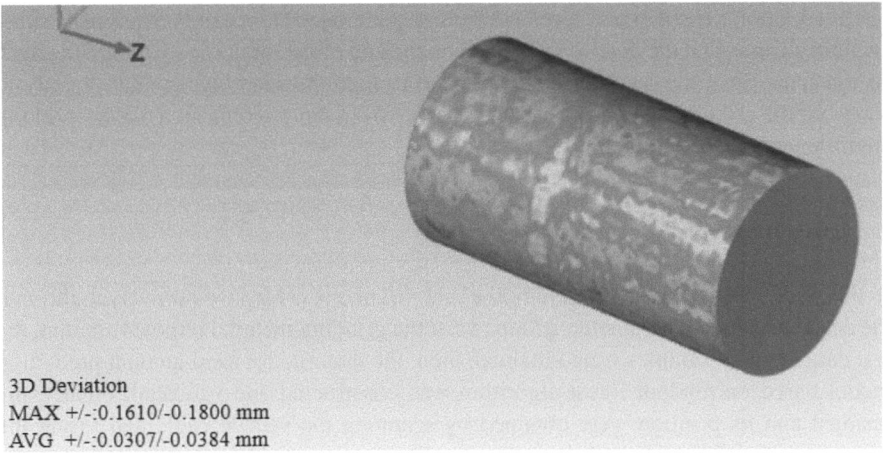

Fig. 11. Maximum residual measurement result of the high-voltage cable insulation layer sample after grinding 10 times

Fig. 12. Surface roughness of the high-voltage cable insulation layer sample after grinding 10 times

The roundness of the high-voltage cable insulation layer is about 0.4–2 mm and the Ra of surface roughness of the high-voltage cable insulation layer is about 0.4–3.2 μm by manual grinding process in a related industry. The roundness of the high-voltage cable insulation layer is about 0.16–0.18 mm and the the Ra of surface roughness of the high-voltage cable insulation layer is about 0.3–0.4 μm by using the robot and force-controlled grinding system. It is shown that the method is effective to improve the roundness, surface quality and consistency of the high-voltage cable insulation layer, and finally improve the reliability of the high-voltage cable insulation layer.

In addition, the robot and force-controlled grinding system can be equipped with a vacuum cleaner, and the dust cover is fixed on the end of the robot for absorbing the dust. At the same time, the operator does not need to hold the sand belt grinder directly to carry out the grinding operation, can be far away from the grinding area, so the working environment can be improved.

6 Conclusions

In this paper, based on the grind of 500 kV high-voltage cable insulation layer, through the design of process parameters group to test the grinding material removal amount, the test data of small samples were obtained, then, the material removal amount prediction model based on random forest algorithm was constructed and validated. Finally, the residual and its position were obtained by scanning the sample cable and fitting the target cylinder, then selected the corresponding process parameter group to carry on the residual controllable grind to high-voltage cable insulation layer sample, through adopting the dynamic measurement-grind method to carry on the grind to the cable sample many times, the grinding effect is good, it is of great significance to apply robot grind in the grinding field of high-voltage cable insulation layer, to improve the grinding quality of high-voltage cable insulation layer and to improve the level of intelligentization of the grind of high-voltage cable insulation layer.

Acknowledgment. The results were supported by China Yangtze Power Co., Ltd. (Z422302030).

References

1. Li, X.W., Rao, W.L.: Research on material removal of robotic constant-force grind and polish. Mach. Tool Hydraulics **49**(4), 31–36 (2021)
2. Zhou, L.M., Liu, M.X., Ma, C.Y.: Technology of robotic automatic grinding internal surface in aircraft structural parts. Sci. Technol. Eng. **19**(36), 128–133 (2019)
3. Jia, X.Z., Du, L.F., Wang, Y.: Research on efficiency and force of grinding steel castings with industrial robot. Mod. Manuf. Eng. **4**, 93–98 (2021)
4. Yuan, S.: Random gradient boosting for predicting conditional quantiles. J. Stat. Comput. Simul. **85**, 3716–3726 (2015)
5. Bastos, J.A.: Predicting credit scores with boosted decision trees. Forecasting **4**, 925–935 (2022)

A Peg-in-Hole Assembly Method Based on Hybrid Visual Information

Jian Zhang and Yongpeng Tian[✉]

School of Mechanical Engineering, Tongji University, Shanghai 201804, China
2230239@tongji.edu.cn

Abstract. Visual information is widely used in peg-in-hole assembly due to the features that can quickly reduce the uncertainty of the position and the lack of contact with the target hole surface. This paper proposes a peg-in-hole assembly method based on hybrid visual information. Firstly, we acquire 3D point cloud data, and based on the RANSAC algorithm, we obtain the direction vectors of the holes, to calculate the required orientation of the end-effector. Then we propose a two-stage target detection network that can directly extract the position of the target hole, and to alleviate the large amount of time required to collect and label the real images, we train on the synthetic dataset and part of the real dataset obtained from the constructed virtual assembly scene. The method was trained and tested on the constructed simulation platform, proving that the assembly strategy can be effectively applied to robot peg-in-hole assembly.

Keywords: Peg-in-hole · Deep Learning · Point Cloud · Synthetic data

1 Introduction

Most of the current studies divide the peg-in-hole assembly task into two phases - search and insertion, the most important of which is the search phase, i.e., the positioning of the hole; theoretically, if the search phase is sufficiently accurate in terms of localization, the insertion phase only requires the control of the actuator to move in the vertical direction.

The existing control strategies can be categorized according to the starting point of control: passive compliance control (PCC) [1], manual teach-in control (MTC) [2], and active control (AC) [3]. Among them, passive compliance control fixes a flexible device on the end-effector to naturally adapt to the contact force due to the positional error of the shaft and the hole during the shaft assembly process; manual teach-in control implements the next assembly by recording the data during the manual teach-in assembly process (Cartesian trajectory and recording the change of the contact force of the end-effector), which is then used as a reference; and active control generally applies the vision/sensors in the scenarios to actively control peg-in-hole assembly by establishing the relationship between sensor data and assembly state.

The search strategy based on contact sensing will inevitably cause contact friction between the end of the shaft hole and the mating surface, in addition, the force/torque

Table 1. Table captions should be placed above the tables.

Method	Accuracy	Speed	Success rate	Contact	Complexity	Cost
Contact	Medium	Slow	High	Yes	High	High
Plane vision	Medium	Fast	Medium	No	Low	Low
Spatial Vision	High	Faster	High	No	Medium	Medium
Laser Sensing	*Higher*	Faster	Higher	No	Higher	Higher

sensor is generally larger, and the solid connection with the end-effector will result in a significant increase in the volume and mass of the end-effector, which will lead to a certain degree of reduction in the robot's precision and workspace, so the search strategy based on contact sensing is suitable for the mating surface of the regular size and precision assembly scenarios with no special requirements. Therefore, the search strategy based on contact sensing is ideal for regular size and precision assembly scenarios with no special requirements for the mating surface; the search strategy based on planar (2D) vision generally adopts the mounting method of a monocular camera fixed on the end-effector (Eye-in-hand), which is the same as that of the force, torque sensor but with the greatly reduced volume and mass, and the faster imaging speed. Still, it will be affected by the illumination and obstruction. Assembly scenarios; the search strategy based on spatial (3D) vision generally adopts binocular cameras, which are also more flexible in location and have improved accuracy but will also be affected by light to a certain extent, so it is suitable for assembly scenarios with good lighting conditions; the search strategy based on laser sensing generally requires the installation of a special laser device on the surface of the object to be measured, and the cost is high, so it is usually applicable only to the structured scenes. A comparison of the various methods is shown in the Table 1.

2 Method

2.1 Target Orientation Determination Based on 3D Information

Although it is possible to fit the point cloud data into the cube based on PCA and RANSAC [4, 5] algorithms, it is not easy to directly obtain the location and orientation of the holes because the point cloud image acquired by a single orientation camera cannot completely cover the whole cube, but a more accurate orientation vector of the center axis of the holes can be obtained based on the features of the cylinder.

The RGBD image is acquired globally using a depth camera, and then the RGBD image is converted to 3D point cloud data based on Open3D, and then the axis orientation calculation is performed based on the acquired 3D point cloud data.

The depth camera is utilized in the simulation environment (Coppeliasim) to acquire the depth map as shown in Fig. 1.

RANSAC (Random Sample Consensus) is a robust parameter estimation method for estimating model parameters from a set of data containing outlier points. When fitting cylinders, RANSAC can be used to find the cylinder model that best fits the point cloud data while ignoring possible noise or outliers. Principal Component Analysis (PCA) is a statistical technique that can find the direction of data variability by determining standard orthogonal axes to maximize de-correlation of the data and it has been used in many ways for point cloud processing. In this paper, the idea of RANSCA is applied on the basis of using PCA to obtain more accurate information about the orientation of cylindrical axes.

PCA and RANSCA based cylindrical axis extraction algorithm:

First, the Point Cloud Data (PCD) is decentered to obtain the covariance matrix C.

$$C = \frac{1}{k}\sum_{i=1}^{k}(p_i - \bar{p}) \cdot (p_i - \bar{p})^T \quad (1)$$

where $p_i = (x_i, y_i, z_i)^T$ and $\bar{p} = (\bar{x_i}, \bar{y_i}, \bar{z_i})^T$ are, respectively, the ith point of the PCD consisting of k points and their centers of mass, where the value of k is empirically set to be from 1% to 5% of the point cloud span depending on the density of the point cloud.

Then the eigenvalues and eigenvectors of C are solved.

$$\begin{cases} (C - \lambda_j I) = 0 \\ (C - \lambda_j I)v_j = 0 \end{cases}, j = 0, 1, 2 \quad (2)$$

According to the above equation, the eigenvalue λ_j and the eigenvector v_j can be obtained. Where $\lambda_2 \geq \lambda_1 \geq \lambda_0$, the eigenvector v_o is the point the point normal vector $v_0 = n^{(3 \times 1)}$, because it indicates that the point cloud data has the least variation in that direction.

According to the properties of a cylindrical surface: the normal to any point on a cylindrical surface is perpendicular to and intersects the axis of the cylinder, and the two points can determine a straight line.

$$\begin{cases} a \cdot n_1 = 0 \\ a \cdot n_2 = 0 \\ a_s = \beta_1(n_{1e} - n_{1s}) \\ a_e = \beta_2(n_{2e} - n_{2s}) \end{cases} \quad (3)$$

where a is the potential axis, and the starting and ending points of a are $a_s^{(3 \times 1)}$, $a_e^{(3 \times 1)}$; n_1, n_2 are the normal vectors of two different points on the column plane, and the starting and ending points of n_1 and n_2 are $n_{1s}^{(3 \times 1)}$, $n_{2s}^{(3 \times 1)}$, $n_{2s}^{(3 \times 1)}$, $n_{2e}^{(3 \times 1)}$; β_1, β_2 are the coefficients to be determined for the two straight lines. Solving the above equation yields two coefficients, which are substituted into the parametric form of the space linear equation to obtain the potential axis.

$$a = R^{(3 \times 1)}\gamma + T^{(3 \times 1)} \quad (4)$$

where R is the three direction vectors, γ is the parameter, and T is the position vector (which can be $a_s^{(3 \times 1)}$, $a_e^{(3 \times 1)}$).

Iterate as follows: randomly sample two points from PCD and get normal vectors n_1, n_2; Calculate the potential axis a_i according to Eq. (4); Calculate the error $s_i = a_i \cdot n_i$ according to the direction; Judge: whether s_i is greater than the error threshold $\hat{s}$; if it is, delete the point (outlier); otherwise, keep it (inlier), and at the same time, accumulate $inlier_i$, and update a_i with the current maximum value of inlier to the potential axis,, and enter the next loop; based on experience, the error threshold $\hat{s}$ is set to 0.05, and the number of iterations i is set to 20.

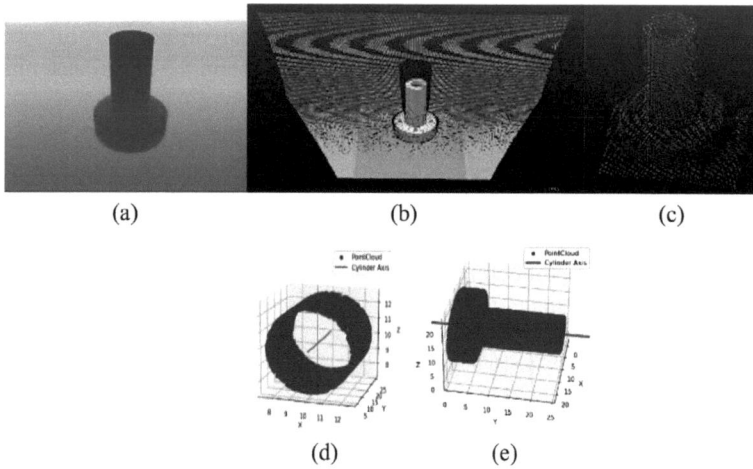

Fig. 1. RGBD to Point Cloud to extract hole direction vectors (a) RGB image acquired in the simulation environment. (b) Point cloud data converted according to the summed internal reference. (c) Cropped point cloud using Cloud Compare. (d) (e) Prediction results using the PCA and RANSAC algorithm.

So far, we have converted the depth map to point cloud data, and according to the PCA and RANSAC algorithm, we get the direction vectors of the cylindrical axes (holes), and then we get the coordinates of the hole axes in the robot coordinate system according to the transformation matrix (calibrated) between the robot base coordinate system and the camera coordinate system, and then we make the direction vectors of the axes on the end-effector equal to them according to R, i.e., the orientation of the holes. In the next section, we obtain the position information of the hole, from the 2D image.

2.2 Target Position Determination Based on 2D Information

To realize high-speed and efficient labor-saving dataset annotation and construction, Blender virtual engine, Coppeliasim, and synthetic data generation methods are used for obtaining a large amount of training data [6], quickly obtaining images, and constructing datasets. Among them, Blender scripts are written to construct a virtual assembly 3D scene; the basic idea of synthetic data generation is to simulate various situations in a real scene to generate corresponding part images. We take a randomized approach to generate data, taking the position and brightness of the light source, which are most likely to affect the image in the real scene, and the surface texture of the model as random variables to generate the virtual dataset [7].

Firstly, the most common round hole flange part is taken as the model, and then considering that the actual light source position is generally at the top of the part, in this paper, the position of the virtual light source is randomly placed at the front top, back top, right top, left top, right top; then considering the brightness of the light source in different scenes, the brightness of the virtual light source is randomized to be bright, medium, and dark; and then considering the surface texture of the model, six types of textures, including the texture of scratched metal, rusted metal, etc., are randomly generated. The six textures including scratched metal, rusty metal texture, etc. are randomly generated on the surface of the model, and then we fix the position of the parts, and the camera randomly takes pictures and collects data within the range of x-axis ±67.5 cm, z-axis ±75 cm, totaling 1,000 virtual pictures for each texture, and then we take multiple pictures with the light angle and luminance as the random variables under the real scenario, and then we generate the synthetic dataset with a ratio of 9:1, and then we randomly After that, we randomly disrupt all the pictures and train the net-work according to the ratio of 9:1 between the training set and the test set.

Some examples of synthetic dataset images are shown in Fig. 2.

Fig. 2. Partially synthetic dataset. The images in the left seven columns are virtual datasets with the following textures from top to bottom: scratched metal, green rusty metal, psychedelic texture, checkerboard texture, Voronoi texture, and noisy texture, with decreasing light intensity and randomly varying light direction from left to right; and the images in the eighth column are real datasets, photographed against metallic and blue backgrounds and with randomly varying light intensity and direction.

Figure 3 illustrates the architecture of the Network. Considering that the network task in this paper is different from the classical target detection task, i.e., there is no need to classify but only to regress the position coordinates and size of the target holes in the image, we use the classical Faster-RCNN two-stage neural network [8], and the input of the network is an RGB image with arbitrary resolution, which is firstly Reshaped to a fixed resolution, then the features are extracted through the as the back-bone part of the VGG-NET to extract features [9]; finally, the regressed prediction frame data is replaced with the pixel coordinates and size of the holes, where the pixel coordinates are converted to the position information of the target holes, and the size is used as the feature data to match the depth information of the holes.

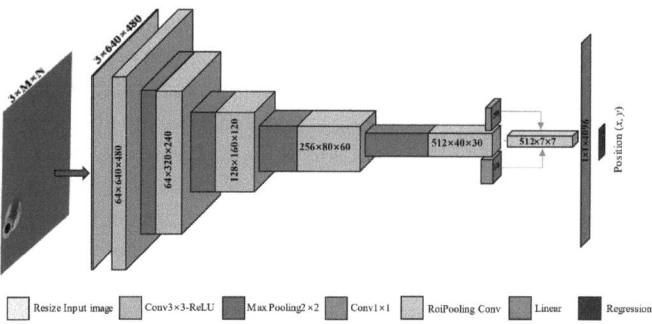

Fig. 3. Architecture of the Network

Then it is summarized as the location information of the hole.

For the loss function, a smoothed *L2 loss* function is used when the regression difference is poor, other-wise an *L1 loss* is used.

$$x = |p_l - g_l| \tag{5}$$

$$r_{loss} = \begin{cases} 0.5\sigma^2 x^2, & x < \frac{1}{\sigma^2} \\ x - \frac{0.5}{\sigma^2}, & x \geq \frac{1}{\sigma^2} \end{cases} \tag{6}$$

where the x is the regression difference, p_l is the predicted value of the location, g_l is the true value of the location, re_{loss} is the value of the loss function, and σ is the hyperparameter, which controls the conversion of the loss function from *L2 loss* (smooth but sensitive to outliers) to *L1 loss* (more robust to outliers but not smooth). According to the characteristics of the task in this paper, the regression localization of peg-in-hole assembly needs to be more sensitive to small errors, and combined with the analysis of many experiments, we set the σ value to *1.2* to have a better training effect. Train loss and Value Loss are shown in Fig. 4 left, with significant convergence within 100 epochs. The robustness of the trained neural network to luminance can be known from Fig. 4 right.

$$\begin{cases} u = bb_u - bb_d \\ v = bb_r - bb_l \end{cases} \tag{7}$$

Pixel coordinate system to the point $(X_C, Y_C, Z_C)^T$ under the camera coordinate system.

$$\begin{pmatrix} X_C \\ Y_C \\ Z_C \end{pmatrix} = \begin{pmatrix} \frac{(u-c_x) \cdot z}{f_x} \\ \frac{(v-c_y) \cdot z}{f_y} \\ z \end{pmatrix} \tag{8}$$

where f_x, f_y is the focal length, c_x, c_y are the principal point coordinates, both obtained from the internal reference matrix (known), u, v are the pixel coordinates, bb_u, bb_d, bb_r, bb_l are the boundingbox pixels, respectively, with the coordinates obtained from the neural network; and z is the depth, which is obtained from the camera parameters;

The camera coordinate system to the world coordinate system under the coordinates $P = (x, y, z)^T$.

$$\begin{pmatrix} x \\ y \\ z \end{pmatrix} = R \begin{pmatrix} X_c \\ Y_c \\ Z_c \end{pmatrix} + t \qquad (9)$$

where R is the rotation matrix and t is the translation matrix, known from the camera calibration [10].

$$L = \mathcal{F}(r) \qquad (10)$$

where L is the insertion depth, r is the hole size, and $\mathcal{F}$ is the mapping relationship, established from the data to be assembled.

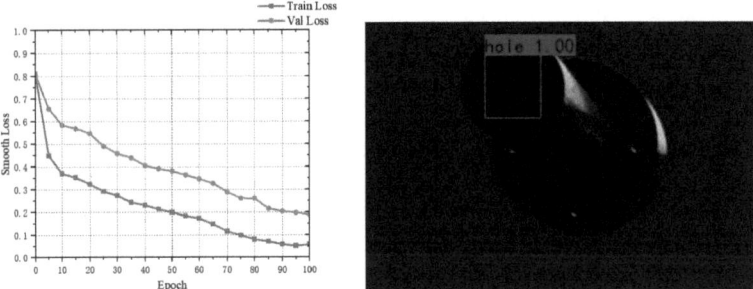

Fig. 4. Loss and Example of target hole detection in low light conditions.

3 Simulation Experiments

First, we use the following configuration for our simulation. Software: Coppeliasim EDU v4.0; Hardware: GPU: NVIDIA RTX A4000 (32 GB); CPU: Intel(R) Silver 4210R 2.40 GHz. RAM: 32 GB 2400 MHz. Actuator: UR5 robotic arm model;

The kinematic inverse solution is performed using the DLS (The damped least squares) algorithm with max iterations = 100 and Damping = 0.1; Virtual camera (Kineticv1) parameters: Resolution = 640*480; Field of view 57° (focal length can be found). The specific simulation environment is shown in Fig. 5

We use the joint simulation environment of Python and Coppeliasim to integrate the point cloud attitude determination algorithm, the trained neural network, the control of the camera, and the robotic arm [11], firstly, the scene is arranged as below, the RGBD camera is controlled to capture the image, and then the image is passed into the point cloud algorithm and the neural network through the joint simulation, respectively, and then the flange holes' coordinates in the time coordinate system are Then the coordinates

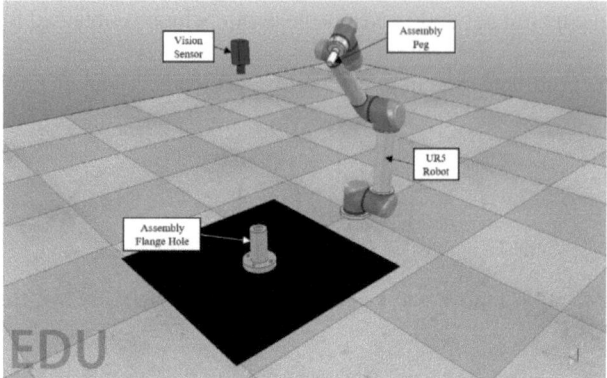

Fig. 5. Simulated assembly scenarios.

of the flange hole in the time coordinate system are passed into the robot motion control module, and the Damped Least Squares (DLS) algorithm based on the inverse kinematics to solve the inverse solution controls the end of the robotic arm to arrive at the specified position and perform the insertion action, and we also configure a force sensor on the end actuator of the robotic arm to obtain the data required for the evaluation. Figure 6 shows snapshots of the assembly process.

The DLS algorithm is a common method for solving the inverse solution of robot kinematics, especially when singularities are encountered or the solution is not unique, it can provide a stable solution. The DLS algorithm introduces a damping factor (damping factor) in the calculation of the inverse solution, which makes the solution more numerically stable.

$$\Delta q = \left(J^T J + \lambda^2 I\right)^{-1} J^T \Delta x \tag{11}$$

where Δq is the amount of change in the joint angle, J is the Jacobi matrix (which is the derivative of the mapping function from the joint angle to the position and orientation of the end-effector with respect to the joint angle), I is the unit matrix, x is the position and orientation vector of the end-effector, and λ is the damping factor (empirically, set to 0.1).

Based on the amount of change in the joint angle, the joint angle can be updated.

$$q^i = q^{i-1} + \Delta q, i = 1, 2, \cdots 100 \tag{12}$$

where i is the current number of iterations. Repeat the above steps until the end-effector position and orientation reach the desired target position and orientation.

In this paper, we focus on the case of gap fit, the assembly gap is taken as: 0.8 mm, 1 mm, 1.2 mm, and 1.5 mm; to avoid the error caused by the difference of the fixed position of the shaft at the end of the arm, we let the size of the shaft remain unchanged, and we only change the size of the holes, to test the assembly of different gaps; and we also take into account that the existence of the chamfer and the position of the flange holes will have a greater impact on the assembly experiment. Considering that the presence

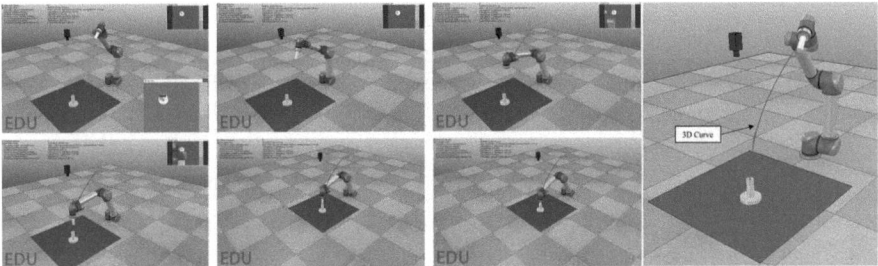

Fig. 6. Snapshots and 3D curve (The Neural network detection is shown in the first image in the top left corner).

or absence of chamfers and the fixed or unfixed flange hole position will have a large impact on the assembly experiment, we carry out the experiment according to the degree of difficulty of the assembly from the chamfered and unfixed flange hole position to the non-chamfered and fixed flange hole position, and the shafts and the different sizes of the flange hole models are modeled using Solidworks and exported to the simulation environment of Coppeliasim; the presence of chamfer size C1; F_Z initial force $= 1.05N$, and the assembly results are shown in the table. Assembly results are shown in Table 2.

Table 2. Assembly experiment results.

Test group	D (mm)	G (mm)	L(mm)	Suc./Test.num	Chamfer	Fixed hole	Maximum resistance of Z (N)
1	32	0.8	100	10/10	Yes	No	7.23
	32	0.8	100	10/10	Yes	Yes	18.85
	32	0.8	100	10/10	No	No	8.44
	32	0.8	100	10/10	No	Yes	22.9
2	32	1.2	100	10/10	Yes	No	4.92
	32	1.2	100	10/10	Yes	Yes	13.91

(*continued*)

In this paper, we measure the smoothness of assembly based on the magnitude of the peak resistance in the Z-direction. From the experimental results, it seems that although all the assemblies are completed, the time-consuming and difficult assemblies increase significantly when the assembly gap increases gradually, especially when there is no chamfer and the hole position is fixed. The specific assembly data is shown in Fig. 7.

Furthermore, the average time taken for assembly is largely independent of the size of the gap, which is mainly affected by whether the chamfer and hole position are fixed or not; compared with the traditional visionless contact assembly method, the method proposed in this paper improves the time taken, and in addition avoids frictional contact between the surfaces.

Table 2. (*continued*)

Test group	D (mm)	G (mm)	L(mm)	Suc./Test.num	Chamfer	Fixed hole	Maximum resistance of Z (N)
	32	1.2	100	10/10	No	No	5.575
	32	1.2	100	10/10	No	Yes	19.13
3	32	1.5	100	10/10	Yes	No	2.54
	32	1.5	100	10/10	Yes	Yes	9.58

(*continued*)

Table 2. (*continued*)

Test group	D (mm)	G (mm)	L(mm)	Suc./Test.num	Chamfer	Fixed hole	Maximum resistance of Z (N)
	32	1.5	100	10/10	No	No	6.01
	32	1.5	100	10/10	No	Yes	13.66

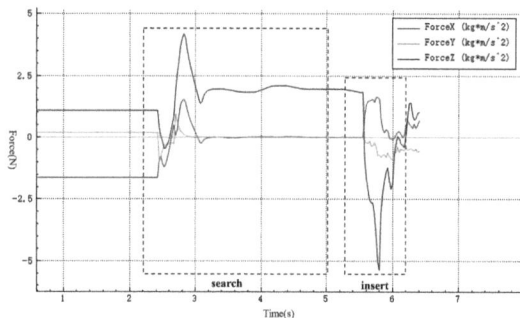

Fig. 7. g = 1.2, Force on the end of the robotic arm during assembly without chamfer and hole position not fixed.

4 Conclusion

This paper proposes a peg-in-hole assembly method based on hybrid visual information. The target pose is acquired based on 3D point cloud data and the target position is acquired based on 2D image data, where the pose acquisition based on point cloud is based on PCA and DBSCAN; For hole position acquisition we propose a two-phase target detection network can directly extract the target hole position, and to minimize the time-consuming problem of building the dataset, we use a stochastic script to obtain a synthetic dataset in the constructed virtual assembly scene and use it in proportion to the real dataset for network training. Finally, the assembly experiments are co-simulated based on Python and Coppeliasim and the proposed method is validated. Future research directions can go deeper into the peg-in-hole assembly of different shapes to realize a wide range of applications for unstructured assembly scenarios.

References

1. Park, H., Park, J., Lee, D.H., Park, J.H., Bae, J.H.: Compliant peg-in-hole assembly using partial spiral force trajectory with tilted peg posture. IEEE Rob. Autom. Lett. **5**(3), 4447–4454 (2020). https://doi.org/10.1109/LRA.2020.3000428
2. Song, J., Chen, Q., Li, Z.: A peg-in-hole robot assembly system based on Gauss mixture model. Rob. Comput. Integr. Manuf. **67**, 101996 (2021). https://doi.org/10.1016/j.rcim.2020.101996
3. Zhao, Y., Gao, F., Zhao, Y., Chen, Z.: Peg-in-hole assembly based on six-legged robots with visual detecting and force sensing. Sensors **20**(10), 2861 (2020). https://doi.org/10.3390/s20102861
4. Martínez-Otzeta, J.M., Rodríguez-Moreno, I., Mendialdua, I., Sierra, B.: Ransac for robotic applications: a survey. Sensors **23**(1), 327 (2022). https://doi.org/10.3390/s23010327
5. Li,C., Chen,P., Xu, X., Wang, X., Yin, A.: A coarse-to-fine method for estimating the axis pose based on 3D point clouds in robotic cylindrical shaft-in-hole assembly.Sensors **21**(12), 4064 (2021).https://doi.org/10.3390/s21124064
6. Shen, Y., Jia, Q., Wang, R., et al.: Learning-based visual servoing for high-precision peg-in-hole assembly, actuators. MDPI **12**(4), 144 (2023). https://doi.org/10.3390/act12040144
7. Triyonoputro, J.C., Wan, W., Harada, K.: Quickly inserting pegs into uncertain holes using multi-view images and deep network trained on synthetic data. In: 2019 IEEE/RSJ International Conference on Intelligent Robots and Systems (IROS). Macau, China. pp. 5792–5799 (2019). https://doi.org/10.1109/IROS40897.2019.8968072
8. Ren, S., He, K., Girshick, R., Sun, J.: Faster R-CNN: towards real-time object detection with region proposal networks. IEEE Trans. Pattern Anal. Mach. Intell. **39**(6), 1137–1149 (2016). https://doi.org/10.1109/TPAMI.2016.2577031
9. Simonyan, K., Zisserman, A.: Very deep convolutional networks for large-scale image recognition (2014). arXiv preprint arXiv:1409.1556
10. Zhang, Z.: Flexible camera calibration by viewing a plane from unknown orientations. In: Proceedings of the Seventh IEEE International Conference on Computer Vision. Kerkyra, Greece. IEEE, 1, 666–673 (1999). https://doi.org/10.1109/ICCV.1999.791289
11. Wang, Y.: Research on robotic grasping and intelligent assembly based on deep reinforcement learning. Shen Yang University of Technology PhD dissertation (2023). https://doi.org/10.27322/d.cnki.gsgyu.2022.000374

Robotic Grasping Object Recognition Method Based on 3D Point Cloud in Multi-object Stacking Scenes

Bingyuan Zhu, Minglun Dong, Yongpeng Tian, and Jian Zhang[✉]

School of Mechanical Engineering, Tongji University, Shanghai, China
2232711@tongji.edu.cn

Abstract. Robotic grasping in multi-object stacking scenes is an important aspect of robot intelligence. In this paper, an object recognition method based on 3D point cloud is proposed, which can be used for robot to recognize the object in the stacking scenes and complete the subsequent grasping operation. Firstly, the classical PointNet++ model is improved to make it more suitable for stacking objects in terms of feature sampling quantity and accuracy. Then, based on the transformation relationship between CAD model and point cloud, a dataset containing 200 sets of stacking scene point cloud was build. Using the dataset to train the improved PointNet ++ model, we get 96.97% training accuracy and 87.47% testing accuracy, which are 0.37% and 1.08% higher than the classical PointNet ++ model respectively. Finally, 30 sets of point cloud data of stacking objects were captured with a 3D camera in real scenes to validate the segmentation performance of the model. Experiments show that the average segmentation accuracy of this method is 84.74%, and the highest segmentation accuracy can reach 90.75%, which satisfies the requirements of industrial applications.

Keywords: Point cloud object recognition · multi-object stacking scene · robotic grasping

1 Introduction

At present, autonomous grasp is an important research direction in the field of robotic control, and it is also the basis for robots to acquire, move and transport objects [1]. However, due to the superposition and occlusion between objects, how to accurately identify the target object and complete the grasp is one of the most challenging problems [2]. In the process of object recognition, the traditional method is to obtain 2D images by using 2D vision sensor. However, with the development of 3D imaging technology and the emergence of 3D sensors (such as depth camera, lidar, 3D scanners, etc.), it has become a reality to obtain 3D data with rich geometric shapes and scale features [3], which greatly improves the efficiency and flexibility of robotic operation.

Compared with 2D data, 3D data has more abundant structural information, which can more fully represent complex scenes. As the primary representation of 3D data, point clouds can be acquired directly by 3D sensors or generated by stereoscopic multi-view images. However, due to the disordered and unstructured characteristics of point cloud, how to effectively use point cloud to recognize the objective world is a challenging task.

In order to complete the robotic grasping in the multi-object stacking scenes, the first step is to identify the target object correctly, which means to separate the target point cloud from the original point cloud. Traditional point cloud segmentation methods can be generally divided into the following three categories [4]: model-based segmentation [3], edge-based segmentation [4, 5] and region-based segmentation [6, 7]. However, it is often difficult to get complete 3D point cloud information in the stacking environments, the segmentation results of traditional methods are often not ideal. In recent years, deep learning methods based on 3D vision have been applied to the classification, segmentation and detection of point clouds. For example, PointNet [8], PointNet++ [9], and PointCNN [10] have been widely used in point cloud feature extraction, and have shown good results. However, these methods are limited in the size of dataset and application situation.

The classical PointNet++ point cloud segmentation model is improved in this paper to accurately identify the target object from the multi-object stacking scenes, so as to prepare for the subsequent robotic grasping operations.

2 Related Research

2.1 Point Cloud Preprocessing

When obtaining point cloud data with 3D sensors, due to the impact of equipment accuracy, operator experience, and environmental factors, the initial point cloud data usually contains some invalid regions (such as noise points, outliers, etc., as shown in Fig. 1a), which will reduce the speed and accuracy of object recognition. Therefore, it is important to eliminate these ineffective areas.

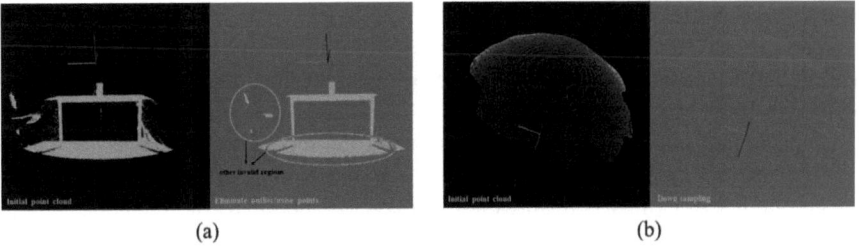

Fig. 1. Point Cloud Noise Reduction and Point Cloud Downsampling.

In addition, if the density of point cloud is too high, it is necessary to down sample the point cloud data for lower processing time and algorithm complexity, which means reducing the number of points and keeping the overall geometric characteristics of the point cloud, as shown in Fig. 1b.

In view of the above cases, the Statistical-Outlier-Removal filter in PCL library is firstly used to remove outliers and noise points in the initial point cloud. By setting the filter radius, the points that did not reach enough neighbors within the given radius range were removed. Due to environmental factors, the filtered point cloud may also contain some invalid regions such as the background and shadow, as shown in Fig. 1a. The segmentation algorithm based on European clustering is used to eliminate these regions. The Voxel-Grid filter in PCL library is used to down-sampling if the density of point cloud is too high. By selecting the appropriate voxel size V, the number of points can be appropriately reduced.

2.2 The Classical PointNet++ Model

The core idea of PointNet++ is to use PointNet to extract features repeatedly in the local area of the initial point cloud, so as to achieve multi-level feature learning. When Pointnet++ is used for point cloud segmentation, the whole model can be divided into two parts: encoder and decoder. The encoder is mainly composed of a series of Set Abstraction (SA) modules, each SA module is composed of three parts: sampling layer, grouping layer and PointNet layer, which is responsible for down sampling of the point cloud.

The decoder is mainly composed of a series of FP (Feature Propagation) modules. The process includes three parts: interpolation, feature concatenation and feature transformation. Finally, the output features are reduced to the class number by MLP, and the class probability of each point in the point cloud is obtained by Softmax.

2.3 The Improved PointNet++ Model

At present, PointNet++ has achieved good segmentation results on some indoor scene point cloud datasets, and can also realize the classification of single object. However, this paper is to realize the object recognition in the multi-object stacking environment, so more features need to be collected. Therefore, this paper makes some improvements on the classic Pointnet++ model to make it better applicable to stacked object point clouds. The improved model parameters are shown in Table 1.

According to the modified model parameters, the point cloud segmentation model of stacking objects. It can be seen that the improvements made in this paper for the classic PointNet++ model are as follows:

The sampling number and sampling radius of the model are increased, so that the model can extract the global features of stacking objects more effectively.

The number of extracted features in each layer is modified, and the concatenation operation in the classical PointNet++ is replaced by residual connection. In this way, the differences between the two layers can be considered at the same time. In addition, the problem of gradient disappearance can be effectively alleviated when the number of layers is large (Fig. 2).

Table 1. Comparison of model parameters before and after improvement.

Name	Classical PointNet++ model			Improved PointNet++ model		
	Sampling number	Sampling radius	Feature number	Sampling number	Sampling radius	Feature number
SA1	512	0.2	64	1024	0.2	128
SA2	256	0.4	128	512	0.4	256
SA3	128	0.8	256	256	0.8	512
SA4				64	1.6	1024
FP4				—	—	512
FP3	—	—	256	—	—	256
FP2	—	—	128	—	—	128
FP1	—	—	128	—	—	64

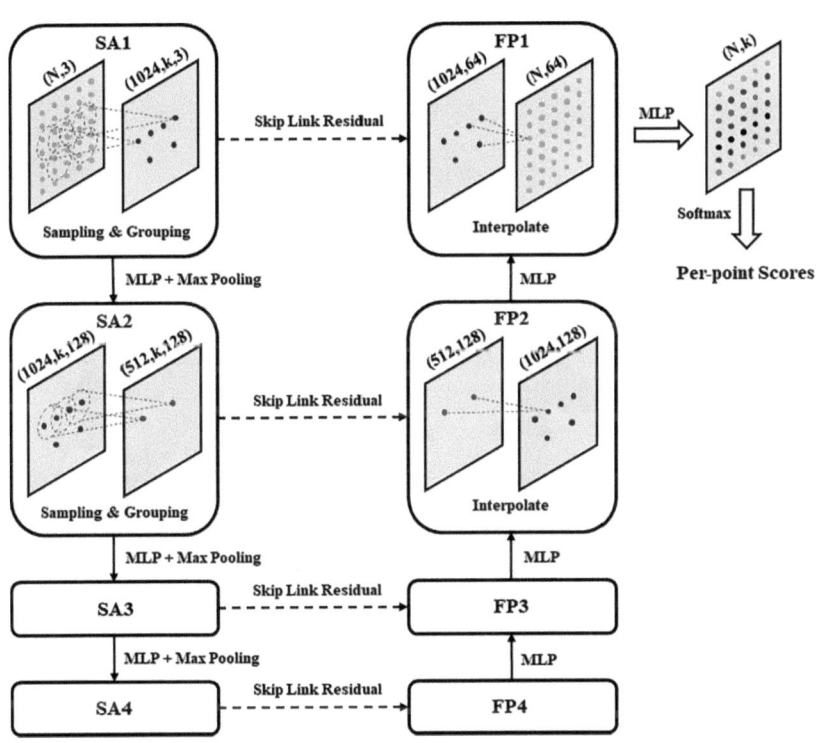

Fig. 2. The improved PointNet++ model.

3 Experiments

3.1 Preparation of Dataset

In order to verify the performance of the point cloud segmentation model proposed in this paper, it is necessary to train on a suitable dataset. A good dataset should contain a rich amount of data, and should be labeled and classified correctly.

Acquisition of Point Cloud. In general, the point cloud data can be obtained by scanning with a 3D camera. However, this method usually has the phenomenon of missing data. 3D scanning is not suitable for large data collection due to its low efficiency and high cost. Therefore, this paper uses CAD software to model the stacking objects, and then converts the 3D model into point cloud data, which not only ensures the integrity of point cloud data, but also improves the efficiency of dataset production.

Firstly, the Solid Works (SW) software was used to model stacking objects, and five different types of parts were randomly stacked, as shown in Fig. 3. Each stacking scene corresponds to a set of point cloud, and the stacking object point cloud dataset is built by combining a sufficient number of stacking scenes.

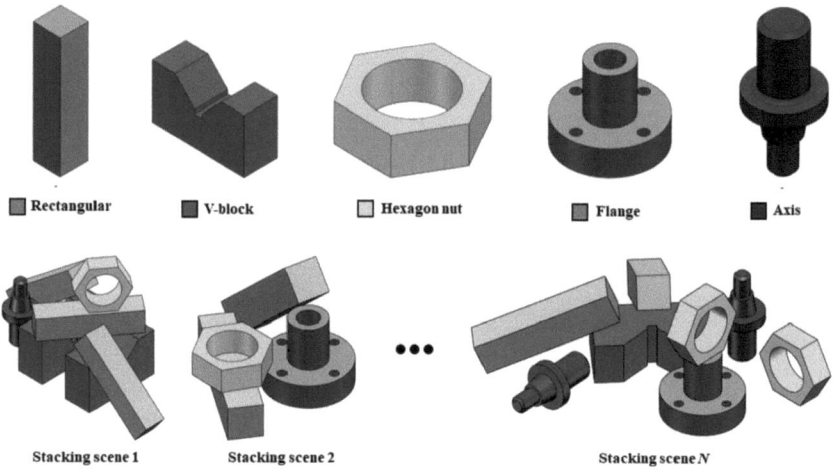

Fig. 3. Random stacking scene based on 3D CAD model.

After finishing the 3D modeling, save them as STL format, and then convert the STL files to OBJ files with the ScanTo3D. There is a corresponding executable file in the PCL library to convert the OBJ file into a point cloud file.

Centralization and Normalization of Point Cloud. After the above process, a point cloud file in PCD format can be obtained. The obtained point cloud data need to be centered and normalized.

The centralization of point cloud data refers to the subtraction of the mean value from the sample data, which is expressed by the formula 1:

$$\begin{cases} x'_i = x_i - \mu_x = x_i - \frac{1}{n}\sum_{i=1}^{n} x_i \\ y'_i = y_i - \mu_y = y_i - \frac{1}{n}\sum_{i=1}^{n} y_i \\ z'_i = z_i - \mu_z = z_i - \frac{1}{n}\sum_{i=1}^{n} z_i \end{cases} \quad (1)$$

where, x_i, y_i, z_i represent the initial coordinates of the point cloud. x'_i, y'_i, z_i' represent the coordinates of the centered point cloud. μ_x, μ_y, μ_z represent the mean value of sample data.

The normalization of point cloud data refers to subtracting the minimum value and then dividing it by the range of the sample, which is expressed as formula 2:

$$\begin{cases} x^i_{norm} = \frac{x_i - x_{min}}{R_x} = \frac{x_i - x_{min}}{x_{max} - x_{min}} \\ y^i_{norm} = \frac{y_i - y_{min}}{R_y} = \frac{y_i - y_{min}}{y_{max} - y_{min}} \\ z^i_{norm} = \frac{z_i - z_{min}}{R_z} = \frac{z_i - z_{min}}{z_{max} - z_{min}} \end{cases} \quad (2)$$

where, x_i, y_i, z_i represent the initial coordinates of the point cloud. $x^i_{norm}, y^i_{norm}, z^i_{norm}$ represent the normalized point cloud coordinates. $x_{min}, y_{min}, z_{min}$ represent the minimum sample; $x_{max}, y_{max}, z_{max}$ represent the maximum sample.

Point Cloud Segmentation and Annotation. After the centralization and normalization process of point cloud data is completed, the point cloud needs to be segmented and labeled before training. In this paper, Cloud Compare software is used to label the point cloud data of stacking objects.

According to the types of 3D models, this paper divides each stacking scene into 5 categories: cuboid, V-block, hexagon nut, flange, and shaft. Figure 4 shows two labeled stacking object point clouds randomly selected from the dataset.

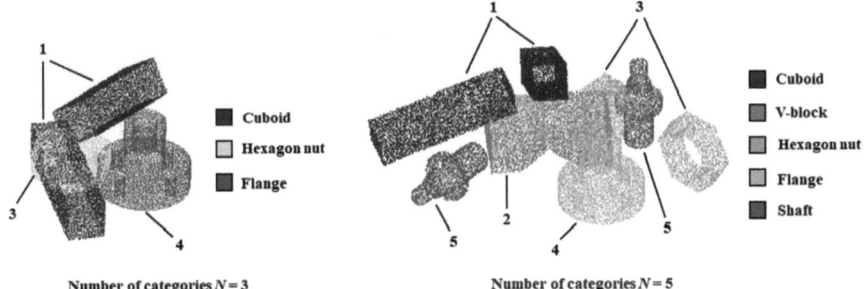

Fig. 4. The stacking objects point cloud after labelling.

Build of Datasets. After the above process, the point cloud of 230 stacking scenes is finally built. 200 point clouds are obtained through 3D model conversion for model training. 30 Point clouds are obtained by scanning actual stacking scenes to verify the segmentation effect of the network model. The 200 point clouds are divided into the training set and the test set according to the ratio of 4:1, which are used for iterative solution and result verification of the network model respectively

3.2 Model Training

This paper uses the Adam optimizer based on Pytorch framework to improve the PointNet++ model. During training, the batch size is 8, the epoch is 400, the initial learning rate is 0.001, the decay rate of learning rate is 0.5, and the decay rate of weight is 0.01.

In the iterative solution process, 160 groups of data are used for model training. Since the batch size is 8, 20 iterations are required for each epoch, with a total of 8000 iterations. In order to verify whether the model converges, the loss function value of the network model after per iteration is recorded, as shown in Fig. 5a. As can be seen from the figure, the loss value in the first iteration of the model is around 1.78, showing a downward trend on the whole, and finally converging to the range of 0.08 ~ 0.1. In addition, the model showed obvious oscillations at the initial stage of training (such as 75th, 206th, 410th, 500th, 723 iterations), indicating that the model had some overfitting phenomenon at the initial stage.

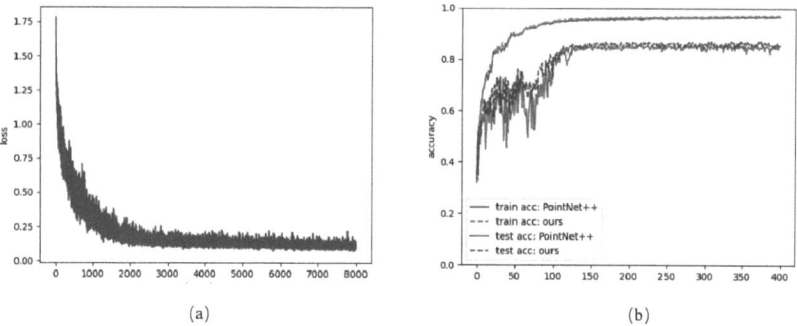

Fig. 5. The loss function (a) of the model and the changes in training and testing (b) results

In order to verify the performance of the model, classical PointNet++ and improved PointNet++ networks were used to train on the stacking object point cloud dataset respectively. The curve of the accuracy of training and testing as the epoch changes is shown in Fig. 5. The experimental results show that the training accuracy of the improved model is almost consistent with the classical model in the overall trend of change, and the accuracy can reach 96.97%, which is 0.37% higher than the classical model. However, the accuracy of the improved model is more gentle and the oscillation phenomenon is weakened, and the accuracy can reach 87.47%, which is 1.08% higher than the classical model.

3.3 Analysis and Visualization of Segmentation Results

In order to verify the performance of the improved PointNet++ model, a 3D camera was used to scan 30 sets of stacking object point clouds in real scenes, input the trained weight parameters for testing, and observe the segmentation effect of the output point clouds. The whole collection and processing process is shown in Fig. 6.

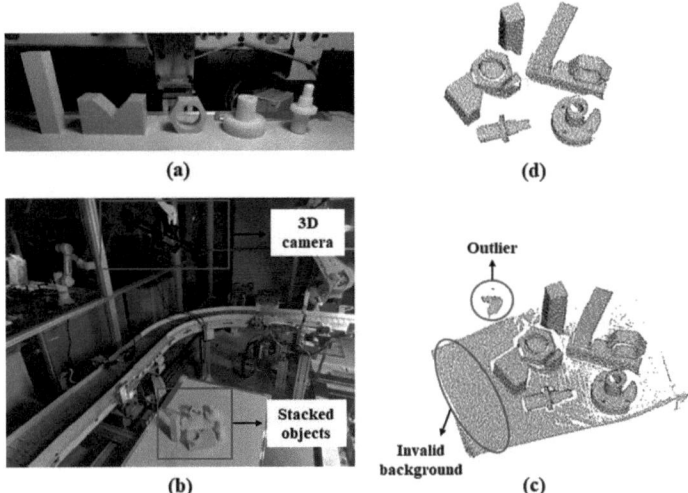

Fig. 6. Using the 3D camera to scan point cloud in the real scene and the subsequent process: (a) Real object models (1:1 size ratio to CAD models). (b) Scanning point clouds in real stacking scenes with a 3D camera. (c) The scanned initial point cloud. (d) The pre-processed point cloud.

The improved PointNet++ model was used to segment and predict the 30 scanned stacking object point clouds, and the segmentation effect was evaluated by comparing whether the prediction label of each point was consistent with the real label. The segmentation and prediction results of each stacking scene were shown in Table 2.

Table 2. Segment prediction results of stacking object point clouds in the real scene.

Scene number	Total	Correct	Accuracy	Scene number	Total	Correct	Accuracy
1	3467	3041	87.71%	16	6021	5004	83.11%
2	6199	5197	83.84%	17	5874	5205	88.61%
3	5514	4673	84.75%	18	6021	4995	82.96%
4	7540	6427	85.24%	19	6216	5585	89.85%
5	5395	4776	88.53%	20	5237	4335	82.78%
6	4392	3689	83.99%	21	6182	5026	81.30%
7	6448	5601	86.86%	22	7412	6170	83.24%
8	6029	5276	87.51%	23	5113	4079	**79.78%**

(*continued*)

Table 2. (*continued*)

Scene number	Total	Correct	Accuracy	Scene number	Total	Correct	Accuracy
9	5412	4462	82.45%	24	5600	4885	87.23%
10	4900	4131	84.31%	25	5779	4794	82.96%
11	5013	4523	90.23%	26	6535	5292	80.98%
12	5695	4761	83.60%	27	5695	4620	81.12%
13	6723	5656	84.13%	28	6427	5250	81.69%
14	6058	5294	87.39%	29	5191	4711	**90.75%**
15	6377	5230	82.01%	30	5377	4478	83.28%

Average accuracy: **84.74%**.

As shown in Table 2, the average segmentation accuracy rate of real stacking object point cloud using the improved PointNet++ model is about 84.74%.

In summary, by observing the segmentation results of 30 stacking scenes, it can be found that when there are fewer types of stacking objects, or the occlusion and superposition between objects are not serious, the segmentation accuracy of the point cloud is higher, up to 90.75%. On the contrary, when the stacking situation between objects is more complicated and the occlusion phenomenon is serious, resulting in the acquisition of too incomplete point cloud, the segmentation accuracy of the point cloud is low, the lowest is 79.78%.

4 Conclusion

This paper introduces a 3D object recognition method based on machine vision, which is used for robotic multi-object grasping in complex environments. First, based on the original PointNet++ model, improvements were made to increase the number of connection layers, sampling radius, and sampling number. In the process of feature transformation, interpolation and residual connection methods were used to obtain point-wise features of the point cloud. The model is more suitable for stacking object point cloud data in terms of feature extraction quantity and receptive field. Secondly, the improved PointNet++ model was trained and tested based on the self-made stacking object point cloud dataset, the training accuracy was 96.97% and the test accuracy was 87.47%. Compared with the classical model, the accuracy is improved by 0.37% and 1.08% respectively. Finally, a 3D structured light camera is used to scan multiple sets of stacking object point clouds in the real scene, the captured point cloud data is input into the improved model to verify the segmentation effect, and the segmentation accuracy of 84.74% is obtained.

From the segmentation results, the improved PointNet++ model proposed in this paper can better realize the automatic segmentation of stacking objects; and can help the robot quickly identify and grasp the target object in the stacking environment. In the future, we will increase the variety of grasping objects and consider better network architectures to improve the segmentation performance.

References

1. Sanchez, J., Corrales, J.A., Bouzgarrou, B.C., Mezouar, Y.: Robotic manipulation and sensing of deformable objects in domestic and industrial applications: a survey. The Int. J. Roboti. Res. **37**(7), 688–716 (2018). https://doi.org/10.1177/0278364918779698
2. Zhang, X., Li, X., Zhou, J., Zhou, X.: Robotic grasping method based on 3D vision for stacked rectangular objects. In: Thirteenth International Conference on Digital Image Processing (ICDIP 2021), Vol. 11878, pp. 488–494. SPIE, Singapore (2021)
3. Schnabel, R., Wahl, R., Klein, R.: Efficient RANSAC for point-cloud shape detection. In: Computer graphics forum, Vol. 26, No. 2, pp. 214–226. Blackwell Publishing Ltd., Oxford, UK (2007). https://doi.org/10.1111/j.1467-8659.2007.01016.x
4. Sappa, A.D., Devy, M.: Fast range image segmentation by an edge detection strategy. In: Proceedings Third International Conference on 3-D Digital Imaging and Modeling, pp. 292–299. IEEE (2001). https://doi.org/10.1109/IM.2001.924460
5. Wani, M.A., Arabnia, H.R.: Parallel edge-region-based segmentation algorithm targeted at reconfigurable multiring network. J. Supercomput. **25**, 43–62 (2003). https://doi.org/10.1023/A:1022804606389
6. Vo, A.V., Truong-Hong, L., Laefer, D.F., Bertolotto, M.: Octree-based region growing for point cloud segmentation. ISPRS J. Photogramm. Remote. Sens. **104**, 88–100 (2015). https://doi.org/10.1016/j.isprsjprs.2015.01.011
7. Xiao, J., Zhang, J., Adler, B., Zhang, H., Zhang, J.: Three-dimensional point cloud plane segmentation in both structured and unstructured environments. Robot. Auton. Syst. **61**(12), 1641–1652 (2013). https://doi.org/10.1016/j.robot.2013.07.001
8. Qi, C.R., Su, H., Mo, K., Guibas, L.J.: Pointnet: Deep learning on point sets for 3d classification and segmentation. In: Proceedings of the IEEE conference on computer vision and pattern recognition, pp. 652–660 (2017). https://doi.org/10.48550/arXiv.1612.00593
9. Qi, C.R., Yi, L., Su, H., Guibas, L.J.: Pointnet++: Deep hierarchical feature learning on point sets in a metric space. Advances in Neural Information Processing Systems, 30 (2017). https://doi.org/10.48550/arXiv.1706.02413
10. Xiang, Y., Schmidt, T., Narayanan, V., Fox, D.: Posecnn: A convolutional neural network for 6d object pose estimation in cluttered scenes. arXiv preprint arXiv: 1711.00199 (2017). https://doi.org/10.48550/arXiv.1711.00199

Time-Optimal Trajectory Planning of a Robotic Arm Based on an Improved Adaptive Inertia Weight Particle Swarm Algorithm

Sirui Liu[1,3], Hua Zhang[2], Gang Zhao[2], and Kai He[3(✉)]

[1] Key Laboratory of Metallurgical Equipment and Control Technology of Ministry of Education, Wuhan University of Science and Technology, Wuhan 430081, China
`joker_three@foxmail.com`
[2] Hubei Key Laboratory of Mechanical Transmission and Manufacturing Engineering, Wuhan University of Science and Technology, Wuhan 430081, China
`jasonzhao@wust.edu.cn`
[3] Shenzhen Institute of Advanced Technology, Chinese Academy of Sciences, Shenzhen 518055, China
`kai.he@siat.ac.cn`

Abstract. A time-optimal 3-5-3 polynomial interpolation trajectory planning approach using the Improved Adaptive Inertia Weighted Particle Swarm Optimization (IAIWPSO) algorithm is developed for the time-optimal trajectory planning challenge of a robotic arm. The method enhances the algorithm by incorporating chaotic mapping for population initialization, an adaptive S-curve for nonlinearly decreasing inertia weight, and a trigonometric function for the asynchronous learning factor, thereby significantly improving convergence accuracy and speed. The experimental findings indicate that the strategy has considerable benefits in minimizing robot operational time and improving production with increased efficiency and stability.

Keywords: robot arm · trajectory planning · particle swarm algorithm · time-optimal · polynomial interpolation

1 Introduction

Robotic arms face challenges such as poor stability and long running times, resulting in high accident rates and low efficiency. To address this, suitable trajectory planning algorithms are needed [1]. Common methods include polynomial interpolation [2] and B-spline interpolation [3]. For example, time-safe collisions of manipulator trajectories were optimized using fifth order B-spline interpolation [4] and robotic arm trajectory smoothness was optimized using fifth order polynomials [5].

Traditional algorithms often struggle with computational complexity and non-convexity, making intelligent optimization algorithms preferable. Particle Swarm Optimization (PSO) algorithms are notable for their simplicity. Innovations like SimplexPSO

[6] and GL-PSO [7] have shown promise in improving search capabilities and efficiency. Time-optimal trajectory planning can be optimized using advanced algorithms. WOA-GA [8] and ISPSO [9] algorithms enhance efficiency and accuracy but often require complex parameter tuning.

This work presents an Improved Adaptive Inertial Weighted Particle Swarm Optimization (IAIWPSO) algorithm-based time-optimal 3-5-3 polynomial interpolation trajectory planning approach. It includes logistic chaotic mapping for population initialization, an adaptive S-curve inertia weighting strategy to avoid local optima, and a trigonometric asynchronous learning factor to enhance convergence speed. This method's supremacy and efficacy are confirmed by comparisons with four different algorithms.

2 Robotic Arm Model

The robotic arm shown in this research is seen in Fig. 1. The robotic arm has six degrees of freedom, designated from the base to the apex as joints 1 through 6 sequentially. Firstly, the conventional DH method kinematic modeling of the robotic arm is carried out, and the exact parameters are presented in Table 1. Secondly, the building of the objective function must fulfill the kinematic constraints of the robotic arm, and the range of the kinematic parameters of the robotic arm has to be addressed in the formation of the optimization model, which is particularly specified in Table 2. Ultimately, the robotic arm is modeled using the Matlab program in the Robotics Toolbox to model the robotic arm, as illustrated in Fig. 2, which offers a crucial basis for subsequent application and optimization.

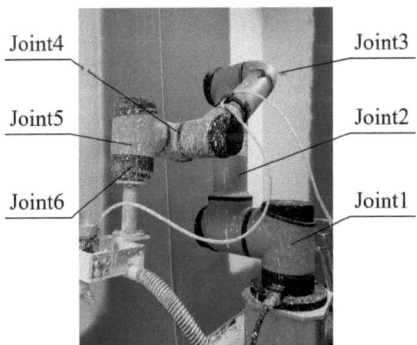

Fig. 1. Robotic arm object

Table 1. D-H parameters

i	θ/rad	d/mm	a/mm	α/rad
1	$pi/2$	163	0	$pi/2$
2	$pi/2$	0	480	$pi/2$

(*continued*)

Table 1. (*continued*)

i	θ/rad	d/mm	a/mm	α/rad
3	0	0	370	pi
4	pi/2	123.5	0	pi/2
5	0	117.5	0	-pi/2
6	0	103.5	0	0

Table 2. Range of robotic arm kinematic parameters

Joint	Range of motion(°)	Maximum speed(°/s)
Joint 1	± 175	180
Joint 2	± 175	180
Joint 3	± 175	267
Joint 4	± 175	180
Joint 5	± 175	180
Joint 6	± 175	180

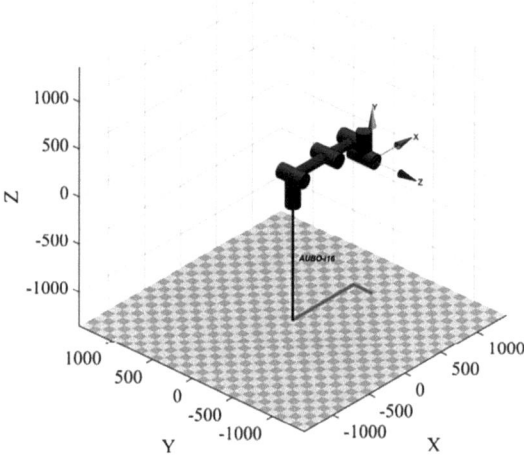

Fig. 2. Robotic arm simulation model

3 Description of the Problem

3.1 Definition of the Objective Function

The goal of this research is to minimize the robotic arm's trajectory planning time, which is the sum of the arm's trajectory and joint running times [10]. The robotic arm's working path is first interpolated using a specified mathematical model, and each joint's running time between the interpolation locations is then minimized using an optimization technique. The purpose of this work is to apply an enhanced particle swarm optimization algorithm to accomplish the robotic arm path to complete the motion in the shortest time through the interpolation points under the satisfaction of kinematic constraints.

The following is the mathematical model used:

$$T = \min \sum_{i=1}^{n} t_i \tag{1}$$

The limitations pertain to the velocities of each joint during the robotic arm's movement, accompanied by the subsequent constraint equation:

$$\left|\dot{\theta}_i\right| \leq v_{\max} \tag{2}$$

where T denotes the overall running time, t_i represents the 3-segment interpolation duration for the joint i, $v_{\max}$ signifies the joint limiting velocity, and $\dot{\theta}_i$ indicates the real-time velocity of the polynomial trajectory segment.

3.2 3-5-3 Polynomial Interpolation

The individual joint angles of the robotic arm's end joint as it goes through the route points may be calculated using the kinematic inverse solution method [11]. To calculate the joint angles, velocity, and acceleration kinematic parameters between the route points, as well as to determine the joint trajectory interpolation function, the trajectories between the path points must be planned [12].

To lower computing complexity and successfully guarantee the stability of the robotic arm as it travels through numerous route points, this work uses 3-5-3 segmented polynomial interpolation for trajectory planning. Segmented polynomial interpolation, split into three steps, is used in trajectory planning. Third-degree polynomial interpolation is used in the first and third phases, and fifth-degree polynomial interpolation is used in the second stage.

Taking joint 1 of the robotic arm as an example, the generalization of the 3-5-3 segmented polynomial is shown as follows:

$$\begin{aligned} h_1(t) &= a_{13}t^3 + a_{12}t^2 + a_{11}t + a_{10} \\ h_2(t) &= a_{25}t^5 + a_{24}t^4 + a_{23}t^3 + a_{22}t^2 + a_{21}t + a_{20} \\ h_3(t) &= a_{33}t^3 + a_{32}t^2 + a_{31}t + a_{30} \end{aligned} \tag{3}$$

where $h_1(t)$, $h_2(t)$), $h_3(t)$ correspond to the polynomial trajectories adopted in the first, second, and third segments of each joint, three, five, and three times, respectively; and the coefficients a_{1i}, a_{2i}, and a_{3i} in the polynomials of the first, second, and third segments of the trajectories of each joint denote the first coefficient, respectively.

Constraints need to be considered in trajectory planning, covering the velocity and acceleration at the start point θ_0, the intermediate points θ_1 and θ_2, and the termination point θ_3 of each joint. Maintaining the continuity of the velocity and acceleration between the path points, the relationship between the coefficient a and the interpolation point can be derived as Eqs. (3), (4) and (5), where θ_m denotes the interpolation position of the current joint, and m denotes the ordinal number of the interpolation point, $m = 0, 1, 2, 3$.

$$A = \begin{bmatrix} t_1^3 & t_1^2 & t_1 & 1 & 0 & 0 & 0 & 0 & 0 & -1 & 0 & 0 & 0 & 0 \\ 3t_1^2 & 2t_1 & 1 & 0 & 0 & 0 & 0 & 0 & -1 & 0 & 0 & 0 & 0 & 0 \\ 6t_1 & 2 & 0 & 0 & 0 & 0 & 0 & -2 & 0 & 0 & 0 & 0 & 0 & 0 \\ 0 & 0 & 0 & 0 & t_2^5 & t_2^4 & t_2^3 & t_2^2 & t_2 & 0 & 0 & 0 & 0 & -1 \\ 0 & 0 & 0 & 0 & 5t_2^4 & 4t_2^3 & 3t_2^2 & 2t_2 & 1 & 0 & 0 & 0 & -1 & 0 \\ 0 & 0 & 0 & 0 & 20t_2^3 & 12t_2^2 & 6t_2 & 2 & 0 & 0 & 0 & -2 & 0 & 0 \\ 0 & 0 & 0 & 0 & 0 & 0 & 0 & 0 & 0 & t_3^3 & t_3^2 & t_3 & 1 \\ 0 & 0 & 0 & 0 & 0 & 0 & 0 & 0 & 0 & 3t_3^2 & 2t_3 & 1 & 0 \\ 0 & 0 & 0 & 0 & 0 & 0 & 0 & 0 & 0 & 6t_3 & 2 & 0 & 0 \\ 0 & 0 & 1 & 0 & 0 & 0 & 0 & 0 & 0 & 0 & 0 & 0 & 0 \\ 0 & 0 & 1 & 0 & 0 & 0 & 0 & 0 & 0 & 0 & 0 & 0 & 0 \\ 0 & 1 & 0 & 0 & 0 & 0 & 0 & 0 & 0 & 0 & 0 & 0 & 0 \\ 0 & 0 & 0 & 0 & 0 & 0 & 0 & 0 & 0 & 0 & 0 & 0 & 1 \\ 0 & 0 & 0 & 0 & 0 & 0 & 0 & 0 & 1 & 0 & 0 & 0 & 0 \end{bmatrix} \quad (4)$$

$$\theta = \begin{bmatrix} 0 & 0 & 0 & 0 & 0 & 0 & \theta_3 & 0 & 0 & \theta_0 & 0 & 0 & \theta_2 & \theta_1 \end{bmatrix}^T \quad (5)$$

$$a = A^{-1}\theta = \begin{bmatrix} a_{13} & a_{12} & a_{11} & a_{10} & a_{25} & a_{24} & a_{23} & a_{22} & a_{21} & a_{20} & a_{33} & a_{32} & a_{31} & a_{30} \end{bmatrix} \quad (6)$$

4 Improved Adaptive Inertia Weight Particle Swarm Algorithm (IAIWPSO)

4.1 Traditional PSO Algorithm

Particle Swarm Optimization (PSO) is an algorithm that utilizes the collective behavior of bird groups as inspiration for solving problems. Through the exchange of knowledge among group members, the group is motivated to consistently explore the most favorable solution within a multi-dimensional objective search space. In the initial stage, a particle is randomly generated. During the iterative process, each particle continuously adjusts its position and speed. This adjustment is derived from two crucial factors: the most advantageous individual position and the most advantageous population position. The ultimate objective is to get the worldwide best solution. The updating process is described by the subsequent equation:

$$v_{id}^{k+1} = \omega v_{id}^k + c_1 r_1 (p_{id}^k - x_{id}^k) + c_2 r_2 (p_{gd}^k - x_{id}^k) \quad (7)$$

$$x_{id}^{k+1} = x_{id}^k + v_{id}^{k+1} \tag{8}$$

where w is the inertia weight, representing the degree of memory of the original speed of the particle; c_1 and c_2 are the learning factors, representing the weights of the particle action from its own experience part and the group experience part, respectively; r_1 and r_2 are the uniform random decimal between (0,1); k is the number of iterations; v is the speed of the i particle in the kth iteration; x is the position of the i particle in the k iteration; p_{id}^k is the individual particle optimal extreme value and p_{gd}^k is the population optimal extreme value.

4.2 Population Initialization for Logistic Chaotic Mapping

In traditional particle swarm optimization (PSO), random initialization of particle positions and velocities lacks guidance, leading to uneven distribution and reduced population diversity, complicating the search and slowing convergence. Logistic chaotic mappings are well traversed and randomized, and through their intrinsic nonlinear dynamics, initial populations with higher complexity and uniform distribution can be generated [13]. This paper uses logistic chaotic mapping to initialize the population and generate chaotic sequences.

$$z_{n+1} = 4z_n(1 - z_n) \tag{9}$$

$$x_{id} = x_{max} z_{n+1} - x_{min} \tag{10}$$

where x_{id} is the position of the d-dimensional component of the i particle, z_n is the chaos value at the n moment, and x_{max} and x_{min} are the upper and lower bounds of the allowed flight space of the particle, respectively. Logistic chaotic mapping for population generation does not depend on the initial value, and z_n can be a random number between [0,1].

4.3 Adaptive S-curve Inertia Weights Nonlinearly Decreasing Method

Inertia weight is key in particle swarm optimization (PSO). Initially large, it enhances global optimization and accelerates population evolution. As iterations progress, the weight decreases, aiding local optimization and improving convergence accuracy.

This paper proposes a new strategy: a nonlinear decreasing S-curve inertia weight based on adaptive population updates. To prevent local optima, random variables adjust the inertia weight if the global optimum remains static, extending the search range and maintaining algorithm diversity for comprehensive solution space exploration. A nonlinear decreasing S-curve inertia weight changes more gradually in early and late iterations than linear methods [14]. Larger initial values aid global search, while smaller later values enhance local optimization. This dynamic adjustment improves overall search efficiency. An adaptive weight update method combines random variables with the nonlinear S-curve approach.

When the judgment algorithm falls into a local optimum, the inertia weights are updated by random variables to jump out of the local optimal solution:

$$w = w_{min} + rand\,(w_{max} - w_{min}) \tag{11}$$

When the judgment algorithm does not fall into a local optimum, the inertia weights are updated by nonlinearly decreasing S-curve:

$$w = w_{min} + \frac{(w_{max} - w_{min}) \cdot \left(1 + \tanh\left(\frac{2-4k}{maxgen}\right)\right)}{2} \tag{12}$$

where w_{min} is the minimum inertia weight value, w_{max} is the maximum inertia weight value, $rand()$ is a random integer in the range $(0,1)$, $tanh()$ is the hyperbolic tangent function, k is the current number of iterations, and $maxgen$ is the maximum number of iterations.

4.4 Trigonometric Asynchronous Learning Factors

The learning factor c_1 in the conventional particle swarm optimization (PSO) method regulates a particle's reliance on its own experience, whereas c_2 controls its reliance on the experience of the group. These factors are varied asynchronously using a delta function during iterations.

Early in the algorithm, increasing c_1 helps particles focus on their own optimal solutions, enhancing global search capability and avoiding premature convergence to local optima. Later, increasing c_2 encourages particles to learn from the social optimal solution, reducing dependence on their own experience, speeding up convergence, and increasing the likelihood of finding the global optimum. The proposed formula for changing learning factors is as follows:

$$\begin{cases} c_1 = 2(\cos(\frac{k\pi}{2 \cdot maxgen}))^2 \\ c_2 = 2(\sin(\frac{k\pi}{2 \cdot maxgen}))^2 \end{cases} \tag{13}$$

where k indicates the number of iterations that are being carried out at the moment, and $maxgen$ indicates the maximum number of iterations.

4.5 IAIWPSO Algorithm Steps

The trajectory interpolation model, which integrates the suggested 3-5-3 polynomial trajectory interpolation with the enhanced technique mentioned above, is included into the simulation verification process. The time t and matrix a in Eq. (6) are the variables in the text. When matrix a is used as the independent variable, the algorithm's dimension is 14. Given the substantial complexity of the algorithmic measures, this study explicitly seeks to optimize time by reducing the dimension to three, hence decreasing computational requirements. The algorithm's stages are as follows:

Step 1: Set parameters. Maximum number of iterations *maxgen*, number of particles *sizepop*, dimension of fitness function D, maximum inertia weight w_{max}, minimum inertia weight w_{min}.

Step 2: Initialization. Initialize the particle location and velocity, compute the fitness value of each particle and record the optimum particle.

Step 3: Population creates 3D particle time variables t_1, t_2, t_3.

Step 4: Solve matrix a by putting the combination of time variables into Eq. (4)-Eq. (6).

Step 5: Substitute the coefficients of matrix a into the 3-5-3 polynomial while evaluating if the velocity restriction is met.

Step 6: Introduce the speed limitation, and if it is not fulfilled, assign it to a bigger fitness value and the algorithm changes it each iteration.

Step 7: Repeat the steps till the maximum number of iterations.

5 Simulation and Analysis

Due to the small displacements of joints 1, 5, and 6, the simulation focuses on joints 2, 3, and 4 to validate the algorithm. Four predetermined locations in Cartesian space were employed for trajectory planning, as Table 3 illustrates. These points were converted to joint space angles using inverse kinematics to ensure accurate trajectory tracking. The corresponding angles are listed in Table 4.

Table 3. Cartesian space path point (mm)

Starting point	Intermediate point 1	Intermediate point 2	Ending point
−87, −746,600	−87, −746,400	−87, −746,200	−87, −746, 0

Table 4. Joint space interpolation points (rad)

Joint	Starting point	Intermediate point 1	Intermediate point 2	Ending point
Joint 2	0.8196	0.9759	0.8281	0.5427
Joint 3	0.2367	1.0925	1.3962	1.4582
Joint 4	−0.5829	0.1166	0.5681	0.9156

PSO, LPSO, SPSO, SIWSPSO and IAIWPSO are selected for trajectory planning simulations. For all algorithms, the particle population size is set to 30, the number of iterations is set to 70, the maximum inertia weight is set to 0.9, the maximum inertia weight is set to 0.4, and the particle position is constrained at [0.1, 3], and the specific parameter settings for each algorithm are shown in Table 5.

Table 5. Algorithm Parameter Setting

Algorithm	Parameter Setting
PSO	$c_1 = c_2 = 0.05, w = 0.5(1 + rand)$
LPSO	$c_1 = c_2 = 2$
SPSO	$c_1 = c_2 = 2, w = 0.8$
SIWSPSO	$w_{max} = 0.9, w_{min} = 0.4$
IAIWPSO	$w_{max} = 0.9, w_{min} = 0.4$

IAIWPSO improved joint 2's trajectory interpolation time, and Fig. 3 displays the running times of each iteration for joint 2 iterations. The particle swarm is shown to converge quickly after around 20 repetitions. Table 6 summarizes the findings achieved by optimizing the trajectory interpolation times of the remaining joints using the same methodology.

Table 6. IAIWPSO Optimized Optimal Running Time for Each Joint

Time/s	T_{i1}	T_{i2}	T_{i3}
Joint 2	0.284621	0.1	0.314212
Joint 3	0.543623	0.1	0.1
Joint 4	0.677017	0.151568	0.344927

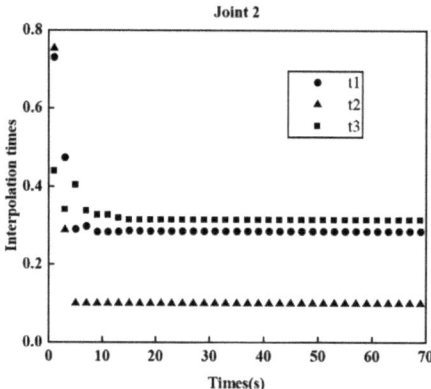

Fig. 3. Joint 2 optimum iteration diagram for particles

The robotic arm has several joints that move concurrently. Therefore, to guarantee that every joint arrives at the same moment, the maximum interpolation duration of each joint segment is chosen. $T_1 = max\{T_{i1}\}, T_2 = max\{T_{i2}\}, T_3 = max\{T_{i3}\}, (i = 1,2,3)$.

According to IAIWPSO, $T_1 + T_2 + T_3 = 1.173513s$ is the overall running time of the robotic arm. $T_1 = 0.677017s$, $T_2 = 0.151568s$ and $T_3 = 0.344927s$. Additionally, the PSO, LPSO, SPSO, and SIWSPSO algorithms are used sequentially to improve the interpolation time of each joint segment of the robotic arm. Table 7 provides an overview of the runtime outcomes from 50 separate runs of each of the five methods.

Table 7. Running time of the five algorithms

Algorithm	BEST/s	MEAN/s	STD/s
PSO	1.433012	1.583866	0.078053
LPSO	1.320416	1.338365	0.011350
SPSO	1.314445	1.403870	0.035088
SIWSPSO	1.245384	1.306505	0.030916
IAIWPSO	1.173513	1.179005	0.004864

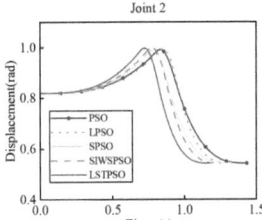 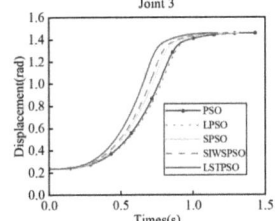 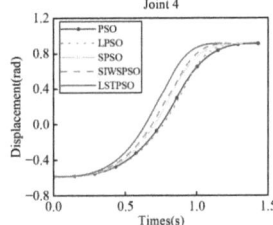

Fig. 4. Joint displacement curves

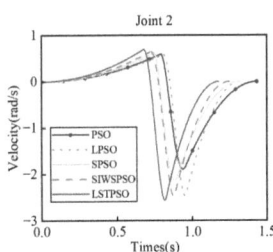 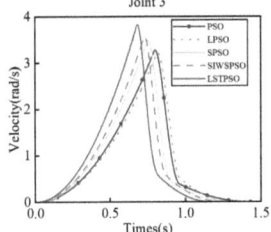 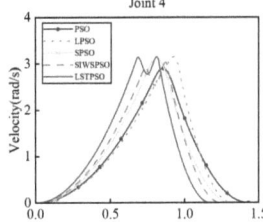

Fig. 5. Joint velocity curves

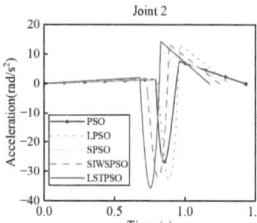 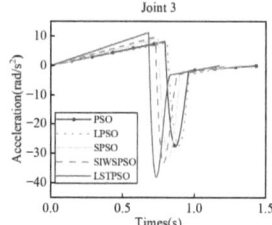 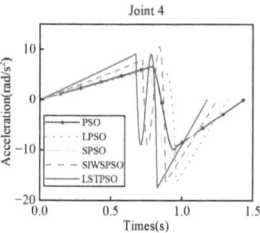

Fig. 6. Joint acceleration curves

The benefits of the IAIWPSO trajectory planning approach in raising the robotic arm's operational efficiency are evident when comparing the trial results. The IAIWPSO algorithm has far better performance when compared to the other four algorithms. In particular, the IAIWPSO algorithm performs 18.1% better than PSO and 11.1% better than LPSO. The running time of the robotic arm is reduced from 1.433012s with conventional PSO and 1.320416s with LPSO to 1.173513s. The running times of SPSO and SIWSPSO with random inertia weights are 1.314445s and 1.245384s, respectively, compared to 1.173513s for IAIWPSO. IAIWPSO improves about 10.72% and 5.77% over SPSO and SIWSPSO, respectively. The IAIWPSO trajectory planning method has higher stability. The average running time of IAIWPSO is 1.179005 s, whereas the averages of the other four algorithms are 1.583866 s, 1.338365 s, 1.403870 s, and 1.306505 s, respectively. This further comparison of the mean and standard deviation data reveals a significant advantage of IAIWPSO over the average of the other four algorithms. In addition, the standard deviation of the IAIWPSO algorithm is only 0.004864, which is much lower than that of the other four algorithms, further demonstrating its superiority in stability.

Figures 4, 5 and 6 illustrate the displacement, velocity and acceleration curves of each joint of the robotic arm, which are derived by various methods and exhibit smooth and no sudden changes. Comparing the joint velocity graphs in Fig. 5, it is found that the IAIWPSO algorithm tends to the limiting velocity but does not exceed the limiting velocity under the velocity constraints of the optimized joints, which performs well in comparison with other algorithms, and the joints operating efficiency is improved. The acceleration comparison of each joint is presented in Fig. 6, and the acceleration at the start and finish joints is 0. This continual acceleration assures the stability of the joint motion and also decreases the incidence of vibration. Based on the analysis of the above simulation results, the following conclusions can be drawn: the IAIWPSO trajectory planning method significantly reduces the task execution time, improves the productivity, and at the same time effectively ensures the continuity and stability of the robotic arm work.

6 Conclusions

The "3-5-3" interpolated trajectory planning method is used to try to solve the challenge of time-optimal trajectory planning for the robotic arm. Based on this, the IAIWPSO algorithm is introduced to time-optimize the planning approach. The performance of the

IAIWPSO method is then assessed by comparing the optimized time trajectories with the ideal time trajectories scheduled by the other four algorithms.

The results demonstrate that the IAIWPSO trajectory planning approach greatly decreases the running time and increases the running efficiency. The efficiency of the IAIWPSO algorithm is enhanced by 18.1% compared to PSO and 11.1% compared to LPSO. And all of them exhibit evident benefits and gains in comparison with other optimization techniques. This indicates that IAIWPSO converges quicker and more precisely. The optimized trajectory displacement and velocity profiles are smooth and steady, and the acceleration profile is continuous and without sudden shifts. Therefore, the method has substantial use in the area of time-optimal trajectory planning, which can effectively minimize the running time, enhance the productivity, and effectively maintain the continuity and stability of the robotic arm.

Acknowledgments. This work was supported by the Fund of National Natural Science Foundation of China (Grant NO. 52175480).

References

1. Ekrem, Ö., Aksoy, B.: Trajectory planning for a 6-axis robotic arm with particle swarm optimization algorithm. Eng. Appl. Artif. Intell. **122**, 106099 (2023)
2. Xu, J., Ren, C., Chang, X.: Robot time-optimal trajectory planning based on quintic polynomial interpolation and improved Harris Hawks algorithm. Axioms **12**(3), 245 (2023)
3. Sun, H., et al.: Multi-objective trajectory planning for segment assembly robots using a B-spline interpolation-and infeasible-updating non-dominated sorting-based method. Appl. Soft Comput. **152**, 111216 (2024)
4. Cheng, Q., Hao, X., Wang, Y., Xu, W., Li, S.: Trajectory planning of transcranial magnetic stimulation manipulator based on time-safety collision optimization. Robot. Auton. Syst. **152**, 104039 (2022)
5. Wang, C., Yao, X., Ding, F., Yu, Z.: A trajectory planning method for a casting sorting robotic arm based on a nature-inspired Genghis Khan shark optimized algorithm. Math. Biosci. Eng. **21**(2), 3364–3390 (2024)
6. Bera, R., Mandal, D., Kar, R., Ghoshal, S.P.: Optimal design of single and multi-ring planar array antenna using simplex-PSO. IETE J. Res. **63**(6), 881–892 (2017)
7. Gong, Y.J., et al.: Genetic learning particle swarm optimization. IEEE Transactions on Cybernetics **46**(10), 2277–2290 (2015)
8. Wang, F., Wu, Z., Bao, T.: Time-jerk optimal trajectory planning of industrial robots based on a hybrid WOA-GA algorithm. Processes **10**(5), 1014 (2022)
9. Hu, X., Wu, H., Sun, Q., Liu, J.: Robot time optimal trajectory planning based on improved simplified particle swarm optimization algorithm. IEEE Access **11**, 44496–44508 (2023)
10. Madridano, Á., Al-Kaff, A., Martín, D., De La Escalera, A.: Trajectory planning for multi-robot systems: Methods and applications. Expert Syst. Appl. **173**, 114660 (2021)
11. Zhao, G., et al.: A tandem robotic arm inverse kinematic solution based on an improved particle swarm algorithm. Front. Bioengin. Biotechnol. **10**, 832829 (2022)
12. Aristidou, A., Lasenby, J., Chrysanthou, Y., Shamir, A.: Inverse kinematics techniques in computer graphics: A survey. In Computer Graphics Forum, Vol. 37, No. 6, pp. 35–58 (2018)
13. Du, Y., Chen, Y.: Time optimal trajectory planning algorithm for robotic manipulator based on locally chaotic particle swarm optimization. Chin. J. Electron. **31**(5), 906–914 (2022)
14. Chen, S., Zhang, C., Yi, J.: Time-optimal trajectory planning for woodworking manipulators using an improved PSO algorithm. Appl. Sci. **13**(18), 10482 (2023)

An Automatic Generation Method for Business Process Specification Based on Large Language Models

Kai Wang[1], Shan Li[2(✉)], Lizong Zhang[1], Yongjian Zhang[1], Baobing Xia[3], Lei Zhang[1], and Yihong Qian[1]

[1] State Grid Zhejiang Electric Power Co., Ltd., Hangzhou, China
[2] State Grid Information and Communication Industry Group Co., Beijing, China
lishan@sgitg.sgcc.com.cn
[3] Beijing SGITG-Accenture Information Technology Co., Ltd., Beijing, China

Abstract. A comprehensive understanding of business processes is essential for their digitization and optimization. This thesis presents a novel approach for automatically generating Business Process Model and Notation (BPMN) 2.0 diagrams from natural language descriptions, specifically focusing on Chinese business process documents. By integrating Large Language Models (LLMs) with enhanced rule-based natural language processing (NLP) techniques, we address the complexities inherent in Chinese texts, including filtering irrelevant information, recognizing conditional sentences, and converting implicit actions into explicit ones. Our method significantly improves the accuracy and reliability of BPMN diagram generation.

Keywords: Natural Language Processing · Large Language Models · Business Process Modeling · BPMN 2.0 · Chinese Text Processing

1 Introduction

Business Process Management (BPM) focuses on enhancing the efficiency and organization of workflows. These processes are often documented in unstructured text formats. Transforming these documents into structured process models facilitates the identification of inefficiencies, detailed analysis, strategy development, and overall operational improvement.

Research on automated business process specification generation has primarily focused on several key technologies. Template-based methods, such as those used in tools like Sterling B2B Integrator, rely on predefined templates to generate business process specifications. However, these methods require manual creation and maintenance of templates, which limits their flexibility [1]. Model-driven generation methods utilize Model-Driven Engineering (MDE) techniques to automatically produce detailed business process specifications from high-level models, enhancing efficiency and consistency but struggling with complex business scenarios [2]. Process mining techniques extract and generate business process models from business data, but they are less effective when dealing with complex and unstructured business descriptions, such as those found in the power systems domain.

Extensive application of rule-based NLP methods has been made to automate the generation of business process specifications. Tools like Stanford CoreNLP [3], FreeLing [4], and NLTK structure text content by extracting predicates and actors using Semantic Role Labeling (SRL), performing Word Sense Disambiguation (WSD), resolving coreferences, and establishing action sequences. Despite their effectiveness, these tools often fall short in semantic tasks and unrestricted domains, especially when dealing with technical and regulatory documents that contain complex vocabulary. Additionally, interpreting legal texts requires domain-specific knowledge, which standard NLP systems often lack.

The Generative Pre-trained Transformer (GPT), developed by OpenAI, has advanced to more sophisticated versions like GPT-4, which are capable of generating high-quality text. GPT-4 can preprocess text to normalize descriptions [5], followed by rule-based NLP methods to extract detailed, structured information. This paper presents an approach that integrates GPT-4 for text preprocessing, employs rule-based NLP techniques to extract relevant information from Chinese business process documents, and uses BPMN 2.0 for visualization.

2 Method

This section outlines our approach to automating the generation of business process specifications using a combination of LLM and rule-based NLP techniques, as shown in Fig. 1. The following sections delve into each phase and their respective tasks in detail.

2.1 Pre-processing

Pre-processing converts raw data into a format suitable for analysis. The first step in pre-processing is refining and normalizing textual descriptions using an LLM. Key tasks include text normalization, specifying conditional statements, and converting implicit information into explicit information.

Relevance of Information. We created the Irrelevant Information Criteria (IIC) classification system. The IIC includes:

1. Company Mission Statements. Sentences that describe company goals are filtered out as they do not specify process steps.
2. Goals or Results of Activities. Information about goals or outcomes is irrelevant for flowcharts and can lead to overly detailed representations.
3. Example Information. Sentences providing examples, such as "For example, 'power limit exceeded by xxx watts' can be logged," are not part of the flowchart and must be excluded.
4. Citations from Other Articles or Paragraphs. Information citing other documents is irrelevant and should be filtered out.

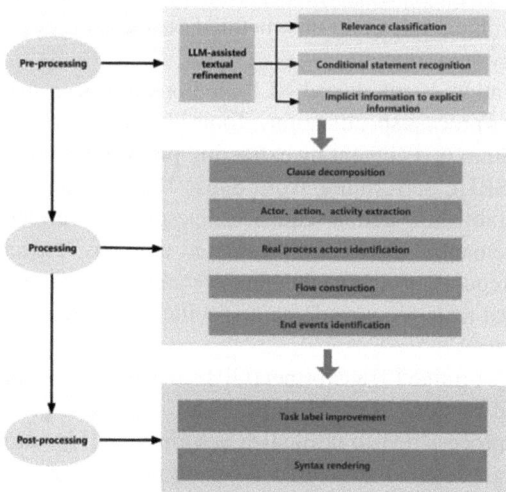

Fig. 1. Overview of the text2BPMN steps

We utilize LLMs for selective filtering, leveraging SpaCy's sentence segmentation to break down text into individual sentences. Each sentence is classified based on the Irrelevant Information Criteria (IIC). The LLM then removes irrelevant content, ensuring only essential information remains.

Conditional Statement Recognition. In Chinese, conditional statements often omit explicit markers, making sentences fluid and succinct but challenging for rule-based NLP techniques that rely on keywords to identify conditional blocks. By employing the LLM, we can detect these implicit conditional statements and transform them into explicit ones, thereby enhancing text clarity and improving the understanding of conditional logic. This approach ensures that the intended meaning is clearly conveyed, even in the absence of explicit conditional markers.

Implicit Information. Natural language often uses implicit information, leading to ambiguity and making it difficult to extract necessary steps for flowcharts accurately. Understanding the causal relationship requires semantic understanding beyond simple syntactic parsing.

We use LLMs analyze sentences to identify and transform implicit actions into explicit ones, ensuring clarity and accurate process diagrams. After refinement, the sentences are reassembled into a complete text, optimized for creating detailed process diagrams.

Pre-processing is central to our approach to automatic process extraction from natural language descriptions. During this stage, we refine technical and regulatory documents into a format suitable for further analysis. These steps, referred to as "LLM-Assisted Textual Refinement (LLM-ATR)," leverage advanced language model capabilities to optimize text data, ensuring it is well-prepared for subsequent processing stages.

2.2 Processing

The processing phase uses a rule-based extraction methodology to convert the refined input from the pre-processing stage into a structured format for post-processing visualization.

Identification of Real Actors in Process Descriptions. Traditional approaches often struggle to accurately label all actors in process descriptions, resulting in incomplete lane generation in BPMN diagrams. We propose broadening the definition to include places, locations, professions, and occupations, facilitating a more comprehensive identification of actors. The integration of an LLM allows for adaptive learning from large datasets, recognizing nuanced distinctions in actor categorization. We improve actor identification accuracy using:

1. Presence *in a Predefined Corrector List*. Checking if the actor is listed in it.
2. Synonym *and Hypernym Analysis*. Generating synonym sets and deriving hypernyms for identified actors, cross-referencing with "REAL_ACTOR_ DETERMINERS" categories like "person", "social_group", and "software_system".
3. LLM *Classification*. The LLM classifies actors based on predefined criteria as real or non-real actors.

Context-Driven Identification of End Events. Current methods for determining end nodes in process diagrams follow a structured approach, categorizing activities or blocks of activities and designating the last structure as the end activity. For conditional blocks, each branch is iterated to determine the process end, supported by hypernyms categorizing the verb or its synonym under "结束" (end) or "完成" (finish). However, this approach is simplistic and lacks contextual understanding.

To improve end activity identification, we propose a more sophisticated context analysis, considering activities, surrounding context, and each activity's role within the broader process flow. Our approach leverages a Large Language Model to interpret process contexts and identify potential end activities by assigning each activity an attribute that indicates whether it specifically represents process completion ("is_finish_activity").

2.3 Post-processing

Task Label Optimization. This section presents strategies for improving the quality of syntax and BPMN diagrams. The context understanding ability of LLM is used to improve the task labeling and make the process diagram clearer. For subprocesses, LLM merges "first activity" tasks describing the same object and clarifies fuzzy descriptions. LLM directly generates fluent Chinese flowchart grammar without additional annotations, which enhances the clarity of the chart and facilitates the understanding of complex processes. The post-processing stage focuses on presenting and visualizing the obtained data.

3 Experiment

3.1 Data Set

We use a dataset of 54 texts of technical regulations in the power industry. Each document details various power system workflows, including routine maintenance, complex operations, and emergency protocols.

3.2 Results

In this subsection, we will present partial results using our approach.

The procurement material receiving process is shown in Fig. 2.

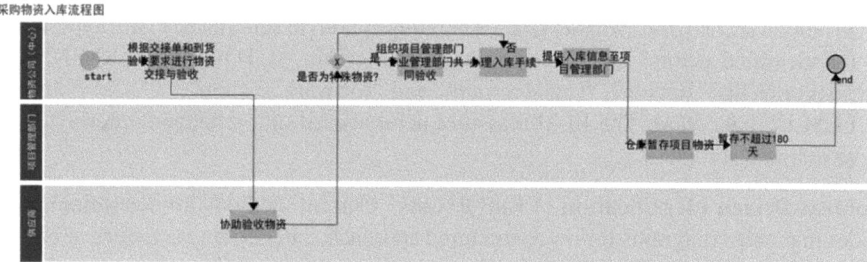

Fig. 2. Procurement material receiving process

The daily inspection process is shown in Fig. 3.

Fig. 3. Daily inspection process

3.3 Evaluation

This chapter evaluates our method for automatically generating BPMN models from natural language descriptions. We compare our models with manually created BPMN models from power industry documents, using metrics such as accuracy, recognition, and F1 score to assess performance.

We measure model performance on: lanes (L); task and event nodes (N); parallel and exclusive gateways(G). These metrics are formally defined as:

$$\text{Precision} = \frac{\text{True Positives}}{\text{True Positives} + \text{False Positives}} \tag{1}$$

$$\text{Recall} = \frac{\text{True Positives}}{\text{True Positives} + \text{False Negatives}} \quad (2)$$

$$F1 = 2 \cdot \frac{\text{Precision} \cdot \text{Recall}}{\text{Precision} + \text{Recall}} \quad (3)$$

We introduced a novel method combining LLMs with rule-based NLP techniques for automating business process specifications. The baseline solely relies on the rule-based NLP approach, without LLMs. We will present the evaluation process, as shown in Table 1, comparing precision, recall, and F1 scores to assess our novel method against the baselines, determining the effectiveness and reliability of each approach.

Table 1. Performance Comparison Between Baseline and Proposed Method

	N			G			L		
	Recall	Precision	F1	Recall	Precision	F1	Recall	Precision	F1
Baseline	0.6722	0.5172	0.5847	0	0	0	0	0	0
Proposed method	0.8218	0.7981	0.8098	0.7142	0.7142	0.7142	0.3636	0.8889	0.5162

Evaluation of Gateway Identification (G). Compared with the baseline model which completely fails in identifying gateways, the proposed method significantly improves the gateway identification ability. This improvement is attributed to the integration of context-driven recognition methods and large language models like GPT-4 that accurately understand implicit conditional logic and the broader context.

Evaluation of Nodes Identification (N). In node identification, our method achieves a recall of 0.8218, precision of 0.7981, and F1 score of 0.8098, which outperforms the baseline model. These enhancements result from LLM-assisted textual refinement during pre-processing, which normalizes and clarifies text, ensuring consistent terminology. Additionally, combining LLMs with enhanced rule-based NLP techniques allows better handling of complex and unstructured business descriptions, leading to more accurate node identification.

Evaluation of Actors Identification (L). In actor identification, our method shows nuanced improvements over the baseline model. Our method achieves a recall of 0.3636, precision of 0.8889, and F1 score of 0.5162. This improvement stems from a broader definition of actors and LLM-assisted classification, which better distinguishes between different types of actors based on context, ensuring more accurate identification and categorization.

4 Conclusion

Our research has demonstrated significant advancements in the automatic generation of business process specifications from natural language descriptions, particularly for Chinese texts. By integrating Large Language Models (LLMs) such as GPT-4 with rule-based NLP techniques, our method has achieved notable improvements compared to the baseline model. In gateway identification, the context-driven approach combined with LLMs allowed for a deeper understanding of implicit conditional logic. For node identification, LLM optimizes the preprocessing to make the text more standardized and clear, which facilitates NLP to process complex business descriptions.

This method solves the traditional limitations and lays a solid foundation for business process management, which can be expanded to more languages and fields in the future, promote the progress of automatic specification generation, and provide efficient solutions for modern business.

Acknowledgment. This work is supported by the State Grid Corporation of China Limited Scientific and technological innovation projects (Digital integration of workflow and standards Technical research and application, No.5700-202319836A-4-2-KJ). We would like to thank the company for providing funds and hardware and software support for this study.

References

1. IBM Corporation: Connectivity integration and SOA. Sterling B2B Integrator (2024). Published 4 June 2024. https://www.ibm.com/docs/en/b2b-integrator/6.2.0?topicsbio-sterling-b2b-integrator-overview
2. Delgado, A., Calegari, D., García, F., Weber, B.: Model-driven management of BPMN-based business process families. Softw. Syst. Model. **21**, 2517–2553 (2022). https://doi.org/10.1007/s10270-022-00985-3
3. Manning, C.D., et al.: The Stanford CoreNLP natural language processing toolkit. In: Proceedings of the 52nd Annual Meeting of the Association for Computational Linguistics: System Demonstrations, pp. 55–60. Baltimore, Maryland (2014). https://doi.org/10.3115/v1/P14-5010
4. Padró, L., Stanilovsky, E.: Freeling 3.0: Towards wider multilinguality. In: Proceedings of the Language Resources and Evaluation Conference (LREC 2012), pp. 2473–2479. Istanbul, Turkey (2012). https://aclanthology.org/L12-1242
5. Zhang, H., Dong, Y., Xiao, C., Oyamada, M.: Large Language Models as Data Preprocessors. arXiv:2308.16361 [cs] (2023). Available: http://arxiv.org/abs/2308.16361. Visited on 19 October 2023

Design of a Smart Wearable Power Supply Scheme for Abrasive Water Jet Equipment in Troubleshooting Condition

Xianding Xue[1,2](✉), Shiyou Xu[2], and Shenglin Wu[2]

[1] National Technical University of Ukraine "Igor Sikorsky Kyiv Polytechnic Institute", Kyiv, Ukraine
714555901@qq.com

[2] Guangzhou Institute of Science and Technology, Guangzhou 510540, China

Abstract. This paper introduces a 5V charging device for wearable AI, designed to harness mechanical energy from human movement. It efficiently converts this energy into electrical power using rectification and energy storage technologies. The device aims to provide stable power in environments lacking traditional charging facilities. Key innovations include a pendulum and permanent magnet transmission system to minimize energy loss and optimized rotor coils for enhanced conversion efficiency. The structural design and principle analysis highlight advancements in kinetic energy harvesting, particularly in linear motion energy harvesters. This solution prioritizes performance, weight reduction, and user comfort, ensuring practical and reliable power support for wearable AI devices in everyday use.

Keywords: Pendulum · Ratchet transmission · Power supply for artificial intelligence devices · Human mechanical energy harvesting

1 Introduction

Wearable artificial intelligence devices have seen a surge in their integration into daily life, offering unparalleled convenience and functionality. However, despite their growing popularity, these devices frequently confront the significant challenge of battery power limitations, particularly during extended outdoor usage scenarios. This limitation can severely impede their operational capabilities and user experience. To tackle this pressing issue, our research endeavors are concentrated on the development of an innovative mechanical energy-based charging device. This device is designed to capitalize on the abundant mechanical energy naturally produced by the user's movements, encompassing activities such as walking, running, and other ambulatory actions. By efficiently converting this kinetic energy into electrical power, the device aims to provide a reliable and consistent power supply to wearable AI devices, thereby eliminating the dependency on external charging infrastructure. This approach not only enhances the autonomy and usability of wearable devices but also aligns with the broader trend towards sustainable and self-sufficient technology solutions [1]. Furthermore, the integration of such a charging mechanism fosters a seamless user experience, as it negates the need for frequent recharging or carrying additional power banks, which can be cumbersome and impractical, especially in outdoor settings [2–4].

Our design encompasses a sophisticated wearable device intended to be securely strapped to either the wrist or ankle of the user. This device incorporates a groundbreaking pendulum and ratchet drive system, which represents a significant advancement in energy harvesting technology. The pendulum, responsive to the natural movements of the limbs, oscillates with each step taken by the user, thereby harnessing the kinetic energy embedded within these movements. The ratchet drive system, in turn, functions as a crucial intermediary, efficiently converting this captured kinetic energy into electrical energy in real-time, ensuring minimal energy loss during the conversion process.

By seamlessly integrating this innovative mechanism into the wearable device, our solution is capable of continuously charging wearable AI devices throughout the duration of outdoor activities. This continuous charging capability significantly extends the operational duration of these devices, allowing them to remain functional for extended periods without the need for frequent recharging. Furthermore, this approach enhances user convenience by eliminating the anxiety associated with battery depletion and the inconvenience of carrying additional charging equipment. Consequently, our design effectively addresses the growing demand for prolonged device usage in scenarios where access to traditional power sources is limited or unavailable, thereby contributing to the advancement of wearable technology and enhancing the overall user experience.

2 Design of the Solution

2.1 Pendulum Design

Functional Requirements. This device is lightweight and flexible, designed for easy attachment to the wrist or ankle, optimizing portability and wearability. It is tailored for personalized electricity generation and reliably produces stable low-voltage DC for continuous operation of wearable AI devices in various environments.

Performance specifications include: Rated voltage DC $19V \pm 5V$, rated current 1A. Voltage variation $\leq 10\%$, efficiency $\geq 30\%$ for energy conversion. Operating noise ≤ 67 dB to minimize disturbance. Safety features include overcurrent protection (1.5A), with additional functionality (1.6 to 2.5A), and uninterrupted overvoltage protection. It includes robust reverse discharge protection and operates reliably from $-10\,°C$ to $55\,°C$, suitable for harsh conditions.

Functional Requirements. The human body mechanical energy-based motion power generation device operates on the fundamental principles of Faraday's law of electromagnetic induction, effectively transforming external mechanical vibrations into electrical energy. This innovative device is comprised of two primary systems: the energy harvesting system and the energy conversion system. The energy harvesting system is tasked with capturing external vibration energy, which it accomplishes by inducing forced vibrations that, in turn, convert mechanical energy into electrical energy. This conversion process is facilitated by the relative movement of a permanent magnet in relation to coils, which alters the magnetic flux and subsequently generates an electromotive force. The core components of the device are seamlessly integrated, with a permanent magnet and induction coil serving as the pivotal elements for energy conversion, as evidenced in existing literature [5–7].

The structural design chapter delves deeply into two distinct bracket schemes, meticulously optimizing materials and structures to enhance the performance of the vibration energy harvester. A novel approach is proposed, featuring a pendulum-mounted permanent magnet, which is designed to improve user comfort while maintaining efficiency. This chapter considers two primary wearing methods to cater to diverse user preferences and applications. The theoretical foundations supporting the electromagnetic vibration energy harvester's construction design are laid out in detail, encompassing comprehensive analyses of mechanical vibration characteristics and voltage output properties. These analyses provide a robust understanding of how the device operates and ensures that the design meets the required specifications and performance standards.

Energy Transmission Design. The ratchet mechanism presents a multitude of advantages in the realm of power generation systems, primarily stemming from its unique unidirectional input capability. This capability allows the mechanism to convert intermittent motion into a continuous and stable energy output, thereby significantly enhancing the overall efficiency of energy utilization. The simplicity of its structure is another notable benefit, as it minimizes energy losses during transmission. This not only boosts the reliability of the system but also facilitates ease of maintenance, reducing downtime and operational costs.

Furthermore, the ratchet mechanism demonstrates remarkable adaptability to a wide range of loads and speed fluctuations. This versatility ensures that the mechanism can maintain consistent performance under varying conditions, making it an ideal choice for a diverse array of applications. Through optimized design, the ratchet mechanism can significantly enhance energy harvesting density, maximizing the amount of energy extracted from a given source. These characteristics collectively position the ratchet mechanism as an exceptionally effective component for augmenting the performance of energy harvesting systems. Consequently, its integration into such systems has been extensively studied and documented in the scientific literature, further validating its utility and potential [8].

Upon designing a ratchet mechanism for an energy harvesting system, we can evaluate its performance based on the following parameters: a pendulum mass of 1 kg swinging with an amplitude of ± 30° at a frequency of 1 Hz. The ratchet transmission efficiency is 90%, while energy loss without the ratchet mechanism is approximately 20%. Under these assumptions, we can calculate that each swing incurs an energy loss of 0.1 J without the ratchet mechanism and achieves an energy conversion efficiency of 0.45 J with the mechanism [3].

If we assume the linear speed of pendulum swing is 1 m/s, then:
Energy loss per swing without the ratchet mechanism: $E_{loss} = (mv2)/2 \times 20\% = 0.1$ J.
Energy conversion with the ratchet mechanism: $E_{conv} = (mv2)/2 \times 90\% = 0.45$ J.

Through comprehensive analysis and rigorous computation, we have thoroughly examined the design of this ratchet mechanism in the context of power generation systems and conclude that it is indeed rational and highly beneficial. Firstly, the incorporation of the ratchet mechanism results in a substantial enhancement of energy conversion efficiency, increasing it from 80% to 90%. This significant improvement translates into a considerable reduction in energy losses during the conversion process, thereby maximizing the utilization of available energy sources.

Secondly, the mechanism's simplified structure plays a pivotal role in reducing the overall component count. This, in turn, leads to lower manufacturing costs and diminished maintenance requirements, as fewer parts mean fewer potential points of failure. This aspect not only enhances the overall reliability of the system but also simplifies the maintenance process, thereby extending the lifespan of the components.

Moreover, the adaptability of the ratchet mechanism is a standout feature, enabling it to maintain stable operation across a diverse range of environments and conditions. This versatility ensures that the mechanism can continue to perform efficiently, regardless of external factors such as temperature, humidity, or load variations. Additionally, through meticulous optimization of the design, the energy harvesting density is markedly increased, further boosting the overall performance of the power generation system.

Ease of maintenance is another crucial advantage of the ratchet mechanism. The simplified structure and reduced component count contribute to reduced long-term operational costs, as maintenance tasks become less frequent and less complex. This aspect is particularly important in industries where downtime and operational costs can have a significant impact on profitability.

Finally, the ratchet mechanism provides a stable and predictable energy output, which is essential for devices and systems that require a continuous and reliable power supply. This consistency ensures that the power generation system can meet the energy demands of connected devices without any interruptions or fluctuations, thereby enhancing overall system performance and user satisfaction.

Combining all these advantages, it is evident that the design of the ratchet mechanism not only meets the growing demand for high-efficiency energy conversion but also ensures system reliability and cost-effectiveness. These attributes collectively demonstrate the rationality and effectiveness of the ratchet mechanism in the design of power generation systems, making it a valuable and innovative contribution to the field of energy technology.

2.2 Shaft Design

Structural Design of the Shaft (Fig. 1). The structural design of a shaft typically encompasses two primary aspects: its geometric configuration and dimensional specifications. These design considerations must fulfill specific criteria: (1) Ease of machining to facilitate straightforward installation, adjustment, and disassembly of mounted components on the shaft; (2) Mitigation of stress concentration through appropriate loading to ensure operational durability; (3) Precise positioning and secure fastening of components mounted on the shaft; (4) Alignment with optimal manufacturing practices to enhance efficiency.

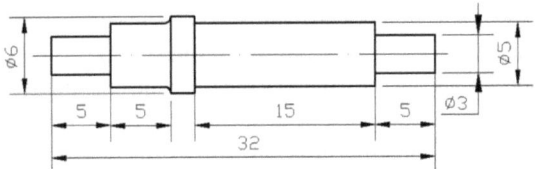

Fig. 1. Engineering Drawing of Shaft.

Selection of Shaft Material. In motion power generation devices, the shaft serves a pivotal role by supporting the pendulum and enduring substantial radial forces with minimal axial loads. The decision to utilize 45 steel for the shaft stems from its balanced attributes, offering a harmonious blend of manufacturability and cost-effectiveness. This material boasts excellent mechanical properties, including high tensile and yield strengths, which enable it to withstand significant radial loads without deformation. Additionally, 45 steel's machinability allows for precise manufacturing, ensuring that the shaft meets stringent specifications and tolerances crucial for optimal device performance. Its widespread availability and established manufacturing processes further contribute to its economic viability, making it an ideal and practical choice for large-scale production in motion power generation devices.

Shaft Assembly Structure (Fig. 2). In the design of the motion power generation device, the shafts and housings are assembled with a transition fit to facilitate occasional maintenance inspections and ensure ease of disassembly. The pendulum, crucial for collecting human kinetic energy through regular swinging, is connected to the shaft via bearings to minimize friction and maximize energy transfer efficiency. An interference fit between the pendulum and shaft is avoided to prevent undesired energy loss, as it would cause the shaft to move with the pendulum. For a clearer understanding, Fig. 2 illustrates the assembly diagram of the shaft, detailing the arrangement and fit of the components.

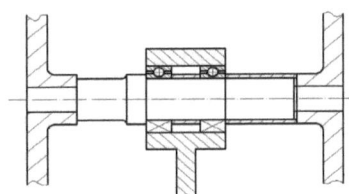

Fig. 2. Assembly Structure Diagram of Shaft for Human Body Mechanical Energy-based Motion Power Generation Device

2.3 Design of the Magnetic Field

Introduction to Relevant Concepts. Permanent magnet materials, crucial in energy harvesting systems driven by human body motion, provide essential magnetic fields for energy conversion. They significantly influence the electrical output characteristics of such systems. Various types include aluminum-nickel-cobalt, rare earth cobalt, and neodymium-iron-boron magnets [9, 10]. Key performance parameters include coercive force (Hc), which indicates resistance to demagnetization; remanence induction (Br), reflecting retained magnetic induction after external field removal; and maximum energy product ((BH)max), defining stored magnetic energy per unit volume [9]. The selection of permanent magnet materials hinges on coercive force, remanence induction, and maximum energy product. Higher values of these parameters enable dimensional reduction, amplify magnetic flux variation in induction coils, bolster induced electromotive force, and thereby elevate induced current levels.

The Selection of Permanent Magnet Materials. Rare earth permanent magnets [11, 12], such as sintered neodymium-iron-boron magnets, offer superior characteristics compared to traditional materials like aluminum-nickel-cobalt and ferrite magnets. They feature high coercive force, exceptional energy product, and robust mechanical strength, resulting in compact size, reduced weight, and consistent performance. Neodymium-iron-boron magnets, notably the N35 Grade, stand out for their high cost-performance ratio among various types, making them ideal for this application.

Arrangement of Permanent Magnets. The efficiency of energy conversion in devices heavily depends on how permanent magnets are arranged, affecting the distribution of magnetic fields. Optimal efficiency occurs when coils move perpendicularly to magnetic flux lines, maximizing magnetic flux cutting and inducing larger currents (Fig. 3). Neodymium-iron-boron magnets (30 × 10 × 2 mm), magnetized along their largest faces with NS poles on these surfaces, reduce the number of magnets needed and overall device mass. Positioned on the outer side of the pendulum according to Sect. 2.3, these magnets accommodate practical manufacturing and assembly tolerances and operational wear between shaft and housing. Creo Simulate 1.0 Analysis determined an optimal 1.5 mm distance between fixed housing magnets and coils for this design.

The ratchet mechanism is seamlessly integrated onto the power output shaft, which functions as the primary conduit for the transmission of mechanical energy. This energy, efficiently harnessed by the ratchet, is then conveyed through a precisely engineered secondary gear assembly to the axis that houses the winding assembly. The meticulous arrangement and alignment of these components are crucial to facilitating the precise interaction required for the conductors to effectively cut through the magnetic flux lines. This precise interaction is essential for generating an induced electromotive force, thereby exemplifying the conversion of mechanical motion into electrical energy. A schematic representation of this intricate process, delineated in Fig. 3, illustrates the orchestrated sequence of energy transfer and transformation, demonstrating the seamless integration and functionality of each component in the system.

2.4 Circuit Design

This chapter focuses on the design of the energy storage circuit for a kinetic energy harvesting device, emphasizing the selection of the cost-effective MAX846 battery charging controller due to its versatility and suitability for the application. The design, as illustrated

Fig. 3. Optimal Method of Transmission and Relative Motion of Permanent Magnets

in Fig. 4, incorporates a three-phase bridge rectifier filtering circuit and charging setup, ensuring efficient and stable energy transfer. For the energy storage solution, a reliable lithium-ion battery, which is widely used in modern electronic devices, is employed. The choice of this battery further enhances the overall efficiency and performance of the kinetic energy harvesting device, underscoring the importance of careful component selection and design in energy harvesting systems.

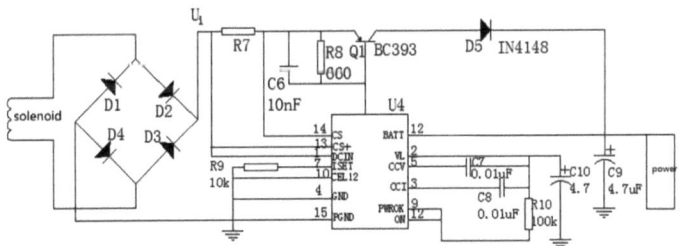

Fig. 4. Rectification and Charging Circuit Diagram

3 Theoretical Design Calculations

3.1 Calculation of DC Generator Electromotive Force

Calculation of Magnetic Flux

(1) Magnetic Flux Density $B = \mu H$.

where μ is the magnetic permeability of the medium, in units of (H/m); in air, $\mu_0 = 4\pi \times 10^{-7}$ H/m; H is the magnetic field strength.

Alnico is a widely used permanent magnet material in motors.

Assume Alnico 32, B = 1.2T, HC = 44 kA/m, and the permeability is 3.2–4.5 μ0. (2) Magnetic flux area A = πR, where R is the average radius of the motor coil.
In summary:
If magnetic leakage is neglected, $\Psi = BA = \mu H \pi R^2 = 4\pi \times 10^{-7} \times 44 \times 10^{-3} \times \pi \times 0.001^2 = 1.7 \times 10{-4} Wb$.

Calculation of Rotor Speed

To begin with, the calculation of the angular velocity (ω) is essential for determining the rotor speed in a gear-based kinetic energy harvesting system. Given that the gear ratio (n) is a crucial factor, along with the human walking speed and the degree of rotation per step, we can derive the angular velocity. Here, the human walking speed is specified as 1.5 steps per second, and each step causes a 60-degree rotation.

By considering these parameters, we can deduce that the rotor speed (n) is 180 revolutions per minute (rpm). This is achieved by multiplying the number of steps per second by 60 (to convert seconds to minutes) and then by 120 (since 60 degrees per step translates to 120 degrees per full revolution, given that a full circle is 360 degrees). Thus, the rotor speed of 180 rpm corresponds to an angular velocity (ω) of 15π radians per second. This calculation provides a clear understanding of the rotor's speed based on the human walking input, demonstrating the efficiency and mechanics of the gear-based energy harvesting system.

Calculation of Average Induced Electromotive Force

In the given formula, various parameters are defined to represent key components of an electrical machine. Specifically, P denotes the number of magnetic poles, with a value of 1 in this context. N represents the total number of conductors in the armature winding, which is crucial for the electric current flow. The term 2a signifies the number of parallel paths through which the current can flow, influencing the machine's performance and efficiency. Φ stands for the flux per pole, which is a measure of the magnetic field strength. Lastly, n represents the rotor speed, indicating the rotational velocity of the machine. These parameters collectively contribute to the overall functionality and output of the electrical machine, as demonstrated through their inclusion in the formula.

Therefore, the average induced electromotive force of a DC motor

$$E_a = \frac{PN\Psi n}{60a} = \frac{1 \times 2 \times 500 \times 1.7 \times 10^{-4} \times 180}{60 \times 1} = 0.51V$$

Utilizing both clockwise and counterclockwise generators results in a significant enhancement in power generation, doubling the output compared to a setup employing a single generator. This improvement stems from the ability to harness energy from both directions of rotation. Furthermore, the incorporation of a bidirectional overrunning clutch mechanism leads to an additional increase in power generation, amplifying it by a factor of three to four. This mechanism exploits relative motion between the components, thus maximizing energy extraction. Consequently, the combined effect of these innovations results in a summed voltage of E = 1.53 V from the two parallel generators, underscoring the effectiveness of the combined approach in boosting power production.

3.2 Calculation of Output Voltage

Calculation of Circuit Resistance
(1) Coil Resistance R = $\frac{\rho L}{S} = \frac{0.0175 \times 30}{0.1 \times 10^{-3}} = 52.5 \, \Omega$.
(2) The circuit resistance is initially taken as R0 = 2000 Ω.

Calculation of Output Voltage

$$\text{Output voltage } U = \frac{E \times R_0}{R + R_0} = \frac{1.53 \times 2000}{52.5 + 2000} = 1.49 \text{V}$$

Note: the voltage provided is an average estimate. Due to operational errors and power factors, the actual average voltage may be slightly lower than calculated. Human walking speed varies in a wave-like pattern similar to a sine wave, causing fluctuations in the estimated voltage ranging from 1 V to 3 V.

3.3 Circuit Diagram Design

During the process of walking, joint swing irregularities introduce variations in the generated voltage, resulting in a fluctuating output that resembles a sine wave. This fluctuation causes the voltage to range from 1 V to 3 V, posing challenges for direct utilization in devices that require a stable power supply. For instance, a mobile phone battery necessitates a constant charging voltage of 4.7 V to ensure efficient and safe charging. Therefore, to address this issue, voltage stabilization and boosting techniques are essential. These methods are crucial for converting the fluctuating voltage into a stable and sufficient level that meets the charging requirements of the mobile phone battery, thereby enabling reliable and efficient energy harvesting from walking-induced motion.

Upon powering up, capacitors C1 and C2 charge through resistors R1 and R2 respectively. Once C1's voltage is sufficient, Q1 turns on, enabling Q2 to conduct and current flows through transformer T's primary winding. C1 then discharges until Q1 can no longer conduct, turning off Q1 and Q2 and reducing primary winding current. Simultaneously, inductive current starts flowing through T's secondary winding. As primary winding current ceases, C1 begins recharging, restarting the oscillation cycle and inducing voltage in T's secondary winding.

A 1N4733 Zener diode is chosen for 4.7 V voltage stabilization.

4 Conclusion

In a series of tests conducted on the device, key data was collected to assess its safety and reliability. Firstly, environmental temperature testing demonstrated that the device maintains voltage stability under extreme temperature conditions (-10 °C to 55 °C), with fluctuations within ± 0.05 V and ± 0.1 V, respectively. This confirms the device's excellent temperature adaptability and potential for application in harsh environments.

Furthermore, to rigorously assess the device's stability and durability, it underwent both continuous operation and overload tests. During an extended period of continuous operation spanning 1000 h, the device demonstrated exceptional long-term operational reliability, with a performance degradation rate that remained below 2%. This result underscores its capacity to maintain high performance levels over an extended timeframe. Additionally, when subjected to overload conditions equivalent to 150% of its rated capacity, the device's protection mechanisms responded swiftly, initiating within 5 s to effectively mitigate potential damage. These test outcomes further validate the robustness and reliability of the device, ensuring its suitability for demanding applications requiring sustained performance and resilience under stressful conditions.

Lastly, vibration and electrical safety tests highlighted the device's stability and safety in practical use. Even under vibration conditions of 3 g acceleration, the device exhibited voltage stability with fluctuations of only ± 0.02 V, ensuring stable energy supply during simulated human movement. In terms of electrical safety, the device responded swiftly to short circuit, overcharge, and over-discharge conditions, with response times of less than 0.5 s. The overcharge protection activation voltage ranged from 4.8 V to 5.0 V, and the over-discharge protection activation voltage ranged from 3.0 V to 3.2 V, significantly reducing usage risks.

In conclusion, based on rigorous testing and the collected data, we conclude that this device excels under various environmental conditions and ensures high levels of safety and reliability during long-term use and electrical anomalies.

Acknowledgments. First and foremost, I would like to express my gratitude to all the members of the project team who participated in this research and experiment. The hard work, innovative thinking, and professional abilities of each member have been decisive to the success of this study. Special thanks are also extended to colleagues responsible for data analysis and equipment maintenance, whose technical skills and dedication have been instrumental in ensuring the smooth progress of the research.

I am also grateful to all the colleagues within the laboratory and research group. The open exchanges and continuous cooperation among us have pushed the research work deeper, and everyone's contribution has been indispensable in this process.

Furthermore, I would like to express my deepest appreciation to my family. Their support and encouragement have been a pillar of strength for me, especially during challenging and difficult times. The understanding and accommodation shown by my parents, spouse, and children have allowed me to focus on my scientific endeavors and pursue excellence without distractions.

I am deeply grateful to the scientific research institutions and funding organizations that have generously provided financial support for my research endeavors. Their monetary assistance has played a pivotal role in not only facilitating the seamless execution of this study but also ensuring the timely acquisition of essential experimental equipment and materials. This crucial support has been instrumental in advancing my research objectives, enabling me to conduct comprehensive experiments and analyses with the highest quality tools and resources available. By enabling access to these vital resources, the funding received has significantly contributed to the success and robustness of my research findings, underscoring the indispensable role of these institutions and organizations in fostering scientific advancement and innovation.

Lastly, I appreciate everyone who has shown concern and support for me. Thank you for your trust and encouragement. I will continue to strive for progress and make more contributions to exploring power supply schemes for wearable artificial intelligence devices.

Once again, I thank all those who have helped and supported me. Your efforts have made the successful completion of this research possible.

Project Name: Water Jet Cutting Technology.

Item No.: 2023XZXK70.
Project Name: Abrasive Waterjet Cutting Quality Study for Composites.
Item No.: 2023KYQ173.

References

1. Allam, S., Nadikattu, A.K.R.: AI economical wearable smart device to alert real time health reports to doctors. Int. J. Creat. Res. Thoughts (IJCRT), ISSN, 2320-2882
2. Bai, S., Cui, J., Zheng, Y., et al.: Electromagnetic-triboelectric energy harvester based on vibration-to-rotation conversion for human motion energy exploitation. Appl. Energy **329**, 120292 (2023)
3. Zhao, L.C., Zou, H.X., Wei, K.X., et al.: Mechanical intelligent energy harvesting: from methodology to applications. Adv. Energy Mater. **13**(29), 2300557 (2023)
4. Gao, Y., Xu, B., Tan, D., et al.: Asymmetric-elastic-structure fabric-based triboelectric nano-generators for wearable energy harvesting and human motion sensing. Chem. Eng. J. **466**, 143079 (2023)
5. Ali, A., Shaukat, H., Bibi, S., et al.: Recent progress in energy harvesting systems for wearable technology. Energ. Strat. Rev. **49**, 101124 (2023)
6. Hou, J., Qian, S., Hou, X., et al.: A high-performance mini-generator with average power of 2 W for human motion energy harvesting and wearable electronics applications. Energy Convers. Manage. **277**, 116612 (2023)
7. Wang, T., Shen, Y., Chen, L., et al.: Large-scale production of the 3D warp knitted terry fabric triboelectric nanogenerators for motion monitoring and energy harvesting. Nano Energy **109**, 108309 (2023)
8. Malozyomov, B.V., Martyushev, N.V., Sorokova, S.N., et al.: Mathematical Modeling of Mechanical Forces and Power Balance in Electromechanical Energy Converter. Mathematics **11**(10), 2394 (2023)
9. Nuzzo, S., Bolognesi, P., Decuzzi, G., et al.: A consequent-pole hybrid exciter for synchronous generators. IEEE Trans. Energy Convers. **36**(1), 368–379 (2020)
10. Sriwannarat, W., Seangwong, P., Lounthavong, V., et al.: An improvement of output power in doubly salient permanent magnet generator using Pole configuration adjustment. Energies **13**(17), 4588 (2020)
11. Coey, J.M.D.: Perspective and prospects for rare earth permanent magnets. Engineering **6**(2), 119–131 (2020)
12. Sagawa, M., Fujimura, S., Yamamoto, H., et al.: Magnetic properties of rare-earth-iron-boron permanent magnet materials. J. Appl. Phys. **57**(8), 4094–4096 (1985)

Design of an Automatic Take Tooth Threading Robotic Arm Based on Solidworks

Shiyou Xu, Xianding Xue, Yunfeng Wu, and Ruyi Wang[✉]

Guangzhou Institute of Science and Technology, Guangzhou 510000, China
{xushiyou,xushiyou,wangry}@gzist.edu.cn

Abstract. This study developed an automated rake toothed robotic arm to meet the automation assembly requirements of grid cleaning machines, aiming to solve the labor-intensive and error rate problems in traditional assembly processes. Designed using Solidworks software, this robotic arm is suitable for the rake tooth assembly of a three-rope grid machine. The structural design of the robotic arm considers stability and cost-effectiveness, and the control system uses Siemens S7–1200 PLC combined with a touch screen to ensure ease of operation and real-time monitoring. After virtual assembly and motion simulation verification, the robotic arm has demonstrated good operational performance and interference free assembly process.

Keywords: Non-standard automated assembly · Solidworks · Motion simulation

1 Introduction

Grid screen machine is an important equipment for sewage treatment plant, which can be divided into rotary arm, swing arm, rotary arm, three-rope type according to the condition of traction parts. Among them, three-rope grid machine, shown in Fig. 1, using a unique rake teeth assembled into a group of rotary grating chain, driven by the motor reducer, the rake teeth chain rotary movement against the direction of the water flow, and then salvage the scum. Applicable to a variety of width and depth of the grating mobile for wide grating, grid by grid removal. Because of its easy maintenance and repair, can be applied to a variety of width, depth of the grating, a wide range of advantages, widely used in the market [1].

In terms of grating machine assembly, the traditional three-rope grating machine assembly process is complex and labor-intensive. The seven-axis three-rope grid machine involves the assembly of three types of rake teeth: side rake teeth, middle rake teeth and small rake teeth, which are assembled to the shafts according to a specific cross sequence. This process is extremely labor intensive and time consuming as the number of layers of rake tines can be upwards of a hundred. There have been a series of research results in the industry on automated pickup technology for industrial products [2]. Chen [3] have designed a gripping stacker robot equipment, which realizes the full automatic control of stacking the tablets through the fully automatic pneumatic transmission method, and solves the sticking problem of the tablet materials when picking up the tablets through the jittering control program. Wu [4] have designed the main and vice suction cup manipulator for deformed round plate, which improves the positional accuracy of deformed embryo material round plate sent to the center of the hydraulic press from the centering mechanism through the positioning of the main suction cup and the vice suction cup auxiliary grasping, and realizes the stable handling of the high precision with the positioning accuracy of 1 ~ 4 mm. Zhu [5] designed an automatic loading and unloading robot by modifying the slotting machine to realize the automated operation of motor punching. Chen [6] designed an automatic loading and unloading robot for brake pad stamping, and verified the accuracy of the robot design by determining the robot's end trajectory, positional attitude, and key speed information through motion simulation of ADAMS software. The above studies mainly focus on the development of loading equipment for industrial products, however, there are few in-depth discussions in the research field of integrating sheet loading with automated piercing process.

Fig. 1. Three-rope grid machine.

In this paper a kind of automatic wear rake teeth manipulator equipment of grating machine is designed, which is important for the development of automated assembly technology for improving the production efficiency of grating machine, ensuring the safety and reliability of the equipment and reducing the cost of labor [7].

2 Design of Automatic Rake Threading Robot Requirements

2.1 Basic Functions

Automatic rake teeth robot for seven shafts of the three-rope grating machine is mainly used for stainless steel rake teeth processing after the completion of the assembly process. After the rake teeth stamping processing is completed, the rake teeth are stacked into the designated loading equipment. Through the robot, the side rake teeth will be threaded into the corresponding shaft according to the actual installation requirements. Rake teeth are divided into three kinds of side rake teeth, rake teeth and small rake teeth. Odd layer consists of two side rake teeth and two small rake teeth, side rake teeth assembled on the shaft 1, 4, 5, small rake teeth assembled on the shaft 2, 3, 6, 7. Even layer consists of two in the rake teeth and two small rake teeth, in the rake teeth assembled on the shaft

1, 2, 5, 6, small rake teeth assembled on the shaft 2, 3, 7, the rake teeth layer totaling 128 layers. The design requirements of the device include ensuring the reliability of the upper material and perforation, to meet the requirements of each layer of the type of rake teeth, the realization of the rake teeth assembly automation, to ensure the safety and reliability of the equipment and equipment operating efficiency.

2.2 Composition

The device consists of key components such as bearing base, rotary feeding mechanism, picking and threading mechanism and control system. The core function of the bearing base is to provide stable support for the seven axes. The rotary feeding mechanism automates the feeding process of the rake sheet, which is easy to be absorbed by the rake tooth robot. The rake tooth robot is responsible for accurately picking up the rake teeth and putting them on the corresponding shafts in a predetermined order. The control system is responsible for the time scheduling of the entire process and consists of components such as a PLC controller and touch screen.

2.3 Introduction to Rake Teeth Products

The rake teeth of the three-rope grating machine can be divided into small rake teeth, medium rake teeth and side rake teeth according to its design. These teeth are usually made of nylon or 304 stainless steel, as shown in Fig. 2.

According to the specific needs of the application, the thickness of the rake teeth can range from 1 mm to 4 mm, the length range of 185 mm to 285 mm. Rake teeth made of 304 stainless steel, the weight of a single piece is about 40 g to 120 g between.

Fig. 2. Nylon rake teeth and 304 stainless steel rake teeth

3 Automatic Wear Rake Teeth Manipulator Structure Design

3.1 Overall Structural Design

This equipment is designed to thread 128 side rakes, 128 medium rakes and 256 small rakes, totaling 512 rakes, into seven shafts in a defined sequence. When selecting the drive, the machine had to fulfill the requirements of low noise, easy control and high running accuracy. In order to ensure the high precision and smooth operation of the rotary loading equipment and the gearing robot, this design adopts servo motor as the core power source. In terms of material selection, in order to ensure the stability of the process of wearing rake teeth, the base of the equipment and the support of the manipulator using the heavier weight of the cast iron material. The rake teeth baffle plate in the rotary loading equipment is made of acrylic while other parts are made of aluminum alloy based on strength and cost considerations, shown in Fig. 3.

The design of the control system is based on reliability and stability, and the compact, economical and easy-to-maintain Siemens S7–1200 PLC is selected, and equipped with a touch screen to enhance the human-computer interaction [8].

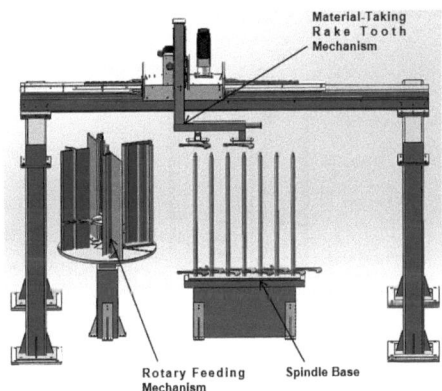

Fig. 3. Overall structure of automatic rake tooth threading robot

3.2 Spindle Base Design

In the automatic wearing rake teeth process, in view of the shaft body is long, the traditional manual operation is usually seven shafts side by side flat, one end of the pad to form a certain angle with the horizontal plane, in order to facilitate the rake teeth into the, as shown in Fig. 4. In automated equipment, the shafts need to be fixed vertically in order to simplify the rake teeth penetration operation. For this reason, the design of the end of the shaft has been improved, and the length of the shaft head has been extended from 30 mm to 80 mm to enhance the stability of the shaft during the assembly process. Before starting the machine, the operator needs to manually insert the seven shafts into the corresponding holes in the base.

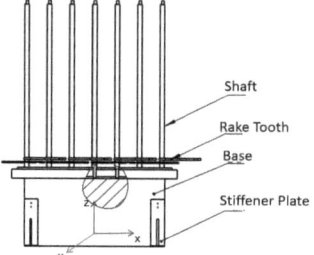

Fig. 4. Spindle base

3.3 Design of the Rotary Feeding Mechanism

The rotary feeder has a rotary cylinder mounted on the base of the rotary feeder to achieve a precise 90° rotation of the rotary table. The rotary table has a combination of customized fixed plates, baffles and rake lifting plates for stable stacking of the rakes, with grooves on the table surface to ensure accurate positioning of the baffles. The fixed plate, baffle plate and lifting base plate are all customized according to the contour of the rake sheet to ensure the stability of the rake sheet installation, as shown in Fig. 5.

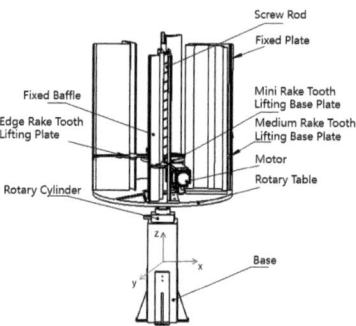

Fig. 5. Rotating feeding mechanism

The loading mechanism is equipped with a total of four rake sheet placement station, of which the small rake sheet with two symmetrical workstations, respectively, located in the X-axis direction, the side rake sheet and the middle rake sheet each occupies a workstation, symmetrically distributed in the Y-axis direction. Wear rake teeth robot first suck located in the x-axis of a pair of small rake sheet, and then rotary cylinder will rotate the rotary table 90°, so that the side rake sheet and the middle rake sheet aligned with the x-axis for the robot to pick up materials. After picking, the rotary cylinder turns the table 90° again to return to the original position. After a layer of rake sheet picking is completed, the motor drives the lifting base plate to move upward by 10 mm, which matches the thickness of the rake sheet to ensure that the manipulator can smoothly pick up the next layer of rake sheet.

3.4 Material-Taking Rake Tooth Mechanism

The operation of the picking and threading mechanism is dominated by the loading lifting arm, which is responsible for the overall movement control of the manipulator. The width adjusting cylinder is responsible for the width adaptation of the harrow teeth when they are inserted. These two components work in tandem to realize the precise feeding and insertion of the rakes.

For the design of the loading lifting arm, the transverse and longitudinal transmission modes adopt the rack and pinion design, which guarantees the smooth transmission when it wears the rake teeth, and the noise of its transmission is small, and it will not produce obvious impact sound and vibration. According to the actual working conditions, the design speed of Z-axis v_{max} is 1.28 m/s, the maximum acceleration a_{max} is 3.2 m/s^2, the load mass m_z is 48 kg, and the mechanical efficiency η is 0.9. The torque T required under the maximum acceleration is:

$$T = \frac{m_z * g * (1 + \mu) + m_z * a_{max}}{\eta} \tag{1}$$

Considering the dynamic torque demand, performance and economy of the structure, the Z-axis and X-axis motors are selected from the Hechuan X2-MH series with a power of 1,000 W servo motors.

The width adjustment cylinder is responsible for adjusting the size of the pick-up tine structure to fit the tines on the rotary loading mechanism. The cylinder retracts when picking up the rake teeth to ensure smooth pickup and extends when threading into the specified shaft to ensure size matching. SMC standard 40 mm diameter JMDB system cylinders are used for precise width adjustment.

The rake teeth are sucked up by a vacuum suction cup, and when the suction cup contacts the rake teeth on the rotary loading mechanism, a vacuum pressure of approximately −25 kPa is applied to realize the suction. When the rake teeth are moved to the top of the bearing for penetration operation, the suction cup stops adsorption and performs reverse blowing, which promotes efficient and precise penetration of the rake teeth into the target shaft. The structure is shown in Fig. 6.

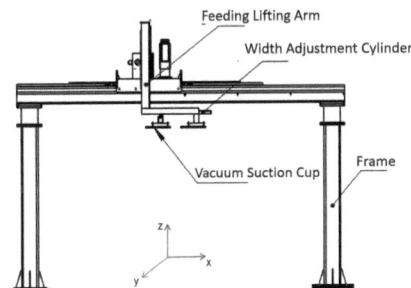

Fig. 6. Material-taking rake tooth mechanism

4 Action Flow and Efficiency Analysis

4.1 Overall Action Flow

The overall control of the device adopts Siemens S7–1200 PLC as the control core and KTPT00 Basic touch screen as the human-machine interface to realize precise control, and the overall control process is shown in Fig. 7.

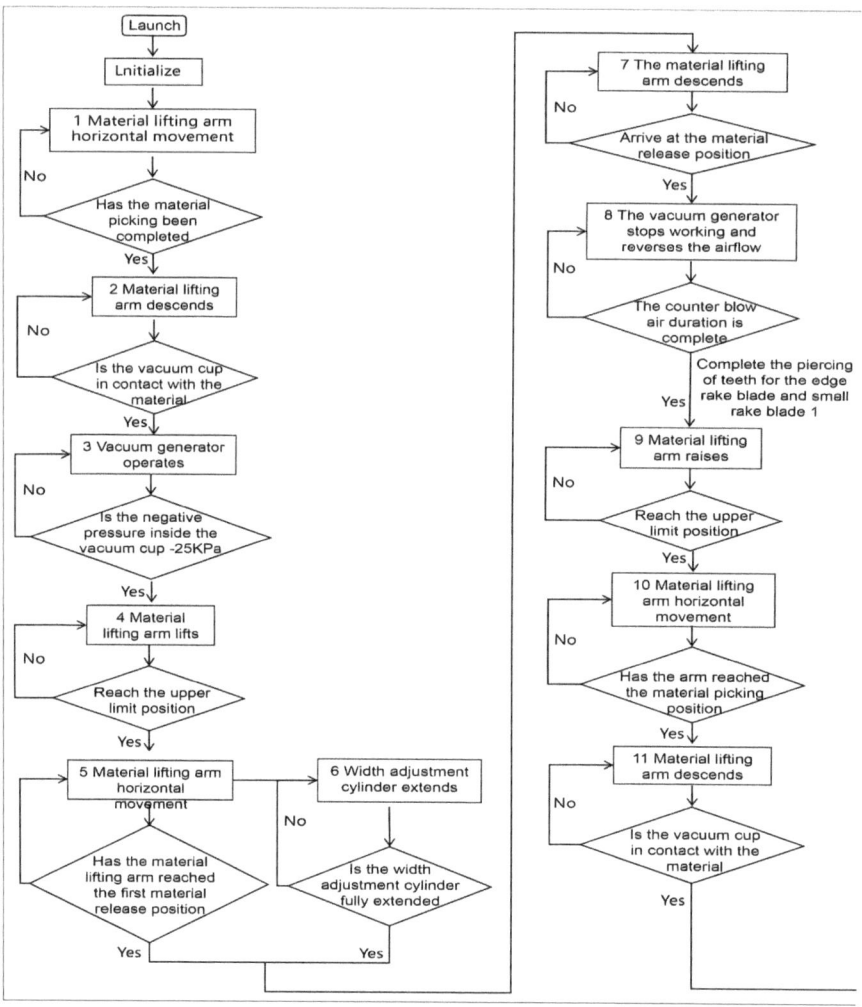

Fig. 7. Control flow chart

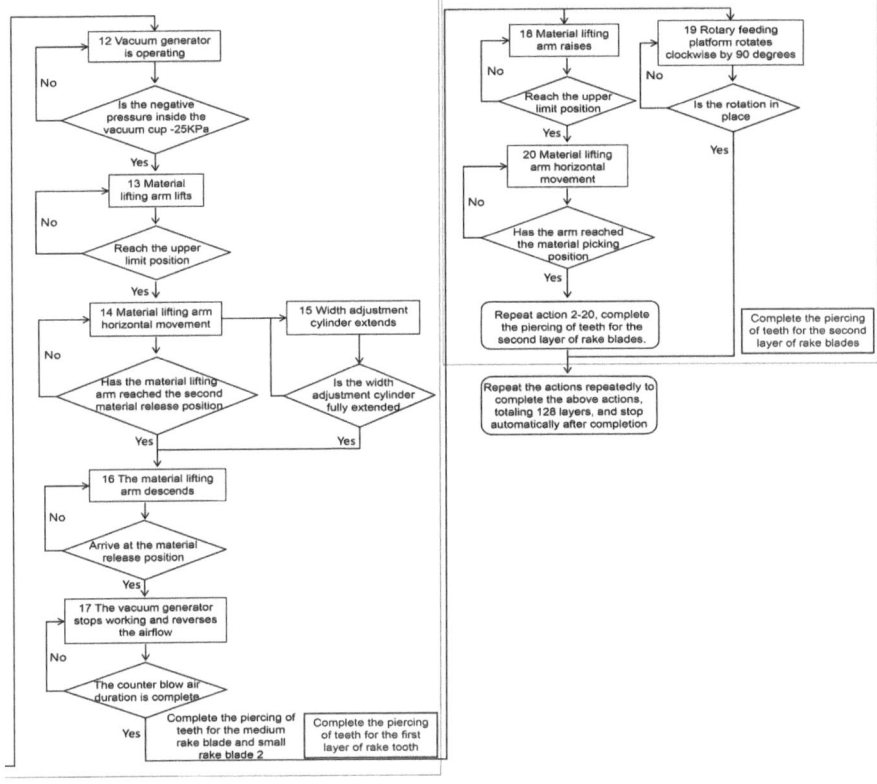

Fig. 7. (*continued*)

4.2 Analysis of Work Efficiency

The assembly feasibility of the product design is analyzed and verified by virtually assembling each component of the automated rake-through-tooth manipulator. Motion simulation test. The results show that the operation of the components is good, no interference phenomenon, and the articulation between the sections is appropriate, and it can efficiently complete the functions of picking up materials and wearing rake teeth.

As shown in Table 1, the total time required by the automated rake piercing manipulator to perform rake piercing operations in odd-numbered layers is approximately 10.1 s per layer. The time required for each layer of the even numbered layers is the same as that of the odd numbered layers, which is also about 10.1 s, and there are 64 layers for each of the odd numbered layers and even numbered layers. The rake tooth stack loading and bearing fixing is done manually and takes about 60 s. After putting on the rake teeth, unloading the bearings that have been put on the rake teeth is also a manual operation, which takes 30 s. In total, the time required to complete the automatic rake teeth assembly is 23 min.

The detailed procedure and time consumption for a skilled worker to manually thread rake teeth are as follows: Securing one end of seven shafts, positioning them horizontally at a certain angle, and resting them on a fixed bracket requires 50 s. Subsequently, threading the rake teeth layer by layer, with each layer taking approximately 17.5 s, results in a total threading time of 2240 s for 128 layers of teeth. After threading, the manual unloading of the shafts with threaded teeth takes an additional 30 s, culminating in a total assembly time of 23 min. On average, without errors, a set of teeth is manually threaded in approximately 38.5 min.

In comparison to manual assembly, the use of an automated rake tooth threading robotic arm enhances the assembly efficiency by a factor of 1.67 and eliminates the possibility of errors during the assembly process.

Table 1. Statistics of time per layer for penetrating rake teeth.

Action 1: Material Lifting Arm Horizontal Movement - 1.1 s	Action 2: Material Lifting Arm Descends - 0.5 s	Action 3: Vacuum Generator Operates - 0.5 s	Action 4: Material Lifting Arm Raises - 0.5 s
Actions 5–6: Material Lifting Arm Horizontal Movement while Width Adjustment Cylinder Extends - 1.1 s	Action 7: Material Lifting Arm Descends - 0.5 s	Action 8: Vacuum Generator Stops Working and Reverses Airflow - 0.3 s	Action 9: Material Lifting Arm Raises - 0.5 s
Action 10: Material Lifting Arm Horizontal Movement - 1.1 s	Action 11: Material Lifting Arm Descends - 0.5 s	Action 12: Vacuum Generator Operates - 0.5 s	Action 13: Material Lifting Arm Raises - 0.5 s
Actions 14–15: Material Lifting Arm Horizontal Movement while Width Adjustment Cylinder Extends - 1.2 s	Action 16: Material Lifting Arm Descends - 0.5 s	Action 17: Vacuum Generator Stops Working and Reverses Airflow - 0.3 s	Actions 18–19: Material Lifting Arm Raises while Rotary Feeding Platform Rotates Clockwise by 90° - 0.5 s

4.3 Analysis of Work Efficiency

The control system, utilizing a Siemens PLC, is characterized by high reliability and stability, ensuring stable operation under adverse working conditions. The equipment's adjustability is commendable, as the size of the grid machine often necessitates specific adjustments based on the depth of the pool and the width of the teeth. Consequently, the automated rake tooth threading robotic arm must also be correspondingly adjusted for the number of shafts and teeth. These adjustments can be precisely made by modifying the control program. For instance, in cases of deeper pools, the design of the grid machine is longer, requiring up to 192 layers of teeth. Manual assembly for threading these teeth is estimated to take approximately 57.3 min, whereas the automated robotic arm is projected to complete the task in approximately 33.8 min, reflecting a 1.69-fold increase in efficiency.

5   Conclusion

Aiming at the current rake teeth grating machine in the assembly process rake piece assembly difficult, easy to make mistakes, designed a kind of automatic wear rake teeth device. It has the advantages of simple structure, reasonable layout of components and high degree of automation. Realize the rake teeth pickup and wear teeth process of full automation, the simulation of assembly test, production efficiency increased to 23 min per group, manual assembly efficiency of 1.67 times. In addition, the device has the flexibility, according to the different specifications of the grating machine, by adjusting the program to adapt to the actual needs of different bearing lengths and the number of rake pieces, effectively reducing labor input and significantly improve the work efficiency.

Acknowledgments. This work was supported by Guangzhou Institute of Science and Technology public elective course project (No. 2023XGXK011).

References

1. Li, W.: Research on failure problem analysis and solution measures of grating remover. Technology and Market **31**(2), 118–120.46,1854 (2024)
2. Yuan, L., Kumar, P., Makhatha, M.E., et al.: Optimization design of micro-motor rotor core feeding mechanical system based on electrical automation. Electrica **22**(3) (2022)
3. Yan, C., Feng, Z.: Design of robotic system for CZC-1 new type tablet material gripping and stacking machine. Food and Machinery **30**(2), 88–90 (2014)
4. Xiaojun, Z.H.U., Zheng, W.A.N.G., Xiaofeng, G.A.O.: Modification of automatic punching robot loading and unloading system for silicon steel sheet of large-sized motor. Shanghai Large and Medium-sized Electric Machinery **2**, 58–60 (2021)
5. Tie, C.H.E.N., Jiuxiang, Y.A.N., Jie, S.U.N., et al.: Kinematic modeling and simulation of brake pad loading and unloading robot based on ADAMS. Shandong Science **32**(4), 114–120 (2019)
6. Costa, R., Sousa, V.F.C., Silva, F.J.G., et al.: A Novel Robotic Manipulator Concept for Managing the Winding and Extraction of Yarn Coils. Machines **10**, 857 (2022)
7. Azamfirei, V., Psarommatis, F., Lagrosen, Y.: Application of automation for in-line quality inspection, a zero-defect manufacturing approach. J. Manuf. Syst. **67**, 1–22 (2023)
8. Sun, L., Guilin: Application of SolidWorks software assembly on virtual prototype design of agricultural machinery. Agricultural Mechanization Research **45**(4), 229–232 (2023)

Author Index

B
Bai, Kang II-51
Bao, Mingzi II-3

C
Cai, Zongyou I-59
Calderon, Aldrin D. II-139
Chai, Xiaoli I-184
Chang, Hui I-86
Chen, Bo II-81
Chen, Boxuan I-211
Chen, Hongji II-115
Chen, Jianhao I-235
Chen, Jie I-266, II-127
Chen, Liang I-75
Chen, Ru I-3
Chen, Shuang I-92
Chen, Tao II-174
Chen, Yuyu I-243
Chen, Zhengyang II-188
Chen, Zhixi II-188
Cheng, Rongjian II-3
Cheng, Siyuan II-188

D
Dai, Zhengxing II-3
Devaraj, Madhavi I-52
Di, Xu I-199
Ding, Heng I-21
Ding, Yufeng II-162
Dong, Minglun II-246
Du, Jiaxin I-92
Du, Xuefei I-59
Duan, Kailin II-223
Duan, Yanhua I-119

F
Fang, Bojian II-188
Fei, Wei I-199
Feng, Yan II-162
Feng, Yaohua II-188

G
Guo, Feng II-43

H
Han, Baoxing I-86
Han, Jinjiang II-29
Hao, Hong I-103
He, Chao II-210
He, Kai II-256
He, Shengdang II-18
He, Shuanglong II-10
Hu, Yanbing II-58
Hu, Yi I-151
Hu, Zhiqiang II-174
Huang, Chaosheng I-131
Huang, Lijun II-139
Huang, Xiabing II-3

J
Jia, Jingli II-223
Jian, Jianming II-198
Jiang, Youhang I-59
Jiang, Zhujun II-127
Jin, Fenghua II-101
Ju, Kaihuan II-198

L
Lei, Bin II-29
Li, Chuanyu I-266
Li, Hui I-69
Li, Jiayan I-92
Li, Jing I-59
Li, Jun I-131
Li, Li I-75
Li, Meiyan II-150
Li, Shan II-268
Li, Weibo I-69
Li, Wenwei I-3
Li, Xin II-3
Li, Yonghong I-119
Li, Yuan I-131

Li, Zexia I-254
Li, Zhifeng II-10
Liang, Jianan I-3
Liao, Lu II-101
Lin, Kaiyan I-266
Lin, Li I-199
Liu, Aihua I-103
Liu, Guang II-81
Liu, Hailu II-43
Liu, Hong Yuan I-223
Liu, Jiazhen I-143
Liu, Jinjiang I-151
Liu, Qichao I-176
Liu, Sirui II-256
Liu, Tongyang I-254
Liu, Xiangyang II-10
Liu, Yang II-29
Liu, Yiqiang II-3
Liu, Yusheng II-3
Liu, Zesheng II-81
Lu, Honghao I-52
Lu, Xiaohu II-51
Luo, Qianhua II-115
Lv, Min I-162

M
Mei, Fei I-266
Meng, Xianghe I-119

N
Niu, Xia Hong I-223
Nurmemet, Yolwas I-176

P
Peng, Cheng II-18
Peng, Furong I-243
Peng, Yan I-109

Q
Qi, Hongfang II-174
Qian, Qianyi I-235
Qian, Yihong II-268
Qu, Dong I-109
Qu, Jiachen I-33

S
Sha, Shuang I-15
She, Mi II-223
Shi, Jie II-51

Si, Huiping I-266
Song, Juan I-44
Su, Kaishun II-115
Sun, Dong II-94, II-107

T
Tan, Bin II-43
Tan, Haoran I-235
Tan, Qijin II-51
Tang, Haoran I-235
Tang, Jun-ao I-162
Tang, Xiuying II-198
Tao, Jinlei I-103
Tian, Yongpeng II-235, II-246
Tian, Zhijia I-15
Tian, Ziyang II-198

W
Wang, Ben II-3
Wang, Bo II-223
Wang, Debo II-210
Wang, Fang II-174
Wang, Feiyu II-94, II-107
Wang, Jingtong I-33
Wang, Jun II-29
Wang, Kai II-268
Wang, Lili I-254
Wang, Lingyu II-58
Wang, Minghui II-81
Wang, Qingping II-29
Wang, Ruyi II-286
Wang, Xiaofeng I-235
Wang, Zhiguang II-70
Wu, Junhui I-266
Wu, Kai II-198
Wu, Shenglin II-275
Wu, Yueyang I-184
Wu, Yunfeng II-286
Wu, Zhuoping I-59

X
Xia, Baobing II-268
Xia, Shaoxuan II-3
Xiao, Yang II-210
Xie, Hongkai I-235
Xie, Jian I-59
Xiong, Huafeng I-75
Xu, Shilong I-211
Xu, Shiyou II-275, II-286

Author Index

Xu, Xiang II-29
Xu, Xun I-162
Xu, Zhangliang II-10
Xue, Liu I-199
Xue, Xianding II-275, II-286

Y

Yan, Bo II-223
Yan, Lipeng I-59
Yan, Yonghuan II-115
Yang, Chengbo II-29
Yang, Hua I-151
Yang, Pengfei I-52
Yang, Xuerong II-188
Yao, Yongge I-143
Yasenjiang, Jiarula II-210
Ye, Fuqiang I-254
Ye, Nan II-51
Yin, Junming II-198
Yu, Shusong II-43
Yuan, Ruihong II-70
Yuan, Yanhua II-150
Yue, Xintong I-86

Z

Zhang, Bo II-94, II-107
Zhang, Hua II-256

Zhang, Jian II-235, II-246
Zhang, Jie I-69
Zhang, Lei II-268
Zhang, Ling II-29
Zhang, Liyan I-92
Zhang, Lizong II-268
Zhang, Mi I-86
Zhang, Xiaojie II-81
Zhang, Xinghui I-75
Zhang, Xinyu I-131
Zhang, Xinzhe I-86
Zhang, Yansheng II-115
Zhang, Yonggang I-131
Zhang, Yongjian II-268
Zhang, Zhenguo II-81
Zhao, Gang II-256
Zhao, Pingping II-150
Zhao, Xiaowei II-127
Zheng, Mao II-29
Zheng, Yonghang I-109
Zheng, Zhiguo II-127
Zhong, Zhenyu I-3
Zhou, Yu-peng I-162
Zhu, Bingyuan II-246
Zhu, Hai II-223
Zhu, Hongwei II-43
Zou, Yuanyuan I-211, II-18

MIX
Papier aus verantwortungsvollen Quellen
Paper from responsible sources
FSC® C105338

If you have any concerns about our products,
you can contact us on
ProductSafety@springernature.com

In case Publisher is established outside the EU,
the EU authorized representative is:
**Springer Nature Customer Service Center GmbH
Europaplatz 3, 69115 Heidelberg, Germany**

Printed by Libri Plureos GmbH
in Hamburg, Germany